DEBATING

**Longman Series in
College Composition and Communication**
Advisory Editor: Harvey Wiener
LaGuardia Community College
The City University of New York

DEBATING,
APPLIED RHETORICAL THEORY

Theodore F. Sheckels, Jr.
Randolph-Macon College

Longman
New York & London

To Marie

DEBATING
Applied Rhetorical Theory

Longman Inc., 1560 Broadway, New York, N.Y. 10036
Associated companies, branches, and representatives throughout the world.

Copyright © 1984 by Longman Inc.

All rights reserved. No part of this publication may be reproduced, stored in a retrieval system, or transmitted in any form or by any means, electronic, mechanical, photocopying, recording, or otherwise, without the prior permission of the publisher.

Developmental Editor: Gordon T. R. Anderson
Editorial and Design Supervisor: Barbara Lombardo
Production/Manufacturing: Ferne Y. Kawahara
Composition: C. L. Hutson Co., Inc.
Printing and Binding: Malloy Lithographing, Inc.

Library of Congress Cataloging in Publication Data

Sheckels, Ted.
   Debating, applied rhetorical theory.

   (Longman series in college composition and communication)
   Includes index.
   1. Debates and debating. I. Title.
PN4181.S36   1984   808.53   83-22172
ISBN 0-582-28387-6 (pbk.)

Manufactured in the United States of America
Printing: 9 8 7 6 5 4 3 2 1   Year: 92 91 90 89 88 87 86 85 84

Table of Contents

Preface ix
Acknowledgments xiii

Chapter 1   Why Debate? Why Study Rhetoric?   1
  The Benefits of Debating   2
  What Is Rhetoric? A Brief History   5
  What Classical and Modern Rhetoric Add to Debate   5

Chapter 2   Exploring the Resolution   9
  Policy Resolutions and Value Resolutions   9
  Understanding the Resolution by Defining its Key Terms   10
  Understanding the Resolution by Using Heuristics   14
  Exercises in Exploring the Resolution   19

Chapter 3   Research   21
  Shortcuts   22
  Preliminary Research   23
  Is Access to a Good Library a Problem?   28
  Research in the Library   29
  Research Outside the Library   38
  Preparing for Competition   49
  Exercises: Evaluating Evidence   53
  Ongoing Research   59
  When the Season is Over   61

Chapter 4   The Affirmative Case   62
  The Stock Issues   63
  The "Needs Case"   65

The "Comparative Advantages Case" 65
The "Goals Case" 68
Nestorian Order 69
Inherency and Cases Other than the "Needs Case" 70
Attitudinal Inherency 71
Using the Standard Case Structures as a Heuristic 72
Exercises: Generating Affirmative Argumentation 73
Choosing among the Standard Case Structures 73
Exercises: Choosing among the Standard Case Structures 74
Two Innovative Approaches 75
The Plan 78
The Affirmative Case in Value Debate 80

Chapter 5 Writing the First Affirmative Speech 88
A Word on the Teaching of Writing 88
Using an Outline 89
Drafting 89
Revising 90
Preparing the Finished Copy of the Speech 107

Chapter 6 Refutation 111
A General Heuristic for Refutation 112
Exercises: Challenging Arguments I 123
Topoi for Argumentation 124
Exercises: Generating Arguments 127
More on Analyzing the Logic of Arguments 127
Exercises: Challenging Arguments II 133
Exercises: Challenging Arguments III 138
Exercises: Challenging Arguments IV 142

Chapter 7 The Negative Task I 144
The Negative Team as Policy Advocates:
  Judicial versus Legislative Paradigms 145
Going "Straight Negative"; Defending the Status Quo 146
Defending the Status Quo with Repairs 155
Exercises: Refuting the Affirmative Case 156
The Traditional Counterplan 157
Innovative Approaches to the Counterplan 158
Challenging the Innovative "Alternative Justifications"
  Case 161
Defending a Negative Policy in a "Net Benefits" Debate 162
Still Newer Ground for Counterplans 164
Value Debate 165
Exercises: Refuting the Affirmative Case in Value Debate 171

Observations   171
Two Common, Related Observations   174

Chapter 8   The Negative Task II   177

The Negative Division of Labor   177
Challenging the Affirmative Plan   180
Exercises: Challenging Plans   189
Value Debate and the Second Negative Constructive Speech   189
Briefs   191
Some Special Negative Problems   195

Chapter 9   The Entire Debate   201

An Overview   201
Case Side, Plan Side   203
Modifications   203
In Value Debate   211
Planning Rebuttals   211
Exercises: Challenging Plan Attacks   217
Exercises: Grouping Plan Attacks   219
Flow Sheets   222
Judging Criteria   226

Chapter 10   Cross-examination   232

Some Don'ts   232
Procedural Matters   233
The Uses of Cross-examination   234
Special Goals for Questioners   237
Applying an Opponent's Responses in the Speeches that Follow   243
Preparation for Cross-examination   244
Cross-examination and *Ethos*—A Brief Word   246

Chapter 11   Alogical Dimension of Argumentation   249

Ethical Appeal   250
Pathetic Appeal   252
Formal Appeal   253

Chapter 12   Delivery   258

Human Communication or Information Processing   258
Conceiving of the Speech as a Whole   260
First-Time-Final Strategies for Speaking   262
Rate   265
Jargon and Shorthand   269
Small Points   270

Chapter 13 Four Case Studies   **275**

Case One—Should the Government Maintain Files
  on Suspected Homosexuals   275
Case Two—Should the U.S. Navy Be Revamped   282
Case Three—Should the Government Give Subsidies to the
  Fledgling Solar Energy Industry   291
Case Four—Should Political Activism by Religious Organizations
  Be Restricted   298

Glossary of Debate Terms   **306**
Glossary of Rhetorical Terms   **313**
Appendix: Policy Debate versus Value Debate   **317**
Index 320

Preface

Very few activities remain static. Think of sports. Since, let's say, 1965, football has changed; baseball has changed; tennis has changed; track has changed. New rules are written, new strategies are devised. Debating is like these sports in its dynamism. Debating, however, is perhaps more dynamic.

Why? Because, in the early 1970s, debating unfortunately found itself becoming an increasingly elite activity. Debating demanded more and more of students in terms of research time as well as intelligence. Furthermore, the best debaters began demanding more and more of themselves. They pushed themselves. Not only did this pushing mean more research, it also meant more preparation in general, a more frantic pace during actual competition, and a new emphasis on strategy.

These developments did not totally delight the men and women involved in forensics education. They saw the advantages of the hard work, and they were not sad that strategic thinking was gaining a place in the activity; however, they felt the dynamics were such that the value of debating as training in thinking and communicating was being diminished. They were also distressed that the dynamics were excluding many interested students from the activity.

These educators have taken two separate courses. Some have abandoned what debating has become and tried to recreate what debating, in their view, was meant to be; others have tried to reform the activity, keeping the good things the 1970s brought and discarding the bad.

Debating: Applied Rhetorical Theory is very supportive of both courses. Although this text has more to say about traditional policy debate and what it ought to be, this text respects the newer value debate and tries to give you sound guidance no matter whether you're involved in a debate program committed to reforming traditional policy debate *or* a debate program which has abandoned traditional policy debate and embraced the newer value debate *or* a debate class where you may try the one, the other, or both. This text also stresses that the common ground between the rival modes of debating is extensive and devotes a great deal of time to exploring that common ground.

Given the changing face of debating, you need thorough, nonprescriptive guidance. The guidance must be thorough in the sense that it must be rooted in theory. *You*—if you choose to debate for more than just a semester—will be involved in determining how the activity should change in the years ahead; in order for you to participate intelligently in the deliberations, you need to understand the theory underlying what you are doing. The guidance must also be nonprescriptive because, right now, aside from certain fundamental procedures, much in debating is a matter of opinion. I do not—I must confess—totally refrain from offering mine; however, I have tried to offer the contrary ones too. *You* will have to make many informed decisions—as you read this text, and afterwards as you debate.

The changes which are ongoing not only invite you into the process of determining what debating ought to be, they also complicate the activity. If you skim the table of contents, you will realize how complex debating is. To make the activity as comprehensible to you as possible, this text has a pronounced process-orientation. I have tried to teach you the necessary skills in the order that you will need to learn them. You will be surprised at first that the overall structure of a debate is not discussed until Chapter 9; however, there are many matters you must master before you need to know about the obligations of the different speakers and the rules which govern competition if you are to become a truly good debater. And by "truly good," I mean a *thinking* debater. The organization of this text mirrors the process you will be going through as you learn to debate.

The text is process-oriented in another way. Before you debate, you engage in a number of thinking processes; as you debate, you engage in even more. The text specifically addresses these processes and helps you engage in them by offering numerous heuristic charts to guide your thinking and numerous exercises to help you practice your thinking.

The real exercises, however, are not to be found in this textbook or any textbook. The real exercises are to be found in actual debates. This textbook is designed, *first*, to be a prelude to such debates.

You should, however, find *Debating* valuable after you begin debating as well. Then you will be able to return to what I have said, understand it more fully, and profit more from it. I would expect you to be able to review *Debating: Applied Rhetorical Theory* throughout your career as a debater; each new look should prompt greater understanding and send you back into composition with stronger skills. This textbook, then, is, *second*, a reference work which should help you in the months and years to come.

In those months and years, change will certainly continue, especially in value debate. This text has been written in such a way that it can coexist with change. I have tried to stick to the fundamental without neglecting the theoretical roots;

furthermore, I have treated those recent developments that have struck me as enduring because they contribute significantly to the art of debating.

I hope you will find this text a useful introduction to that art, as well as a valuable guide in constantly refining your skills in debate and rethinking the art's theory and practice.

Acknowledgments

A textbook such as this is rarely the product of one person's mind. In the course of reviving the Franklin Debating Society at Randolph-Macon College, I have read numerous full-length and short-length discussions of various aspects of debating. Although *Debating: Applied Rhetorical Theory* reflects my own ideas and views on the art of debating, I must acknowledge the work of those who have preceded me in writing on the subject, for their views have undoubtedly helped me form mine.

I have several more particular acknowledgments to make.

I am indebted to the numerous scholars in the fields of composition and rhetoric who visited the campus of Beaver College in Glenside, Pennsylvania. These scholars came to Beaver College as part of a three-year faculty development program funded by the National Endowment for the Humanities. I was a member of the Beaver College faculty then, and the lessons I learned from these visiting scholars and the process-orientation of the Beaver College Writing Program are reflected not only in Chapter 4, which focuses on writing, but throughout the book.

The work of one of these scholars, Ohio State University rhetorician Edward P. J. Corbett, as well as one member of the Beaver College faculty, logician Finbarr W. O'Connor, have particularly influenced the discussion of argumentation in this text. Corbett's influence is particularly noticeable in Chapter 6, when I discuss syllogistic reasoning, and in Chapter 11, when I discuss the use of rhetorical schemes to enhance persuasion. O'Connor's influence is particularly noticeable in Chapter 6, when I discuss the charting of argumentation. O'Connor also introduced me to the work of Stephen Toulmin, whose new approach to logic is discussed in many places in this text.

As a teacher of freshman composition for many years, I have taught library research procedures to hundreds of freshmen. This teaching was improved considerably several years ago thanks to Beaver College Reference Librarian Josephine Charles. I thank her and two Randolph-Macon College faculty members: Reference Librarian Douglas W. Cooper, who has helped me handle some of the special problems researching debaters have, and Professor Bruce M. Unger, who has shared with me and my debaters his expertise as a researching and publishing political scientist.

I would also like to acknowledge the contributions made—largely unknowingly—by numerous coaches and judges in NDT District VII. Through conversations, their judging philosophy statements, and their ballots when judging Randolph-Macon teams, they have helped shape many of my thoughts. I must also acknowledge the contributions made by the debaters I have worked with at Randolph-Macon College during the past three years. Their problems, questions, and ideas have also helped shape many of my thoughts. I also must acknowledge Professor Harvey S. Wiener, the advisory editor of the Longman Composition and Communication series. It was he who suggested, three and a half years ago, that I write this book. He has also encouraged me along the way to its publication.

Finally, I must acknowledge and thank my wife Marie. As a former debater and someone with a great deal of common sense, she was a good sounding board for numerous ideas that both are and are not a part of this book. Furthermore, she endured the many, many hours I spent holed up in my office reading, thinking, planning, writing, revising, and typing. I speak in Chapter 1 of the many good things debating can lead to. I do not mention there that you can meet future wives or husbands through debating. I do, however, mention that possibility to my own debaters. I tell them that, "You just might meet someone as helpful and as understanding as my wife Marie through debating." It is to her that this book is dedicated.

CHAPTER 1
Why Debate? Why Study Rhetoric?

In this chapter, you will learn:

- what debating can do for you;
- what rhetoric is and how the study of it can make you a better debater.

You are, with this chapter, beginning your training in an activity that has a long history in American and British education. This activity—debating—mixes the excitement and satisfaction of interscholastic or intercollegiate sports with the challenge of a course of study that demands that you use your mental ability to the fullest. One of my debaters commented not too long ago that none of his fraternity brothers understood why he returned home from a weekend's debating both "high" and exhausted. Once you begin debating, you will understand, perhaps not right away, because learning the required procedures and overcoming your natural nervousness do take some time, but you will before too long. Then you will begin to understand why competitive debating has been a popular activity among high school and college students for well over a hundred years. You will also begin to sense what the activity teaches. Many famous men and women—presidents, senators, distinguished jurists—have testified to debating's value. However, presidents, senators, and distinguished jurists are fairly remote from your present situation. You may dream of being United States Senator from your state; however, you are naturally much more concerned with the beginning of your career than its culmination. So, let me talk briefly about two former debaters and how debating helped them *begin* their careers.

The first debater always had an interest in politics. Capitol Hill—its excitement, its glamour, its involvement in the important issues of the day—attracted her. The press has reported that a newly elected representative, the day after election, will find over a thousand resumés awaiting consideration. All of these aspirants want a place on the new representative's staff. This former debater's resumé made cut after cut; she was eventually hired as an aide right out of college with no government experience. Why? The representative said he hired her because he was impressed with her background as a debater. He was convinced that she could think, and he felt that after a bit of orientation, she could forcefully present his office's point of view before the press and other public audiences. The representative's confidence was not unfounded. Within a very short time, this former debater was managing the congressman's district office and representing him before numerous community audiences.

The other former debater had his eyes set on a traditional goal of many debaters: law school. However, not just any law school would do. He wanted to go to one of the nation's best—a law school halfway across the nation. He had good grades and a good LSAT score, but this particular law school was state-supported and therefore had to admit a sizeable in-state group. Furthermore, this law school looked very closely at the law school track records compiled by graduates of an applicant's undergraduate institution when deciding which few of the out-of-state applicants to accept and this student had very few predecessors from his university at this law school. This student was admitted. Why? The law school admissions committee noticed his participation in high school and college debating and decided that he was well worth the risk. The story does not end with this former debater's admission to the prestigious law school. Once there, he used his debate-trained mind to distinguish himself. He graduated second in his class and chose among several lucrative job offers from some of the East Coast's most distinguished firms. He attributes his success largely to his training as a debater. Data supports this debater's feeling that his participation in debate helped him get ahead. The results of a recent survey of those responsible for hiring at a variety of Midwest businesses listed debating first among twenty other activities and academic specializations that an applicant might present on a resumé. Debating was the *overwhelming* first choice of those responsible for recruiting and hiring for law firms. Moreover, debating was ranked very high by a wide variety of businesses.[1]

The Benefits of Debating

The above survey did not ask the respondents to indicate why they ranked debating so high; however, their reasons are rather easy to guess. Debating provides numerous benefits from which both the participant and his or her future employer will profit.

Debating Teaches Research Skills

All students write research papers. However, the research process too often stops with the card catalog and *The Reader's Guide to Periodical Literature*. Unlike many college-educated students, debaters know the numerous other resources a good library contains; debaters also know how to get information from the government and the courts. Well-trained debaters can get the information quickly, too. Too many students think library research ends when one graduates from college. Not so. Business executives, lawyers, physicians, and scientists—to name just a few groups of professionals—engage in library research and their effectiveness as researchers has a great deal to do with their success and their firms' success. In scientific research and business, for example, a company does not spend money to repeat someone else's work, so a research scientist or business executive goes to the company library or to a larger library before expending the company's time and money by repeating work.

Debating Educates Citizens

When you debate, you discuss questions of national importance. Whether the debate topics are policy-oriented matters such as nuclear waste control and import restrictions or value-oriented matters such as the right to die and censorship, debating will necessarily bring to your attention the relevant issues citizens should understand if they are to support intelligent courses of action by their society and their elected officials.

Debating Encourages Perspective

Too often, a person will jump to a conclusion on an important question and vehemently support that conclusion. However, debaters must, for an entire year or semester, take both sides of a question. Debaters, therefore, develop the ability to understand and advocate an opinion they might not personally hold. This aspect of debating—that you must offer arguments in which you do not believe—often bothers beginners. What these beginners come to understand before too long is that there are two sides to most questions. They also come to understand that a clear, rational understanding of the opposite point of view is a necessity in successful argumentation. If one wishes to present a truly compelling argument, one needs to anticipate and answer the counterargument. This understanding is also essential in real-world situations where good policy is typically developed through compromises made possible only when the policymakers involved can understand opposed points of view. The ability to distance yourself from your own opinions and view them and the views of others objectively is called perspective. Debate helps you develop perspective.

Debating Teaches Important Thinking Skills

A good debater is *not* the loudest talker; neither is he or she the most persistent advocate of a position. Rather, a good debater is one who can think through a problem and develop a strong case for a particular solution. A good debater is also one who can look at an argument with an analytical eye and quickly see its weaknesses and then point them out so that a listener understands why the argument is invalid. The good debater, then, is a master at investigating and solving problems, at analyzing and scrutinizing argumentation, and at forceful but rational challenging of others' arguments. A good debater is a master at a number of thinking skills which are useful in *all* academic disciplines as well as in *all* careers.

Debating May Teach a Truth-Seeking Method for Nonscientific Realms

In the sciences and, to a less extent, the social sciences, the scientific method and fairly well-established procedures governing experimental design and the statistical analysis of gathered data provide researchers with a method for establishing "truth." We can know the "truth" about a given chemical's effects on animal tissue or the correlation between a high aptitude for learning foreign languages and success in learning computer programming. True, another experiment or more data may alter our view of the situation—thus the quotation marks around the word "truth." Nonetheless, we do feel we are objectively seeking facts. Can we know the "truth" about the effect of a guaranteed annual income on the rate of inflation or the "truth" about the effect of a Nicaraguan-backed Communist takeover in Honduras on Mexican-American relations? We cannot simply hypothesize, experiment, and study data when dealing with such questions. But some sense of the "truth" is needed if we are to make the best decisions. The back-and-forth dialectic activity of debating may provide the necessary truth-seeking method. The power of such an activity to lead to the "truth" has long been recognized in business where corporate executives toss ideas back and forth in brainstorming sessions. Debaters are uniquely qualified for this kind of activity because they have experienced the dynamics of just such a session during a typical debating season.

Debating Sharpens Communication Skills

A debater must stand before an audience and speak clearly and persuasively. The first time you debate, you are understandably nervous; the more you debate, the more comfortable you become. You then start to acquire poise, a sharper sense of audience, and style. Most debating is extemporaneous: using just a few notes, you speak in an organized, compelling manner. The training you receive in extemporaneous speaking will prove especially beneficial. How often in a career does one deliver a written oration? Not that often. But extemporaneous speeches are given at business meetings, sales presentations, training sessions, and include remarks to a judge or jury, an intern's report on a patient's condition to a supervising doctor, and questions and comments at any kind of meeting, whether it be that of a political group, a church group, or the PTA. The list goes on. You will use the extemporaneous speaking skills you acquire while debating in numerous situations.

If you want to acquire all these benefits, you must do more than just argue. Practice does indeed help, but practice alone does not make perfect. Just as in athletics, practice must be coupled with training. Fortunately, since ancient times, an art has existed which deals specifically with persuasive writing and speaking—the art of rhetoric.

What Is Rhetoric? A Brief History

Different historians will designate different beginnings for the art of rhetoric. The consensus is that the art began with the teaching of some rather unscrupulous Greeks who recommended to all who would listen many ways to twist facts and manipulate audiences. These unscrupulous teachers, known as "sophists," were condemned repeatedly by Socrates; however, Aristotle, the star pupil of Socrates' own star pupil, believed that the "sophistic" art could be transformed into something respectable. In his *Rhetoric*, Aristotle does just that.

Since Aristotle's time, the art of rhetoric has had its ups and downs. In the *Rhetoric*, Aristotle concerns himself with three major dimensions of the persuasive act: the searching for arguments or *invention*; the arrangement of arguments or *disposition*; and the stylistically effective presentation of arguments or *elocution*. After Aristotle, attention gradually came to focus on the third dimension to the virtual exclusion of the other two. As a result, the art of rhetoric was viewed for several centuries as a mere decorative art. However, in the twentieth century, the art of rhetoric has regained its original breadth. Researchers and theoreticians are offering valuable insights on invention *and* disposition *and* elocution. And since these men and women know a great deal more about how the human mind works than Aristotle did, their insights tend to be richer.

What Classical and Modern Rhetoric Add to Debate

As you learn to debate, you should learn the relevant lessons taught by the art of rhetoric—the ancient lessons and the contemporary lessons. This text presents those lessons as you need them to sharpen your debating skills. Let me give you a few examples of how the art of rhetoric will help you.

Aristotle and Ethical Appeal

Aristotle talks in the *Rhetoric* about three different kinds of arguments or appeals the persuader makes: logical appeals, emotional appeals, and ethical appeals. Since humans are a rational *and* emotional species, every persuasive artist needs to recognize the usefulness of a mixture of logical and emotional arguments in a persuasive speech or essay. The persuader must also be alert to the power of ethical appeals: these are appeals a speaker or writer makes because of his or her character. This character is known as one's *ethos*. If you come across as sincere, honest, and reasonable, you are making a powerful ethical argument. The use of emotional appeals and ethical appeals is discussed at length in Chapter 11.

Heuristics Old and New

Heuristics are formulae or set procedures for discovering arguments. Aristotle listed a number of places, or *topoi*, where a persuasive artist ought to look for arguments. Contemporary rhetoricians have offered heuristics ranging from the free-wheeling to the rigidly systematic. Some of these heuristics are presented in this text; more important to you as an apprentice debater, numerous heuristics designed specifically for the debating situations are offered to you. These heuristics will help you discover what you might say when your turn comes to stand up and speak; they will allow you to think through any position an opponent might toss at you and see where that position can be challenged.

Kenneth Burke and Formal Appeal

A very important contemporary rhetorician, Kenneth Burke, has written about the persuasive appeal particular forms or structures or organizations have. Burke has alerted persuasive writers and speakers to two very important lessons: first, the goal is not simply to organize, but rather to organize in the most effective way, given the specific nature of the argument you are making; second, an argument's structure can be a thing of beauty, and the audience's aesthetic pleasure when reading or listening to it can enhance the persuasion. Burke's observations on formal appeal are discussed in Chapter 11.

Stephen Toulmin and the Search for Warrants

Flemish logician and rhetorician Stephen Toulmin has made a significant contribution to our understanding of argumentation. Like many other contemporary logicians, he sees the mathematical and the nonmathematical as very different rhetorical realms. According to Toulmin, many of the procedures used by traditional logic are based on mathematical reasoning and are inappropriate to nonmathematical reasoning. Because he felt this way, he examined arguments in areas such as law, government, the natural sciences, business, and the arts, and, based on what he saw, he outlined the requisite elements and the standards for evaluating arguments in each one. Then Toulmin began working with students, helping them analyze arguments into those elements and establish an argument's validity or invalidity based on whether the elements met the established standards or not.

The six elements—claim, grounds, warrant, backing, modality, and rebuttals—will be discussed in detail in Chapter 6. So will other traditional and not-so-traditional concerns of applied logic.

Linda Flower and Issue-Treeing

Teachers of writing have for generations asked students to prepare outlines. Research has revealed that formal outlines, if prepared too early, can actually be a detriment. Why? Outlines do not always reveal a true hierarchical or logical arrangement of ideas; outlines *look* hierarchical and logical, but looks can be quite deceiving. Linda Flower, a leading researcher in writing at Carnegie-Mellon University, recommends that writers try "issue trees" when thinking through a presentation and planning its disposition or organization. This very visual sketch of the relationships among ideas can give a persuasive speaker an accurate view of the hierarchy and logic of his or her ideas. Issue-treeing and other recommendations for improving the logical organization of a persuasive speech are presented in Chapter 5.

Before you are ready to learn and apply these lessons (and many others) drawn from the art of rhetoric, you need to understand how to approach a debate topic or resolution to figure out what issues it raises. You also need to understand how to engage in effective, efficient research on these issues. The following two chapters focus on these two important preliminary tasks: exploring the resolution and researching the issues it raises. But before you begin the process of learning how to debate, let me emphasize the fun of debating. Yes, preparing for debating is hard work, and many debates will strain and expand your intellectual capabilities. However, the competition is exciting. You can "wow" an opposing school's team with your well-thought-out arguments; *or* you can find critical flaws in the seemingly airtight position an opponent has taken; *or* you can decide to use an unconventional, risky strategy in a given debate.

Debates typically take place at tournaments. Anywhere from ten to a hundred schools convene to debate. Most tournaments last a couple of days; many will require traveling long distances. The average active high school team will journey to two or three "big" tournaments a year; the average active college team will drive or fly to ten or twelve tournaments a year. The travel is fun—not the hours on the highway, but the experience of going new places with your close friends on the team and interacting with students from other schools during the tournament day and later on at planned and spontaneous parties at the host school or at the motel housing the debate tournament participants.

My own philosophy as a debate coach is to get beginners on the road and into competition as soon as possible. Why? Because then, as the research and lessons in rhetoric continue, the fun of debating and the fun of going to tournaments will keep the energy level high. Try to keep the fun of debate in mind as you now begin your instruction.

After reading Chapter 1, you know:

- how debating can equip you for your future by
  —teaching you research skills;
  —informing you about important public issues;
  —encouraging perspective;
  —teaching you important thinking skills;
  —teaching you a truth-seeking method for nonscientific realms;
  —sharpening your communication skills.
- that rhetoric is the art of writing and speaking persuasively and that the study of it can help you, among other tasks,
  —know what to say;
  —plan how to organize it;
  —know how to analyze an argument you wish to challenge.

Notes

1. Don B. Center, "Debate and the Job Market," *Debate Issues* 15, no. 8 (May 1982), pp. 4–6.

CHAPTER 2
Exploring the Resolution

In this chapter, you will learn:

- what kinds of resolutions you may debate;
- how to understand the issues a debate resolution raises by defining key terms;
- how to understand the issues a resolution raises by using heuristics.

When you debate, you debate a specific question or resolution. Two different types of resolutions are common in competitive debating—policy resolutions and value resolutions.

Policy Resolutions and Value Resolutions

Policy resolutions call for the adoption of a particular course of action. The following are policy resolutions:

Resolved: That government information-gathering should be significantly curtailed.
Resolved: That United States foreign military commitments should be significantly increased.
Resolved: That the United States should reduce its commitment to Israel.
Resolved: That the penal system in the United States should be significantly improved.

Each calls for the adoption of a policy: a law against CIA wire-tapping; federal appropriations for additional troops to be stationed in Western Europe; a law prohibiting the sale of "high tech," potentially offensive weaponry to Israel; state appropriations for greatly expanded maximum-security prison systems.

Value resolutions call for the affirmation of a judgment based on the acceptance of a particular value or values. The following are value resolutions:

Resolved: That the rights of the mother are more important than the rights of the fetus.
Resolved: That affirmative action programs have been deleterious in their effects.
Resolved: That American television has sacrificed quality for entertainment.
Resolved: That a United States foreign policy significantly directed toward the furtherance of human rights is desirable.

Each resolution calls for the acceptance of a judgment based on a value or set of values. Respectively, the affirmative must argue that the mother's pursuit of happiness is more valuable then the fetus' right to live; that job efficiency is more valuable than justice for minorities; that the enrichment of the mind is more valuable than simple, perhaps mindless relaxation; and that fundamental human rights are more important than deterring the expansion of Communism.

These summary statements of the value conflict and the debate that these representative value resolutions might lead to should make two troublesome aspects of value resolutions clear to you. First, the decision between competing values—e.g., job efficiency and justice for minorities—is a tough and very emotional one. Both sides in the debate may be able to construct and present equally compelling arguments. The judge's decision will be a difficult one, and he or she may be unconsciously swayed to one side or the other by his or her personal emotional attachment to the value or values that one of the teams is defending. In other words, the judge may have a more difficult time maintaining objectivity when the debate is on a value resolution than when it is on a policy resolution. Second, affirming many value resolutions implies the advocacy of a policy. This is the case because the division of debate resolutions into policy resolutions and value resolutions is arbitrary. Policy resolutions imply values; value resolutions imply policies. The division is made by those who govern competitive debating so that there will exist a form of debating where values are central, not incidental (as they often are when a definite policy must be presented and defended). So, if you are debating a value resolution, realize that there usually are policy implications, but also realize that your focus should be on the values, not the specifics of public policy.

Understanding the Resolution by Defining its Key Terms

The Two Types of Key Terms

Every debate resolution has key terms. The terms are of two types: (1) those which are in need of definition; (2) those whose definitions *seem* clear. Consider the policy resolution "Resolved: That the United States should implement a comprehensive policy to maintain the nation's infrastructure." Only one term falls into type one, "infrastructure." Many people are not familiar with this rather technical term which refers to our sewer, water, and highway systems. Four terms fall into type two: "implement," "comprehensive," "maintain," and "the nation's." Does "implement" mean devise *and* administer or just the latter? Does "comprehensive" imply that all systems embraced by the term "infrastructure" must be covered by the proposed policy or that all aspects of one system—e.g., water—may be covered? Does "maintain" mean that the proposed policy must not call for additional construction? Does "the nation's" mean that the policy need only deal with those systems owned and operated by the federal government and therefore can ignore the vast state, county, and municipal infrastructure? To get a handle on the resolution, one must understand what the key terms might mean and, based on those possible meanings, what issues the resolution raises.

Let's consider the value resolution "Resolved: That *compulsory national service* for all *qualified United States citizens* is *desirable*." I have italicized the key terms. Three are obviously in need of definition. What in legislative circles is meant by "national service"? What is the official definition of "United States citizens"? What standards will be used to determine whether something is "desirable" or not? Other terms are not so obviously in need. Does "compulsory," used legally, admit any exceptions? What might "qualified" mean? Is the term to be defined in terms of not having any physical or mental limitations that would make service impossible? Or is "qualified" to be defined in terms of having suitable training, background, or aptitude? Which way a particular debater interprets the term may well determine whether he or she is talking about a program for almost all Americans or a program for the few who possess special qualifications, e.g., computer programming skills, the ability to speak Russian, IQ above 120, etc. Those programs would be very different. Again, to get a handle on the debate resolution and all of the issues it raises, you need to think about all of the reasonable ways the key terms could be defined.

Your own mind, your fellow debaters (especially those with some competitive experience), and your instructor or coach can help you examine the key terms. Printed resources can also help. Yes, you can look up the terms in a dictionary. But make sure it is a good desk dictionary such as *The Random House Dictionary of the English Language* or *Webster's New Collegiate Dictionary* or a larger, longer, more definitive dictionary such as *Webster's Third International Dictionary of the English Language*. Small dictionaries, although handy, do not provide you with all of a word's uses. Furthermore, no matter what dictionary you turn to, be alert to how that reference work orders the meanings it lists. Some dictionaries, such as *Webster's New Collegiate* and *Webster's Third International*, arrange the listed meanings in historical order, with the oldest use first; other dictionaries, such as *The Random House Dictionary*, arrange the meanings in order of use, with the most frequently used meaning first. You need to be alert to the principle of arrangement because you would be on weak ground if you defined a term based on an old meaning that has almost disappeared from usage or a very rare meaning. You can find out a particular dictionary's principle of arrangement by looking at its front matter—i.e., the written explanation of how the dictionary works, which is usually offered as a preface to the A through Z listing of words.

Regular dictionaries can help; however, frequently superior for debating are specialized dictionaries such as *Black's Law Dictionary*. These specialized reference works define the term as it is used, not in general, but in the specific context you may be interested in—law, economics, philosophy, etc. These dictionaries are prepared for specialists; therefore, reading an entry in them will require time and patience. You may even have to consult with your instructor or coach about these "technical" definitions, or perhaps even a specialist in the field in question. This consultation will prove well worth the time, for, once a specialized definition is understood, it will give you a specialist's sense of the debate resolution and provide you with powerful ammunition to defend your sense of the resolution and challenge that of others.

The goal of defining the resolution's key terms is to discover what the resolution might be thought to mean. A handy way to meet this goal is to construct a "definitions chart." Turn an 8½" × 11" sheet of paper sideways, so that the 11" side is the horizontal. Print the resolution across the top. Underscore every key term, whether obviously in need of definition or not-so-obviously, and list beneath each term the possible meanings you have uncovered. If you number the meanings, you can generate all the possible permutations and see what the resolution might be interpreted to mean. Figure 2.1 provides you with a sample "definitions chart" for the policy resolution "Resolved: That all United States military intervention into the internal affairs of any foreign nation or nations in the Western Hemisphere should be prohibited." By selecting sequence 3-2-2-1-1-2, you come up with an interpretation that would not have been apparent to many: that the sending of money and arms by United States citizens to the Irish Republican Army for its use in terrorist activities in Northern Ireland be made illegal. By selecting sequence 2-3-2-4-1-1, you come up with another unusual reading: that the secret monetary support given to out-of-power groups in certain Central American nations by American corporations, which are seeking tax and other favors from the rebels once they gain power, be declared illegal.

You may wonder at this point whether the goal of debating is to discuss the important issues implicit in the resolution or to find a very unusual interpretation of the resolution to discuss—one which opponents would not be "up" on. Actually, the goal is to reach a compromise between these two goals—to discuss the truly important issues so as to reap the full benefits of debating *and* to choose an aspect of the resolution to focus on that would give you a strategic advantage over opponents. But, in discussing your selection of an aspect to focus on, we are getting ahead of ourselves, into the matter of Chapter 4. Right now, all we are trying to do is unlock the resolution and discover all that might be stored in it.

RESOLVED: That all

	United States	military	intervention	into the	internal affairs	of	any foreign nation or nations	in the	Western Hemisphere	should be prohibited.
1	funded by the government	involving armed forces	hostile action		internal politics		any single nation or a set of nations		North, Central, and South America (including Caribbean islands)	
2	involving U.S. corporations	involving weaponry	outside interference, even if requested		internal economics		any single nation or all nations (including the U.S.)		everything between the Greenwich Meridian on the East and the International Dateline on the West	
3	involving money from U.S. citizens	involving financial assistance for operations involving armed forces	mediation		anything within geographical boundaries		all nations without exception			
4	involving U.S. citizens	involving any government agency with a direct military role			anything over which a sovereign nation has jurisdiction		any single nation but not necessarily the government of that nation			

Figure 2.1 Sample definitions chart.

13

"Should" and Fiat Power

The word "should" appears often in policy resolutions. I have not treated it as a key term in need of definition because its definition in debating is fairly standardized. "Should" means "ought to but not necessarily will." This standardized definition implies two important conventions of debate: (1) that the team advocating the resolution *does not* have to show it will be adopted; (2) that the team advocating the resolution *does not* have to show that a Constitutional amendment will be passed by Congress and ratified by the requisite number of states if an amendment is necessary for the presented or implied policy to take effect. Both of these conventions are subsumed under the term "fiat power." The team advocating a policy is permitted to command or "fiat" the presented or implied policy into operation, bypassing, as it were, the necessary legislative actions. This convention has long been observed in debating so that attention will be directed toward the merits of the resolution, not the political dimensions any presented or implied policy possesses. Beginning debaters need to know about this convention so that they do not waste time discussing whether Congress will or will not pass a policy.

Understanding the Resolution by Using Heuristics

The Problems Perspective as a Heuristic

The "definitions chart" should—i.e., ought to but not necessarily will—give you a good sense of what the debate resolution might mean. However, other heuristics ought to be used to ensure that the sense you acquire is as complete as possible. I will present four such heuristics. The first asks you to take a problems perspective and is suitable for both policy and value propositions. Ask yourself what problems would lead one to make the judgment or advocate the policy embodied by the resolution. Let's try out this heuristic with both policy and value propositions. First, a policy proposition. The resolution calls for a curtailment of labor union power. Why might someone advocate that kind of policy? Brainstorm—i.e., rapidly fire forth anything that comes to mind. Brainstorm by yourself or brainstorm with teammates. Some—*only some*—of the answers to the question are listed below:

High inflation
The near failure of the U.S. automotive industry
The near failure of the U.S. railroad industry
The high cost of federal construction projects
The violation of the rights of dissident union members who do not want their dues contributed to union-selected political causes and candidates
The violation of the rights of those forced to join unions in order to work

Union violence
Corruption in union pension fund administration

Each of these answers would lead to a very different debate.

Let's try a value resolution—the Spring 1976 Cross-Examination Debate Association (CEDA) resolution which judged United States education to be a failure. Why might one make this judgment? A brainstorming session might lead to a list containing the following reasons:

Declining SAT scores
Mathematics and science education inferior to that received in the Soviet Union
Poor teaching
Violence in the schools
A lack of preparedness for the world among high school graduates
A lack of control of "the basics" among high school graduates
Limited computer science education in most American high schools
Poor foreign language education at all levels

Again, each problem would lead to a very different debate.

The Plans Perspective as a Heuristic

In policy debate, a policy is advocated. Rarely is the policy simply a restatement of the resolution; usually, the policy is a more specific statement. For example, if the resolution called for the federal government to share its income tax revenue with the states, the policy would explain on what basis this revenue-sharing should occur—population, degree of poverty, the severity of winter weather, etc. Or, if the resolution called for the United States to "beef up" its military, the policy would explain exactly how the military should be strengthened: more missiles, more submarines, new bombers, higher salaries and therefore more men, more aircraft carriers, etc. In a policy resolution, numerous plans are hiding. If you adopt the plans perspective and brainstorm to discover *all* the possible plans, you will achieve a greater understanding of the policy resolution you are going to be debating.

Let's try the plans-perspective heuristic with a policy resolution advocating alternative national service. What kinds of service could be mandated for those who object to serving in the military? The list might include the following:

Working in hospitals
Working with the elderly
Rebuilding America's sewers, water pipes, and roads
Rebuilding America's inner-city slums

Teaching in remote areas
Serving as a member of a new natural disaster relief corps
Working in dangerous but important coal mines
Working in federal parks and forests

The Divide-and-Conquer Heuristic

Quite a few resolutions, both policy and value, contain key terms which permit the debaters to narrow down the discussion. For example, the policy resolution in Figure 2.1 permits the debaters to choose any western hemisphere nation they want. A value proposition declaring "That a U.S. foreign policy directed toward the furtherance of human rights is desirable" permits debaters to choose the specific human rights they wish to discuss. To gain as full an understanding of a debate resolution as possible, debaters should identify such divisible terms and divide them into all the realistic choices.

Consider the policy resolution concerning U.S. military intervention in "any nation or nations in the western hemisphere." What western hemisphere nations might be realistic choices? What nations are we presently intervening in militarily? The list that debaters would generate would include El Salvador, Guatemala, Honduras, Panama, Uruguay, and other nations.

Consider the value resolution on human rights. What human rights might be focused on? The list would include the right to vote, the right to speak one's mind, the right to print antigovernment views, the right to justice, the right to humane treatment, the right to privacy from government spying, and other rights.

Dividing key terms such as "any nation or nations" and "human rights" gives one a high degree of command over a debate resolution. The debaters who have intelligently used the "divide and conquer" heuristic should know on what issues debating will focus and where their research energies should be spent.

The Values Perspective as a Heuristic

Almost all propositions involve conflicting values. True, value propositions do so more explicitly, but most policy propositions imply the acceptance or rejection of values. To fully understand a debate resolution, you should understand the values that it raises. A recent CEDA resolution, "That the American judicial system has overemphasized the rights of the accused," raises such values as justice, safety, innocence (until proven guilty), and freedom from coercion. All of these values are time-honored ones in this nation, but the resolution suggests that you must select the first two as being more important that the latter two if you are to defend the resolution. The policy resolution dealing with U.S. military intervention in the western hemisphere raises such valued objectives as the economic prosperity of the United States and its citizens, the human rights of the citizens of nations we may be aiding, our national security, and the preservation of global freedoms from the threat of Communism. Again, the resolution suggests that you must select the first two valued objectives and reject the latter two if you are to defend the resolution.

When exploring a debate resolution, you should brainstorm to discover the values implicit in affirming the resolution and in negating the resolution. Let's try out the heuristic procedure on a value resolution, and then on a policy resolution.

Consider the value proposition "That American television has sacrificed quality for entertainment." If you embrace that judgment, what values do you embrace? Education, culture, aesthetic pleasure. If you reject that judgment? Relaxation, laughter, excitement. Consider the policy proposition "That the executive power over U.S. foreign policy should be significantly limited." If you embrace that policy statement, what values do you embrace? Democracy, public awareness, fiscal responsibility. If you reject that policy statement? National security, strength, efficiency.

Undoubtedly, some of you will ask why you have to choose. Can't television be defended as educational and exciting, cultural and humorous, aesthetically pleasing and relaxing? Can't the conduct of U.S. foreign policy be democratic but conducive to national security, open but strong, fiscally responsible and efficient? By asking these questions, you are intuitively sensing how a debater who is dealing with values will often proceed: that debater will try to show that there is no value conflict, but rather that the values implicit in affirming and denying the resolution can be maintained by the judgment or policy he or she advocates. This debater argues, for example, that limiting executive control over U.S. foreign policy will ensure democracy but not at the expense of national security if he or she is on the affirmative side. *Or* this debater argues that strong executive control is necessary to maintain national security and that this control, as it has been exercised over the past half-century, does not in any way jeopardize democracy.

I recommend that you think of the implicit values on the opposite sides, not because many actual debates will focus *exclusively* on a simple choice between education and relaxation or fiscal responsibility and efficiency, but, rather, because it is useful to know what values a resolution implies if you are to arrive at a truly complete understanding of the resolution and all the issues it raises.

Combining Perspectives

I have introduced you to four separate heuristics for exploring the debate resolution: the problems-perspective heuristic, the plans-perspective heuristic, the divide-and-conquer heuristic, and the values-perspective heuristic. Figure 2.2 combines the four in such a way that they can now work together as one "super heuristic." Column 1 lists the problems, column 2 the plans, column 3 the divisions of any divisible key terms, and column 4 the values implicit in advocating the resolution.

	Problems	Plans	Divide and Conquer (on "defense and defense-related industries")	Values (in affirming the resolution)
1	The damage to the economy done by strikes	Binding, final-offer arbitration	Basic metals	National security
2	Inflationary wage settlements	Government-imposed contract by Presidentially-appointed panel	Aerospace	Prosperity
3	National security threatened	Contract imposed by U.S. Department of Labor	Electronics	Freedom from Communism
4	Damage to smaller businesses as strikes have ripple effect on those who supply the affected industry	Cost-of-living increase mandated by law (no more, no less) except upon special appeal to the President	Computers	Justice for all workers
5	"Blackmail" by unions in key industries who know they are vital	A cooling-off period; mediation; finally, government-imposed contract with terms somewhere in between final positions of two sides	Fuels	Economic health

Figure 2.2 "Super heuristic" for exploring the resolution.

Exploring the Resolution

The same game you played with the "definitions chart" can be played here. Choose a four digit number (five if you have two divisible key terms), and then see what approach to the debate resolution you have discovered. Figure 2.2 applies all four heuristics to a policy resolution calling for the arbitration of labor-management disputes in any defense-related industry or industries. If you choose 1-1-3-1, you come up with an approach that will discuss the evils of strikes, propose binding final-offer arbitration for just the electronics industry, and stress the superiority of national security to the workers' democratic rights.

Some permutations will yield nonsense—i.e., four or more ingredients that just do not mesh. Devising and then playing intelligently with a chart like Figure 2.2 can, however, yield a very full understanding of what approaches are possible to a given resolution.

Exercises: Exploring the Resolution

1. Construct a "definitions chart" for the following debate resolutions:
   A. Resolved: That active participation in organized athletics promotes maturity.
   B. Resolved: That mandatory school prayer is desirable.
   C. Resolved: That the federal government should more fully regulate the American trucking industry.
   D. Resolved: That laser technology should be limited to peaceful applications.
2. Construct a "definitions chart" for the debate resolution you will be debating this year or semester.
3. Brainstorm, using the problems-perspective heuristic. List the problems that a debater might cite to justify the following debate resolutions:
   A. Resolved: That intercollegiate football has not proved its worth.
   B. Resolved: That America's schools are dangerous places.
   C. Resolved: That the federal government should more strictly regulate the activities of large American corporations.
   D. Resolved: That the United States should embark upon a policy of unilateral nuclear disarmament.
4. Brainstorm, using the plans-perspective heuristic. List the possible policies a debater might advocate if defending the following resolutions:
   A. Resolved: That the American criminal justice system for juvenile offenders should be significantly improved.
   B. Resolved: That the American presidential election process should be significantly improved.
   C. Resolved: That the United States should strengthen its nuclear defense capability.
   D. Resolved: That the United Nations should be reorganized in order to significantly increase its efficacy as a peacekeeping body.
5. Brainstorm, using the divide-and-conquer heuristic. List some of the divisions of the italicized key terms in the following debate resolutions:

A. Resolved: That our *electoral process* encourages corruption.
B. Resolved: That the United States should share its *resources* with developing nations.
C. Resolved: That *federal tax laws* should be significantly revised.
D. Resolved: That the United States should revoke the most-favored-nation trading status from *any nation or nations abusing its special privileges.*
6. Brainstorm, using the values-perspective heuristic. Draw out the values implicit in affirming and denying the following debate resolutions:
   A. Resolved: That legal protection of accused persons in the United States unnecessarily hinders law enforcement agencies.
   B. Resolved: That NATO is an anachronism.
   C. Resolved: That the United States should reduce its commiment to Israel.
   D. Resolved: That the federal government should guarantee an annual subsistence income to all United States citizens.
7. Use the four heuristics presented in this chapter to devise and and construct a "combination chart" for the resolution you will be debating this year or semester. (Note: the plans-perspective will not be appropriate if the resolution is a value resolution.)

After reading and studying Chapter 2, you know:

- the difference between policy resolutions and value resolutions;
- how defining terms obviously in need of definition *and* terms not-so-obviously in need of definition can lead to an understanding of the issues a debate resolution raises;
- how to use (1) the problems-perspective heuristic, (2) the plans-perspective heuristic, (3) the divide-and-conquer heuristic, and (4) the values-perspective heuristic.

CHAPTER 3

Research

In this chapter, you will learn:

- how to begin your research;
- how to engage in serious research in an academic library;
- how to gather materials *beyond* the confines of the academic library;
- how to read when researching and how to prepare your evidence and your evidence file;
- how to engage in research as the debate season progresses.

You now know how many issues are contained in a typical debate resolution. Debating "Resolved: That the powers of labor unions should be significantly curtailed" would require that you become conversant with labor-management relations in a host of industries. It would also require that you become knowledgeable about laws governing violence during strikes, procedures for setting wages for workers on government construction projects, and regulations establishing how unions can contribute to political campaigns. Debating "Resolved: That United States military intervention into the internal affairs of any foreign nation or nations in the western hemisphere should be prohibited" would require that you become conversant with the governments of just about every Central American and South American nation as well as U.S. policy toward them.

These two resolutions are policy propositions. Many people suggest that debating a value resolution requires less research because you are dealing with opinions about values, not facts. Consider, however, the value proposition: "That unauthorized immigration into the United States is seriously detrimental to the nation." If you were to debate this resolution successfully, you would have to know a great deal about the economies of the states illegal immigrants flock to—Florida, Texas, California. You would also have to investigate the conditions these immigrants are fleeing and the numerous strains they place on the welfare and educational systems where they settle. So, whether you are debating policy questions or value questions, you will have to engage in research. This chapter is designed to guide you in that research.

Shortcuts

There are shortcuts you can take. They do save time, but you do not end up learning as much—about your subject matter and about research itself—if you rely too heavily on shortcuts.

Handbooks

Several educational materials companies publish handbooks on national high school and national college policy topics. They typically contain a brief introduction to the resolution and hundreds of pieces of evidence—statements of fact and statements of opinion. Although some of these handbooks contain some evidence of questionable value, the handy-dandy evidence can provide you with a helpful *start*. The questionable evidence you might see and should discard is characterized by any one of the following flaws: (1) a citation lacking the author's name or where the statement was published (i.e., in what journal) or when the statement was published or the page or pages upon which the statement is to be found; (2) ellipses so numerous that the original meaning of the quoted statement may well have been lost; (3) a statement so brief that neither the context nor the author's reasons for an opinion are clear.

Into the same category as handbooks fall collections of evidence, already on 4" × 6" cards, which many of the same publishers market. Again, these cards can help you get started; however, you need to scrutinize each piece of purchased evidence very closely. If it is flawed, discard it. If you cannot figure out what the author meant, don't guess; rather, use the full citation, go to the original, and read the quoted statement's full context before you use the statement as evidence in an actual debate.

In a debate, you are responsible for the integrity of each piece of evidence you use. If that evidence is in some way flawed, that flaw may cost you the debate.

Institutes

Many colleges and universities sponsor summer institutes for high school and college debaters. At these institutes, you receive instruction and intensive coaching; you debate the new academic year's topic or, in value debate, a practice topic; you also begin to accumulate your evidence cards. Many institutes provide a system whereby a debater comes home with not only his or her evidence but with that of everyone in his or her small group. As with handbook evidence, this material can help you get started; however, you need to exercise caution when using evidence obtained from someone else, whether he or she is also at the institute or someone from your school who went to one of these institutes. If the borrowed evidence is flawed, toss it out; if you aren't sure of its precise meaning, check it out. *You* are fully responsible for any evidence you use.

Preliminary Research

Evidence acquired via the shortcuts I discussed above can help you get started. You will get a better start, though, if you do your own research. The bulk of this chapter will guide you. The advice is specific to the debater's situation.

Background Reading

The first task is to acquire some familiarity with the topic you will be debating. You cannot engage in effective library research blindly; you must know the fundamentals. For background information, you can go to three different sources.

Special Studies. To encourage debating, different think tanks have, over the years, prepared special introductions to the national high school and college policy resolutions. The American Enterprise Institute (AEI), a conservative think tank based in Washington, D.C., used to put its expert staff to work to prepare what AEI calls a "special analysis." A few years ago, AEI stopped publishing one of the college handbooks, but the AEI special analysis on the high school topic is still prepared and provides an excellent, objective introduction to the year's debate resolution. Write the American Enterprise Institute, 1150 17th Street N.W., Washington, D.C. 20036, for a copy. At the moment, nothing comparable exists for either the college NDT resolution or the college CEDA resolutions.

Editorial Research Reports. Many libraries subscribe to a valuable series called *Editorial Research Reports*. Every month, the Congressional Quarterly publishes a 100+-page booklet on a particular public issue. The May 1983 issue, for example, focused on *The World Economy*; the September 1981 issue focused on *Education in America*. All *Editorial Research Reports* offer a brief bibliography as well as an objective, to-the-point overview of the issue under discussion.

Monographs. If you are not fortunate enough to find a special study or an *Editorial Research Report*, you'll have to go the old-fashioned route. You will have to search for a good book on your general topic. You find out what books are available to you by using your library's card catalog and *The Library of Congress Subject Headings Index*. This index is a two-volume reference work, and you will generally find it near the card catalog. Look up a subject in it; it will tell you what heading the card catalog uses. If you look up a heading the card catalog does indeed use, *The Library of Congress Subject Headings Index* lists for you related headings that you might also want to consult in the card catalog.

Figure 3.1 is a sample page from *The Library of Congress Subject Headings Index*. Look at it for a moment. If you had looked up "foreign policy" in it, you would have discovered that the card catalog uses the heading "international relations," not "foreign policy." If you had looked up "foreign trade regulations" in *The Library of Congress Subject Headings Index*, you would have discovered that the card catalog does indeed use "foreign trade regulations" as a subject heading; you would have also discovered that "export controls" and "import quotas" are two other possible subjects to look under for information related to "foreign trade regulations."

Once you've got the correct subject heading, you can see what the library has. For example, if the subject is immigration, you may find six monographs (that is, single-authored, book-length discussions) on the subject. What then? You're at a very early stage in the research process. You need a monograph that accomplishes two missions for you: first, provides you with a thorough, not overly detailed introduction to the topic; second, provides you with recent information. Look at the six available monographs. To see a monograph's coverage, look at its Table of Contents; to see a monograph's date, look at the copyright page (usually the back of the title page).

You will not always make the best choice. A book may look general and introductory, but prove to be closely tied to the author's particular, rather complex thesis concerning, for example, various microeconomic dimensions of immigration. If you made a bad choice, put it aside and go back to the library shelves. There are two ways to avoid wasting time. First, you can consult with someone at your school who is knowledgeable in the field you are investigating; he or she might be able to direct you to the best introductory monograph(s). Second, you can work as a team. Isolate the best-looking four, five, six, or seven monographs; have each team member read one. Then, stage a symposium at which each member presents his or her findings to the group in writing and orally. Lots of time should be allotted for questions and discussion.

Additional Symposia

The idea of staging symposia need not be limited to presentation of preliminary research findings. On college campuses, quite a few members of the faculty who are not involved with the debating program are more than willing to share their expertise with that school's debate squad or class. At the college where I teach, several members of the faculty have been generous with their time and have helped debaters shape their preliminary thoughts about a debate topic. For example, the debaters have been guided in their thinking on several foreign policy topics by an internationally known expert on disarmament. He led the debaters (and myself) to realize, first, how superficial their initial thinking on the topic was,

Foreign offices
   sa *names of individual foreign offices, e.g.*
      United States. Dept. of State
   xx Diplomatic and consular service
      International law
      International relations
Foreign opinion of the Catholic Church in the United States
   See Catholic Church in the United States—Foreign opinion
Foreign opinion of the United States
   See United States—Foreign opinion
Foreign physicians
   See Physicians, Foreign
Foreign policy
   See International relations
      subdivision Foreign relations *under names of countries*
Foreign policy and trade-unions
   See Trade-unions and foreign policy
Foreign population
   See Emigration and immigration
      Libraries and foreign population
      Minorities
      subdivisions Emigration and immigration *under countries, and* Foreign population *under countries, cities, etc.*
Foreign propagandists in the United States *(JX1896)*
   Here are entered works on foreign agents active as propagandists as defined in the foreign agents registration act of 1938, as amended. Works on foreign business agents are entered under the heading Commerical agents.
   x Agents of foreign principals in the United States
      Foreign agents in the United States
   xx Diplomatic and consular service
      Lobbyists
      Propaganda
Foreign property
   See Alien property
Foreign radio stations *(Indirect)*
   x Alien radio stations
      Radio stations, Foreign
Foreign relations
   See International relations
      subdivision Foreign relations *under names of countries, e.g.* France—Foreign relations
Foreign relations administration
   See *subdivision* Foreign relations administration *under names of countries, e.g.* United States—Foreign relations administration
Foreign relations law (United States)
   See United States—Foreign relations—Law and legislation
Foreign service
   See Diplomatic and consular service
Foreign students
   See Students, Foreign
Foreign study
   sa Students, Foreign
   xx Education
      Students, Foreign
Foreign tax havens
   See Tax havens
Foreign teaching positions
   See American teachers in foreign countries—Employment

Foreign trade and employment *(Indirect)*
   sa Investments, Foreign, and employment
      Trade adjustment assistance
      Unemployed
   x Employment and foreign trade
   xx Commerce
      Investments, Foreign, and employment
      Labor supply
      Trade adjustment assistance
      Unemployed
   — Underdeveloped areas
      See Underdeveloped areas—Foreign trade and employment
Foreign trade control
   See Foreign trade regulation
Foreign trade policy
   See Commercial policy
Foreign trade promotion *(Indirect)*
   sa Export controls
      Export credit
      Export premiums
      Export processing zones
      Fairs
      Foreign exchange
      Foreign trade regulation
      Import substitution
      Insurance, Export credit
      Subsidies
      Trade missions
   x Export promotion
      Export trade promotion
   xx Commercial policy
      Export sales
      Foreign trade regulation
      Industry and state
      Subsidies
   — Evaluation
      Example under reference from **Evaluation**
   — Underdeveloped areas
      See Underdeveloped areas—Foreign trade promotion
      GEOGRAPHIC SUBDIVISIONS
   — United States
      sa Domestic international sales corporations
Foreign trade regulation *(Indirect)*
   sa Commercial treaties
      Customs administration
      Export controls
      Foreign exchange—Law
      Foreign trade promotion
      Import quotas
      International clearing
      Tariff—Law
   x Export and import controls
      Foreign trade control
      Import and export controls
      Import restrictions
      International trade control
      International trade regulation
      Prohibited exports and imports
   xx Commercial law
      Commercial policy
      Foreign trade promotion
      Trade adjustment assistance
   — Criminal provisions
Foreign trade zones
   See Free ports and zones
Foreign-trained lawyers
   See Lawyers, Foreign
Foreign-trained medical personnel
   See Medical personnel, Foreign

Figure 3.1   Sample page from *The Library of Congress Subject Headings Index*.

and then, how some of their ideas could be translated fairly quickly into sophisticated rationales for public policies.

The original symposium was conducted by Socrates. After a good meal, spurred on by fine wine, Socrates and other distinguished citizens of Athens would debate an issue that was important to them. The debates, or sessions, held by the nineteenth-century literary societies at American colleges were not unlike the original symposium chronicled by Socrates' student Plato. Even though today's competitive debating, which grew out of meets between rival literary societies, is far more elaborate and sophisticated than these earlier meetings, we need not totally forget what our predecessors did. The meetings or debates these societies held can be transformed into sessions in which debaters (with or without their coach) speak persuasively on the year's resolution based solely on their initial research. A firm insistence on a degree of formality will prevent such sessions from degenerating into something farcical.

The goal at this stage in the research process is to get minds going, working with some research accomplished, but not too much. This preliminary research, these symposia, and the heuristic exploration of the resolution (outlined in Chapter 2) will lead debaters to the point where they can engage in efficient, effective, *serious* library research.

Preparing a Good Bibliography

The last preliminary activity you need to engage in is the preparation of a good bibliography to guide you in your serious library research. A good bibliography has three characteristics. First, it is dominated by recent books and articles. Notice that I said *dominated*. Contrary to the thinking of far too many debaters, a five- or ten-year-old study is not worthless if it is (a) a theoretical or historical discussion, (b) authored by a preeminent figure in the field, or (c) considered to be, in some way, definitive. Second, a good bibliography does not list books and articles that treat a very small aspect of the subject. You are not ready to make use of the microscopic treatment given some subjects by some scholars. If you have a reason to read such treatments later in the season, you can return to them. Third, a good bibliography permits continual expansion. As you read the first ten studies you've listed, you will find references to four or five others. Add these to your bibliography if they look useful and then read them.

Does a Good Bibliography Already Exist? We're getting ahead of ourselves in talking about adding to the bibliography. How do you put the initial bibliography together? You can go to a good library and dig. (I will give you detailed advice on how to do that.) However, before you work entirely from scratch, you should spend a little time exploring some research shortcuts.

Perhaps a good bibliography is already in print. You are not researching a strange topic, but rather an issue of considerable public interest; therefore, it is likely that several bibliographies exist. You can find them by consulting the

Bibliography Index issued periodically by the H. W. Wilson Company; most academic libraries subscribe to it. Look up your subject or several related subjects in it, starting with the most recent issue of the index. The index will refer you to existing bibliographies. If the bibliography is in a book, you will have to consult your library's card catalog to see if that book is in its collection; if the bibliography is in a periodical, you will have to consult the library's list of periodicals. Different libraries list their periodical holdings in different ways, so consult a librarian if you do not know how your library lists the magazines and journals it has collected.

Be skeptical when examining the bibliography or bibliographies you find. Make sure they are good ones. Combine the ones you find, and add to this list, especially with the titles of recently published books and articles. Follow the instructions given a bit later in this chapter concerning library research in finding titles to add.

Computer Searches. Finding a good bibliography already in print is one shortcut. Conducting a computer search is another. More and more libraries are subscribing to national and regional information networks. These networks consist of a central computer file and numerous subscribers who, by paying an initial membership fee and service fees each time the central file is tapped, have access to the stored information. There exist *numerous* indices to published books and articles. You are undoubtedly familiar with the most general index, *The Reader's Guide to Periodical Literature*. But there are more specialized ones such as the *Business Periodicals Index* and the *Public Affairs Information Service Bulletin*, and still more specialized ones such as the *Quarterly Cumulative Index Medicus* and the *Index to Legal Periodicals* for medicine and law. For government documents, there is the *Monthly Catalog of Government Documents*; for doctoral dissertations, there is *Dissertation Abstracts International*. A good central computer file will contain all of these and still others.

You will probably have to work with a librarian to conduct a computer search for the books and articles useful to you. The more efficiently one sends instructions to the central computer file, the lower the cost of the search, and librarians are trained to proceed as efficiently as possible.

You can increase efficiency and further reduce the cost if you understand how a search is typically conducted. First, you need to select a data base. Which of the indices in the central computer file do you wish to search through? Select carefully, for the more you select, the more time the computer will need; the more computer time, the higher the cost. Not long ago, one of my debate teams was researching the effect of work rules on the railroad industry. The team hoped to prove that these rules, which established the size of a crew, the number of miles a crewman could travel in a work day, the geographic boundaries of freight districts, and the like, were unreasonable and financially harmful to the railroad industry. Tapping the computer network DIALOG, a reference librarian searched for useful material. The team chose a rather specialized index, the *Transportation Research Information Service*, as its data base.

After you select a data base, you select time parameters. How far back in time do you want to go? How far forward? Since the data base they chose only began in 1977, the team decided to search the entire data base.

Next, you select descriptors. The team first selected "Rail Transport" or "Railroad." The computer told them that 7,618 items in the selected data base had those words or phrases among their descriptors. The team then asked the computer how many of the 7,618 also had "labor" in the list of descriptors. The computer responded four hundred. Then, the team asked how many of the four hundred also had "work rules." The computer responded forty-eight. Feeling that forty-eight was a manageable *and* affordable number, the team ordered the computer to print out those forty-eight. In a few days, the print-out arrived by mail from DIALOG's headquarters in Palo Alto, California. (The total computer time for that search was, by the way, .061 seconds.) The forty-eight items provided the team with an excellent bibliography. Despite its excellence, they were still able to add to it by their own digging in the library.

Is Access to a Good Library a Problem?

The procedures I have described thus far and will describe below are useful in just about any college library. They have been followed at two small (i.e., fewer than one-thousand students) college libraries as well as at a large state university library. It is part of the folklore at many medium- and small-size colleges that their libraries are inadequate. That belief, however, is fiction, fed by some students who'd rather curse the library than dig through its holdings. If you are a college debater, your institutional library has much to offer.

To supplement its collection, you can visit nearby large public libraries or university libraries. These libraries are usually happy to help you; in many cases, they will have made arrangements with your school which allow you to borrow books you might need. Such visits are possible in metropolitan areas where public libraries are large and colleges and universities are numerous. If you are not in such an area, however, you need not despair. You can gain access to needed materials through your library's interlibrary loan services. Give your librarians a list of books and articles you need. Using printed and computerized lists, they can find out what libraries own the books and journals you need. They can then request the book or a copy of the article from a library that has it. Sometimes there is a charge for such services, sometimes not. Your librarians will inform you if there will be a charge before the request is made.

Even if you are in a metropolitan area, you may need something that is not available at any of the area libraries or you may not have the time or the transportation to get it. Interlibrary loan services can help you. Two words of caution: (1) interlibrary loan services cannot be as tolerant of overdue books as your own college library may be because *your entire school's* borrowing privileges may be cancelled if books are not returned on schedule; (2) interlibrary loan services can be slow for many legitimate reasons and may take a few weeks to get the book or article to you.

If you are a high school debater, you will have to go somewhere other than your school's library to do your research. School libraries are designed and stocked to supplement the instruction offered in the school. Debating involves you in subjects at a far more sophisticated level than is possible in most high school classes. Therefore, you will have to go to a more sophisticated library.

You will probably find the public libraries of limited utility, unless you go to a large one—for example, the central public library in a large city. Your best bet is a nearby college or university library. Most will permit high school students to come in under certain circumstances or at certain times. The reluctance of many colleges and universities to admit high school students to their libraries is due to their belief that high school students will not conduct themselves in a sufficiently serious manner and that they really do not require the resources of a college library to do their work. High school debaters are the exception to these beliefs: they usually are sufficiently serious about their work, and they do indeed need what a college library offers. If you present yourself as a high school debater to the person in charge at a college library, you may find that doors that were closed will be opened and rules that were firm will be bent.

Your path can be paved for you by your instructor or coach. He or she can contact the head librarian or reference librarian at a nearby college or university library on your behalf. He or she could also contact the debate coach at that institution and ask for assistance on your behalf. Most college debate coaches are enthusiastic supporters of debating at all levels and would go out of their way to assist high school programs in their community. You might even want to contact the college or university's debate coach on your own.

Research in the Library

You now are ready to engage in serious library work. You've done some preliminary research. You may be in your library; you may be in a strange library. You may have a bibliography in hand and be seeking to supplement it at the same time you are searching for the items on it; you may be compiling a bibliography from scratch. No matter which situation you're in, the advice that follows should help you get your job done. An effective, efficient research strategy usually proceeds from the general to the specific. This way, when you reach very specific material, you will have a general framework in which to place that material. In offering the following advice, I will follow this time-honored, time-proven strategy.

Monographs

You have already searched for monographs using the *Library of Congress Subject Headings Index* and the card catalog. Your goal then was to find general, introductory discussions of your topic. Now you are looking for specific items on your bibliography. To find them, use either the author card catalog or the title card catalog (many libraries combine them). You are also compiling a bibliography or adding more specific, more sophisticated discussions to your bibliography. For example, a monograph entitled *The Wetback Problem: Illegal Immigration in the American Southwest* might have interested you in the preliminary stage of research on the topic of illegal immigration. Now, a monograph entitled *Mexican Immigrants and Social Services in Cameron County, Texas* might interest you. Use the subject card catalog and look at all the cards filed under the "official" heading for your subject as well as the "official" subject headings related to your subject.

Make sure you copy down the necessary bibliographical information on each monograph: author's full name, the monograph's full title, an edition number if there is one, the city of publication, the publishing firm's name, and the date of publication. You will need some of this information in an actual debate; you will need all of it if the monograph is checked out or lost and you have to request its return or turn to interlibrary loan services.

Magazine Articles

Magazines are written and published for general audiences. *Newsweek, Time,* and *U.S. News and World Report* are probably the most general magazines you will cite frequently as a debater. They are all written for the general public. Other magazines are *The New Republic, The National Review, The Congressional Digest,* and *Current History*. They are written for a sophisticated public with very special interests. None of these periodicals is written exclusively for scholars in the field. Periodicals written for a scholarly audience are referred to as "journals." We will discuss them separately.

To find magazine articles listed in your bibliography, consult the library's list of its periodical holdings. That listing should tell you what magazines and what dates of those magazines the library has; that listing will probably also tell you where in the library the magazine is to be found. If it does not, ask. Libraries usually house their nonrecent periodical holdings in one of three ways: (1) bound, supplied with a suitable catalog number, and shelved with books; (2) bound and shelved alphabetically in an area separate from the books; (3) microfilmed and stored near microfilm readers. Recent issues of periodicals are typically shelved separately: in some libraries, you have immediate access to them; in others, you must go to a desk to request and sign them out.

To add magazine articles to your bibliography, you should use the familiar *Reader's Guide to Periodical Literature*. As with all periodically issued indices, you should work *back* from the most recent issue of the index to earlier issues. Figure 3.2 is a sample page from *The Reader's Guide*. Using it, you would find an article entitled "Jurors' Blurred Views of Insanity" on page 14 in the November 1982 issue of *Psychology Today*; you would also discover an article entitled

Industry and the environment
See also
Mining industry—Environmental aspects
Environmental protection: job-taker or job-maker? R. Kazis and R. L. Grossman. bibl f il Environment 24:12-20+ N '82
Industry and theater. See Theater and industry
Infant formula boycott case. See Nestle SA—Infant formula boycott case
Infant obesity. See Obesity
Infant psychology
Discrimination and imitation of facial expressions by neonates. T. M. Field and others. bibl f il Science 218:179-81 O 8 '82
Infantry
See also
United States. Army. Infantry
Infants
Crying
Coping with crying. R. B. McCall. il Parents 57: 114 N '82
Equipment
See also
Snugli, Inc.
Those unpredictable babies [baby market suppliers] J. A. Byrne and P. B. Brown. il Forbes 130:203+ N 22 '82
Growth and development
Asymmetrical brain activity discriminates between positive and negative affective stimuli in human infants. R. J. Davidson and N. A. Fox. bibl f Science 218:1235-7 D 17 '82
Nutrition
See also
Nestle SA—Infant formula boycott case
Vision
See Vision
Infants, Deformed. See Deformities
Infants, Newborn
Preparing for the homecoming. R. B. McCall. il Parents 57:100 O '82
Hospital care
Artificial wombs [monitoring premature infants to prevent retrolental fibroplasia] E. Horton. Sci Dig 90:53 D '82
Infants' friends. See Friendship
Infectious endocarditis. See Heart—Diseases
Inflation (Finance)
Bringing inflation under control. [P. A. Volcker] por Time 121:41 Ja 3 '83
Deflation and stock prices. A. Bladen. il Forbes 130:232-3 O 25 '82
Growth without inflation. G. Tyler. New Leader 65:9-15 O 18 '82
Inflation—a necessary condition for achieving substantial budgetary relief? F. S. Weaver. Change 14:10-11 O '82
Is inflation really cured? L. C. Thurow. il Newsweek 100:101 N 22 '82
"Sclerosis" blamed for economic stagnation [caused by special interest groups; theory of M. Olson] E. Marshall. il por Science 218:357-8 O 22 '82
Two unpleasant possibilities. A. Bladen. il Forbes 130:270-1 N 8 '82
Where inflation is slowing down [Consumer Price Index statistics] U S News World Rep 93:1 N 8 '82
Who's winning race with inflation. il U S News World Rep 93:82 N 22 '82
Influenza
Flu watchers keep a weather eye out. E. Keerdoja. Newsweek 100:27 O 18 '82
How to ride out a cold or the flu. il Glamour 80:48 D '82
Vaccines and vaccination
Reassortment virus derived from avian and human influenza A viruses is attenuated and immunogenic in monkeys. B. R. Murphy and others. bibl f il Science 218:1330-2 D 24 '82
Information display systems
See also
Dorman Bogdanoff
Information Management Exposition and Conference. See Computers—Exhibitions
Information services
See also
Brokers—Information services
Information storage and retrieval systems
About that card file... C. Warren. Comput Electron 20:102-3 N '82
The brave new world of videotex; A teletext/videotex primer. R. C. Morse. il Ms 11:94-6+ O '82

The coming great electronic encyclopedia. P. Rossman. il por Futurist 16:53-7 Ag '82; Same abr. Educ Dig 48:54-6 D '82
Dial-up software networks. H. Friedman. il Radio-Electron 53:131-4 O '82
Information services [access by home computer] Money 11:81 N '82
Videotex: instant info from your TV. N. Shapiro. il Pop Mech 158:102-3+ N '82
Advertising use
Broadcast teletext: the next mass medium? K. Edwards. il por Futurist 16:21-4 O '82
Biological use
Two tracks: information storage and retrieval. J. A. Behnke. BioScience 32:837 D '82
Legal use
Success story [Lexis system analyst, M. L. Skolnick] P. Gerber. il por Work Woman 7:26+ D '82
Infrared astronomy
Too much to swallow? [infrared detection of swallows in direction of Corona Austrinae] il Sky Telesc 64:542 D '82
Ultraviolet, optical and infrared astronomy. E. J. Wampler. il Phys Today 35:44-51 N '82
Infrared equipment
See also
Thermography
Infrared radiometers. See Radiometers
Infrastructure. See Public works
Inglestam, Margareta
Can Swedish culture survive U.S. media imports? P. Rossman. il Christ Century 99:860-1 Ag 18-25 '82; Discussion. 99:1022-4 O 13 '82 *
Ingres, Jean Auguste Dominique
Looking at paintings [Mrs. Charles Badham] H. Brown. bibl f il Am Artist 46:68-9+ D '82 *
Inheritance (Biology) See Heredity
Injections
The stop-smoking shot [work of N. Bachynsky] M. Siegel. il pors Health 14:28-31 O '82
Injections, Lethal (Capital punishment) See Executions and executioners
Inland water transportation
History
The Christmas tree ship [Rouse Simmons, Lake Michigan schooner] M. E. Pourchot. il Am Hist Illus 17:12-14 D '82
Inman, Bobby Ray
Admiral Bobby Inman drops out of the 'eyes only' world and takes a hard look at U.S. spy efforts [interview] M. Bonnett. il pors People Wkly 18:63-4+ N 22 '82 *
U.S. intelligence agencies still suffering from scars [interview] il por U S News World Rep 93: 37-8 D 20 '82 *
Inmarsat system. See Communications satellites—Maritime use
Innervation of hypothalamus. See Hypothalamus—Innervation
Innes, Jocasta
Paint magic [excerpt] il por Fam Handyman 32:26-31 O '82
Inquisition
The Galileo affair [cosmological dispute with the Catholic Church] O. Gingerich. bibl(p 150) il map Sci Am 247:132-8+ Ag '82; Discussion. 247:6+ D '82
Insanity
Jurisprudence
Insanity as a defense—should we end it? [J. Hinckley case] D. Pawelek. il por Sr Sch 115:13-15 O 29 '82
The insanity defense is insane. O. G. Hatch. Read Dig 121:199-200+ O '82
Jurors' blurred views of insanity [study by Norman J. Finkel] S. Witty. il Psychol Today 16:14 N '82
Men and madness: some thoughts on the violence factor. P. Slater. Ms 11:100 O '82
Mental disabilities and criminal responsibility [Hinckley trial; interview with H. Fingarette] D. McDonald. por Cent Mag 15:8-16 N/D '82
Inscriptions
See also
Tablets (Paleography)
Insect bites and stings
Colony defense by Africanized and European honey bees [stinging behavior] A. M. Collins and others. bibl f il Science 218:72-4 O 1 '82
Insect communication
Aggressive signal in courtship chirps of a gregarious cricket. C. R. B. Boake and R. R. Capranica. bibl f il Science 218:580-2 N 5 '82
Flea talk via sound waves [research by James Amrine and Mark Jerabek] il Sci Dig 90:22 O '82

Figure 3.2 Sample from *Readers' Guide to Periodical Literature.* Copyright © 1983 by The H. W. Wilson Company. Material reproduced by permission of the publisher.

"Growth without Inflation" on pages 9-15 in the October 18, 1982 issue of *New Leader*.

Again, make sure you conscientiously record all of the relevant bibliographical information: the author's name (if there is one), the article's title, the magazine's name, its date, and the article's inclusive page numbers. You will need some of this information in actual debates; you will need *all* of it if you are going to request a copy of the article through interlibrary loan services.

Compendia

Compendia are edited collections of articles by several authors bound together like a monograph. Not everyone has a book in him or her about illegal immigration, but many scholars have something valuable to say about small aspects of the large problem—for example, the impact of Cuban exiles on the Ft. Chaffee, Arkansas, area, or the impact of illegal immigration from Mexico on the price of California-grown vegetables.

If you have a compendium in your bibliography, use the author card catalog and look under the compendium's editor's name. Or, use the title card catalog and look under the compendium's title. If you are adding to or compiling a bibliography, you should use the subject card catalog to search for compendia. If the compendium's overall title suggests its value, add it to your bibliography. If you are adding or compiling, you have a second route available to you: the *Essay and General Literature Index*, which is published periodically by the H. W. Wilson Company. Figure 3.3 is a sample page. This publication indexes the articles in compendia, not the compendia themselves. Using it, you will discover compendia which, despite their unattractive titles, contain valuable material; using it, you will discover compendia that the library you are in does not hold. For example, the sample points you to "Human Rights and Development: A Difficult Relationship" by L. Pasara in *Development, Human Rights, and the Rule of Law*. Your library might not have this compendium.

As with monographs, make sure you record all the relevant bibliographical information: the editor's name, the compendium's full title, the article's author, the article's full title, the place of publication, the publishing firm's name, the date of publication, and the article's inclusive page numbers.

Journal Articles

Journal articles are written for scholars; these articles, therefore, are more specialized, technical, and complex than magazine articles. The word *journal* sometimes appears in the journal's title—e.g., *The Journal of Political Economy* and *The Journal of Economic Geography*—but not always. *Foreign Policy* and *The American Economist* are both journals. Having engaged in preliminary background research and having looked at more general sources such as monographs, magazine articles,

Cit (The Sanskrit word)
Hacker, P. Cit and noûs. *In* Neoplatonism and Indian thought, ed. by R. B. Harris p161-80

Cities and towns
Hoffer, E. Cities and nature. *In* Hoffer, E. Between the devil and the dragon p50-55
See also Sociology, Urban; Urbanization

Biblical teaching
Clark, D. L. The mythic meaning of the city. *In* Jacques Ellul, ed. by C. G. Christians and J. M. Van Hook p269-90

History
Hoffer, E. The birth of cities; excerpt from "First things, last things." *In* Hoffer, E. Between the devil and the dragon p43-49

History—Historiography
Burrow, J. W. Teutonic freedom and municipal independence. *In* Burrow, J. W. A liberal descent p155-92

Planning
See City planning

Mexico
Call, F. J. Problems and cooperation between U.S. and Mexican border cities. *In* United States relations with Mexico, ed. by R. D. Erb and S. R. Ross p74-85

United States
Call, F. J. Problems and cooperation between U.S. and Mexican border cities. *In* United States relations with Mexico, ed. by R. D. Erb and S. R. Ross p74-85

Cities and towns, Movement to. See Urbanization

Citizenship. See Civics; Freemen

City and town life

Georgia
Vance, R. B. Stuart-Harmon: social distance in twin towns. *In* Vance, R. B. Regionalism and the South p3-18

City government. See Municipal government

City life. See City and town life

City planning

France—Le Mans
Teyssot, G. Planning and building in towns: the system of the bâtiments civils in France, 1795-1848. *In* The Beaux-arts and nineteenth-century French architecture, ed. by R. D. Middleton p35-49

Greece—History
Kidson, P. Architecture and city planning. *In* The Legacy of Greece, ed. by M. I. Finley p376-400

New England
Geiser, K. R. Reformulation of the cities. *In* New England prospects, ed. by C. H. Reidel p178-204

United States
Berman, M. In the forest of symbols: some notes on modernism in New York: The 1960s: a shout in the street. *In* Berman, M. All that is solid melts into air p312-28

Civic, American. See Civics

Civic planning. See City planning

Civics
See also Political ethics

Study and teaching
Engelhardt, C. L. Religion, morality, and citizenship in the public schools: Iowa, 1858-1930. *In* Ideas in America's cultures from Republic to mass society, ed. by H. Cravens p45-57

Civil disobedience. See Government, Resistance to

Civil liberty. See Liberty

Civil-military relations. See Militarism; Sociology, Military

Civil rights
Becker, L. C. Individual rights. *In* And justice for all, ed. by T. Regan and D. VanDeVeer p197-216
Bedau, H. A. International human rights. *In* And justice for all, ed. by T. Regan and D. VanDeVeer p287-308
Ennals, M. Amnesty International and human rights. *In* Pressure groups in the global systems, ed. by P. Willetts p63-83
Gerstein, R. S. Do terrorists have rights? *In* The Morality of terrorism, ed. by D. C. Rapoport [and] Y. Alexander p290-307
Rawls, J. The basic liberties and their priority. *In* The Tanner Lectures on human values, p1982 p 1-87
Regan, T. What sorts of beings can have rights? *In* Regan, T. All that dwell therein p165-83
See also Due process of law; Equality before the law; Freedom of movement; Liberty

Civil rights (International law)
Alston, P. Development and the rule of law: prevention versus cure as a human rights strategy. *In* Development, human rights and the rule of law p31-108
Buergenthal, T. To respect and to ensure: state obligations and permissible derogations. *In* The International Bill of Rights, ed. by L. Henkin p72-91
Dias, C. J. Realizing the right to development: the importance of legal resources. *In* Development, human rights and the rule of law p187-97
Dinstein, Y. The right to life, physical integrity, and liberty. *In* The International Bill of Rights, ed. by L. Henkin p114-37
Espiritu, A. C. Keeping human life human: altering structures of power economic benefits and of institutions. *In* Development, human rights and the rule of law p175-80
Galtung, J. What kind of development and what kind of law. *In* Development, human rights and the rule of law p121-29
Kiss, A. C. Permissible limitations on rights. *In* The International Bill of Rights, ed. by L. Henkin p290-310
Partsch, K. J. Freedom of conscience and expression, and political freedoms. *In* The International Bill of Rights, ed. by L. Henkin p209-45
Pásara, L. Human rights and development: a difficult relationship. *In* Development, human rights and the rule of law p181-85
Pechota, V. The development of the Covenant on Civil and Political Rights. *In* The International Bill of Rights, ed. by L. Henkin p32-71
Ramphal, S. S. Key-note address. *In* Development, human rights and the rule of law p9-24

and compendia essays, you are ready for the specialized, technical, and complex treatment of issues found in scholarly journal articles.

You will find journal articles the same way you found magazine articles: go to your library's list of periodical holdings, and, if your library has the needed journal and the needed volume of it, go to wherever the particular journal is housed. I said "needed volume," not date, because journal articles are listed in bibliographies not by months and year, but rather by volume number and year if the several issues which comprise the volume are numbered consecutively (i.e., the second issue starts with page 98, not page 1) *or* by volume number, issue number, and date if the several issues are numbered separately (i.e., the second issue in a volume starts with page 1, not page 98). When you examine a bibliography, this difference should enable you to differentiate between magazine articles and scholarly journal articles.

If you are trying to add journal articles to your bibliography, you should not—I repeat, *should not*—go to the *Reader's Guide*. You should turn to one of a number of more specialized periodical indices. If your debate topic is a philosophical one, you might try *The Humanities Index*; if it involves important social issues or has psychological dimensions, try *The Social Science Index*. Quite a few recent debate resolutions have concerned the quality of American education; *The Education Index* would be the best index for journal articles on these issues. Although there has always been a tendency to steer clear of aesthetic questions and technological or scientific questions on the part of those who select the different national resolutions, there is some indication that this tendency will soon no longer govern the selection process. Therefore, *The Art Index*, *The General Science Index*, and *The Applied Science and Technology Index* might be of use to debaters in future seasons. Quite a few resolutions take debaters into economics and American and international business. The best index for such resolutions is *The Business Periodicals Index*. All of these specialized periodical indices are published by the H. W. Wilson Company; they follow the same format as the familiar *Reader's Guide to Periodical Literature*.

Perhaps the most useful specialized periodical index is one not published by H. W. Wilson. It is the *Public Affairs Information Service Bulletin (PAIS)*. Like the others, it is published at regular intervals; like the others, it is most effectively used if you start with the most recent issue and work backwards in time. *PAIS*'s focus is on public issues—hence, its value to debaters who are concerned with just such issues. Figure 3.4 is a sample page from *PAIS*. Using it, you could add an article by Arnold and Virginia L. Binder entitled "Juvenile Diversion and the Constitution" to your bibliography. That article, you should note, appeared on page 1 through page 24 of the first issue of volume 10, the 1982 volume of *The Journal of Criminal Justice*.

Abstracts

In some scholarly areas, you can read a summary of a journal article and then decide whether to read the full article or not. These summaries are called abstracts.

Juvenile courts. (cont.)

† United States. Dept. of Justice. Office of Juvenile Justice and Delinquency Prevention. Services to children in juvenile courts: the judicial-executive controversy. Pettibone, John M. and others. '81 xi+204p bibls il chart (Major Issues in Juvenile Justice Info. and Training) (Stock no. 027-000-01103-9) (LC 80-70835) pa U.S.,$4.75; elsewhere $5.95 —*Supt docs*
Published by the Academy for Contemporary Problems, Columbus, Ohio, for the National Institute of Juvenile Justice and Delinquency Prevention.

JUVENILE DELINQUENTS
See also
Runaway boys and girls.
Youth and law.

Rojek, Dean G. and Maynard L. Erickson. Delinquent careers: a test of the career escalation model. bibl tables *Criminology (Sage)* 20:5-28 My '82

Sigelman, Lee and others. Social service innovation in the American states: deinstitutionalization of the mentally retarded [and juvenile offenders]. bibl tables *Social Science Q* 62:503-15 S '81

Tokoro, Kazuhiko. Change in traditional society and "delinquencization" [juvenile delinquency in Japan]. chart *Japan Q* 28:362-9 Jl/S '81

† United States. Dept. of Justice. Office of Juvenile Justice and Delinquency Prevention. Removal of juveniles from adult jails and lock-ups: a review of state approaches and policy implications. Mr '81 58p pa —*Washington, DC 20531*
Prepared by Arthur D. Little, Inc., Washington, D.C.

† United States. House. Com. on Educ. and Labor. Subcom. on Human Resources. Oversight hearing on juvenile restitution programs: hearing, March 3, 1981. '81 iii+477p bibls il tables charts (97th Cong., 1st Sess.) pa —*Washington, DC 20515*
Work projects for juvenile offenders to repay victims and government agencies for the damages and costs of their offenses.

† United States. Nat. Inst. for Juvenile Justice and Delinquency Prevention. Juvenile criminal behavior in urban, suburban, and rural areas. Laub, John H. and Michael J. Hindelang. F '81 vi+118p bibl il tables charts (Analysis of Nat. Crime Victimization Survey Data to Study Serious Delinquent Behavior. Monograph 3) (SD Cat. no. J 26.15/2:V 66/2/Monograph 3) (Stock no. 027-000-01094-6) pa U.S. $4.50; elsewhere $5.65—*Supt docs*
Prepared by the Criminal Justice Research Center, Albany, N.Y.

† United States. Senate. Com. on the Constitution. Subcom. on Juvenile Justice. Early identification and classification of juvenile delinquents: hearing, October 22, 1981, on oversight hearing to remove the juvenile from a crime cycle. '82 iii+170p bibl tables charts (97th Cong., 1st Sess.) (Serial no. J-97-70) pa—*Washington, DC 20510*
Extent to which future criminality can be predicted from juvenile delinquency behavior; whether any form of social intervention is likely to alter the process.

† United States. Senate. Com. on the Judiciary. Subcom. on Juvenile Justice. Violent juvenile crime: hearing, July 9, 1981, on the problem of juvenile crime. '81 iv+190p tables chart (97th Cong., 1st Sess.) (Serial no. J-97-48) pa—*Washington, DC 20510*

Conferences

† National Symposium on Youth Violence. Focus on youth: team action youth involvement programs to decrease violence; [proceedings of the] first . . ., November 9-12, 1980, Reno, Nevada. '80 vi+173p bibl il charts plastic bdg $6—*Community Development, Division of Continuing Education, University of Nevada, College Inn, Reno, NV 89557*
Sponsored jointly with various organizations and government agencies.

Legislation

† California. Laws, statutes, etc. California laws relating to youthful offenders, 1981: including the Youth Authority Act, the juvenile court, 1980 legislative changes, the juvenile court rules. Lew, Richard and Walt Jones, comp. ['81] 309+[59]p index pa $2.75 —*Documents Section, P.O. Box 1015, North Highlands, CA 95660*
Published by the Cal. Department of the Youth Authority.

Rehabilitation

United States. Dept. of Justice. Office of Juvenile Justice and Delinquency Prevention. Programs for the serious and violent juvenile offender. Jl '81 51p pa—*633 Indiana Av., N.W., Washington, DC 20531*

Weinrott, Mark R. and others. Cost-effectiveness of teaching family programs for delinquents: results of a national evaluation [a commuity-based group home approach]. bibl tables *Evaluation R* 6:173-201 Ap '82

Wilson, Robert L. Seriously troubled youth: North Carolina confronts the problems. il *Popular Govt* 47:28-33 Summer '81

JUVENILE JUSTICE
See also
Directories - Juvenile justice.

Bean, Philip. Punishment: a philosophical and criminological inquiry. '81 viii+215p bibl index (ISBN 0-85520-391-9)—*Martin Robertson*
Examines three of the major theories of punishment: retribution, rehabilitation and deterrence, and relates them to the concept of justice, especially juvenile justice.

Binder, Arnold and Virginia L. Binder. Juvenile diversion and the Constitution [question as to how early in the procedural chain for juveniles various due process rights should enter]. bibl *J Criminal Justice* 10:1-24 no 1 '82

Coates, Robert B. Deinstitutionalization and the serious juvenile offender: some policy considerations [programming for the violent offender within a community-based system]. *Crime and Delinquency* 27:477-86 O '81

Conrad, John P. Can juvenile justice survive? [findings of Project MIJJIT--Major Issues in Juvenile Justice Information and Training, a program of the Academy for Contemporary Problems, Columbus, Ohio]. *Crime and Delinquency* 27:544-54 O '81

Costello, Jan C. and Nancy L. Worthington. Incarcerating status offenders: attempts to circumvent the Juvenile Justice and Delinquency Prevention Act [critical of the incarceration of offenders for actions which are not criminal for adults]. *Harvard Civil Rights-Civil Liberties Law R* 16:41-81 Summer '81

Kiersh, Edward. Minnesota cracks down on chronic juvenile offenders [under a law that permits repeat juvenile offenders to be certified as adults and sentenced to state prisons]. il *Corrections M* 7:21-3+ D '81

Pierce, James R. Relinquishment of jurisdiction for purposes of criminal prosecution of juveniles. *Northern Ky Law R* 8:377-93 no 2 '81

Taylor, Ronald B. The kid business: how it exploits the children it should help. '81 xviii+303p index (LC 81-6292) (ISBN 0-395-30515-2) $12.95—*Houghton*
Emphasis on problems in the foster care and juvenile justice systems; United States.

† United States. Dept. of Justice. Office of Juvenile Justice and Delinquency Prevention. Programs for the serious and violent juvenile offender. Jl '81 51p pa—*633 Indiana Av., N.W., Washington, DC 20531*

Legislation

Ross, Charles A. Post-conviction proceedings under New York's juvenile offender laws: a due process critique. *New York Law School Law R* 26:773-818 no 3 '81

Sobie, Merril. The Juvenile Offender Act: effectiveness and impact on the New York juvenile justice system [1978 state law that allows children to be prosecuted for serious offenses in criminal courts]. tables *New York Law School Law R* 26:677-722 no 3 '81

JUVENILES. See Youth.

K

Figure 3.4 Sample from *The Public Affairs Information Service Bulletin*.

In some scholarly journals, an abstract will be published with an article, either at the article's beginning or as part of the issue's Table of Contents. There are also reference works you should be familiar with that publish nothing but abstracts. They exist in scientific and technical fields—*Chemistry Abstracts* and *Biological Abstracts*; of more value to debaters, they exist in the social sciences—*Sociological Abstracts* and *Psychological Abstracts*. If your bibliography contains journal articles in these academic areas, you might want to read a one-paragraph abstract and then decide whether the thirty-page article is sufficiently valuable to be read carefully. Abstracts can save a researcher some time by permitting him or her to get to and study the needed materials, while avoiding materials of questionable value.

If you are adding to a bibliography, a volume of abstracts can be used in much the same fashion as an index to periodicals. The abstracts are arranged under broad subject headings; find the appropriate heading or headings and read the citation and abstract. If the article looks valuable, copy down the citation and plan on reading the article in its entirety. Like indices to scholarly journals, abstracts are published periodically. So, begin with the most recent issue and work backwards in time.

Pamphlets

Most academic libraries maintain what they often refer to as "vertical files." "Vertical files" are usually nothing more than a euphemism for a number of standard three- or four-drawer file cabinets pushed together. These files contain valuable information: government pamphlets, newspaper or magazine clippings, news releases. Usually the reference librarians maintain these files; oftentimes, faculty members contribute materials in their areas of academic specialization. A political scientist who specializes in disarmament will contribute pamphlets and other materials that he or she either gathers or is sent: an economist who specialize in international trade restraints will contribute pamphlets and other materials he or she has. And so on for the education professor with a special interest in science education, the philosophy professor with an interest in business ethics, and the physics professor with an interest in nuclear waste disposal.

There is no predicting how rich or how poor these vertical files will be. There is considerable variation from academic institution to academic institution. Furthermore, within an institution, there may be marked differences in quantity and quality from file category to file category. Look at your library's vertical files or pamphlet files. You may find a treasure; you may find very little of value.

The cataloging system used for vertical files will vary. Many libraries have prepared a guidebook similar in format to *The Library of Congress Subject Headings Index* for their vertical files. Ask if there is such a guide; if there is, use it to establish the correct heading to look under as well as other pertinent headings. Add the materials you find to your working bibliography, noting where they are to be found in the library.

Special Reference Works

The library resources discussed thus far are ones that you would include in a bibliography—books, articles, etc. There are other library resources that you should know about. You will find them helpful as you research the debate resolution. The reference area of a library—even a small library—contains many sources students discover only accidentally. Four are worth mentioning in particular.

The first two are *NewsBank* and *Keesing's Contemporary Archives*. Published by NewsBank, Inc., every month, *NewsBank* provides reprints of particular news stories as covered by news services or major newspapers. *Keesing's* focuses on world events. Each monthly number reviews the events of every part of the globe. The major "plus" of these summary treatments is their currency. Monographs, journal articles, and essays in compendia are usually written months, maybe years, before they see print. Thus, some information in them is simply no longer accurate. During the 1982-83 NDT season, I judged a junior varsity debate in which a team argued strenuously that the United States should not provide military assistance to Guatemala. This team had very good evidence concerning human rights abuses in Guatemala—evidence taken from authoritative monographs and reputable scholarly journals; however, a few months before the debating season began, a coup d'etat had occurred in that Central American nation. The oppressive dictator this team had indicted had been replaced by an Evangelical Christian who promised reform. When the opposing team pointed to the change in government, this team was flustered and embarrassed. If this team had had current information, such as that provided by *Keesing's*, the embarrassing situation would have been prevented.

The third is *Editorials on File*. Opinion evidence is not always the best kind to use, and *Editorials on File* does present editorial opinion—perhaps twenty or more editorials from around the nation on a single topic, one that was important during a two-week period. Certainly these editorials can be quoted (although as the opinion of a source without expert credentials, they are not especially strong evidence). The real value, however, of these compiled editorials is the arguments they contain. They are all persuasive pieces; they usually compress a fairly long, reasonably sophisticated argument into a rather small space. You may find a compilation on a topic related to your debate resolution; if so, the arguments contained there will probably provide you with some interesting new ideas on and approaches to the topic.

The fourth handy special reference work is *The Congressional Quarterly's* weekly review. This source compiles and summarizes very recent news on the issues that the Congress is at that time considering. Again, the big plus is currency. Especially in policy debate, where you must know what present U.S. policy is, you need to know if Congressional action has changed that policy or soon will.

Statistics

The reference room of a library is also your source for any statistics you might need; there are compilations of statistics galore. If you need to know how many members of a particular religion are under the age of twenty-one, you can find out; if you want to know how many instances of arson there were in Chicago in 1981, you can find out; if you want to know the incidence of smallpox in underdeveloped nations, you can find that out too. A good reference collection has shelves of books containing data of different sorts. Some are general, such as almanacs; others are more particular, such as the United Nation's Annual *Demographic Yearbook*, which provides vital data on all the world's nations.

The best single source of statistics on domestic matters is *The Statistical Abstract of the United States*, published annually by the U.S. Department of Commerce. On approximately one-thousand pages, *The Statistical Abstract* presents data under thirty-four headings including population, education, law enforcement, labor force, prices, national defense, and transportation. In *The Statistical Abstract*, you can find out the number of legal immigrants since 1820 or the number of Cuban immigrants since 1961 if your debate resolution concerns immigration; you can find out the amount of state tax revenue in states with and without an income tax if your debate resolution concerns improving state and local revenue collecting. *The Statistical Abstract* is, furthermore, considered the definitive source of data.

Research Outside the Library

Not all of the necessary research can be done in the safe confines of a school library. There are resources that are often unavailable in a college or university library that you may want to consult. They may already be on your bibliography; you may add them as you continue your research outside the walls of the academic library.

Studies by Think Tanks

A think tank is a place where specialists and scholars research, think, and write. Some think tanks are for hire. The Rand Corporation is a major American think tank which has undertaken a number of special studies for the U.S. Department of Defense. Other think tanks are either endowed or supported by substantial contributions. Two of the nation's most prestigious ones fall into this second category, the conservative American Enterprise Institute (AEI) and the liberal Brookings Institution. Both are headquartered in Washington, D.C., just a few blocks from each other.

Both the AEI and Brookings publish numerous studies on important public issues. Some eventually make it to academic library shelves, but by that time they may no longer be as pertinent. The debater, however, does not have to wait for library acquisition; he or she can purchase copies of especially pertinent studies directly from the AEI or Brookings. Both publish an annual catalog of publications and both regularly publish updates to it. A shrewd researcher will write the AEI (1156 17th Street, N.W., Washington, D.C. 20036) and Brookings

(1775 Massachusetts Avenue, N.W., Washington, D.C. 20036) and request a current catalog. If a study is very recent and looks especially valuable, the debater should order it. The money will be well spent for AEI and Brookings studies are respected for their thoroughness. They are the studies our lawmakers in the nation's capital read. A few recent AEI titles should demonstrate the cogency of good think-tank work: *Government and the Corporation* by Ralph K. Winter; *The Federalization of Presidential Primaries* by Austin Ranney; *Dismantling the Parties: Reflections on Party Reform and Party Decomposition* by Jeane K. Kirkpartrick; and *National Security Challenges to Saudi Arabia* by Dale R. Tahtinen.

Materials from Special Interest Groups

AEI and Brookings might be considered special interest groups insofar as each think tank brings on board only specialists and scholars who are philosophically compatible with the think tank's overall political outlook. Nevertheless, the objectivity and authority of AEI and Brookings studies are so rarely questioned that it seems unfair to place the "special interest group" label on them. A special interest group is a strong defender of a particular interest, whether it be that of manufacturers, gun owners, consumers, or civil libertarians. The National Association of Manufacturers, The National Rifle Association, The Consumer's Union, and The American Civil Liberties Union are special interest groups.

Many special interest groups publish materials which might be relevant to a particular debate topic. If the resolution deals with labor unionism, both the National Association of Manufacturers and the AFL-CIO will have relevant material available, as a public service, on opposite sides of the question. If the resolution deals with abortion, the Right-to-Life organization and the National Organization for Women will have relevant materials available—again on opposite sides. Quite often, your debate coach will receive the materials without having requested them. But you will often have to write to ask for the material an organization might have. A sample letter of inquiry is included as Figure 3.5. Most public and college libraries will have a Washington, D.C., telephone directory and a ZIP code directory in their reference collection, so you can obtain the correct full address.

A great deal of the material you receive from a special interest group will be of no use to you as a debater. A debater accomplishes nothing by quoting materials authored by a special interest group or by an official of the group. The suspicion of prejudice is simply too strong against the special interest group. These groups, however, often ask noted authorities to write an essay or a pamphlet which they will publish; special interest groups also frequently reprint articles written by noted authorities and published elsewhere. It is these materials you are hoping to get. If you get them and use them, quote the authority and deemphasize the publisher or republisher. If the authority has decent credentials, then the issue of the publisher's prejudices is irrelevant.

Box 6072
Randolph-Macon College
Ashland, Virginia 23005
November 24, 1983

Mr. Steven E. Hall
Director of Public Information
National Association of Railroads
1400 16th Street NW
Washington, D.C. 20037

Dear Mr. Hall:

I am an intercollegiate debater at Randolph-Macon College in Ashland, Virginia. This year's national debate resolution concerns the power of labor unions. As the season has progressed, other Randolph-Macon debaters and I have become increasingly interested in the railroad unions. } *introduce yourself*

We hope to argue that labor union power has adversely affected this nation's railroads. I am writing you in hope that you will be able to provide us with information that will help us in making our case. } *explain your situation*

We need information specifically on the effects of unionism on the railroads. However, any information on the nation's railroads would prove helpful because if we argue that the power of railroad unions should be curtailed, we will be pushed by our opponents to prove the following:

1) the importance of railroads to American commerce;
2) the superiority of rail transportation of goods to other methods of transportation;
3) the shaky economic status of many American railroads;
4) the excessiveness or unreasonability of railroad union demands.

} *make a specific request*

Please send us any free information you have—e.g., pamphlets, speeches, news releases, booklets—that might contain useful material. } *indicate how the request can be met*

We hope to be discussing the railroads and the unions fairly soon. I would therefore appreciate your quick response. Thank you for your assistance. } *thank the person*

Sincerely yours,

Figure 3.5 Sample letter of inquiry.

Law Review Evidence

Particularly on policy resolutions and particularly on domestic topics, questions of law interpretation do arise. The courts are empowered to interpret the laws, and they do. Legal professionals, however, write and offer their interpretations of these interpretations. Their views are published in law reviews.

Law reviews vary in quality because authorship varies from review to review. In some cases, the law review articles are authored and edited by a law school's outstanding students; in other cases, the law review articles are authored by distinguished jurists and professors and edited by the school's outstanding students who often append "discussions" to the articles. A law review article authored by a student, no matter how outstanding, is a questionable source of evidence. After all, the author still lacks the fundamental training in his or her chosen profession. A law review article authored by a distinguished jurist or a professor is another matter: it is good evidence, as good as the author's credentials. The appended discussions are especially suspect pieces, for not only are these student works but they tend to be student speculation as opposed to solid student research. Less seems to be on the line when you are a student member of a law review staff and appending a brief commentary to an article than when you are presenting your views in full in an article of your own.

Law review evidence, then, is very much like materials obtained from special interest groups: some may be good, and some is suspect. Whether or not an article is good depends on its authorship. So, be very careful when combing through law reviews. Turn to only those articles that you are sure you can defend. And make sure you have and offer full citations, including the author's credentials. When a law review is quoted without an author's name given (as debaters *often* do), the judge will assume that it's a student discussion of an article (usually followed with the student's initials) and probably discredit it. When a law review article is quoted with an author's name but without any credentials, many judges will assume that the source is a law student and discredit the evidence.

I have voiced caution about using law review evidence, but I haven't told you how to get to it. Law libraries, not public or college libraries, subscribe to law reviews, so, to research law reviews, you must gain access to a law school library. Gaining access is all but impossible for high school students. I know a former high school debater whose father was a law professor; this debater had his father bring home pertinent review issues. I am sure other high school debaters have had older brothers and sisters in law school photocopy articles for them. These routes raise ethical problems because not all high school debaters have the opportunity to pursue them. As a consequence, I would rule law evidence out of high school debates.

College debaters can usually gain access to a law library. Their special need for the library's resources, their seriousness, and their pledges to follow the rules will usually gain them access. (In law schools of state universities, their access may be guaranteed them as citizens of that state.) A debate coach or instructor can sometimes make the path smoother by contacting a law school and requesting access to the library on his or her debaters' behalf. Because most persistent intercollegiate debaters can get to law reviews, the ethical problem does not exist.

Once in a law library, debaters should quietly seek out the *Index to Legal Periodicals*. This is a periodically issued index to law reviews and other law-related journals. It works the same way as the different indices we have already discussed. Look under any heading where information on your topic may be found.

Court Decisions

You can find copies of court decisions in two places. Supreme Court decisions and lower federal court decisions are the easiest to locate, for they are recorded in *The Supreme Court Reporter*, to which most academic libraries subscribe. This periodically issued work lists all cases brought to the U.S. Supreme Court and major cases brought to lower federal courts.

In Supreme Court cases, if the case is referred to a lower court, that disposition is noted; if the case is heard, the majority decision, any concurring views, and any dissenting views are offered. When quoting a Supreme Court decision, it is important to identify the author of the part you are quoting and whether he or she is speaking for the majority, concurring, or dissenting, and the precise case name, and the decision date.

The Supreme Court is the court of final jurisdiction in federal cases; thus, cases frequently reach the Supreme Court on appeal from the federal district courts. A Supreme Court decision will cite the lower court decisions but will not quote them at length. To get to these lower court decisions, you will have to go backwards in *The Supreme Court Reporter*. You will have to know the date of the decision and its exact name and number to find the text of the decision in earlier issues of *The Supreme Court Reporter*, if it is to be found there.

Federal cases involve federal crimes, such as kidnapping and mail fraud, and crimes committed in a federal jurisdiction, such as the District of Columbia. There are far more state cases than federal cases: these state cases deal with most of the common crimes ranging in severity from murder and rape to petty theft. State supreme courts (or their equivalents) are the courts of final jurisdiction in state cases. To get the text of a state supreme court decision, you can try a law library. Frequently, however, a given law library will hold the records only for the state supreme court of the state in which it is located.

The U.S. Supreme Court does, however, hear some of these state cases on appeal. In these instances, the U.S. Supreme Court is a court of special jurisdiction, special because, in the Supreme Court's judgment, constitutional issues *may* be involved in the particular case. Many of the landmark Supreme Court decisions involving the rights of the accused, Miranda *v.* Arizona, for example, which requires that those arrested be read their rights, made it to the Supreme Court from state supreme courts because a Constitutional right was thought to be in question. The same is true for many cases concerning citizen privacy. The U.S. Supreme Court claims special jurisdiction because it is uniquely empowered to interpret the U.S. Constitution. If a case does get to the U.S. Supreme Court via this route, you will find the decision in *The Supreme Court Reporter*.

To search for any court decisions, you again need to know what decisions you are looking for. Fishing expeditions through *The Supreme Court Reporter* or a law library are foolish wastes of time. A good job of library research should precede your search for the text of court decisions. Monographs, scholarly journal articles, and law review articles should refer you to the major court decisions. The texts of major decisions will in turn refer you to related court decisions.

Government Documents

The federal government is an incredibly prolific publisher of studies on important public issues. Executive departments such as the Department of State and congressional committees publish numerous documents you may want to consult. Under the Freedom of Information Act, these documents are available to you, many free of charge. How do you find out what's available and how do you obtain what you want?

Using the Monthly Catalog. The Government Printing Office (GPO) publishes a monthly catalog of available documents. The GPO lists these documents under the name of the agency or committee responsible for them. The GPO also prepares a subject index for each monthly catalog. Figure 3.6 is a sample from this index. Skim it. You'll see headings such as "Energy policy—Canada" and "Energy storage—United States—Security measures." Skimming this sample should give you a sense of how the index works; skimming the index to a monthly catalog should give you an idea of the range of government documents.

Figure 3.7 is a sample from the actual catalog. As you can see, the entries are arranged by issuing agency or committee. They are also arranged numerically: this system allows you to move directly from the index to the description of the publication you are interested in. The listings give you full bibliographical information on each government publication, including, usually, length. Some, you will notice, are reports several hundred pages long; others are no more than pamphlets. The listing also gives you the item number to use in ordering. Before you order, call or write the issuing agency or committee. They often have copies available free-of-charge to industrious researchers. If you write, adapt the sample letter in Figure 3.5 to meet your situation. If you want to call an agency, get the appropriate number from a Washington, D.C., telephone directory. If it is a congressional committee, call the main number for the Senate or the House of Representatives and ask for the committee by name. The operator will connect you.

Energy consumption U.S. Statistics Periodicals.   Subject Index

Residential energy consumption survey. Consumption and expenditures /, 83-7074

Energy crops.
Facts about ethanol /, 83-6445

Energy crops — United States.
Energy research for the farm : an overview /, 83-6362

Energy development — United States.
An implementation study of the SBA's energy loan program /, 83-8506

Energy development — United States — Finance.
Fiscal years 1983 and 1984 Environmental Protection Agency research and development authorization : hearings before the Subcommittee on Natural Resources, Agriculture Research, and Environment of the Committee on Science and Technology, U.S. House of Representatives, Ninety-seventh Congress, second session, February 24, March 2, 19, 1982., 83-8502

Energy industries — Employment — United States — Statistics — Periodicals.
Energy manpower factbook /, 83-7047

Energy industries — Statistics — Yearbooks.
International energy annual., 83-7070, 83-7071

Energy policy — Canada.
Impact of Canadian energy and investment policies on U.S. commerce : report together with dissenting views / 83-8412

Energy policy — United States.
Analysis of energy reorganization savings estimates and plans : summary : report to the Congress /, 83-7369
Creating energy choices for the future : energy policy., 83-7255
Energy and urban policies/programs : official transcript of public briefing and addendum, April 27, 1978, Washington, D.C., 83-7046
Federal energy guidelines : FERC statutes & regulations, proposed regulations, 1977-1981., 83-7065
Federal energy guidelines : FERC statutes and regulations, regulations preambles, 1977-1981., 83-7064
Fiscal year 1983 Department of Energy budget review : hearings before the Subcommittee on Energy Development and Applications of the Committee on Science and Technology, U.S. House of Representatives, Ninety-seventh Congress, second session., 83-8497
Natural gas regulation study /, 83-8410
Synthetic Fuels Corporation and oil inventories policy : hearings before the

Subcommittee on Fossil and Synthetic Fuels of the Committee on Energy and Commerce, House of Representatives, Ninety-seventh Congress, second session, on H.R. 3057, H.R. 5441, and H.R. 5833 ... April 2 and June 9, 1982., 83-8422

Energy storage — United States.
Energy storage : energy conservation., 83-7254

Energy storage — United States — Security measures.
Security assessment of power systems, including energy storage., 83-7259

Energy tax credits — United States.
The role of business incentives in the development of renewable energy technologies : hearing before the Subcommittee on Energy Development and Applications of the Committee on Science and Technology, U.S. House of Representatives, Ninety-seventh Congress, second session, July 13, 1982., 83-8504

Energy transfer.
The Energy exchange project /, 83-7028

Engelmann spruce.
Variation in growth of Engelmann spruce seedlings under selected temperature environments /, 83-6410

Engineering geology — United States.
Engineering geology and geomorphology of streambank erosion /, 83-6903

Engineers — Employment — United States — Periodicals.
Science and engineering personnel., 83-7949

English language — Study and teaching — United States.
Children's English and services study : educational needs assessment for language minority children with limited English proficiency /, 83-7078

Environmental engineering — United States — Periodicals.
Pacific Northwest Laboratory annual report for ... to the DOE Office of Energy Research, 83-7042
Pacific Northwest Laboratory annual report for ... to the DOE Office of the Assistant Secretary for Environmental Protection, Safety, and Emergency Preparedness /, 83-7042

Environmental health — Research — United States — Periodicals.
Pacific Northwest Laboratory annual report for ... to the DOE Office of Energy Research /, 83-7043

Environmental health — United States.
Health implications of coal related energy development : mining impacts /, 83-7125

Environmental health — United States — Congresses.
The 1981 White House Conference on Aging : executive summary of technical committee on the physical & social environment and quality of life., 83-8345

Environmental health — Utah — Millard County.
Community health associated with arsenic in drinking water in Millard County, Utah /, 83-7101

Environmental law — United States.
Environmental compliance guide : guidance manual for Department of Energy compliance with the Fish and Wildlife Coordination Act., 83-7058

Environmental law — United States — Periodicals.
CFR. 40, Protection of environment, 83-7413, 83-7414
Code of federal regulations. 40, Protection of environment., 83-7413, 83-7414
Protection of environment, 83-7413, 83-7414

Environmental laws — United States.
Environmental compliance guide : guidance manual for Department of Energy compliance with Corps of Engineers permits on dredging and filling activities., 83-7059, 83-7060, 83-7061

Environmental policy — New Mexico — Maps.
San Juan River coal region, environmental impact statement /, 83-7574

*Environmental Pollutants — toxicity — periodicals.
Health hazard evaluation summaries /, 83-7547

Environmental protection — United States.
Environmental quality : environmental protection and enhancement., 83-6822

Environmental protection — United States — Periodicals.
CFR. 40, Protection of environment, 83-7413, 83-7414
Code of federal regulations. 40, Protection of environment., 83-7413, 83-7414
Protection of environment, 83-7413, 83-7414

Epidemiology.
Principles of analytic epidemiology., 83-7533

Page I-446   Do not order from index; see indicated entry

Figure 3.6 Sample from subject index of *The Monthly Catalog of Government Documents*.

Government Publications — March 1983

**BUDGET, Committee on the,
Senate
Washington, DC 20510**

83-8391

Y 4.B 85/2:F 31/5

United States. Congress. Senate. Committee on the Budget.
Federal block grants and revenue sharing : the advantages and disadvantages for the state of Iowa : hearing before the Committee on the Budget, United States Senate, Ninety-seventh Congress, second session, Des Moines, Iowa, February 18, 1982. — Washington : U.S. G.P.O., 1982.
iii, 133 p. : ill. ; 24 cm. ●Item 1035-A-1, 1035-A-2 (microfiche)
1. Budget — United States. 2. Block grants — Iowa. 3. Economic assistance, Domestic — Iowa. 4. Revenue sharing — Iowa. I. Title. II. Title: The advantages and disadvantages for the state of Iowa. OCLC 09142564

83-8392

Y 4.B 85/2:G 76

Grassley, Charles.
Views of Senator Grassley on the budget waiver for Radio Broadcasting to Cuba Act / Committee on the Budget, United States Senate. — Washington : U.S. G.P.O., 1982.
iii, 2 p. ; 24 cm. At head of title: 97th Congress, 2d session. Committee print. "September 30, 1982." ●Item 1035-A-1, 1035-A-2 (microfiche)
1. Radio broadcasting — Cuba. 2. Budget — United States. 3. Radio — Law and legislation — United States. I. United States. Congress. Senate. Committee on the Budget. II. Title. OCLC 09114977

**BUDGET, Committee on the,
House
Washington, DC 20515**

83-8393

Y 4.B 85/3:C 76/6/982

The Congressional budget process : a general explanation / Committee on the Budget, U.S. House of Representatives. — Washington : U.S. G.P.O., 1982.
iii, 210 p. ; 24 cm. At head of title: Committee print. "December 1982." "CP-17." ●Item 1035-B-1, 1035-B-2 (microfiche)
1. Budget — United States. I. United States. Congress. House. Committee on the Budget. OCLC 09126359

**COMMERCE, SCIENCE, AND
TRANSPORTATION,
Committee on, Senate
Washington, DC 20510**

83-8394

Y 4.C 73/7:97-129

United States. Congress. Senate. Committee on Commerce, Science, and Transportation. Subcommittee on Science, Technology, and Space.
National materials and minerals policy : hearing before the Subcommittee on Science, Technology, and Space of the Committee on Commerce, Science, and Transportation, United States Senate, Ninety-seventh Congress, second session, on oversight of national materials and mineral policy, June 23, 1982. — Washington : U.S. G.P.O., 1982.
iii, 109 p. : 1 map ; 24 cm. "Serial no. 97-129." ●Item 1041-A, 1041-B (microfiche)
1. Strategic materials — United States. 2. Mineral resources conservation — United States. 3. Mineral industries — United States. 4. United States — National security. 5. United States — Economic policy — 1981- 6. Metals — Conservation — United States. I. Title. OCLC 09135265

**DISTRICT OF COLUMBIA,
Committee on the, House
Washington, DC 20515**

83-8395

Y 4.D 63/1:97-13

United States. Congress. House. Committee on the District of Columbia. Subcommittee on Judiciary and Education.
Federal budget impact on a small school district : oversight hearing before the Subcommittee on Judiciary and Education of the Committee on the District of Columbia, House of Representatives, Ninety-seventh Congress, second session, on the effect of federal budget reductions on a small school district, April 2, 1982. — Washington : U.S. G.P.O., 1982.
iii, 84 p. : maps ; 24 cm. "Serial no. 97-13." ●Item 1014-A, 1014-B (microfiche)
1. Budget — United States. 2. Federal aid to education — California. 3. Education — California — Finance. I. Title. OCLC 09138312

**JOINT ECONOMIC COMMITTEE
Washington, DC 20510**

83-8396

Y 4.Ec 7:C 76/982

United States. Congress. Joint Economic Committee.
Consumer price index : hearings before the Joint Economic Committee, Congress of the United States, Ninety-seventh Congress, second session, May 21 and June 22, 1982. — Washington : U.S. G.P.O., 1982.
iii, 101 p. : ill. ; 24 cm. ●Item 1000-B, 1000-C (microfiche)
1. Price indexes. 2. Inflation (Finance) and public expenditures. 3. Indexation (Economics) 4. Index numbers (Economics) I. Title. OCLC 09150301

83-8397

Y 4.Ec 7:Eu 7/9/pt.2

East European economic assessment : a compendium of papers / submitted to the Joint Economic Committee, Congress of the United States. — Washington : U.S. G.P.O. : For sale by the Supt. of Docs., U.S. G.P.O., 1981-
v. : ill. ; 24 cm. At head of title: 97th Congress, 1st session. Joint committee print. "July 10, 1981"—Pt. 2. Includes bibliographies. Contents: pt. 2. Regional assessments. ●Item 1000-B, 1000-C (microfiche) S/N 052-070-05531-6 @ GPO (pt.1) ; 052-070-05607-0 @ GPO (pt.2) $8.50 (pt.1) $9.00 (pt.2)
1. Europe, Eastern — Economic conditions — 1945- 2. Europe, Eastern — Economic policy. 3. United States — Foreign relations — Europe, Eastern. 4. Europe, Eastern — Foreign relations — United States. I. United States. Congress. Joint Economic Committee. HC244.E2 81-601663 // r82 330.947 ¢2 19 OCLC 07924676

83-8398

Y 4.Ec 7:M 74/9/982

United States. Congress. Joint Economic Committee. Subcommittee on Monetary and Fiscal Policy.
Monetary policy : hearing before the Subcommittee on Monetary and Fiscal Policy of the Joint Economic Committee, Congress of the United States, Ninety-seventh Congress, second session, June 16, 1982. — Washington : U.S. G.P.O., 1982.

Figure 3.7 Sample from *The Monthly Catalog of Government Documents*.

For some documents, you will indeed have to order from the GPO, by mail or, if you are using a credit card, by telephone. When the *Monthly Catalog* listing does not include the price, call the GPO information number (202-783-3238) for that additional information.

Before you order, make sure you look in your library for a copy. Just because it is a government document does not mean it will not be in your library. Look the report up as if it were a book: use the title card catalog, and check the vertical files. Also, before you order and pay, try to get the document from another library (especially one designated as a government documents depository library—such libraries are listed in the front of the *Monthly Catalog*). Either go there or work through interlibrary loan services. Don't, however, expect a great deal of efficiency from interlibrary loan services in this case. Through computer networks and published volumes, libraries are letting each other know what books, magazines, and journals they hold. Government documents, however, are frequently omitted from these lists because they are considered of temporary value and not part of the library's permanent collection.

Using Legislative Calendars and Committee Catalogs. The *Monthly Catalog* is a valuable, albeit cumbersome resource, because it is fairly thorough and because it is available in most libraries. For almost all debate resolutions, there will be certain congressional committees in whose activities you will be particularly interested. The *Monthly Catalog* will give you some sense of what these particular committees are up to; however, you can easily obtain a more detailed look. Congressional committees that deal with legislation issue legislative calendars. If you are debating a foreign policy resolution, you would be interested in the activities of the Senate Foreign Relations Committee and the House Foreign Affairs Committee. Both publish legislative calendars. If you are debating a resolution dealing with federal aid to education, you would be interested in the activities of the Senate Committee on Labor and Human Relations and the House Committee on Education and Labor. Both issue legislative calendars. A good almanac should list for you the names of the different congressional committees.

Legislative calendars follow no firmly set format, but they all keep track of every piece of legislation referred to a committee. Hundreds of pieces of legislation are introduced during a session of Congress (a session lasts a year) and referred to a committee for action. Most die in committee. The fortunate pieces of legislation fall into two categories. The first kind of legislation is so simple or routine that, after a brief discussion, the committee can send it to the full Senate or House of Representatives for action. The second kind is deemed sufficiently significant that committee hearings are held on it and, based on these hearings, the committee issues a report. If the committee approves the legislation, it sends the legislation with the accompanying report to the full Senate or House for action. It is this second type of legislation you will be interested in, for hearings and reports are published and available to the public. A legislative calendar tells you what hearings and reports are presently available or will be available soon.

You should write or call any congressional committees that deal with legislation related to your topic and ask for a legislative calendar. If you see any hearings or reports in the calendar, call or write again. Sometimes they will send you the requested documents; sometimes they will refer you to the superintendent of documents' room. If you're referred, call or write the superintendent of documents' room at the United States Capitol. Capitol Hill personnel are usually very cooperative; however, occasionally, you may feel you are getting the runaround. If you feel that way, write or call one of your Senators or your Representative and ask him or her to assist you in acquiring the desired documents. Senators and Representatives usually have one or more people on their staffs responsible for what is called constituency service: it is these aides' job to do anything they can to assist the citizens whom the legislator represents.

Not all congressional committees deal with legislation. These committees, oftentimes designated "special" or "joint," conduct studies. Their studies are designed to help lawmakers understand important public issues. These committees do not publish legislative calendars; rather, they issue catalogs, usually annually, of their publications. These catalogs can be requested by mail or telephone.

One of the major committees of this type is the Joint Economic Committee. Its catalog lists recent and older studies, including many which may be obtained free of charge from the committee's office and some which must be purchased from the Government Printing Office. A study is usually printed in more than sufficient numbers for congressional and limited public distribution: these are the free copies. If a particular study proves to be in demand, especially years after it was published, another printing is ordered. Studies printed at this later date are the ones you must purchase from the Government Printing Office. Again, before purchasing, check your library and other libraries, either in person or through interlibrary loan services.

Using the Congressional Research Service

Our nation's lawmakers require information. Committees such as the Joint Economic Committee help provide it; so do respectable think tanks such the AEI and Brookings. In particular, the Library of Congress was originally established to provide information to legislators, hence its name. The Library has a special division called the Congressional Research Service (CRS).

The CRS periodically publishes a guide to important public issues called *Update*. You might want to ask your Senator or your Representative to help you get it. It is available to all members of Congress as well as to members of the general public who demonstrate a need for it. You must demonstrate the need to your elected representatives; they, in turn, request *Update* on your behalf. *Update* will provide you with valuable summary information; it will also list CRS issue briefs and information packets which you can obtain upon request. They will prove even more valuable than the material in *Update*. *Update*, then, is a key to other information.

The CRS publishes many special reports. Unfortunately, these are technically available *only* to members of Congress. Unless a particular report is designated by special legislation as available to a larger audience, CRS reports are off limits. You *might* be able to somehow wangle a copy of a CRS report intended for the eyes of the nation's lawmakers; however, the use of that report raises ethical questions. Only material available to all debaters should be cited in competition; quoting a CRS report not available to the general public could lead to an automatic loss if the violation of the American Forensic Association code of ethics were detected.

Thanks to special legislation, two reports per year are prepared especially for high school debaters and college NDT debaters. The high school topic for the succeeding year is announced in early May. Approximately a month later, the CRS issues an annotated bibliography on the resolution; then late in the summer, the CRS issues a report on the resolution. This report is a compendium of reprinted CRS materials, congressional documents, think-tank reports, journal articles, and monograph excerpts which the CRS researchers have felt to be especially pertinent to the year's debate topic. The college NDT topic is announced in early July. Approximately a month later, the CRS issues an annotated bibliography; in the early weeks of the debate season, the CRS issues a compendium of materials on the resolution. As with CRS' *Update*, these reports are available only through the offices of your U.S. Senators and Representatives.

The Faculty as a Resource

We first discussed the resources available to you in your library—monographs, magazines, journals, etc.; then we discussed the resources available to you outside your school library—studies by think tanks, materials from special interest groups, law review articles, court decisions, and various government documents. These outside resources are only as close as the nearest law school or Washington, D.C. There is, however, a resource close by: the faculty.

I mentioned before how faculty members might be asked to participate in early-season symposia, but faculty members can play a role throughout the debating season. On your campus there are men and women who know a great deal about different aspects of your debate resolution. Many will be willing to share their expertise if asked by you or by your debate coach or instructor. These men and women may also have their own private libraries and may be willing to share their collected resources with serious, enthusiastic, trustworthy students.

If your resolution involves U.S. foreign policy toward the People's Republic of China, specialists in international relations, international commerce, and Chinese history might be called upon. If your resolution involves capital punishment, specialists in criminology, sociology, psychology, philosophy, and religion might be called upon. If your resolution involves the nation's water resources, specialists in geology, engineering, and government might be called upon. Right outside your library's doors, there is expertise aplenty. Don't overlook it. Debaters should be very visible on campus, and seek to increase their understanding of the issues a debate resolution raises. Engaging in this kind of personal research will also significantly enhance the debater's education.

Preparing for Competition

How to Read While Researching

Research can be both tedious and exciting—exciting when you discover a treasure; tedious when you're digging and digging. If you've tried to follow the research procedures I have outlined above, you now have before you an extensive bibliography of monographs, magazine articles, compendia, journal articles, and pamphlets you want to read. You also know about some other library resources and know that you want to consult them eventually. You also have before you (or on the way) studies by think tanks, materials from special interest groups, and a host of government documents. You know how to find law review articles and court decisions and you anticipate that your reading of printed material and, perhaps, your discussions with experts on your faculty will help you pinpoint what decisions you want to read and read about.

You are now ready to read. Reading what you have gathered is a large, but crucial task. You must complete it if you are to be the best debater you can be. Mere glibness will get you only so far; to rise to the top of debating competition, you must understand the issues that the resolution raises. Completing the reading is not, however, just a matter of plowing through. Three important strategies ought to be kept in mind.

First, proceed from general to particular. If you read a very focused, very specialized piece too early, you will not know what its relevance is. The general reading is necessary if the specialized reading is to prove meaningful. There is a strong temptation to jump to the specialized discussions: if you are reading sophisticated reports rather than general commentaries, you feel you're really getting somewhere. However, if those specialized reports lack relevance or full meaning for you, you are really getting nowhere. Second, alternate close reading and skimming. If something is proving extremely useful, slow down and read it very carefully; however, if something strikes you as not being helpful or if it confuses you, start skimming. Otherwise you will become bored and/or discouraged.

Keep in mind that there is *far* more information on your topic than you can possibly hope to read. Your goal should be to read as much useful material as possible in as little time as possible. In business and government circles, this goal is referred to as "optimizing" your research. Third, you should make the material your own if possible. If you have acquired the material or if you have made your own photocopy of library material, mark that material up. Underline, highlight, make notes in the margin. Keep in mind that, before too long, you will want to return to the material and know what passages are useful in it and why they are useful.

Think in Terms of Evidence Cards While Researching

When I speak of "useful," I am referring to actual debating. Debaters quote studies, statistics, and authoritative views quite often in competition. The quotations they might want to use are prepared on file cards. When you are marking your material as you're reading it or when you're copying down quotations from material you cannot mark up, keep these file cards in mind. You want to mark off or copy passages which are neither too brief nor too long; you also want to mark off or copy passages which prove one point. You do this to facilitate filing.

Initially, you will find yourself only somewhat able to pick out passages in what you read that will make useful material during an actual debate. The more you debate, however, the more you will come to understand what is useful in actual competition and what is not. But, from the very beginning of your career as a debater, try to think in terms of useful evidence cards when reading.

The Research Notebook

During the research process, I recommend that you maintain a research notebook. In this notebook, you compile your working bibliography; you also take notes on the material you read. What kinds of notes should you take?

First, you should note factual information you think a debater dealing with your particular resolution should know. If you are debating U.S. military intervention in Western Hemisphere nations, you might be reading a very general monograph on politics in Latin America. The book goes nation-by-nation and discusses such matters as its present government, its economy, its foreign policy problems, and its domestic policy problems. Although you may have a difficult time finding a single useful quotation in the presentation, the information is invaluable background. You also might run across an historical review of the changes in government in Guatemala. Record the facts. If you are discussing the quality of American television, you might find an article in which there is a listing of Emmy award-winning dramatic and comedy series since 1955. That list might well prove useful—for example, in arguing that television programming has improved in quality since 1955.

Second, you should note the contents of every book, article and report you read. What does it cover? What arguments does it make? You will frequently find yourself saying, several months into the debate season, that you read an article on a subject months before. The article's information did not seem important then; but now, months later, opponents are talking about precisely what that article covered. You will want to return to that article. If you noted the article and its contents in your research notebook, you can easily find it. If you did not note the article and its contents, you will have rely entirely on your memory to get to that now valuable article. Most people's memories are not anywhere near as reliable as written notes.

Third, you should transcribe the information you think ought to go on file cards (from sources you cannot mark up) for use in competition. You may wonder why I don't recommend transcribing the information directly onto cards. It is not recommended because you will probably initially write down many, many potential evidence cards that, upon later scrutiny, you realize are lacking in value. Between the time you scribble the material down and the time you evaluate it as an evidence card, you establish distance and objectivity. You are better able to see its worth. Transcribing from the source to the notebook and then to the file card will prevent you from filling up a file box with evidence that simply will not be useful. A file box full of cards may impress some people, but if you cannot find the valuable evidence cards for all the valueless ones, your debating will rather quickly change their minds.

The material you place on file cards—copied from the marked-up source or copied from the research notebook—will be evidence of one of two general kinds: empirical evidence, the reported results of research; and opinion evidence, the views of authorities. When evaluating information as potentially useful evidence, you must consider not only the passage's length and its focus on one fully developed argument, but also whether it is good evidence of its kind.

Empirical Evidence

Empirical evidence usually presents the conclusions of studies, either in plain language or in statistical terms. Evidence of this kind should be scrutinized from four perspectives.

First, you should look closely at the design of the study. You should question the sample size and the adequacy of the controls along the following lines:

- Whether a researcher is trying to demonstrate the superiority of tax incentives over government contracts as an economic stimulus, or that brain activity is higher while watching a dramatic television program than when watching a comedy, that researcher must look at a sufficient number of cases. How many businesses has the researcher examined? How many television viewers?
- Has the researcher taken care to make comparisons truly valid? If 100 companies were examined, fifty given tax incentives and fifty given government contracts, were the two groups otherwise equal? If the businesses given tax incentives were initially financially stronger or larger or concentrated in a particular geographic region, the groups were not at all equal and any comparisons are highly questionable.
- Enthusiastic researchers can sometimes cause the predicted results to occur by saying too much to subjects. Perhaps in the case of the television viewers, the assembled group was aware of the hypothesis before the experiment began. The results might then be nothing more than a self-fulfilling prophecy, not a valid empirical conclusion.

Second, if results are presented in plain language, you should look closely at the language for qualifiers such as "usually," "often," or "frequently." These qualifiers indicate that there are exceptions to the researcher's conclusion. Look also for words that imply a degree of uncertainty on the researcher's part, words like "seems to indicate" and "would lead one to believe." When the results of empirical studies are presented in this kind of hesitant language, you would be well-advised to find out what the exceptions might be and, specifically, why the researcher is hesitant in presenting his or her conclusions before you use the study as evidence in a debate.

Third, you should consider the very complex question of causality carefully. Empirical studies frequently seem to claim that "a" acting on "b" causes "c." In a very carefully regulated scientific environment, researchers can make firm causal statements because they are sure that only "a" and "b" were present and that only "a" acted on "b." When the study's subjects are human beings, not chemicals, researchers try to scientifically rule out all other possible elements besides "a" that might act on "b" to cause "c." However, it is frequently practically impossible to rule out totally what is termed "alternative causality" in studies involving human activity. Therefore, researchers present conclusions cautiously. If there is an alternative cause that comes readily to your mind and if it is not explicitly ruled out by reported additional experiments, you had better not use the study as evidence. If the alternative cause has dawned on you, it will probably occur to your opponents, as well.

Fourth, if the results are presented in statistical terms, look for statistical significance and be dubious of percentages.

The question of statistical significance is far too complex to go into here. In a nutshell, the concept of statistical significance is based on researchers' recognition that an experiment may show superiority, inferiority, or some kind of relationship due to quirks in the experimental design. If criminals rehabilitated in maximum-security prisons score better on a test of mental discipline than criminals with equal intelligence and similar educational backgrounds but rehabilitated in a minimum-security prison, the better performance may not prove anything unless the difference is a statistically significant one. Any time the statistics look "close," you might want to avoid using the study as evidence.

Percentages sound good, and statistical presentations of empirical research are full of them. Understand that percentages are deceptive. Nation "S" that has decreased the number of human rights violations (according to Amnesty International) from forty-five to twenty-seven has decreased its violations 166 percent. Another nation, nation "T," that has decreased its violations from 6,100 to 1,500 has decreased its violations a little more than 40 percent. Which nation has done more to improve human rights? Which nation should receive the higher praise? With only percentages to base your judgment on, you would probably have said nation "S." Once you saw the numbers, you probably would have said nation "T." So, before you decide to use the conclusions of empirical studies, take a look at the raw numerical data.

Opinion Evidence

Good opinion evidence should present the views of people who are qualified to speak on the subject and who offer not only their views but their reasons for holding these views. Opinion evidence is bad and should be avoided if the author lacks sufficient credentials or has blinding prejudices. Opinion evidence is also bad and should not be used if the author's rationale for his or her view is not given immediately, not given elsewhere, or not clear. In some debates, you may hear speakers denounce all opinion evidence. The widespread use of bad opinion evidence has given rise to—and sometimes acceptance to—such denunciations. These denunciations aside, fully reasoned, authoritative opinion evidence has an important role in debating. These denunciations have, however, given rise to some skepticism concerning opinion evidence. This skepticism should help keep you from choosing to use bad opinion evidence.

Exercises: Evaluating Evidence

Discuss the five pieces of fictitious empirical evidence which follow. Would you use them in competition? If not, why not?

1. "U.S. military intervention has occurred twenty-six times since 1946. In twenty-four of those cases, it proved counterproductive. The intervention seems to have promoted the very conditions it was intended to prevent."
2. "The water of the Potomac River is 310 percent cleaner in 1982 than in 1972 when clean-up efforts began. The damage done by man can be repaired."
3. "The average SAT score of college applicants in 1970 was 1100; the average in 1980 had fallen to 1030. Obviously, high schools are not doing their job."
4. "Grants of immunity from prosecution have increased over 300 percent in the past decade; at the same time, reported felony crimes have increased over 200 percent. The granting of immunity, rather than leading to convictions which deter the criminally inclined, seems to have actually promoted criminal activity."
5. "A survey of a dozen Philadelphia landlords in 1963 indicated that only two would rent an apartment to an unmarried couple. A similar survey of eighty Denver landlords in 1983 indicated that all but eight would. The difference seems to indicate that the moral climate in America has changed significantly over the past two decades."

Discuss the following five pieces of fictitious opinion evidence. Would you use them in competition? If not, why not?

1. "We should keep the petroleum supply lines open, even if it means using U.S. military might."—President Warhawk, in his State of the Union Address, 10 January 1986

2. "Health maintenance organizations (HMOs) may keep the costs of medical care down; however, they tend to provide inferior health care because HMOs tend to only attract the less capable physicians as member doctors."—A. Doctor, President of the American Medical Association, in hearings before the House Subcommittee on Health and Safety, 10 February 1983
3. "Money spent on welfare payments is money poorly spent. The payments deter able-bodied men and women from seeking gainful employment."—U. Boat, Secretary of the Navy, in a speech reported in *The Washington Post*, 10 September 1982
4. "If the United States commits itself to gradual nuclear disarmament, the Soviet Union will follow suit."—Dr. Peace, Professor of International Relations, Delaware State University, in *The Politics of Disarmament* (1981)
5. "True, a few instances of labor union violence are reported each year; in general, however, present laws directed against such violence seem to be doing the job."—J. J. Bureaucrat, U.S. Secretary of Labor, in hearings before the Senate Committee on Labor and Human Resources, 10 July 1983

Obtaining the Necessary Biographical Information

You will find that you have obtained passages of empirical and opinion evidence that you want to put on file cards for use in competition, but that you know very little about the author. You need not toss the possible piece of evidence aside for fear that you will not be able to provide sufficient credentials for the source. There are, in just about all library reference rooms, academic and public, numerous resources to turn to which provide biographical information.

For American sources, the two major resources are *Who's Who in America* and *The Dictionary of American Biography*. Both are issued periodically, so that their contents are up-to-date. The distinction between these two sources is an important one: *Who's Who* is for living Americans, *The Dictionary of American Biography* for deceased Americans.

For British sources (including many in former parts of the British empire— e.g., Australia, Canada, India), the two major resources are *Who's Who* and *The Dictionary of National Biography*. Again, *Who's Who* is for the living, *The Dictionary of National Biography* for the dead. For sources from other nations, information will be a bit tougher to come by. The best bet would be *Who's Who in the World*. When first included in its pages, the person would have been alive. Those chronicled in earlier editions may well now be deceased. To save yourself library time, try to get biographical information on the source when you are reading the monograph, article, etc. Where should you look? If it is a monograph, try the title page or the very end of the author's preface. If it is a magazine article, look right under the author's name, at the foot of the article's first page, or at the article's end. If it is a journal article or an essay in a compendium, also look in the issue's or compendium's front matter. There will sometimes be a list of contributors with brief biographies there.

(D) → 42   SUBS W/ CRUISE MISSILES   ← (C)
                    COMPLICATE ASW

(A) → The addition of antiship missiles to the submarines' armament adds a further complication. These weapons travel much farther than torpedoes. Against the submarines that fire these cruise missiles, ASW [Anti-Submarine Warfare] forces must therefore provide protection at much greater ranges.

(B) → David Kassing, President, Center for Naval Analyses in *Problems of Sea Power as We Approach the Twenty-First Century*, ed. James L. George
Washington, DC: AEI, 1978.
p. 310

Figure 3.8   Sample evidence card.

Preparing the Evidence Cards

You should put *good* evidence on cards. You should also strive to make the quoted passage neither too brief nor too long; you should also strive to have the quoted passage focus on a single argument. These guidelines insure that the evidence cards are optimally useful to you in an actual debate. You can also lay out the evidence cards themselves so as to enhance their value to you in a debate.

Figure 3.8 is a sample evidence card. It has four elements, labeled on the figure as (A), (B), (C), and (D). Each element is important.

(A) is the quoted passage itself. Debaters should be conversant with the conventional ways of using ellipses (spaced periods) to signify deleted words and the conventional ways of using square brackets to signify inserted words. Sometimes it might be necessary to edit a passage using these conventions. You should *never* edit a passage so as to change its meaning; rather, you delete to make the quoted passage easier to read or you insert to make it clearer. You may well be asked in competition to supply the deleted words, so you will find it a useful idea to jot the deleted words down on the evidence card's flipside. Try to edit sparingly. Evidence cards with too many deletions and insertions will strike opponents and judges as suspicious.

(B) is the full citation. Besides noting where the passage came from, it also gives *brief* information about the author. Many debaters find it useful to maintain a separate alphabetical file—perhaps using smaller file cards or different-color file cards—giving more detailed biographical information on authorities they will be quoting.

Below, in summary form, are the elements of a full citation for most kinds of information:

Monograph and single-authored think-tank or government studies:
    Author
    Monograph Title

City of Publication: Publisher, Date of Publication
Page Number(s) of Quoted Passage

Magazine Article:
Author
Article Title
Magazine Name and Date
Page Number(s) of Quoted Passage

Journal Article:
Author
Article Title
Journal Name, Volume Number, Issue Number, Date
Page Number(s) of Quoted Passage

Compendia Essays (including essays in multiauthored think-tank studies and the CRS annual collection for debaters)
Author of Essay
Compendium Title, Editor
City of Publication: Publisher, Date of Publication
Page Number(s) of Quoted Passage

Pamphlets (including most special interest group publications)
Author
Pamphlet Title
Issuing or Publishing Organization, Date of Issuance
Page Number(s) of Quoted Passage

The Statistical Abstract
The Statistical Abstract of the United States for ⎯⎯ (year)
Table Number

Law Review Articles:
Author
Article Title
Law Review Name, Date
Page Number(s) of Quoted Passage

Court Decisions:
Case Name
Court Issuing Decision, Name of Majority Opinion Author
or
Court Issuing Decision, Name of Concurring Author
or
Court Issuing Decision, Name of Dissenting Author
Date of Decision

Congressional Hearings:
Quoted Source
Hearings Conducted by ⎯⎯ (name of committee or subcommittee)

Date of Hearings
Page Number(s) of Quoted Passage

Congressional Reports:
Report of —— (name of committee or subcommittee)
or
Minority Report of —— (author) to the Report of —— (name of committee or subcommittee)
Date of Report
Page Number(s) of Quoted Passage

There are some other kinds of information you might find yourself using (e.g., a printed transcript of a television interview show); the ten kinds listed above, however, are the major ones. *Remember* that you can ethically use only information equally available to all debaters. Comments made by an authority in conversation with you cannot ethically be used; typed-up, mimeographed, and filed-in-the-library lectures by an eminent professor at your school cannot ethically be used. A single violation of the ethics governing evidence can cost you a debate; in addition, that violation will cast a long shadow over all the statements you and your teammates make and all the evidence you and your teammates offer. Be very scrupulous.

(C) is a very brief summary of the quoted passage. Such a summary allows a debater in competition, in a second or two, to know whether or not an evidence card will prove useful. (D) is a code number: it indicates what section of the evidence file a particular card belongs in. The code number aids in refiling at the conclusion of a debate.

Preparing the Evidence File

Most teams maintain at least two evidence files—an affirmative file and a negative file. Actually, three files are better.

The first file would be the affirmative file. When you are affirming a debate resolution, you choose the ground for the actual debate, since you will start off the debate by presenting your case for saying "Yes" to the question implicit in the resolution. Most debaters will devise several cases before a season is over. Each case will contain several arguments you will offer and defend. The most efficient way to organize the affirmative file is according to these arguments.

The second file would be the first negative file. As you will soon discover, a debate team consists of two people. When you deny the resolution, these two people are called the first negative and the second negative. They have different tasks in an actual debate. The first negative responds to the particular arguments in the affirmative's case. There could in theory be as many affirmative cases as there are teams, and a first negative has to be ready to respond to all of them with evidence. The most efficient way to organize the first negative file is according to these many cases. Use major headings for the different kinds of cases you will be debating; use subheadings for the particular arguments usually made in such cases. Reserve some major headings for negative arguments you are likely to voice against most, if not all, affirmative cases.

The third file would be the second negative file. The second negative debater in policy debate raises objections to the particular policy or plan the affirmative team has advocated; the second negative debater in value debate raises general reasons for rejecting the resolution's judgment. For example, if the topic is "Resolved: That moral relativism has had a positive effect on American society," the second negative debater would probably discuss the negative effects of moral relativism; if the topic is "Resolved: That the Puritan work ethic has been overemphasized," then the second negative debater would probably discuss the negative effects of abandoning this ethic. These arguments, in the jargon of value debate, are called "off-case" arguments because they are not directly linked to any of the specific arguments voiced by the affirmative team in presenting its case for adopting the resolution.

Whether debating a policy resolution or a value resolution, a second negative debater will have available to him or her a stock of general arguments he or she will choose among and use in debate after debate. The most efficient way to organize the second negative file is based on these general arguments. Have a section for each and fill it with the evidence cards you will or might use to support that general argument.

Number the categories in the three files using different schemes—i.e., affirmative file, two-digit numbers starting with 10; first negative file, three-digit numbers starting with 100; second negative file, four digit numbers starting with 1000. For subcategories, use letters—i.e., 10A, 10B, 10C, etc. You should follow this advice for two reasons: first, you will know immediately which file a particular card goes in by just looking at the length of its code number; second, you will be readily able to expand the three files as necessary, something that would be awkward if the first file contained numbers 1 to 38, the second file contained numbers 39 to 74, and the third file contained numbers 75 to 118.

In the Future: Can the Computer Help?

Anyone knowledgeable about computer systems sees an ideal application of computer technology to the masses of data debaters accumulate. Two scenarios seem feasible. Debaters could store their evidence in an institutional computer and use remote terminals in competition. By telephone, the remote terminal could be hooked up to the computer. The debaters could electronically thumb through file categories. If debaters carried a portable printer, they could quickly get "hard copies" of evidence they wanted to use while speaking.

Or debaters could use microcomputers with maximum RAM and considerable additional memory for storage. Evidence could be stored on floppy disks and fed into the microcomputer when needed. The debaters could electronically search file categories, and if they had a portable printer, they could have "hard copy" in seconds. No telephone hookup would be needed, saving the team money and logistical problems.

Whether remote terminals or microcomputers are used, searching programs can be written so that the computer searches descriptors on each evidence card and pulls out all cards containing a particular descriptor or combination of descriptors. When searching programs are added, categorization of evidence cards will no longer be necessary.

Remote terminals or microcomputers could also be connected to national data networks. If an opposing debater mentions a particular Supreme Court decision, you could tap a national data base and have a copy of the decision and any dissenting views before you in seconds. If an opposing debater refers to the results of an empirical study on the effects of acid rain on the nutritional value of vegetables, you could tap a data base containing abstracts of studies in the field of agriculture. The abstract of the particular study could be located, and reading it might allow you to note limitations in the study that you otherwise would never have known.

Let me editorialize here, however. Debating, as an activity, could turn to computer technology right now. All of the possibilities I have mentioned are *present* possibilities. Because we pride ourselves on teaching transferable research skills and thinking skills, debaters should not reject too quickly the use of computer technology. In "the real world," computers are used in research, and if what debating teaches is not to become archaic and irrelevant, we need to consider how it will embrace computers.

Consideration is necessary because of the ethical questions the use of computer technology raises. There is nothing unethical in using computer technology in doing research; it may be unfair, however, and therefore unethical for the financially well-off debate programs to go the computer route because they can afford the requisite hardware and software leaving poor programs in the slow, old-fashioned world of 4" × 6" cards. Debaters can, with their instructors and coaches, consider the real possibilities computer technology offers; however, at the same time, they should wrestle with the important question of fairness.

Ongoing Research

Research does not stop when files are assembled and competition begins. Research is an ongoing activity. Three ongoing tasks should be especially noted.

Research to Plug Holes

You cannot possibly discover all of the issues contained in a typical debate resolution while exploring it at the beginning of a year or semester. Unanticipated issues will pop up as the season progresses, and research will be necessary on these issues. Generally speaking, you will want to follow the same general-to-specific, inside-the-library/outside-the-library strategy outlined earlier in this chapter. You will be able to move much more rapidly through the process because you will now be searching for very specific information, because you will be able to skim even more material than before, and because you will be far more conversant with the general subject and most of the issues it raises. As you research to plug holes, use your research notebook. You will undoubtedly find good information on issues other than the one you are researching. Note the exact location of that information in your notebook so that you or someone else can return to it later. Don't let its existence distract you from your particular quest, but don't let it escape your future grasp.

Keeping Up-to-Date

Debate resolutions are chosen because consultants have suggested that the particular question will become controversial and important during the course of the debate season. Events will occur during the season that you will have to know about.

The easiest way to keep up-to-date is to commit yourself to reading a major newspaper every day and a major news magazine every week. Cut out and mark up whatever you find that is relevant to the debate resolution; then transfer the good information to evidence cards.

Some debaters work on keeping up-to-date as a team. Each will be assigned a newspaper or periodical. That person's job is to read the assigned source and pull out of it anything that may be useful.

Revising the Evidence File

The original scheme for organizing the three evidence files rarely lasts an entire season. Be prepared to revise the file whenever its organization becomes more of a hindrance than a help. Each file usually requires a similar kind of revision.

The affirmative file will, before long, contain categories for the arguments that were voiced in an affirmative case long since discarded. Get rid of these categories and refile the evidence cards from them in places where they might prove useful. Otherwise, some valuable evidence cards might become permanently lost.

The first negative file will grow. You will find yourself adding categories to it as you confront new and different affirmative cases for the debate resolution. You'll also find that some categories are no longer used: either you incorrectly guessed that many teams would base their affirmation of the debate resolution on a certain major argument or an approach taken early proved so unsuccessful that teams using it dropped it. Get rid of these categories and refile the evidence cards contained in them. The second negative file will also grow, and second negative debaters will develop better and better general arguments to offer as the debate season progresses. File categories set up to contain the evidence that supported the arguments used early in the season are no longer helpful. Quite a few of the evidence cards contained in them may be quite useful—elsewhere. Get rid of all no longer useful categories and refile the evidence cards where they will prove valuable.

When the Season is Over

By the end of a debate season, you will probably have quite an accumulation of evidence cards. What should you do with them? One debater I know was so tired of the debate resolution by the year's end that she didn't bother to claim the file box from American Airlines upon arriving home from her last tournament trip. She would have been better off keeping the evidence cards. Why? Because they might have enabled her to write a research paper without expending much energy, and because the evidence might come in handy in debate seasons to come. Evidence on the existence or nonexistence of a Communist threat; evidence on the ravages of inflation; evidence on flaws in the U.S. criminal justice system; evidence on the dangers of pollution, nuclear waste, chemical waste, and an energy shortage—this material is useful time and time again. I would use the same rule the Internal Revenue Service demands, that taxpayers follow and keep all records for six years, or the extent of your debating career. After six years, even if relevant, the information is most probably outdated.

After reading and studying Chapter 3, you know:

- about handbooks and institutes, about different places to look for background on your debate topic, and about preparing a good bibliography (using conventional techniques and computer information retrieval);
- how to find monographs, magazine articles, compendia, journal articles, and pamphlets on your topic in an academic library;
- how to acquire think-tank studies, materials from special interest groups, law review articles, court decisions, government documents, and materials prepared by the Congressional Research Service;
- how to read and take notes on the voluminous materials you have gathered as efficiently as possible, evaluate emipirical and opinion evidence, obtain biographical information, transcribe evidence onto 4" × 6" cards, and set up an efficient filing system for the cards;
- that research is necessary as the season progresses to plug holes and keep up-to-date.

CHAPTER 4
The Affirmative Case

In this chapter, you will learn:

- what the stock issues are that an affirmative team must address;
- the conventional ways to structure the affirmative case in policy debate;
- how to choose among the standard case-structures;
- two innovative approaches to the affirmative case in policy debate;
- how to structure a plan in policy debate;
- how to structure the affirmative case in value debate.

Having decided to debate, having explored the debate resolution, and having engaged in some research, you are now ready to begin learning how to debate. You know that there is a resolution; you also have been told that there are two opposed sides of the resolution and thus two teams in a given debate: the affirmative team, which tries to support the resolution, and the negative team, which tries to refute the case the affirmative team presents.

Resolutions are, typically, large statements. For example, "Resolved: That government information-gathering activities should be significantly curtailed" deals with activities undertaken by the CIA, the FBI, the Internal Revenue Service, Senate and House committees, special prosecutors, the Census Bureau, and other federal agencies, as well as the activities of state and local governments. The affirmative, in supporting such a large resolution, is not expected to deal with all of the possibilities it contains. Rather, the affirmative chooses which small area of the resolution it wants to discuss. Focused on the selected area, the affirmative team makes its case for adopting the resolution. The negative must follow the affirmative's lead and refute its particular case. Because the affirmative case sets up the debate, it is the logical starting point when learning to debate.

Several models exist for the affirmative case. For each model, you should try to understand the theory underlying it and its particular advantages. You should also realize that these models are frequently modified a bit in actual competition for a variety of valid (and invalid) reasons.

The Stock Issues

We are going to proceed pretty much in chronological order, telling a story, as it were. Once upon a time, debating was rather simple. An affirmative team had to offer a *prima facie* case for adopting the resolution. Since the status quo (i.e., the present situation) was presumed to be without problems and any change was presumed to be unnecessary, the affirmative team had a barrier to overcome. The affirmative had to present a case sufficiently strong so that, upon first hearing it, a judge would conclude that the status quo is not without problems and that change is indeed necessary. A case that would, at first hearing, overcome presumption in favor of the status quo and against change is a *prima facie* case. Literally translated, *prima facie* means "at first view."

The affirmative team must present just such a case for there to be a debate. If the affirmative team cannot overcome the presumption against it, there is no reason even to consider the resolution. But how does an affirmative case meet its burden of being *prima facie*—i.e., being sufficiently strong to overcome presumption "at first view"? To help debaters write a case that meets this burden, debate coaches dug into rhetorical theory of old, modified it, and came up with the concept of stock issues. Stock issues are those general requirements that the affirmative case must meet if it is to be *prima facie*. The stock issues are five in number: topicality, significance, inherency, plan, and solvency.

A *prima facie* case must be topical. If the judge decides to vote for the affirmative case and thereby adopt the advocated policy, that judge must be voting for and adopting the resolution. To beginning debaters, this stock issue may seem silly. Of course, buying the affirmative team's case and the affirmative team's policy will mean buying and adopting the resolution, you might think. If all debaters interpreted the resolution in the same conventional manner, this stock issue would be silly, superfluous. However, debaters do not always understand the resolution to mean exactly the same thing, and some affirmative debaters try to find unconventional but valid interpretations in order to achieve a strategic advantage over the negative team. So, when pressed, an affirmative team must be prepared to show that its policy represents a reasonable interpretation of the resolution, that the policy in its case is topical.

A *prima facie* case must also be significant. It must point to a significant problem that the status quo is experiencing. Traditionally, the problem was usually presented in an affirmative case as causing serious harms. In the mid- to-late 1960s, as you will see a bit later, debate theorists began to suggest that the status quo's failure to do as good a job as it might and the status quo's failure to meet important goals were significant problems, even though those failures could scarcely be described as "dire harms." This change represented a broadening of the stock issue of significance, not its denial.

A *prima facie* case must have inherency. The significant problem a case presents must be so much a part of the status quo that the status quo cannot solve it; the problem must be inherent in the status quo. Originally, theorists argued that the status quo must be unable to prevent the harms, if the case is to have the requisite inherency. As the stock issue of significance broadened, so did the stock issue of inherency. Now, theorists say that a case has the required inherency (1) if the status quo is unable to prevent the harms, if harms are claimed, or (2) if the status quo is unable to do the job as well as it might, if inferior performance is claimed, or (3) if the status quo is unable to meet important goals, if the failure to meet a goal or goals is claimed.

A *prima facie* case must contain a plan. As the years have gone by, more and more specificity has been demanded of affirmative plans. Vague plans are unacceptable; plans must be specific enough so that their workability can be evaluated.

Finally, a *prima facie* case must have solvency. The plan must be demonstrated to solve the significant problem. If the significant problem was the number of starving elderly citizens due to inadequate social security payments, the plan would have to increase payments so that they have enough to eat if the plan is to be considered solvent. If the significant problem was the government's failure to make defense spending as cost-efficient as possible, the plan would have to do a significantly better job to be solvent. If the significant problem was the failure of the Bureau of Indian Affairs to protect Native American interests as it is mandated to do by law, the plan would have to meet that goal to be solvent. As these examples should indicate, the solvency standard for prima faciality broadened as the standards for significance and inherency broadened to admit cases for changes in public policy other than those based on horrible, horrible problems with ghastly, quantifiable harms.

But whether it is 1960 or 1980, a *prima facie* case still must meet the stock issues of topicality, significance, inherency, plan, and solvency. In 1960, the affirmative team was allowed to unfold its *prima facie* case at a leisurely pace— primarily because the initial negative speaker presented a lengthy negative philosophy and did not engage in much direct refutation; therefore, the case had to be *prima facie* by the end of the second speech which the affirmative team makes for them to stand a chance in the debate. In 1980, the pace is quicker. The case for the resolution must be developed fully and immediately so that the negative team can start refuting it from the word "go." Therefore, the affirmative case must be *prima facie* by the end of the first speech which the affirmative team makes for the affirmative team to stand a chance of winning.

A note to value-resolution debaters. We are proceeding chronologically in talking about the affirmative case. Value resolutions were not debated in 1960 or 1970 when the stock issues gave rise to a standard affirmative case structure and when dissatisfaction with the emphasis on dire harms in that case structure gave rise to alternative case models. Policy debate was the only form of debate.

The "Needs Case"

The oldest case model grew directly out of the stock issues established to give debaters a standard for *prima faciality*; Figure 4.1 outlines it. This old case is called the "needs case." If following this model, a debater would, first, establish the existence of a problem—e.g., rural poverty is an unheralded American problem. Second, a debater would point to the harms—e.g., malnutrition, disease, poor medical care, death at an early age, etc. Third, a debater would demonstrate that the status quo cannot solve the problem (that the problem and its harms are inherent in the status quo)—e.g., there is a marked urban bias in the terms of federal antipoverty programs. Fourth, a debater would present his or her plan—e.g., federal revenue-sharing with the states, the money to be allocated on the basis of how much rural poverty a state has and spent exclusively to alleviate the harms of rural poverty. Fifth and finally, a debater would argue that his or her plan will solve the problem—e.g., that federal revenue sharing will get enough money to the states so that they can address the symptoms of the problem immediately and solve the problem over a ten-year period. As Figure 4.1 shows, this case model exactly parallels the stock issues.

The "Comparative Advantages Case"

The belief that policy changes were made in the real world for reasons other than the existence of dire harms and the dissatisfaction with the emphasis of the "needs case" on harms led to experimentation with new case structures. The first was called the "comparative advantages case."

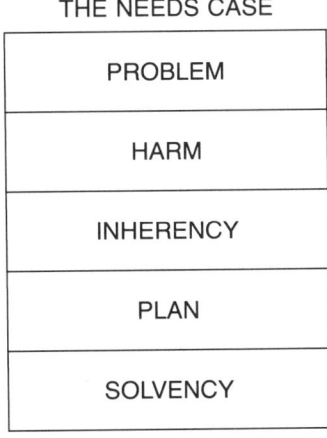

Figure 4.1 The Needs Case model for the affirmative case.

THE COMPARATIVE ADVANTAGES CASE
(Original)

```
PROBLEM (brief)

PLAN

ADVANTAGES:
   Inherency/Uniqueness  ⎫
   Solvency              ⎬  for each advantage
   Significance          ⎭
```

Figure 4.2 The Comparative Advantages Case (original) model for the affirmative case.

Better Performance as an Advantage

Initially, the belief that the status quo's failure to perform adequately was sufficient justification in itself for policy change generated the "comparative advantages case." If following this model (Figure 4.2), a debater would, first, briefly argue that a performance problem exists—e.g., federal mediation is not an effective method of handling labor-management disputes. Second, the debater would present a plan—e.g., compulsory arbitration. Third, the debater would present one, two, or more performance advantages which the plan has, compared to the status quo—e.g., compulsory arbitration *better* keeps inflation under control; compulsory arbitration *better* prevents disruptions in vital services; compulsory arbitration *better* ensures justice. In the course of presenting these advantages, the debater would point out how the status quo is unable to do the job (inherency) and prove that the plan will be able to do the job (solvency). As Figure 4.2 shows, the stock issues are met by a "comparative advantages case"; the "comparative advantages case" is *prima facie*.

Solving a Problem as an Advantage

Gradually, the emphasis in "comparative advantages" cases shifted from improving performance as a rationale for policy change to solving problems as a rationale for policy change. This rationale was the one the "needs case" was premised upon, but the discussion of problems and solving them in a "comparative advantages case" was different in two respects: the problems were not necessarily horrible, and the solving was not necessarily total. Public policy, advocates of the "comparative advantages case" would argue, is made all the time based on less than horrid problems and with partial solution or amelioration the aim.

As Figure 4.3 shows, this modified "comparative advantages case" often began with the plan—e.g., a national fifty-five mile-per-hour speed limit. Then, the debater would present the advantages—e.g., fewer highway deaths and greater fuel economy. In presenting each advantage, he or she would show that (1) a problem exists (highway deaths or a fuel shortage); (2) the status quo cannot take care of the problem (inadequate laws); and (3) the plan will significantly improve the situation (fewer deaths and increased fuel economy). The stock issues are met by this modified version of the "comparative advantages case"; it is *prima facie*. (Note that in this modified "comparative advantages case," the comparison between the status quo and the plan is only implicit.)

Independent Advantages, Add-Ons, Turnarounds

Since the early-to-mid 1970s, a few strategic modifications have been made to the "comparative advantages case." First, case designers have tried whenever possible to come up with advantages that flow independently from the adoption of the plan. For example, the sale of advanced fighter jets to Saudi Arabia might be argued to accrue three significant advantages: (1) the plan improves shaky United States-Saudi relations; (2) the plan better guarantees the flow of Persian Gulf oil to the United States; (3) the plan will reduce U.S. inflation by helping to stabilize the price of gasoline. The three advantages (problem-solving advantages) are *not* independent. Advantage (3) depends on advantage (2), and advantage (2) depends on advantage (1). Therefore, if a negative team can call into question the inherency or solvency of advantage (1), the negative team has beaten all three. If the status quo can accrue advantage (1), then it, by the affirmative's own logic, will gain advantage (2) and advantage (3); or, if the plan cannot accrue advantage (1), it does not establish the basis for advantage (2) and then advantage (3). When advantages are *not* independent, the affirmative is at a strategic disadvantage in a debate. Recall the two advantages claimed to flow from a national fifty-five mile-per-hour speed limit. Those advantages are independent. If, for example, a negative debater denies the inherency of the fuel economy advantage by noting that the status quo can use presently available

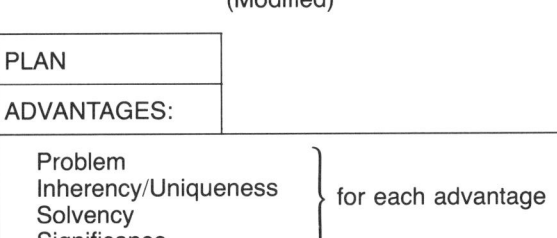

Figure 4.3 The Comparative Advantages Case (modified) model for the affirmative case.

automotive technology to achieve the fuel economy the affirmative claims only a fifty-five mile-per-hour speed limit will, that denial beats the fuel economy advantage but not the safety advantage. The affirmative would correctly claim, from the outset, that it only has to carry one significant, inherent advantage to justify the adoption of the resolution.

The need for only one independent advantage to win has led to the practice of adding on advantages in the affirmative team's second speech. The strategy here is clear: the more independent advantages you have going, the greater your chances of winning one. Offering additional advantages (or "add-ons") is certainly a strategy worth considering. However, let me offer two cautions: first, be careful you do not so enthusiastically pile on "add-ons" that you forget the primary jobs of the second affirmative speaker—to rebuild the case and to refute the arguments the first negative speaker has just offered; second, be aware that some conservative judges will not vote for an affirmative case based solely on an "add-on." Why? Because they feel that "add-ons" cannot be studied thoroughly and discussed as much as necessary because of their relatively late appearance in a debate and are therefore a bit unfair to the negative team.

The need for only one independent advantage to win has also led to the "turnaround." The negative team will, at some point in the debate, offer disadvantages which the affirmative policy allegedly causes. One of the standard affirmative responses to a disadvantage is to turn it around so that, rather than causing problems in a specified area, the plan is shown to be actually beneficial. For example, a negative team might argue that an American pledge of nonintervention into the Central American nation of Nicaragua will lead to that nation's becoming a Soviet client state—a disadvantage of a plan designed to prevent the United States from getting mired in Vietnam-like conflicts. The affirmative might turn the disadvantage around by arguing that, rather than completing Soviet control, the plan will reduce Soviet influence because Nicaragua, free from the threat of U.S. subversion, will no longer feel compelled to seek Russian assistance.

Thus far, the affirmative has simply practiced a time-honored refutation strategy known as the "retort." However, once the disadvantage is "retorted" or "turned around," the plan is further justified by an additional advantage. Not only are there perhaps two or three independent advantages justifying the adoption of the plan and the resolution, but there is that disadvantage which the affirmative has turned into an additional advantage. This kind of additional advantage is referred to in debating jargon as a "turnaround," and, in theory, a "turnaround," if significant and inherent, is an independent justification for voting affirmative. Alone, a "turnaround" can, in theory, win a debate for the affirmative team. I keep saying "in theory" for a reason: not all judges will vote affirmative based exclusively on a "turnaround," especially if it pops up in the debate's last speech.

The "Goals Case"

Dissatisfaction with the traditional "needs case" also led to the development of the "goals" or "criteria" case. (See Figure 4.4.) If using this case model, a

THE GOALS CASE

GOAL/S
EVALUATION OF STATUS QUO
PLAN
EVALUATION OF PLAN

Figure 4.4 The Goals Case model for the affirmative case.

debater would, first, establish the goal or goals a policy should meet. If the status quo has tried and/or is trying to meet the goal or goals, this affirmative argument is easily made and difficult to refute. The affirmative *can* establish, as a goal, something the status quo should have but has not embraced; however, in such a case, the burden of proof on the affirmative is heavier. The affirmative can offer several goals. In such a case, it is important that the affirmative team rank the goals and keep the ranking in mind when evaluating the status quo and the policy the affirmative team is offering. Not meeting the major goal is far more serious a problem than not meeting a secondary but important goal.

An affirmative team might argue that the furtherance of human rights is an important American goal. Then, the affirmative debater using the "goals case" model would argue that the status quo is not meeting the goal—a significant problem—and that the status quo cannot meet the goal—an inherent problem. For example, the affirmative might show that the United States is giving military aid to repressive regimes and that loopholes in foreign assistance laws allow the United States to provide the aid if the President wishes to (and he does).

The third part of a "goals case" is the actual plan, followed by the fourth part—a demonstration that the proposed policy will meet the goal. (Note how the case meets the stock issues.) Totally meeting the goal—complete solvency—was the original standard imposed on goals cases. However, meeting the goal significantly better than the status quo does is theoretically acceptable in the eyes of most judges. In such a situation, the affirmative team is merging the theory behind the "goals case" with the theory behind the "comparative advantages case."

Nestorian Order

If an affirmative team is going to list harms, independent advantages, or goals, the question of order becomes relevant. Sometimes, a natural order is evident, and anything other than that natural order would strike a listener as inappropriate. For example, if the four harms you wish to cite of inept government disaster relief are (1) the failure to address the immediate psychological needs of victims,

(2) the failure to maintain neighborhoods when assigning temporary housing, (3) the failure to provide sufficient privacy in this housing, and (4) the failure to deal with the long-term trauma a disaster may cause, anything other than this pretty-much chronological order would seem odd: there is a natural logic to it. However, quite often, a list is but a list.

In such cases, how should the harms, independent advantages, or goals be arranged? Two ideas should pop into your mind—both bad. You could arrange them in order of importance beginning with the most important. Cognitive psychologists (those who study how the mind works) tell us that the strongest impression is made by the last item in a list. If you begin with the "biggies" and work down, your reader will remember your weakest point the most. You could arrange your items in the reverse order—beginning with the weakest and building up to the strongest. Cognitive psychologists, however, tell us that the second strongest impression is made by the first item in a list and, if the first item is not sufficiently strong, a listener may fade out before the strong latter items are reached. So, what we need is a combination of these two approaches.

Many involved in teaching persuasion have long recognized that a list with the strongest item last, the second strongest item first, and the others in between is the rhetorically strongest possibility. Flemish rhetorician Chaim Perelman named this order "Nestorian." He noticed that Nestor, the masterful persuasive speaker in Homer's *The Iliad*, always arranged his arguments in this particular order.[1] Nestor's success is well worth remembering: Nestorian order thrusts your stronger points forward into prominent positions where opponents and judges will notice them and "hides" your weaker points in less prominent positions where opponents and judges just might not pay extremely close attention to them.

"Inherency" and Cases Other than the "Needs Case"

More than any other stock issue, inherency has caused debaters problems. Originally, theorists argued that for a case to have inherency, a structural barrier must be preventing the status quo from solving the problem and eliminating the harms. This original conception of inherency has been revised on two fronts: first, the advocates of case models other than the "needs case" modified the concept slightly to suit their new models; second, some theorists insisted that barriers other than structural ones could be cited to demonstrate the inherency of a problem. The first modification first.

I have used the word "inherency" in connection with both versions of the "comparative advantages case" and the "goals case." In the latter instance, my use of the word poses no problem at all: theorists generally agree that the status quo's failure to meet the goal must be inherent. Something—a law, a loophole, a Supreme Court decision—must be blocking the status quo from meeting the goal. In the former instance—i.e., in connection with the two versions of the "comparative advantages case," my use of the word "inherency" may pose problems because, although the concepts of "inherency" and "uniqueness" are identical, the latter word is oftentimes preferred when discussing the "comparative advantages" case.

An advantage must be "unique" to the plan; in other words, the plan and the adoption of the resolution are necessary if the advantage is to be accrued. If the status quo can accrue the advantage, the advantage is not unique to the plan or the resolution and neither plan nor resolution is justified. Put another way, the status quo must be blocked by something from accruing the advantage; the status quo's failure to accrue the advantage—either do the job well or solve the problem—must be inherent in the status quo. The status quo's failure must be inherent; the advantage's success must be unique. Inherency and uniqueness are then the same concept viewed from different directions. When offering either variety of the "comparative advantages case" and when refuting cases following these models, the term "uniqueness" is preferred in some circles.

Consider one example. An affirmative team is advocating compulsory arbitration of labor-management disputes and claiming that compulsory arbitration will accrue the advantage of fewer disruptions in vital services. The implied problem of disruptions is inherent insofar as status quo procedures for handling disputes cannot guarantee freedom from disruptions; the advantage is unique in so far as the plan can and the status quo cannot offer the guarantee.

Attitudinal Inherency

The second modification in the concept of inherency is more substantial and less semantic than the first. Traditionally, structural barriers—i.e., a law preventing or no law permitting—were considered to be the only acceptable inherent barriers. But what about intense lobbying? In the real world, intense lobbying can block action. The National Rifle Association, for example, could lobby and block gun control legislation. What about a strong commitment by the President to increasing the U.S. nuclear arsenal? In the real world, this commitment would indeed block nuclear disarmament efforts. What about a President and a Secretary of Labor who have said on numerous occasions that they will not support the repeal of the Davis-Bacon Act, a piece of federal legislation which sets up a wage-setting procedure for all federal construction projects? In the real world, such an absence of support could well block a repeal effort. Are then the problems of the availability of firearms to one and all, of the buildup of nuclear weaponry, of inflationary wages for federal construction work inherent in the status quo or not?

The question is difficult to answer, for there is no established view. To a large extent, debaters will have to acquire a sense of what's what in their district or league as well as a sense of what particular judges will allow. Let me, however, offer what I think the consensus is. Attitudinal inherency—the barrier provided, in the above examples, by the National Rifle Association's attitude, the President's attitude, and the Secretary of Labor's attitude—is acceptable if the attitude can be shown to be sufficiently strong so as to prevent the status quo from solving the specified problem. What is "sufficient" is something for the debate itself to resolve. Here are some guidelines. If the attitude can be shown to be wavering, it is not sufficiently strong; if the status quo can be shown to have overcome the barrier in the past, it is not sufficiently strong. If antigun legislation has become law despite National Rifle Association lobbying, the claim of attitudinal inherency is a weak one; if a particular President's objections and even vetoes have been overridden by Congress, the claim of attitudinal inherency is a weak one.

One crazy quirk to debating using or opposing "comparative advantages cases": whereas the term "uniqueness" seems to be preferred when the barrier is structural, the term "inherency" seems to be be preferred when the barrier is attitudinal. Perhaps "attitudinal uniqueness" just sounded odd.

Using the Standard Case Structures as a Heuristic

Figures 4.1-4.4 present the fairly traditional structural models for the affirmative case. Before they are used as models for organizing, they can effectively be used as a heuristic to help you generate possible arguments.

Let's say you are debating the policy resolution "That victimless crimes should be legalized." You have explored the resolution, and you have decided that, on the affirmative, you want to be a bit daring and controversial and you will therefore focus your case on the sale of pornography to adults. (You carefully exclude pornographic material that depicts those under legal age from your proposed repeal of laws.)

March your chosen case area through the case structures. Looking first at the "needs case," ask yourself what problems the prosecution of pornographers causes? For each problem you come up with—e.g., police diverted from more important duties—ask yourself what the harm is. For each problem, ask yourself why the status quo cannot take care of it—e.g., pressure from citizens' groups to "clean up" the city and a finite number of police officers. What plans are possible—e.g., total legalization or legalization in "combat zones"? How will the plans solve the problems and prevent the harms?

Try the "comparative advantages case" models; ask yourself if legalization will help the status quo do its job more effectively. Might not your plan (1) free police officers for other duty and thereby reduce violent crimes; (2) free jail space and thereby improve the conditions of incarceration; and (3) reduce court clog and thereby provide speedier justice? Why can't the status quo accrue these advantages: the answer is, in these cases, limited funds and public and official resistance to any additional taxation.

Try the "goals case" model. What goals might be relevant: speedy justice, public safety, the right of free expression? Is the status quo meeting these goals? You might answer "no": courts clogged with vice offenders deny speedy justice to all; police digging for pornography are not keeping murderers, rapists, and thieves off the streets; police arresting those who sell pornography are denying them and the materials' authors their constitutionally guaranteed right to free expression. Why can't the status quo meet these goals? Could these goals be met—or met better—if the sale of pornography to adults were legalized?

Marching your basic idea for an affirmative case through the different case structures should bring to the fore many arguments you *might* make, several different slants you could give the case.

Exercises: Generating Affirmative Argumentation

Try out the heuristic procedure just discussed with following resolutions and ideas for specific affirmative cases:

1. Resolved: That restraints on United States foreign trade should be lifted.
   Specific idea: granting most-favored-nation status (a special trading status) to Cuba.
2. Resolved: That the federal government should significantly assist the U.S. coal industry.
   Specific idea: building coal slurry pipelines from the coal fields of the Appalachians to the major coal ports of Hampton Roads, Virginia; St. Louis, Missouri; and New Orleans, Louisiana.
3. Resolved: That the federal government should provide free medical insurance to all U.S. citizens.
   Specific idea: providing catastrophic illness coverage to supplement medical insurance which employers provide or employees purchase.
4. Resolved: That the United States should reduce its commitment to NATO.
   Specific idea: pulling out all of our ground troops from Western Europe.
5. Resolved: That the United States should build a new interocean waterway.
   Specific idea: building a wide, deep canal through Costa Rica.

Choosing among the Standard Case Structures

The case structures we have discussed so far are *not* interchangeable. You should *not* choose one over another because you feel more comfortable with one, appreciate the aesthetic beauty of one, or used that one before. These are not valid reasons for selecting a "goals case" over a "needs case," or a "needs case" over a "comparative advantages case." The standard case structures have very different rhetorical effects on an audience. You should choose your case model based on the rhetorical effect you want to have.

The "needs case" emphasizes harms. You present them in gory detail; you discuss why the status quo cannot address them; and you argue that your plan will prevent them. The harms are structurally focal in the "needs case." If you do not have serious harms to emphasize, you would probably be better off using another case structure. Given how much attention the harms get in the "needs case" structure, qualitative harms (e.g. the psychological damage due to personality testing) and hypothetical harms (e.g. World War III if we pull troops out of NATO) sometimes do not fare well. Too much exposure seems not to serve these important kinds of harms well.

The original "comparative advantages case" emphasizes comparative efficacy. You present a number of ways in which your plan does a better job than the status quo. If you want to emphasize the comparison between plan and status quo, you would find the original "comparative advantages case" a good model.

The modified "comparative advantages case" emphasizes one or more problems and how the proposed policy will take care of them. The problems need not be devastatingly harmful; the solutions need not be total. This case structure may, at first glance, strike you as a rather wishy-washy one. However, of the four standard models, it is probably the most realistic; real problems are not all dire; real policies are good, even if they only partially solve the problems. If you want to talk about problems that are not horrible but are important and/or if you intend to present a plan that will do a better job taking care of the problem than the status quo, even though it may not or will not solve it completely, this third case model is a good model.

The "goals case" emphasizes the goals. They are presented; the status quo is marched past them; the affirmative plan is marched past them. Goals tend to be philosophical statements. The philosophy can be practical—e.g., balance the budget, reduce unemployment to five percent. Or the goals can be very philosophical—e.g., protect freedom of expression, promote human rights globally, ensure justice for all races. If you want to emphasize a goal or a set of goals, the "goals case" is a good model to follow. The "goals case" is also a shrewd case model, for everything hinges on the goal or goals. Once you have established it or them, the evaluation of the status quo and the plan is fairly routine and difficult to refute. Many negative debaters, not well-trained in combatting the fairly rare "goals case," grant the goal/s or ignore the goal/s, not realizing how they have fallen onto strongly defended affirmative ground and made their task very difficult, if not impossible.

Exercises: Choosing Among the Standard Case Structures

Consider the following situations. What would the best case structure be? *Why*?

1. You are debating that victimless crimes be legalized, and you have decided to focus on prostitution. You want to base your case on the argument that fear of arrest actually increases prostitution because young girls turn to the protection of street-wise pimps and then cannot get out of the "business" when they want to. You also want to stress the deleterious effects of long-term prostitution on the girls who are part of a pimp's "stable."
2. You are debating that the United States should alter its trading policies and you have decided to focus on U.S.-Japanese trade. You want to propose

import restrictions and present them as an effective means of saving from bankruptcy numerous American industries.
3. You are debating that the federal income tax system should be reformed. You want to argue that the present procedures unfairly penalize the middle class.
4. Same as #3, except you want to emphasize how draining the wallets of the middle class hurts the overall economy.
5. You are arguing for unilateral nuclear disarmament. You are *not* willing to admit that such a policy poses any risks; you also see it as being a better policy than the continued buildup of more and more sophisticated, destructive weaponry.
6. You are debating that teaching in American secondary schools should be improved. You intend to advocate much higher salaries and argue that money will attract a pool of talented people from which to hire.
7. You are debating that the federal government should take steps to reduce white collar crime significantly. You have decided to focus on crimes involving illegal access to or manipulation of computer-stored data. The problem is real today, but it will be much more serious as years pass. You want to show that the FBI and other law enforcement agencies are virtually powerless. Your plan will recruit and train a special corps of computer crime experts.
8. You are arguing for a moratorium on nuclear power plant construction. You have decided to offer the dangers posed by waste disposal as your rationale for a moratorium.

Two Innovative Approaches

Remember. We are recounting a story, how debating moved from stock issues to the "needs case" to other types of cases. The story does not stop with "turnarounds" as independent advantages and the slowly growing popularity of the "goals case." Debaters and debate coaches are constantly innovating: some innovations will catch on, some probably won't. Let me discuss the two most interesting recent innovations.

The "Net Benefits Case"

The theory behind the "net benefits case" is important, for it is significantly influencing the way debate judges conceive of their situation. Once upon a time, the status quo was conceived of as a static entity. It was presumed to be problem-free and not in need of change, unless an affirmative team, by offering a *prima facie* case, overcame this presumption. The advent of systems analysis as a way of studying public affairs and the application of systems analysis to debating has altered the way the status quo is viewed. Systems analysis denies the existence of static entities: everything is a system and all systems are constantly changing. According to systems analysis, the status quo then is a dynamic system.

So what? If the status quo is a static entity, maintaining it means keeping things the way they are. However, if the status quo is a dynamic system, then maintaining it means keeping things changing in accordance with present policies. Both the affirmative plan and the status quo mean change. The presumption against change, which favored the status quo, now vanishes; the presumption granted the status quo on the assumption that it is problem-free is considerably weakened since the status quo will not be tomorrow what it is today. The only advantage the status quo has is that it is a policy-directed dynamic system which can *really* be studied—really, because the system exists. The affirmative plan, on the other hand, is a policy-directed dynamic system which can only be theoretically studied because it is not in operation. Therefore, when statements are made about where the status quo policy will take us, there is a higher degree of certainty than when statements are made about where the affirmative policy will take us. This advantage that the status quo has does give it a degree of presumption—i.e., a policy which will certainly achieve so-so results is superior to a policy which *might* give slightly better results. However, this is a very different kind of presumption from that traditionally granted the status quo.

In recognition of systems analysis and this different definition of presumption, theorists have developed the "net benefits case." The affirmative debater using this case compares the fairly certain benefits of following present policy, *less* its fairly certain disadvantages or costs, to the less certain benefits of following the affirmative policy, *less* its possible disadvantages or costs. The structure of this case is not as firmly established as that of the traditional cases. Affirmative teams tend to use a three-step approach: (1) the disadvantages/costs of following the present policy, their certainty emphasized; (2) the affirmative's policy; (3) the benefits of following the affirmative policy (including why the present policy cannot accrue them), their predictability argued. The negative team is then left to bring up the benefits of following the present policy (emphasizing their certainty) and the costs or disadvantages of following the proposed policy (arguing their predictability). The judge is left to use the following inequality in making his or her decision. In the inequality, "A" stands for affirmative; "N" stands for negative.

$$(\text{Benefits of A}) (\text{Certainty}) - (\text{Costs of A}) (\text{Certainty})$$
$$<\text{or}>$$
$$(\text{Benefits of N}) (\text{Certainty}) - (\text{Costs of N}) (\text{Certainty})$$

If the inequality favors the affirmative, then the affirmative has demonstrated that its policy is more cost-beneficial than the negative's; if the inequality favors the negative, then the negative has demonstrated that its policy is more cost-beneficial than the affirmative's. I say "negative's policy" for a reason. As you will discover in Chapter 7, the negative team does not have to defend the status quo, but can defend any policy it wants as long as adopting that policy does not mean adopting the resolution. If the negative opts to defend a policy other than the status quo, then the negative forfeits the slight presumption it has because of the higher degree of certainty granted the benefits of the status quo policy.

One cannot say whether the "net benefits case" will acquire a more set form and become a new standard case model. What is clear is that its existence and its theoretical justification in the journals which debate instructors and coaches contribute to and read have led to many judges *not* granting as much presumption to the status quo as formerly, insisting that the negative defend *some* policy system, and using something like the above formula in deciding the outcome of actual debates.

The "Alternative Justifications Case"

If an affirmative team claims that four truly independent and significant advantages accrue if its plan is adopted, then that team could, in theory, abandon three of them in its second speech and devote all of its time to the advantage which the negative team seemed unable to beat. The affirmative team could pull this "trick" because, if the advantages are independent and each is significant, then carrying one justifies the adoption of the resolution. This "trick" is pulled on a larger scale in the "alternative justifications case." If offering this kind of case, the affirmative presents two, three, or more *separate* cases. Each mini-case has its arguments and its plan. One might be a "goals case"; another might be a traditional "comparative advantages case"; all could be "needs cases." Each mini-case is an independent, *prima facie* justification for the resolution. If the affirmative team carries any one, the affirmative team wins. Most affirmative teams who use this tricky case model plan to drop one or more of the mini-cases, depending upon what happens in the actual debate.

Consider the 1982-83 college National Debate Tournament (NDT) resolution "That all United States military intervention into the internal affairs of any nation or nations in the western hemisphere should be prohibited." This resolution seems to permit the affirmative to choose its country. An "alternative justification case" in response to this resolution might consist of four cases recommending that U.S. intervention be prohibited in four separate nations—let's say Nicaragua, El Salvador, Honduras, and Guatemala. If the negative team has lots of evidence and uses it to respond strongly on Nicaragua, El Salvador, and Guatemala, then the affirmative team can base the entire debate on its third mini-case, the one focused on Honduras.

Quite a few judges object to this "trick." The theoretical justification for it may be sound, but that is not what these judges base their objection on. Debate, they argue, is designed to encourage the serious, *in-depth* discussion of important public issues. The "alternative justifications case" does not seem to fit in with this purpose, for, in the first affirmative speech, a little is said about a lot. And then, a large chunk of the first two speeches is tossed out, with the debate's "real" issues getting less attention than they deserve because only half the time remains in the debate. If you choose to offer an "alternative justifications case," beware of the strong feelings against it.

Why, you might ask, aren't judges similarly upset with affirmative teams who offer four independent advantages only to ditch three? Some judges view this practice with disdain, but, when a team offers independent advantages, the team is discussing a single policy. This policy will be discussed throughout the debate; no part of this policy is ditched. Reasons for adopting it may be, but *one policy is under scrutiny the entire time*. Offering an "alternative justifications case" is a similar strategy to offering several independent advantages, but there is that crucial difference.

The Plan

All cases for adopting policy resolutions have a plan as a *prima facie* part. Once upon a time, plans were relatively simple things. Then, negative teams—and judges—kept demanding more and more specificity. Gradually, a formulaic method of presenting a plan emerged. Follow the formula (which I will go over presently) intelligently. If parts of the formula seem irrelevant to your resolution or case, omit them; if you think you can improve your presentation by modifying the formula, go ahead and try.

Planks

Political parties convene every four years to select their candidates for the Presidency and the Vice Presidency. Before they make their selections, they adopt a platform—i.e., those stands on the important issues that their candidates will take. A political platform is said to be built of "planks." By analogy, an affirmative team's plan, the policy that the team will make its stand on, consists of planks.

According to formula, a plan has five planks. *The first plank* specifies how the plan will be administered. Is the affirmative calling for the presidential appointment of a committee or the creation of a new federal agency? Is the affirmative relying on existing mechanisms? *The second plank* specifies the mandates to be given the administering group. What will the group do? What legislation will Congress have to pass for the administrators to act as required? *The third plank* specifies the means that will be used to enforce the administrators' actions or decisions; *the fourth plank* specifies how the administrators' actions will be supported in terms of staff, information, and funding. *The fifth plank* is a technical one, indicating that the affirmative team's explanatory comments on the plan will be used in case of litigation to establish the intent of any new legislation and that the plan will supercede any contradictory laws, regulations, or procedures. This last plank is necessary to prevent the negative team from arguing that the plan's vagueness and/or incompatibility with existing laws, etc., will lead to chaos in the courts.

If the debate resolution called for restrictions on trade with any or all foreign nations, the affirmative team might choose to focus on Japan. If the affirmative team followed the formula for a plan very closely, its plan might read as follows:

Plank I. Administration. Under the auspices of the U.S. Department of Commerce, a three-member Japanese-American Trade Commission will be established. Its members will be presidentially appointed, approved by the Senate, and serve at the President's pleasure.

Plank II. Mandates. (A) The Commission will set import quotas for all items and review them every ninety days. (B) Its goals will be to protect American industry from unfair Japanese competition. (C) "Unfair" will be defined to include the use of cheap labor and "dumping."

Plank III. Enforcement. (A) Importers found in violation of the Commission's decisions will be in violation of federal felony law and prosecuted with the mandatory minimum sentence being one hundred days in prison and a $5,000 fine. (B) Exporters (Japanese) found in violation of the Commission's decisions will be denied licenses to operate through American ports for five years.

Plank IV. The Commission will be provided with all necessary staff and information; funding will be provided by a five percent import duty on imported Japanese steel, automobiles, and electronic systems.

Plank V. Affirmative speeches will serve to establish legislative intent in case of litigation; the affirmative plan will supercede conflicting portions of any existing laws, regulations, or procedures.

Spikes

Return for a moment to our discussion of political platforms. When the political parties speak of platforms, they are speaking metaphorically. Their candidates will make their stands on the party platform just as they will, as they travel from town to town, make their *literal* stands on numerous *literal* platforms made from *literal* planks. If you were building just such a literal platform, what would you use to put the planks together? Nails. But, if the platform might be shaky with just nails holding it together, you might want something bigger and stronger, like spikes.

In debating terminology, "spikes" are extratopical plan planks designed to prevent—or "spike out"—problems the plan might cause—that is, to prevent the plan from being shaky. For example, a negative team might argue that the plan outlined above will cause domestic inflation because the price of the average automobile in the United States will increase because American automobile manufacturers will have no incentive to lower prices. This possible problem or disadvantage could be "spiked out" by adding a plank specifying that the Commission could cite profiteering by American workers or companies and automatically suspend all import quotas for sixty days. This extra provision is not topical—i.e., it is not a restriction on importation; it is in the plan to prevent a possible problem from occurring. A negative team might also suggest that the affirmative plan could prevent electronic components needed for defense purposes from being imported. A provision could be added to the plan exempting imported materials designated by the President as having defense uses. Again, this provision is not topical; it is added to the plan to prevent—to "spike out"—a possible problem of disadvantage the negative team might bring up.

How big can a plan spike be? How many spikes can a plan have? There is no set limit; reasonability should be your guide. Negative teams will cry foul if you get around a major disadvantage by specifying that some *major* action will be taken. If your topical plan providing national comprehensive medical insurance could lead to doctors' significantly raising all fees and you try to spike the problem out by imposing government price controls on all medical services, you have probably gone too far. If your topical plan mandating that attaining a certain score on a national examination be necessary to teach in the public schools could lead to a severe shortage of mathematics and science teachers and you try to spike the problem out by providing federal subsidies to all school districts to raise mathematics and science teachers' salaries eighty percent, you've probably gone too far.

The Affirmative Case in Value Debate

In the early 1970s, the intercollegiate debate group known as the Cross-Examination Debate Association (CEDA) formed. It formed in opposition to a number of trends seen developing in debate programs that were oriented toward winning a berth at the prestigious National Debate Tournament (NDT) and doing well once at "the nationals." One of CEDA's many goals was to encourage the debating of value resolutions. NDT-style debating was—and still is—exclusively on policy resolutions. CEDA's resolutions through 1974 were policy resolutions; since 1975, CEDA has tried to propose value resolutions for debating.

Initially, CEDA affirmative cases were not significantly different from traditional NDT cases. There was less development of arguments, and plans were not as detailed. These differences may well have been due more to the slower speed of CEDA delivery and the shorter length of CEDA speeches than to a difference in fundamental debating theory between NDT and CEDA. However, once value propositions arose, differences in theory *began* to develop.

I say "began" because the theory underlying the debate of value resolutions is still very much evolving. Those of you who will be engaging in value debate need to be aware that there are far, far fewer theoretical verities that can be offered about value debate than about policy debate. What I intend to offer you in this chapter are a few safe guidelines for constructing the affirmative case when the resolution is a value resolution.

Types of Value Resolutions

Three kinds of value propositions seem to exist. First, there is the most common kind, the pre-new policy proposition (PNP) such as "Resolved: That unilateral disarmament is desirable" or "Resolved: That privacy is important." This kind of proposition offers a value judgment which, if adopted, would lead one to perhaps then go a step further and advocate a *new* policy. Second, there is the pre-present policy choice proposition (3PC) such as "Resolved: That environmental protection is more important than energy exploration." Here, the proposition offers a value judgment which, if accepted, would lead one to go a step further and choose between two present policies. Third, there is a different kind of resolution: it is a pre-present policy rejection proposition (3PR) and looks like the following:

Resolved: That American secondary education is not succeeding.
Resolved: That television is a wasteland.

Although it is not necessarily negative in the grammatical sense, it is negative in the sense that you pass a negative judgment on something that exists—e.g., secondary education or television. You also remain noncommittal or silent as to what might be done to improve the situation.

The first two types of value resolutions are handled by the affirmative team in similar ways. The third requires a different abbreviated treatment.

Adapting the "Goals Case" Model for Value Resolutions

When value resolutions first appeared on the debating scene, debaters and debate coaches alike tried to adapt case models used in policy debate to value debate. Since the "needs case" is so very policy-oriented—with its emphasis on eliminating harms by adopting a plan, these debaters and coaches did not look to the "needs case." Rather they looked to the "goals case" and the "comparative advantages case."

The "goals case," with its tendency to emphasize philosophical principles, provided the best model (see Figure 4.5). If a debater were to adapt the "goals case" model to a value resolution, he or she would first establish a value or values. Then, this debater would evaluate the action opposite the action implied by the resolution based on the value(s); then, this debater would evaluate the action implicit in the resolution based on the value(s). These three contentions are acquiring the following names among value resolution debaters and coaches: the definitive contention and the designative contentions. The definitive contention defines a value; the designative contentions designate how something measures up to that value.

Let's consider the Spring 1980 CEDA resolution, "Resolved: That compulsory national service for all qualified United States citizens is desirable" (a PNP resolution). The definitive contention would establish how "desirable" is to be defined in the particular affirmative case. That contention might read, "Patriotism is of value" or "Patriotism is desirable." The first designative contention would establish that the present policy of not requiring national service does not help promote patriotism; the second designative contention would establish the many ways that compulsory national service would help promote patriotism.

Consider the Spring 1982 CEDA resolution, "Resolved: That the American judicial system has overemphasized the rights of the accused" (another PNP

PRE-NEW POLICY PROPOSITION (PNP) e.g., Unilateral disarmament is desirable	PRE-PRESENT POLICY CHOICE PROPOSITION (3PC) e.g., Environmental protection is more important than energy exploration	PRE-PRESENT POLICY REJECTION PROPOSITION (3PR) e.g., American secondary education is not successful
DEFINITIVE CONTENTION World peace is valuable	DEFINITIVE CONTENTION The preservation of life is valuable	DEFINITIVE CONTENTION Education should equip young men and women to live in the modern world
FIRST DESIGNATIVE CONTENTION The arms race is detrimental to world peace	FIRST DESIGNATIVE CONTENTION Energy exploration, if it continues at the present rate, will destroy numerous habitats and pollute the water and air	DESIGNATIVE CONTENTION American secondary education does not equip young men and women to live in the modern world
SECOND DESIGNATIVE CONTENTION Unilateral disarmament will promote world peace	SECOND DESIGNATIVE CONTENTION Environmental protection is necessary to preserve life	

Figure 4.5   Adaptations of the "Goals Case" for use in structuring the affirmative case in value debate.

resolution). The definitive contention might be, "Promoting public safety is valuable." The first designative contention would argue that, thanks to numerous Supreme Court decisions during the Warren years, the judicial system at present overemphasizes the rights of the accused and, as a result, does not promote public safety. The second designative contention would argue that, if some of the restraints placed on police and courts by the Warren Supreme Court were lifted, public safety would be enhanced.

Consider the resolution "That unemployment is preferable to high inflation" (a 3PC resolution). The definitive contention might be, "The economic health of the nation must have primacy over other, more limited economic goals." The first designative contention would argue that measures which fight unemployment but cause inflation do not promote national economic health; the second designative contention would argue that measures which fight inflation but may cause unemployment *do* promote national economic health.

Notice that no plan is offered. Even though all of these resolutions (whether PNP or 3PC) have policy implications, they are value resolutions, which logically *precede* policymaking. They offer a prepolicy value judgment which the affirmative team must support. Even though no plan is presented, the affirmative case following this model must meet the stock issue of solvency, as well as the stock issues of topicality, significance, and inherency in order to be *prima facie*. All of these stock issues have, however, a slightly different meaning or "feel" in value debate than in policy debate. The affirmative case must speak to and defend the value judgment that the resolution offers, not some other value judgment (topicality); the affirmative case must offer sufficient justification for strongly accepting the resolution's judgment (significance). The team must demonstrate that the status quo or the action opposite to the action implicit in the resolution cannot have the value argued for in the definitive contention (inherency). Finally, the affirmative case must demonstrate that the action implicit in the resolution will prove valuable (solvency).

Let's apply these "revised" stock issues to the three value debate cases discussed above. The case for compulsory service based on the importance of patriotism to a society clearly defends the resolution's value judgment concerning the desirability of such service and is therefore *topical*. Either by arguing the importance of national spirit in the definitive contention and/or by suggesting that the United States presently lacks the will to survive if survival requires struggle in the first designative contention, the case would offer a *significant* reason for accepting the resolution. The first designative contention seems to suggest that the failure of the status quo to legally require compulsory national service means its failure to inspire the valuable patriotism and the vital national spirit; thus, the case has a kind of *inherency*. The second designative contention demonstrates that compulsory national service will provide the patriotism and the spirit; this contention gives the case a kind of *solvency*.

The case for a loosening of restraints on the police and the courts because public safety is not served when those restraints overprotect the accused clearly affirms the value judgment in the resolution that our judicial system overemphasizes the rights of the accused. The case is therefore *topical*. The definitive contention's argument for public safety and the first designative contention's criticism of the inability of the status quo to provide public safety offer a *significant* rationale for adopting the resolution. The first designative contention demonstrates that the action opposite to the action implicit in the resolution cannot promote public safety—i.e., that protecting the accused as at present rather than deemphasizing the rights of the accused cannot promote public safety. Therefore, this contention provides the case with its *inherency*. Finally, the second designative contention, which extols the public safety benefits to be accrued if the rights of the accused are in some major ways deemphasized, gives the case its *solvency*.

The case for anti-inflation measures based on their promoting the goal of national economic health better than employment-intensive programs clearly defends the resolution's value judgment as to the preferability of unemployment to high inflation (*topicality*). By presenting why national economic health is crucial in the definitive contention, the case establishes the *significance* of making a good choice. By showing that anti-inflation programs promote economic health in the second designative contention, the case establishes its *solvency*; by showing that the opposite action—employment-intensive programs—does *not* promote economic health, the case establishes its kind of *inherency*.

3PR resolutions, as I indicated earlier, would require a slightly different treatment from PNP and 3PC resolutions. You would have a definitive contention, but only one designative contention. In the instance of the resolution arguing that secondary education has not succeeded, the definitive contention would establish what success means; the designative contention would establish that the present system of secondary education does not and cannot meet that defined standard. In the instance of the resolution arguing that television is a wasteland, the definitive contention would establish what a wasteland is; the designative contention would prove that television is and cannot help but be a wasteland.

To be *prima facie*, the case would have to be topical, significant, and inherent. The first case would point to major failures of American secondary education (*significance*) and prove that the schools cannot or will not overcome these failures (*inherency*). The second case would point to major weaknesses of television (*significance*) and prove that the television industry cannot or will not address these problems (inherency). The stock issue of solvency is irrelevant to a 3PR resolution since you are not arguing that a goal or value will be met by a prospective policy, only that a goal or value is not being met now.

Adapting the "Comparative Advantages Case" for Value Resolutions

An affirmative case cannot always argue that the action opposite to the action implicit in the value resolution absolutely cannot, at least partially, prove valuable;

similarly, an affirmative case cannot always argue that the action implicit in the value resolution will prove totally, perfectly valuable. When an affirmative team feels it is in either of these situations or both, another case model is needed. Both PNP and 3PC resolutions may give rise to this need. Figure 4.6 outlines this model.

This case, an adaptation of the "comparative advantages case," will have definitive and designative contentions. The definitive contention will define the measure of value—e.g., patriotism or public safety or national economic health. Then, there will be a single designative contention or a series of them, in which the affirmative team argues that the action implicit in the resolution measures up better than the opposite action. If the resolution indicts affirmative-action programs (a PNP resolution), the affirmative team might want to establish "work quality" as the measure of the value of a work force; then, the affirmative team would show how basing employment on qualifications, not race, measures up better. Another example. If the resolution affirms environmental protection over energy exploration (a 3PC resolution), the affirmative team might want to establish "providing for our descendants" as the measure of value in the definitive contention and then argue that, although both actions provide for the future, environmental protection provides better.

Again, no plan is offered. The other stock issues are still pertinent—topicality, significance, inherency, and solvency. The affirmative team must defend the value judgment in the resolution and no other. Topically thus looks the same in both the adapted "goals case" and the adapted "comparative advantages case." The affirmative team also must offer a significant reason for adopting the resolution by demonstrating that the action implicit in the resolution will indeed prove to be *significantly more valuable* than the opposite action. Inherency and solvency are tied to significance; the opposite action must be unable to achieve the same measure of value as the implied action, and the implied action must be able to achieve the argued measure of value.

Those of you who are going to engage in value debate need to be much more alert to your debating environment than those who are going to debate policy resolutions. You need to be alert to changes in theory and changes in practice. You also need to be aware that these changes may not be permanent and merely someone's attempts to develop a complete theoretical basis for debating value resolutions. You also need to be very alert to regional differences. There are regional differences in policy debating, but they are relatively easy for debaters and their coaches to pin down. Given the volatility of value resolution debating, the regional differences from California to Colorado to Kentucky to North Carolina are much more difficult to pin down. You may think you know Colorado-style value debating based on a trip to a tournament there two years ago only to find out that, this year, the style has significantly changed. As value debate establishes its theoretical basis, the pace of change will slow and the number of theoretical and practical verities will increase. Until then, stay alert.

PRE-NEW POLICY PROPOSITION (PNP) e.g., Unilateral disarmament is desirable	PRE-PRESENT POLICY CHOICE PROPOSITION (3PC) e.g., Environmental protection is more important than energy exploration
DEFINITIVE CONTENTION World peace and human life are valuable	DEFINITIVE CONTENTION The preservation of human life *and* other life forms is valuable
DESIGNATIVE CONTENTION(S) Unilateral disarmament is more conducive to world peace than the continuation of the present arms race Unilateral disarmament will result in fewer lives lost than the nuclear war the present arms race is pointing toward	DESIGNATIVE CONTENTION(S) Environmental protection helps minimize air and water pollution and thereby helps preserve human life for centuries to come; energy exploration causes such pollution. Environmental protection preserves habitats, and thereby life forms, far better than even the most ecology-sensitive modes of energy exploration

Figure 4.6 Adaptations of the "Comparative Advantages Case" for use in structuring the affirmative case in value debate.

After reading and studying Chapter 4, you know:

- that the stock issues characterizing a *prima facie* case for a policy resolution are topicality, significance, inherency, plan, and solvency;
- that there are four structural models for the affirmative case in policy debate
  —the needs case;
  —the comparative advantages case emphasizing better performance;
  —the comparative advantages case emphasizing solving a problem;
  —the goals case;
- that the first case emphasizes HARMS, that the second and third emphasize a COMPARISON, and that the fourth emphasizes GOALS; *and* that you should choose your case's structure accordingly;
- about the net benefits and alternative justifications approaches;
- about the conventional planks a plan has in policy debate and about plan spikes;
- how the "Goals Case" model and the "Comparative Advantages Case" model have been adapted for use in value debate.

Notes

1. C. Perelman and L. Olbrechts-Tyteca, *The New Rhetoric: A Treatise on Argumentation*, Notre Dame, Indiana: University of Notre Dame Press, 1969, p. 499

CHAPTER 5
Writing the First Affirmative Speech

In this chapter, you will learn:

- how to draft the first affirmative constructive speech;
- how to go about revising that draft;
- how to prepare the finished copy of the speech.

You have now decided what your approach to affirming the resolution will be; you have also chosen a case model to follow in presenting your case. The next step is to write the speech which will kick off an actual debate by presenting your case. This chapter will help you write an effective kick-off speech.

A Word on the Teaching of Writing

Not too long ago, the bulk of writing instruction was based on guesses. Now, some of those guesses were pretty good–offered by men and women who understood how they and other successful writers worked. However, none of those guesses was supported by any research. Writing was taught by English teachers, and it was *not* considered appropriate within the profession of English to engage in the kind of empirical research necessary to validate the way writing ought to be taught. Fortunately for you, the profession of English has experienced a revolution of sorts in the past decade. Now, there are highly regarded writing professionals who engage in the necessary empirical research and who are extremely knowledgeable about cognitive psychology. These professionals have established for the teaching of writing a scientifically sound foundation. Based on this foundation, advice can be offered to those like you who are about to begin a writing task. Some of this advice is the same as that offered a decade ago; some of it flies in the face of that old advice.

Using an Outline

How many of you have been asked by teachers to write an outline and hand it in with a paper? How many of you wrote that outline *after* you wrote the paper? Probably the majority of you. The outline, however, is supposed to precede and guide the actual writing. This rebellion against the tyranny of the outline is not just a product of student laziness; it is also a reflection of students' recognition—perhaps unconscious—of how premature outlining stops thoughts from flowing and ideas from generating more ideas as you write.

But there are outlines, and there are outlines. The outlines that stop thought are the ones with big Roman numerals; A's, B's, and C's; 1's, 2's, and 3's, etc. They are *so* formal, so set, that they freeze the thinking process that naturally does *and should* go on when you are writing. Rough outlines are another matter. A list of your four or five or six major points can guide you without freezing you. Having selected a case model, you have just such a loose, rough outline for the speech that will present your affirmative case—the first affirmative speech. Let that outline guide, but not restrain you, as you draft.

Drafting

Too many writers try to make their first draft a perfect document. Almost no one can accomplish this goal, not even professional writers. The reason is provided by cognitive psychology. We, as human beings, have the capability of focusing on only a handful of things at one time—the number varies between three and seven. Writing a perfect draft requires that you focus on your content, the extent to which you develop your ideas, the way you connect ideas to each other, your overall organization, your paragraphing, your control of your sentences, your grammar, your punctuation, your word choice, your style, the personality you project, your spelling, and much more. Assuming you can make your entire mind available to you as you write, you probably have nearly twenty concerns here to focus on. But your mind can only handle seven at best. Experienced writers have made some of these concerns, such as grammar, automatic; therefore, they are more likely to be able to write a perfect draft than you are. But even experienced writers draft and revise, and revise, and revise. In fact, a recent study by New York University Professor Nancy Sommers showed that experienced writers as a group distinguish themselves from beginners by the amount of revision they engage in.[1]

You should focus, as you draft, on the largest of what Stanford Professor Ellen Nold has called "the elements of choice": what you intend to say, how you intend to develop your ideas, how you will organize the overall presentation, and—maybe, if you can manage—how you will put the smaller elements together. The remaining elements of choice and the "elements of convention"—i.e., those aspects of writing governed by agreed-upon rules—you leave for rounds of revision.[2] If you draft in this manner, you are not overloading and short-circuiting your mind. You are also focusing on the most important matters first.

Draft rapidly. Realize that you will be coming back later to tighten the organization, untangle sentences, find better words, correct grammar and punctuation, and check spelling. Let the creative juices flow; let new ideas come into your mind, and, when they do, try to build them in rather than discarding them because they are not in the outline.

Try to draft the entire speech in one sitting. If you cannot, stop in the middle of a section that you know how to complete. That way, when you return to the business of writing, you will be able to warm up on material that is already under your control.

Revising

As I have already noted, revising is the difference between successful, experienced writers and struggling beginners. Good writers revise extensively and several times. Revising is *not* just polishing up the writing; revising can entail major deletions, additions, and rearrangements. After letting the draft sit a while, you should objectively look at it again. (Revise means "look at again.") Treat the draft as the raw material out of which you will fashion an effective presentation of your affirmative case.

A Collaborative Activity

An author is sometimes not as able to see the problems in a draft or to devise the best solutions as others. The author is too psychologically close to the draft. As a result, the author sometimes insists that something is clear when it objectively is not. The author is not being pigheaded; rather, the author is, without knowing it, supplying missing ingredients as he or she reads. This is a normal authorial tendency. Some writers require weeks away from a draft to overcome it and to finally see the draft as a reader or hear the draft as a listener would. Some writers require less time. For this reason, revision requires some collaboration to be as successful as possible. The author of a drafted first affirmative speech should submit it to the scrutiny of teammates and coach. If the author is being honest, he or she can pinpoint places where he or she senses that things don't quite work and ask for suggestions. The author should want these suggestions. Furthermore, the author should solicit any and all other comments.

It is natural for an author to feel somewhat defensive; however, he or she should put the success of the speech ahead of personal pride in the draft. An author can defiantly say, "Well, it's clear to me!" and refuse to make adjustments that are probably necessary. What an author should say is, "If it isn't clear to them, it probably won't be clear to the judge in an actual debate, and, if it isn't clear to the judge, the case may lose when it deserves to win."

Three areas should almost always be attended to when revising a first affirmative speech: sharpening the organization, improving the use of evidence, and improving the speech's style. We will go over each of these. Spend time on these revising tasks *and* the very important task of clarifying anything that is unclear and strengthening anything that is not sufficiently strong.

Sharpening the Organization

Speeches tend to be more highly organized—i.e., with points labeled "first," "second," etc.—than essays or papers. There is a logical reason for this difference. A reader can vary his or her pace and even reread to make sure he or she is following a presentation. A listener, on the other hand, is totally dependent on the speaker; a listener must proceed at the speaker's pace and cannot "relisten." The typically higher degree of organization of a speech aids the listener. A debate speech tends to be more highly organized than other kinds of speeches. Again, there is a logical reason for this difference. The complexity of an affirmative case's content and the speed at which the first affirmative presentation is made make the listener's job a difficult one. The typically higher degree of organization of a debate speech helps the listener do his or her job.

Effectively organizing a debate speech, however, does not mean using "first," "second," and "third" or "A," "B," and "C." A speech with lots of outline-like markers sprinkled throughout it can be just as—if not more—confusing than a speech with none. Effectively organizing means three things: proceeding logically, setting up and meeting audience expectations, and signposting.

Establishing True Logic. You have already taken the first step toward establishing true logic by choosing the most effective case model for your particular case. To the extent possible, the model should provide you with your major contentions. These will provide you with a skeleton for the speech. Conventionally, these contentions are given Arabic numbers—1, 2, 3, etc. (The plan is not treated as a contention. It is simply labeled "plan"; its planks are conventionally given large Roman numerals and any subpoints under the planks, large letters.)

Under each contention, you will need some substructure. This substructure should reflect the logical development of the contention if the argument is to be as clear as possible and have the requisite impact. Two heuristics can be used to help you find the logical development.

The first heuristic is used by problem-solvers and is recommended to writers by one of the nation's leading researchers in writing, Professor Linda S. Flower of Carnegie-Mellon University.[3] The heuristic is called issue-treeing, and it is premised upon the fact that many ideas and arguments have a hierarchical logic.

Let's construct an issue tree for what would be the contention of inherency in a "needs case" on rural poverty: "3. Present federal programs have an inherent urban bias." (Note: the contention is numbered "3" because, in the "needs case" model, the contention of inherency would typically be the third contention.) At

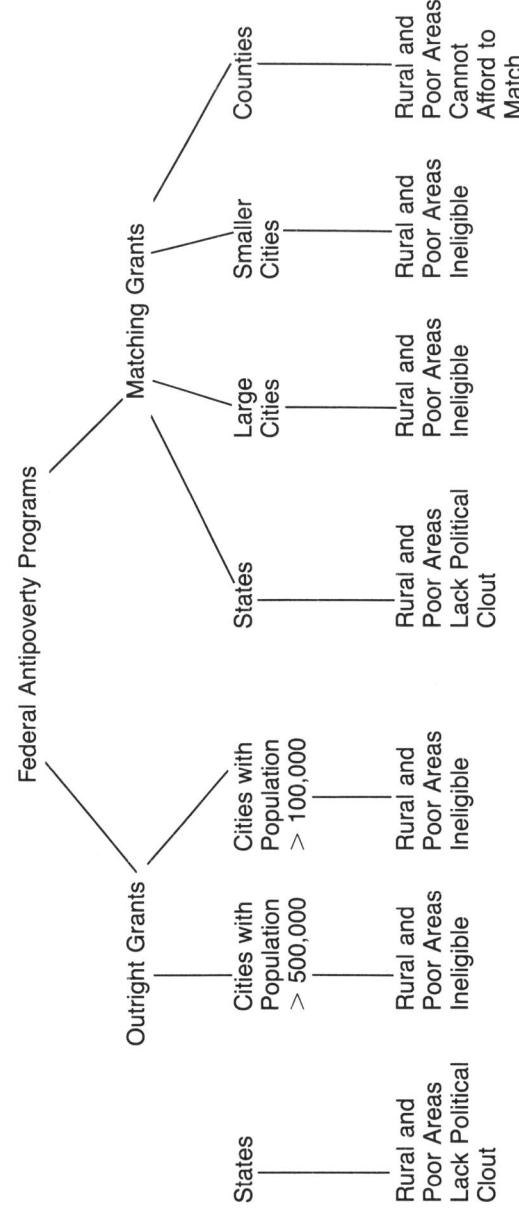

Figure 5.1 Issue tree.

the top of the tree (see Figure 5.1), you would place "federal programs." "Federal programs" divides into: "outright grants" and "matching grants." Perhaps all outright grants presently go to states, cities with populations over 500,000, and cities with populations over 100,000; perhaps matching grants are available to states, large cities, smaller cities, and counties. Why do the rural poor fail to get assistance? Our tree has seven branches at the third level. Rural poverty is concentrated in counties with rather small populations. Since these counties have neither the political power to get their states to apply for an outright or matching grant nor the financial resources to apply for a matching grant on their own, rural poverty goes untreated by federal grants. If we add the reason a particular grant program cannot help alleviate rural poverty, we have a fourth level to our issue tree. The tree allows us to think the issue through and discern the logic which would lead one to accept contention number three:

A. Outright grants cannot help rural poverty:
   i. No outright grants are available directly to counties;
   ii. Poor rural counties lack the political clout to get their states to go after outright grants available to states;
B. Matching grants cannot help rural poverty:
   i. Rural, poor counties do not have sufficient financial resources to meet the matching requirements of grants that are available to counties;
   ii. Poor, rural counties lack the political clout to get their states to go after matching grants to states.

The second heuristic is also used by problem solvers, especially those in business. The heuristic employs a flowchart and is useful in discerning the logic of chronologically, causally developing issues.

Let's construct a flowchart for a designative contention, "Energy exploration in the American Rockies will damage the quality of life of our descendants," in a value debate. Figure 5.2 presents the flow chart: (A) energy exploration leads to deforestation; (B) deforestation reduces the evaporation into the mountain atmosphere; (C) the reduction in evaporation means less built-up moisture in clouds passing over the mountains; (D) the reduced moisture build-up means less rain in the plains; (E) less rain in the plains means a reduced agricultural output; (F) less agricultural output means a reduced domestic food supply; (G) a reduced food supply, especially when linked with a higher population and a lower nutritional content (thanks to pollution and other factors) in all food leads to (H) a reduction in the quality of life.

The flowchart allows us to think the issue through and see the logic necessary to persuasively present the contention. You would not want to present subpoints A through H (with "G" having a "little i" on population growth and a "little ii" on lowered nutrition). Too much structure can be just as baffling as too little. Furthermore, too many links in a logical argument tend to make the argument sound absurd; too many links also expose many spots where the causality might

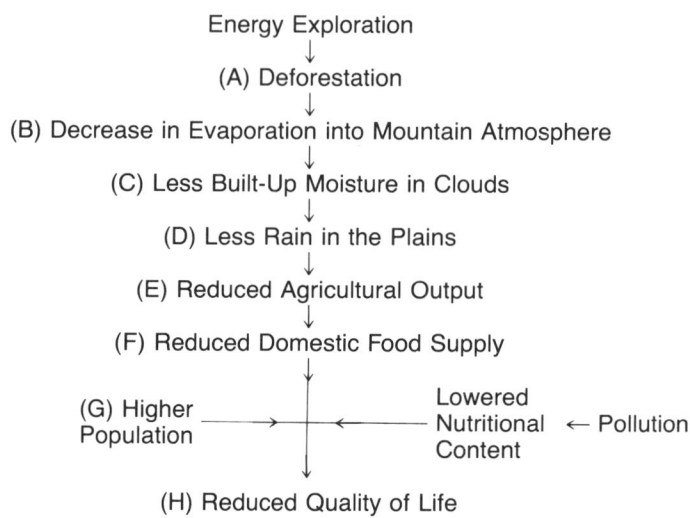

Figure 5.2 Flowchart.

be challenged. The discovered logic might be presented in the following simplified scheme:

2. Energy exploration in the American Rockies will damage the life of our descendants:
   A. Exploration means deforestation;
   B. Deforestation will lead to less rain in our grain-producing region;
   C. With less rain, this region will produce less food for a larger population.

What you have drafted before you try out these heuristics is the raw material you will reshape. If you use these heuristics before you draft, you end up with a *very* detailed outline, and writing becomes a mechanical, fill-in-the-blanks process, not a high-energy thinking process during which new ideas are discovered. So, draft using *just* the contentions as a guide. Then, tighten the organization of your presentation of each contention by using one of these heuristics.

The two heuristics are not interchangeable. Issue-treeing, premised on the hierarchical nature of many ideas and arguments, is suitable for static statements. Establishing that there is a problem, arguing that it and resulting harms are inherent, and suggesting that something should be a goal or a value are static statements. Using a flowchart, premised on the chronological and causal nature of many ideas and arguments, is suitable for dynamic statements. Arguing that a problem leads to harms; contending that a plan will solve a problem, accrue an advantage, or meet a goal; and designating an action as promoting a value are dynamic statements.

Setting Up and Meeting Audience Expectations. In all discourse, you must carry your audience along with you. At every step of the way, the audience must know where you are and have a fairly good idea where you are going. Given a debate's complexity and speed, that your audience be with you is crucial. A logical overall organization modeled on one of the standard case structures helps; so does a logical substructure under each contention. However, the use of other techniques is also necessary.

You need to set up audience expectations. Toward the beginning of your first affirmative speech, you need to provide the listener with an indication of how you are going to proceed. Since the listener is usually a judge knowledgeable in affirmative case structures, the preview need not be overly explicit. The following preview would be useful if your audience was *not* informed about debating:

In this speech, Marie and I will demonstrate, first, that strikes in defense industries are a problem; second, that these strikes are harmful; and third, that the status quo cannot solve the problem and prevent the harms. Then, we will present a new policy, and, finally, we will show how this plan solves the problem posed by strikes in defense industries.

If debating before a trained judge, such an explicit preview is not necessary.

The following previews should do the job if your audience is knowledgeable in debating practices. These previews will set up expectations in the listener's mind:

The problem of strikes in defense-related industries is serious and cannot be solved except by the affirmative plan. Marie and I will show this in four contentions.
Our present controls on the drug industry are inadequate. By adopting the affirmative plan, you will bring about significant improvements in three important areas. First, the plan . . .
This plan [presented first] will accrue the following three independent advantages.
The preeminent goal of U.S. foreign policy should be the furtherance of human rights. The present adminstration's policy toward South Africa does not meet that goal; the affirmative's plan will.
Freedom is the most cherished gift the American Revolution gave this nation. The actions by religious groups in airport lobbies and other public places are endangering this freedom. Some restrictions on these groups are justified to insure freedom for all.

If you studied Chapter 4 carefully, you know what kinds of cases will follow each of these previews and you can guess how they will be structured. The judge, thanks to such previews, has similarly clear expectations. His or her job is, as a result, far easier; he or she is with you from the very beginning.

You have to keep the listener with you. You accomplish this goal by offering brief reminders at points of transition. The crucial points are when you move from contention to contention:

This important American goal, however, is not being met by the status quo.

Not only will the affirmative plan better insure the nation the highways it needs, but it will also reduce unemployment.

Rural poverty exists and is harmful. Unfortunately, nothing can be done about it at present.

If a particular contention is rather involved, a reminder of the course you are taking might be helpful in its midst:

Outright grants offer no assistance; the same is true of federal matching grants, as we note in our second subpoint.

The purpose of these reminders is to keep the listener on course, to keep his or her expectations alive. Such reminders, although they do take a little time, result in a significant increase in comprehension of the speech and the affirmative case.

Finally, it is also helpful to remind your listeners of where they have been at a speech's end:

Strikes in defense-related industries are common and harmful. And the status quo cannot prevent them. As Marie and I have shown, a system of compulsory arbitration can.

United States policy toward South Africa does not promote human rights in that nation. The policy John and I are advocating will further human rights there and bring our foreign policy in line with an important preeminent American goal.

Freedom must be highly valued. To preserve freedom for all, we must restrict the way religious groups solicit funds in public places.

Such a reminder recalls the entire case to the listeners' minds and allows them to see it, one last time, in its entirety. That entire case is not promised, as it was in the speech's organizational preview; rather, the promise is fulfilled. As you briefly recall the case to each listener's mind, he or she recalls not only the points you have made, but also—to some extent—how you developed them. You want the speech to close with such a full view of the affirmative case in each listener's mind, especially the judge's.

Signposting. Previews, reminders, and reviews will help you keep your listener on course. So will signposting. There are four principles of signposting.

First, label each contention or subpoint you are offering and label it the expected way. Conventionally, contentions are labeled with regular Arabic numbers—1, 2, 3, etc., subpoints are labeled with letters—A, B, C, etc., and subpoints of subpoints are labeled with small Roman numerals—i, ii, iii, etc., When subpoints of subpoints are read aloud, the label is read "little one," "little two," etc. Plan planks are labeled with large Roman numerals (read aloud as "one," "two," etc.), and plan subpoints are labeled with letters—A, B, C, etc. The label helps the listener know (1) that a new point is being presented and (2) how the point fits into the hierarchy of the affirmative case. The label also helps your opponents, your judge, and you to refer easily to a particular argument.

The second principle of signposting is to present the actual argument as succinctly as possible. Look back to the inherency contention on page 93. The arguments there are probably not sufficiently abbreviated. Subpoint A should become "Outright grants cannot help"; little i should become "They are not available to counties"; little ii should become "Poor rural counties lack clout." When the arguments are stated succinctly, they can become signposts themselves throughout the debate:

In response to "Poor rural counties lack clout," the first negative had three arguments . . .

The third principle—an optional one—is to use echoes. Echoes follow an argument and offer an abbreviated version of the argument. For example, if a contention were "Political action committees are amassing huge sums of money," an echo might be "PACs amass money"; if a contention were "Anti-abortion laws violate the woman's right to direct the course of her life," an echo might be "laws violate a woman's right." Echoes *can* be a repetition of the complete contention. If the contention is brief, a complete echo makes sense. Usually, however, time is precious in a debate speech and full repetition is an unaffordable luxury.

The fourth principle of signposting—another optional one—is to use stock issues or other tags between the label and the statement of the contention. An inherency contention might then sound as follows: "3. Inherency: present federal antipoverty programs cannot help." A solvency contention might sound like the following: "4. Solvency: binding final-offer compulsory arbitrtion will prevent damaging strikes in defense-related industries." A frequent spot for such tags is before the final subpoint of an advantage (or a disadvantage offered by the negative team); the tag used there is "impact." If the affirmative is claiming to increase employment through a federal program to repair the decaying infrastructure of the cities in the northeastern and east central states, the last subpoint might be, "D. Impact: an improved U.S. economy."

Improving the Use of Evidence

Evidence is essential in debating, so essential that the development of the vast majority of subpoints is centered on one or more pieces of evidence. The evidence should mesh with logic to persuade a listener of the point's validity. Oftentimes, the argument *in draft form* will consist of an explanation of the argument, the evidence, and a recapitulation of the argument beginning with the phrase "As you can see." Too often, the argument remains in this choppy form. When you are revising, you should strive to improve the way the evidence is used to validate your argument.

Expanding the Explanations and Recapitulation. The first step in improving the use of evidence is to expand the explanation and the recapitulation. Too often, both are inadequate. A good beginning debater might offer an argument in the following manner. (I have numbered the sentences so that I can refer to them easily.)

1. Technology is counterproductive.
2. Technology often solves a problem, but, at the same time makes the problem worse.
3. As Barry Commoner tells us in *The Closing Circle* (1971), "Under the impact of heavy use of inorganic nitrogen fertilizer, the nitrogen-fixing bacteria originally living in the soil may not survive, or if they do, they may mutate into non-fixing forms."[4]
4. As you can see, technology makes the problem worse, not better.

I say "good" beginner because many beginners would simply offer sentences 1 and 3, no more. This debater knows that the argument requires some explanation; the debater also seems to sense that there should be some transition between the evidence and the next argument, a transition that helps the listener apply the evidence to the first argument.

In the example above, sentence 2 offers an explanation, but sentence 2 just is not enough to prepare the listener for the statement by Commoner. The debater needs to expand the explanation. Here's a revised sentence 2:

2. Technology often solves a problem, but, at the same time makes the problem worse, as has happened in the case of technologically advanced inorganic nitogren fertilizer designed to enhance the soil's ability to fix nitrogen.

The recapitulation of sentence 4 also does not go far enough: it rushes too quickly from a very specific piece of evidence to a generalization. More is necessary if the evidence's point is to be appreciated by the audience. Here is a revised sentence 4:

4. Technology provided inorganic nitrogen fertilizer, and it did enhance the soil's ability to fix nitrogen; however, at the same time, this new fertilizer further destroyed the soil's own natural ability to do the job, making the fertility problem worse.

Add Your Warrants. Explanation-Evidence-Recapitulation does not, however, adequately reveal an argument's logic. An excellent method for analyzing an argument in order to see its logic has been developed recently by logician-rhetorician Stephen Toulmin.[5] If an argument's logic is fully understood, then it can be fully, adequately presented.

Consider the argument that the defense of Western Europe depends on sea power. In support of that argument, former U.S. Senator William H. Taft, Jr., and present U.S. Senator Gary Hart said, "If the Soviets manage to cut the sea

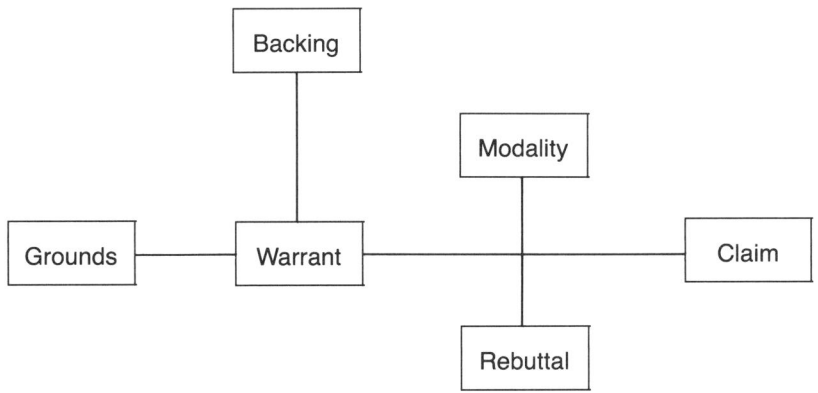

Figure 5.3 The Toulmin analysis of an argument.

lanes to Europe from North America or the Middle East, all the NATO ground forces in Europe will become useless."[6] This piece of evidence certainly supports the contention, but what is the *complete* logic of the argument?

Toulmin analyzes any argument into six parts. First, at the far right side of Figure 5.3, the *claim*. That's the argument: that the defense of Western Europe depends on sea power. Second, at the far left side, the *grounds*. They are the evidence: here, "they" is an "it," a quotation from two U.S. Senators. The *warrant* is the rule of argumentation that justifies the jump from grounds to claim. Here, the warrant would be the credentials Senators Taft and Hart have in foreign affairs. A warrant requires *backing*—the argument that backs the warrant. Here, the *backing* would be the long-demonstrated belief that those with expert credentials are able to make accurate assessments. The last two elements in an argument are the *modality*, the degree of certainty claimed, and the rebuttal, the circumstance/s under which the claim may not be true. In this case, the modality is expressed by the definite "will" in the quotation and the rebuttal is if the sea lanes are not cut. Based on this analysis, the argument's full logic is

Because authoritative testimony has been reliable in the past (*backing*) and because Senators Taft and Hart have expert credentials in the field of foreign affairs (*warrant*), believe their statement (*grounds*) that, unless the sea lanes are not cut by the Soviets (*rebuttal*), then the defense of Western Europe will (*modality*) depend on sea power (*claim*).

This analysis alerts us to the conditions under which the claim will not hold and to the backing all claims based on authority rely on. More important, it encourages us to include the warrant (and maybe its backing) in the argument as well as to emphasize the modality.

As a result, rather than a lame contention-explanation-evidence-recapitulation chain, we expand it into a contention-explanation-*warrant-backing*-evidence (with *modality* stressed)-recapitulation chain. Compare the following two versions of the same argument:

Version 1
The defense of Western Europe depends on sea power. Supplies must reach ground troops there by sea; without those supplies, the troops are useless. As U.S. Senators William H. Taft, Jr., and Gary Hart argued in their 1979 revised *White Paper on Defense*, "If the Soviets manage to cut the sea lanes to Europe from North America or the Middle East, all the NATO ground forces in Europe will become useless." As you can see, the defense of Western Europe depends on having the power to keep the seas open.

Version 2
The defense of Western Europe depends on sea power. Supplies must reach ground troops there by sea; without those supplies, the troops are useless. U.S. Senators William H. Taft, Jr., who was a member of the Senate Armed Services Committee for many years before his retirement, and Gary Hart, who has made foreign affairs his special study in the Congress, support this argument in their 1979 revised *White Paper on Defense*. They offer, without a doubt, their authoritative assessment that, "If the Soviets manage to cut the sea lanes to Europe from North America or the Middle East, all the NATO ground forces in Europe will become useless." Their statement tells us definitely that the defense of Western Europe depends on having the power to keep the seas open.

The second is stronger. Why and how certainly the evidence validates the argument is clearer in it than in the first version—because the warrant has been added and the modality stressed.

Authoritative opinion is common evidence in debating; so are the results of empirical studies. Let's examine the argument that college curricula do not emphasize fundamental skills after the initial year, and, as a result, these skills deteriorate. The evidence is a study conducted by Albert Kitzhaber at Dartmouth College.[7] The level of writing skills peaked after the freshman year only to fall to a level below that of entering freshmen by graduation as students moved through a curriculum in which very little writing was required. If we examine this argument using Toulmin's method, we find that it has the following elements:

Claim: Fundamental skills deteriorate in college if not reinforced throughout the curriculum.
Grounds: This claim is supported by a study conducted by Albert Kitzhaber at Dartmouth College.
Warrant: Sound empirical studies are, within limits, generalizable.
Backing: Examples of valid generalization could be cited or authorities on experimental design could be quoted.
Modality: The study *suggests* the generalization presented in the claim.
Rebuttal: The claim seems possible unless the Kitzhaber study is unsound and unless its conclusions concerning writing skills are invalid for other fundamental skills.

This examination should alert us to a number of weaknesses in the argument. Alert to the shakiness evident in the modality and the rebuttal, the good debater would probably want (1) to beef up the grounds by offering *two* studies and (2) to express and offer backing for the warrant—i.e., the generalizability of empirical studies. In other words, the debater should add his or her warrant and address any weaknesses the Toulmin analysis of the argument revealed.

Vary the Way Evidence Is Incorporated. A third way to improve your use of evidence is to avoid the monotony of continually stopping the flow of your words to insert a one, two, or three-sentence verbatim quotation. Debaters frequently use the word "card" rather than the word "evidence." In cross-examination, a negative debater will ask an opponent if he or she read a card to support an argument rather than asking if he or she read evidence (which just happened to be printed on a file card). As long as debate jargon clearly communicates to all involved and all involved fully realize that the jargon would have no meaning to people outside debating, I have no serious objection to it. I mention this particular use of jargon—the use of "card" to mean "evidence"—at this point because its very use reveals how evidence is seen by many debaters. Evidence is seen as a solid entity that must be submitted just as a prosecuting attorney submits the murder weapon, rather than words that can be responsibly made a part of one's own writing. There are several ways to build evidence into one's writing: stop the flow and quote in full, work the source's sentence into your paragraph, work phrases from the source into your sentences, or ignore the source's phrasing entirely and paraphrase. If you have the complete original close at hand (on a card), you need not fear the accusation that you have presented the source's view inaccurately because you have not presented it in full. If challenged, you can read the full quotation and make the accuser look bad. Furthermore, by building evidence into your speech in varied ways, you avoid the monotony of repetition by offering the freshness and energy of variety. (You can also present more evidence per speech if you do not have to quote every last word.)

The following is a part of a published statement by Allen V. Kneese, Professor of Economics at the University of New Mexico, arguing that the boomtowns that may develop in the American mountain states in conjunction with energy exploration may *not* benefit the region's native people:

Finally, the indigenous labor force in the Rocky Mountain States, more often than not Indians, is usually lacking in the training which could qualify its members for the types of jobs that become available. Therefore they either do not participate at all in the benefits that the economic development would otherwise offer or are consigned to the most menial types of work.[8]

If you were trying to argue that ecological preservation is more valuable than energy exploration, you might want to argue, in a designative contention, that energy exploration is of limited value. One of your subpoints might be "energy exploration does not bring jobs to the indigenous population." You could offer your argument, explain it, offer your warrant (Kneese's credentials), offer Kneese's statement in full, and recapitulate your argument. You might, however, want for the sake of variety to present the evidence in a different way:

D. Energy exploration does not bring jobs to the indigenous population. The jobs require a high degree of skill, and the native population does not possess that skill. Allen V. Kneese, Professor of Economics at the University of New Mexico, internationally known consultant, and the author of *Economics and Environment* (1975) and *Pollution, Prices, and Public Policy* (1975), argues in a 1978 essay that, ". . . the indigenous labor force in the Rocky Mountain states . . . is usually lacking in the training that would qualify its members for the types of jobs that become available." As a result, the indigenous population does not obtain any economic benefits or is "consigned to the most menial types of work." The good jobs that energy exploration advocates suggest will become available to a region's residents simply are not available.

This argument handles Kneese's statement in three ways: first, it fits the initial sentence into the paragraph's flow; second, it paraphrases the first part of his second sentence; third, it borrows a key phrase from the second part of his second sentence. This presentation of the evidence is no less effective than offering the quotation verbatim from beginning to end; in fact, from a stylistic perspective, it's a better presentation because it is far less mechanical and choppy.

If you can improve the way you use evidence by expanding the offered explanation and recapitulation, presenting your argument's warrant, and varying the way you present quoted evidence, you have not only made your reasoning clearer and more persuasive but you have taken several steps toward a better style, which just happens to be our next concern.

Improving Your Style

Books have been written on the subject of improving one's style, so I can only offer you here some of the simplest lessons. Fortunately, these lessons, if learned and followed, will significantly enhance the first affirmative speech you are now revising.

You need, first, to ask yourself who will be delivering the speech you have drafted and are now revising. If you are going to be the only deliverer of the speech, you can get away with those sentences that you know how to deliver but others stumble on. These are sentences tied very closely to some of the quirks of your particular style as a writer and orator. No wonder you can handle them—no wonder others can't.

If one other person or two other people are going to be the deliverers of the speech, then you cannot get away with some sentences that you know you alone can handle. You will have to pinpoint the places where the speech does not go smoothly, where ideas just are not coming across clearly, and revise them. Fortunately, you do not have to guess: you can listen to those who will be delivering the speech in competition deliver it in practice. As you do, note the trouble spots and revise them. You may like—even love—the way an idea is phrased; the attachment is the normal one the creator feels for the created. However, no matter how "nice" the passage is, if it does not work when the speaker reads it, it needs to be revised—perhaps radically revised.

If many others are going to be delivering the speech—for example, if you are writing an affirmative case everyone in your school's debate program will be using—then you will be able to listen to a few future readers but not all. If you are in this situation, a few research-proven principles of effective style should help you. Even if you are writing a speech for yourself or one or two others to read, these principles should help.

Avoid Complex Sentences. Public policy issues are complex: one issue is related to another, and that other is related to a third, etc. You could write sentences, which, in their length and grammatical complexity, reflect the complexity and the interrelatedness of the issues. Such sentences are very difficult for an audience to process. A reader, with the chance to slow down and reread and study, *might* be able to deal with such sentences; however, a listener, who must process sentences immediately, would be hard-pressed to accomplish the task. Such sentences are not "reader-friendly"; even more so, they are not "listener-friendly." Avoid them.

Avoid Preposition Strings. When you hear the phrase "complex sentence," you probably think of an involved combination of clauses and long phrases. Sentences featuring several prepositional phrases do not fit some people's definition of "complex," but such sentences, especially if the phrases are strung together, are very difficult for readers and—more so—listeners to handle.

Consider the following sentence:

The costs of petroleum exploration *in the open waters of the Atlantic and Pacific Oceans* are at present too high to make such exploration a profitable venture *for American companies in the field of crude oil discovery and extraction.*

The first underlined string is only two phrases long; therefore, it is probably not a serious impediment to audience comprehension. Still, it could be revised and improved. The second underlined string is a phrase longer. A revised version of it (and the first string) would make the audience's job easier:

The costs of open water petroleum exploration in the Atlantic and Pacific Oceans are at present too high to make such exploration a profitable venture for American crude oil discovery and extraction companies.

The strategy for revising sentences containing preposition strings is to convert some of the prepositional phrases that follow a noun (are postnominal) into adjectives preceding that noun (are prenominal). I say "some of" intentionally: converting all would probably result in another kind of awkwardness and problems for the reader and listener.

Such strings are especially common when the source of a quotation and the author's qualifications are being cited. In fact, by revising your use of evidence and including the warrant, you may well be creating preposition strings. The following phrase exhibits the problem:

According to Helmut E. Landsberg, noted Professor of Meteorology at the University of Maryland, in his 1981 article in *Parameters* on the effects of weather on the success of military operations in the Persian Gulf area

The two preposition strings here can be shortened by selectively converting postnominal prepositional phrases into prenominal adjectives:

According to Helmut E. Landsberg, noted Meteorology Professor at the University of Maryland, in his 1981 *Parameters* article on weather's effects on the success of Persian Gulf area military operations

Beware of Excess Branching. Sentences can be divided into three categories, depending on where you branch off the main course and place the extra qualifications and explanations. There are left-branching sentences, mid-branching sentences, and right-branching sentences:

Left-branching
Although the buying power of a $20,000 income has changed significantly since 1970, thanks to unprecedented inflation during the 1970s, the Internal Revenue Service still taxes $20,000 as if it were an extremely comfortable income.

Mid-branching
The United States, because of inadequate planning during the years when nuclear power first emerged as a legitimate commercial possibility, is now faced with a nightmarish nuclear waste problem.

Right-branching
No strong federal anti-gun legislation has ever been passed because the National Rifle Association and other lobbying groups have fiercely opposed suggested legislation fearing that any restriction on the free availability of guns would lead to further restrictions.

Each kind of sentence presents problems to the audience if the branching is overdone.

Left-branching sentences present information to the audience *before* the audience knows what the information is attached to. The audience will not know this until the main part of the sentence begins, and must hold the information of the left-branch in memory until the main part of the sentence comes along. The audience can only hold so much unconnected information in memory.

Mid-branching sentences present information to the audience before the thought in the sentence's main part is complete. The audience, therefore, must hold half of the main thought in memory as they process the information in the mid-branch. If the mid-branch contains too much, the audience forgets the first half of the main thought by the time the second half comes along.

Right-branching sentences present necessary qualifications or additional explanations only after the thought in the sentence's main part is complete. While this extra information is being absorbed, the audience needs to remember that thought so that they can connect it to the thought in the next sentence. Remembering a complete thought is far easier than remembering half of a thought; therefore, right-branching is far easier for the audience to handle than mid-branching. However, even right-branching, if overdone, can make the audience's job difficult. Right-branching is also an easier style for a speaker to handle than left- or mid-branching, particularly if the speaker is a beginner. A speech heavy in right- and mid-branching sentences requires considerable skill in pausing and changing pitch, as one moves into and returns from branches, skill often not possessed by the beginner.

Use Transitional Words Heavily. Transitional words, such as "therefore" and "however," are more than simply glue between your ideas. These words can help you convey your argument's logic. Since your audience does not have the ability to study what you are presenting, a heavy dose of these transitional words will help the listener along. Transitional words are not interchangeable; each word signals a particular logical connection between what precedes the word and what follows. Four logical connections are common in affirmative cases.

First, the information following the transitional marker may be the next item in a list. It might be another reason or another advantage or another harm. Transitional words such as "second," "in addition," and "furthermore" would convey the logical connection.

Second, the information following the transitional marker may be the next item in a chronological sequence. Perhaps you are detailing how a harm develops in time or how political forces operate in time to prevent the solution to a problem. Transitional words such as "next," "then," and "later" would convey the logical connection.

Third, the information following the transitional word may be the logical consequence or result of what is said before the transition point. You may be making the transition from a contention arguing that a problem exists to a contention arguing that dire harms result. Appropriate transitional words would be "as a result," "therefore," and "thus."

Fourth, the information following the transitional marker may be contrary to the expectations set up by what is said before the transition point. For example, after establishing in a definitive contention that freedom is of value, you might move to the designative contention by saying. "Freedom is valuable; however, laws which allow unlimited solicitation by nonprofit groups in public places threaten this freedom." One would expect, given freedom's value, that laws, etc., would promote it. Contrary to expectations, laws actually endanger it. Thus, the transitional word "however" is an appropriate choice. A similar situation exists in a "needs case." After establishing the dire harms of water pollution, you might move to the inherency contention by saying, "Water pollution is widely recognized as a serious threat to the health of the American people; nevertheless, the federal government does not act." One would expect a government to respond to a serious threat; that it does not is contrary to one's expectations, and the transitional word "nevertheless" conveys the logical connection. In addition to "however" and "nevertheless," the simple words "but" and "yet" would adequately signal the logical connection.

Use Parallel Structure. Rhetoricians, from the ancient Greeks to contemporary theorists, have devoted some time to the different ways sentence parts can be arranged. Artistic, effective ways of arranging these parts are called "rhetorical schemes." There are hundreds of them, some named by the Roman rhetorician Cicero, some named by later rhetoricians. Rhetorical schemes have a certain power, and debaters should learn how to use them to their advantage. Several of the more useful schemes will be discussed in Chapter 11 and their particular effects will be explored. Right now, I want to discuss a fundamental scheme, parallelism.

Parallelism consists of presenting a series of ideas in the same grammatical form. The effect is to link the ideas immediately together in the listener's mind.

Consider the following two versions of a summary that might conclude a "comparative advantages case" advocating the legalization of marijuana:

Version 1
If the affirmative plan is adopted, the courts will be able to unburden themselves of hundreds of cases which are clogging the docket. The plan will also produce additional revenue for the federal government since the plan calls for a substantial tax on marijuana cigarettes and will prevent the needless ruin of the lives of young men and women.
Version 2
If the affirmative plan is adopted, the courts will unclog, the federal government will gain additional tax revenue, and the lives of many young men and women will not be needlessly ruined.

The second version is more effective because the use of parallel grammatical structure ties the three claimed advantages together.

Consider the following two versions of a summary that might be offered to a contention arguing that nuclear power production is harmful in three ways:

Version 1
Nuclear power production will damage the marine life in the waters used for cooling. It will also make life in the areas near where wastes are dumped dangerous. And a nuclear power plant could, if emergency procedures fail to work, make a huge area uninhabitable.
Version 2
Nuclear power will seriously harm the marine life in the water used to cool the reactors, will seriously harm human life in areas near where wastes are dumped, and will seriously harm all life in an even larger area if emergency procedures fail.

Version 2 uses parallelism; it also uses two other "rhetorical schemes," *anaphora*— beginning a series of parallel items with the same word or phrase—and *climax*—

arranging a series of parallel items so that they build to a climax. Parallelism is a fundamental rhetorical scheme: use it. Chapter 11 will show you how to build other, more sophisticated schemes into your speeches.

Preparing the Finished Copy of the Speech

A great deal of time should have gone into the planning, drafting, and revising of the affirmative case. You should want the appearance of the speech that presents it to reflect this time and effort. Appearances *are* important. Although, technically, only what the case says should matter to the judge, judges will be influenced by how it appears. If it looks sloppy, that sloppiness sends a signal to the judge that this case is not a good one; if it looks professional, that polished appearance sends a signal to the judge that this case is one to reckon with. In addition, a professional-looking finished copy will have the same effect on your opponents—perhaps intimidating them a bit. Furthermore, a professional-looking finished copy will make the first affirmative speaker's job much easier—reading scribbled pages is tough; reading a nicely typed manuscript is easy.

What constitutes professional-looking? The speech should be typed on paper which is substantial in weight. Its dimensions should be the standard 8½" × 11"; the color should be either white or off-white. Since most erasable bond papers smear, you should use nonerasable paper if at all possible. You should leave 1" margins all around—maybe 1½". You should double-space the text; you might want to triple-space if triple-spacing seems to make the particular speaker's task easier. (Be careful though: triple-spacing means more awkward page-turning.)

There are other things you can do in preparing the finished copy to help the person who will be delivering the speech. First, you can use underlining, highlighting, capitalization, and other similar techniques to remind the deliverer when special emphasis is necessary or valuable. Do not, however, mark up the text so much that it becomes difficult to read; overdone, your underlining, etc., can become counterproductive. Second, you can use a slash mark "/" or some other large, dark symbol to remind the speaker of points where pausing is necessary or helpful. Again, do not put in too many such marks: you will make the first affirmative speaker's task difficult, and your professional-looking copy will begin to look messy.

Third and most important, you can make the flipping from page to page correspond with the moving from one argument to another. Between subpoints or between major contentions, there is a transition. If the transition leads *immediately* into the new subpoint or contention, then you should begin the new page with the beginning of the transition. If there is a pause before and after the transition, then you can begin the new page with the transition or end the old page with the transition. If you make the flipping correspond to the moving from argument to argument, you add the physical signal of page-turning to verbal signals of transition and give your case an enhanced sense of organization; you make the speaker's job easier, since he or she will not have to hurriedly flip the page while delivering an argument (perhaps ripping the page in the process); and you make the ongoing job of revising the speech easier, since the way a particular point is presented (the evidence, the logic, the style) can be changed without a great deal of retyping.

One last matter concerning the speech's finished copy. Often, an opposing team will ask to see a copy of your plan (if you are debating a policy resolution) or your entire speech. It is discourteous to refuse, even though you may justifiably feel the team should have listened. You should have a *good* copy of just the plan and a *good* copy of the entire speech ready to give them—ideally, not your only copy or the marked-up copy the first affirmative speaker read. The opposing team will be making sure its notes on your case are accurate; they will also be examining the details of your plan (if you are debating a policy resolution) and the specific words in your evidence (no matter what kind of resolution you are debating). The judge, at the end of the debate, may also want to see a copy of the case—to look closely at either the plan or the evidence or both. For both of these audiences, you *must* make sure your use of evidence is professional. By "professional" in this case, I mean in accordance with the standards of scholarly and professional publication. Your excisions *must* be indicated by ellipses; your interpolations *must* be placed within square brackets. Not following these standards not only makes your opponents' and your judge's job of assessing your evidence difficult, it could also very easily result in your being accused of a violation of the ethics governing competitive debate. A demonstrated violation, intentional or not, would probably lead to an automatic loss; furthermore, that violation would put the team's and the school's reputation under suspicion for a good long while. So, be careful.

The standards you must follow are presented in most writing handbooks and research paper guidebooks as well as in such detailed sources as the *MLA Handbook* (New York: Modern Language Association, 1977); the *Publication Manual of the American Psychological Association* (Washington, D.C.: American Psychological Association, 1974); or *A Manual of Style*, 13th edition (Chicago: University of Chicago Press, 1982).

The two passages below should help you grasp the fundamentals:

According to the January 9, 1981, *Washington Post*, "The Soviet Union has stunned the U.S. intelligence community by launching a new cruise missile-firing submarine [Oscar] which will make American aircraft carriers ten times more vulnerable than they are now . . ."[9]

As U.S. Senators Robert Taft, Jr., and Gary Hart have noted, a weak U.S. Navy " . . . would not only imperil those large sectors of our economy directly involved in importing and exporting, it could bring all of our resource-dependent industry to a standstill. That could be as effective in destroying America's economy . . . as defeat in all-out war."[10]

There are three spots where you might excise something from a quotation in order to improve your speech's flow—at the beginning, in the middle, and at the end. The second passage illustrates the first two; the first illustrates the third. The first passage illustrates how to interpolate clarifying information correctly into a quotation: the code name of the new submarine, presented earlier in the newspaper story, is inserted to aid clarity as well as to link the quotation to the discussions preceding and following it about this new submarine and other new weapons systems.

The speech presenting the affirmative team's case for adopting the resolution is now ready. The negative team will try to undermine it by offering arguments which, the negative team claims, *refute* the affirmative's arguments. Then, the affirmative team will attempt to defend its case and refute the arguments the negative team has raised. Both teams then will engage in refutation. Therefore, before we talk very specifically about what the negative team should try to do in a debate (Chapters 7 and 8), I want to spend a chapter going over important principles of refutation.

After reading and studying Chapter 5, you know:

- to focus on the elements of choice when you draft and to draft rapidly;
- to improve the draft by
    —sharpening the organization by establishing true logic, setting up and meeting audience expectations, and signposting;
    —improving the use of evidence by expanding the explanation and recapitulation, adding your warrants, and varying the way evidence is incorporated;
    —improving your style by avoiding complex sentences, avoiding preposition strings, watching out for excess branching, using transitional words heavily, and using parallel structure;
- that the finished copy should be professional in appearance, easy for the deliverer to work with, and professional in the way quotations are presented.

Notes

1. Nancy Sommers, "Revision Strategies of Student Writers and Experienced Writers," *College Composition and Communication* 31 (1980), 378–388.

2. See Elaine P. Maimon et al., *Writing in the Arts and Sciences*, Cambridge, Mass.: Winthrop, 1981, p. 9.

3. See Linda Flower, *Problem-Solving Strategies for Writing*, New York: Harcourt Brace Jovanovich, 1981, pp. 87–99.

4. Barry Commoner, *The Closing Circle*, New York: Bantam, 1972, pp. 150–151.

5. See Stephen Toulmin et al., *An Introduction to Reasoning*, New York: Macmillan, 1979.

6. William H. Taft and Gary Hart, *White Paper on Defense*, rev. ed., Washington, D.C.: Government Printing Office, 1978, p. 36.

7. Albert Kitzhaber, *Themes, Theories, and Therapy: The Teaching of Writing in College*. New York: McGraw-Hill, 1963.

8. Allen V. Kneese, "The Economic and Economically-Related Aspects of New Towns in Arid Areas," in *Urban Planning for Arid Zones*, ed. by Gideon Golany, New York: Wiley-Interscience, 1978, p. 134.

9. *Washington Post*, January 9, 1981, p. A-1.

10. Taft and Hart, p. 11.

Chapter 6
Refutation

In this chapter, you will learn:

- what options are open to you when you confront an argument;
- how to devise counterarguments;
- three approaches to analyzing the logic of argumentation.

Argumentation is *not* one person standing up and saying something and another person standing up and saying the exact opposite or saying that the first speaker is wrong. Unfortunately, too many debates among beginners feature this kind of interchange. Let's call this kind of interchange *attacking*.

Argumentation is also *not* one person standing up and offering his or her view on an issue and another person standing up and offering his or her view but making no comments on the first speaker's view. Again, too many novice debates feature this kind of no-interchange interchange. Let's call it *ignoring*.

Argumentation is also *not* one person standing up and offering his or her argument and another person figuring out what category among twenty that the particular argument best fits in and then pulling out a preprepared response for that category of argument and standing up and reading it. But again, too many debates—involving beginners as well as experienced debaters—feature this kind of interchange. Let's call it *reading*.

Refutation, the key element in argumentation, must involve thinking—careful thinking. The argument you intend to challenge should be examined carefully from a variety of perspectives. You should come to understand its logic and evidence and to see the possible flaws in either or both; you should note these flaws and why they necessarily lead to a rejection of the argument. *Attacking* does not involve this kind of careful thinking; *ignoring* involves no thinking at all about the arguments you may hear. And *reading*, at best, involves using the results of someone else's or your previous thinking, thinking which may be only partially on target because it was not done in response to the specific argument you are now faced with.

The next three chapters are designed to help you engage in serious refutation, without attacking, ignoring, or reading. This chapter, will deal with refutation in general terms; chapters 7 and 8 will deal with refutation as practiced by the negative team in a debate.

This chapter reviews five different approaches to refutation. First, the chapter offers you a general heuristic for refutation. What options are open to you if you are confronting an argument? How can you proceed? This general heuristic should help you understand and consider the available avenues. Two of the toughest avenues to take are offering a counterargument and challenging the argument's logic. The second approach offered in this chapter should help you think up counterarguments; the third, fourth, and fifth should help you challenge an argument's logic.

A General Heuristic for Refutation

Figure 6.1 is a list of seven strategies you can adopt when confronting an argument. The discussions that follow correspond to these seven strategies.

1. Concede the Point

Not all arguments are debatable. If a team argues that "America was founded on democratic principles," should you deny it? If a team argues that "nuclear weapons are destructive," *can* you deny it? Don't be afraid to concede an argument if the argument is not really a debatable one. In fact, you are better off conceding such an argument because attempting to argue against it takes time and may make you look excessively argumentative rather than sincerely interested in finding the best position on an important issue. Be careful though; some arguments that look undebatable are really very debatable. The argument that "The goal of U.S. foreign policy is to further global human rights" might look to some like a truism. If you look at that argument a little more closely, however, you will realize that what is set up as *the* goal may be just *a* goal and a minor one at that. Conceding that argument *too quickly* could get you into serious trouble in an actual debate.

2. Concede with Qualifications

Some arguments are almost truisms. These arguments you may want to concede with important qualifications. For example, let's say an affirmative team argues that "The rights of the accused are important." You probably would not deny that there is some truth in this statement; however, you might believe that the rights of the general public are more important. Conceding the affirmative's

A GENERAL HEURISTIC FOR REFUTATION

1. Concede the point, noting that it is not really a debatable contention.
2. Concede the point, with important qualifications.
3. Challenge the assumptions lying behind the point.
4. Ask for evidence of a specific kind.
5. Deny and offer counteranalysis and counterevidence.
6. Challenge the evidence:
    a. Have they generalized from evidence either numerically insufficient or unrepresentative?
    b. Have they presented half the truth in evidence?
    c. Have they irresponsibly edited important qualifications out of their evidence?
    d. Have they quoted their authority out of context?
    e. Have they equivocated on a word in a quotation?
    f. Have they quoted some prestigious or well-known person who lacks credentials in the field in question?
    g. Have they quoted a biased source?
    h. Have they quoted a (methodologically) bad study?
    i. Have they used statistics irresponsibly or carelessly?
    j. Is their evidence out of date?
7. Challenge the logic:
    a. Have they inappropriately appealed to the audience's emotions?
    b. Have they attacked a person's character, not the actual argument?
    c. Have they engaged in "bandwagoning"?
    d. Have they jumped from the truth of a general statement to a particular application?
    e. Have they posed a false dilemma?
    f. Have they falsely set up an analogy as proof?
    g. Have they mistaken a sequential relationship for a causal one?
    h. Have they mistaken a sufficient cause for a necessary cause?
    i. Have they mistaken an effect for a cause?
    j. Have they mistaken correlation for causation?

Figure 6.1 General heuristic for refutation.

argument is not what you would want to do; rather, you would want to concede with qualifications by saying, "Yes, the rights of the accused are important; however, the right of the general public to safety is more important."

3. Challenge Assumptions

Many arguments are phrased so as to hide assumptions. Once the assumptions are unveiled, an argument's weakness becomes apparent. Consider the following argument: "The high number of imports is ruining the American automobile industry." A high number of imports does not, by itself, hurt American industry; the affirmative team seems to be assuming that the number of cars available is the crucial matter. Is that assumption valid? No. If foreign products were demonstrably inferior to American products or not demonstrably superior, the number of imports would hardly matter. The assumption that the number of imports is the issue is flawed. When that assumption is challenged, the spotlight shifts from numbers to quality, and the blame shifts from supposedly profit-hungry foreign nations to inferior American engineering and manufacturing.

4. Ask for Evidence of a Specific Kind

Oftentimes, an argument will contain evidence that does not quite provide proof. For example, let's say the affirmative team is outlining the extent of poverty in Appalachia and discussing the reduced buying power that the poor experience. Buying power is one thing in New York City and other urban centers and another in the coal mining regions of Kentucky. Perhaps you suspect that the affirmative's evidence on reduced buying power is urban-oriented, since in the quotation the words "discount chains" and "shopping malls" appear. Ask the affirmative team to provide you with evidence which deals specifically with the buying power of the poor *in Appalachia*. Suggest to your listeners that perhaps the lower cost of living in rural areas mutes the effects of poverty in those areas and makes them less dire than in New York, Philadelphia, or Los Angeles. Suggest that this suspicion justifies your request for evidence of specific kind.

5. Deny and Counter

You will find denying relatively easy: all you essentially have to do is say "No." Denial, however, must be based on something. One basis can be your counter-argument supported by counterevidence. Let's say the argument you are facing is that America's railroads are going bankrupt. You could deny the argument and demonstrate that most (not all) railroads are financially sound and a couple are very profitable. Or, let's say the argument is that the Soviet Union is aggressive. You could deny the argument and point to the fact that Russia has not, in the post-World War II era, invaded any nations except for those already under its control. Or, in a value debate, let's say an affirmative team cites human life as the foremost value in its definitive contention and then argues that the arms race does not promote this value. The negative team might argue that the arms race, insofar as it helps maintain a balance of power which deters aggressive acts, actually preserves life. By exposing the affirmative team's logic as simplistic, the negative team denies and counters the affirmative. This last dramatic instance of denying and countering often goes by the name of a "retort" or a twisting or turning-around because the original argument's logic or evidence is somehow turned against itself.

6. Challenge the Evidence

Figure 6.1 offers you ten very specific questions to ask of a piece of evidence used in a debate to support an argument. Let's review these questions briefly.

The first question alerts you to the common problem of faulty generalization. Does one example of U.S. economic aid being used for military purposes justify an indictment of the entire economic aid program because "money is diverted from economic to military purposes"? Does the Soviet retreat from confrontation with the United States over Cuba in 1962 mean the Soviets will always retreat? Will they retreat over Nicaragua in 1984? No. Times have changed and Soviet power has increased. Does the failure of unionism to gain popular support in Richmond, Virginia, prove the decline of labor union power nationally? No. Virginia has never been a strong union state, unlike Pennsylvania and Ohio. And, besides, one example rarely proves a generalization.

The second question alerts you to the use of incomplete evidence. When evidence is used to demonstrate the existence of a problem in the past, that evidence might go on to discuss how that problem was solved. For example, let's say a team points to the poor financial standing of Conrail, the government-operated merger of several Northeastern freight rail lines, in the 1970s as evidence of the financial failure of business enterprises that are under federal auspices. This evidence presents half the truth, for Conrail has, since the 1970s, improved its financial posture considerably.

The third and fourth questions alert you to two irresponsible and unethical uses of evidence which sometimes do occur. Whenever a crucial piece of evidence has an ellipsis in it, you might want to ask what was excised in preparing the evidence card or the speech. Ask only for important pieces of evidence, and ask only when you have some reason to believe that a crucial phrase has been cut. Questioning excisions too frequently can look like harassment or an unwarranted questioning of ethics to a judge. Whenever a piece of evidence sounds too good to be true *or* if the content of a piece of evidence contradicts facts you know to be true *or* if the opinion expressed in a piece of evidence contradicts the source's usual opinion, you might want to ask to see the original source the evidence was copied from. Perhaps a word or phrase was accidentally deleted during transcription. If the team offering the evidence cannot produce the original, explain why you are questioning the evidence to the judge and ask him or her to join you in your suspicions and reject the piece of evidence. In these same situations, you should ask to see the original context of the quoted passage. Again, if the opposing team can provide it, fine; examine the context and see if the quotation, when removed from context, was misinterpreted. If the opposing team cannot provide the quotation in its original context, explain to the judge why you are questioning the evidence and ask him or her to reject the evidence based on your justified suspicion.

Always give the opposing team the benefit of the doubt: many errors in the copying of evidence are accidental. Always assume that the errors you suspect are not cases of intentional deception. If you do, debating will be a far friendlier activity without your weakening your position against the evidence one bit.

The fifth question alerts you to a special instance of quoting out of context: the accidental or intentional misuse of evidence by misrepresenting the meaning of a word in a quotation. This misuse is known as "equivocation." The word "balance" in a quotation may, in context, refer to the "balance of payments," whereas the team using the evidence is trying to document a claim concerning the "balance of trade." The phrase "the accused" in a quotation may, in context, refer to those who have been indicted for a crime whereas the team using the evidence is trying to document a claim concerning the rights of those who have only been arrested.

The sixth and seventh questions alert you to some common problems with opinion evidence. Oftentimes, beginning debaters will cite someone well-known or holding public office as an authority in a field that person has no special expertise in. Being a U.S. Senator or a member of the House of Representatives *does not* in and of itself qualify one to speak authoritatively on a public policy issue. Former Senator J. William Fulbright of Arkansas, for example, was an excellent source on foreign policy but not especially well-qualified on domestic policy. Senators and Congressmen choose to make one or two areas of public policy their areas of expertise. In these areas, they are authorities; in other areas, they are not. The same can be said about Presidents. They are not experts in all areas of public policy. Some, such as former President Richard M. Nixon, can speak authoritatively on foreign affairs; others, such as Nixon's predecessor, the late President Lyndon B. Johnson, can speak authoritatively on domestic problems and policies.

Sources of opinion evidence must be qualified and objective. Everyone has his or her views, and of course, these views will affect whatever a person says on a particular issue. The influence of one's views on one's statements is not evidence of a lack of objectivity. A lack of objectivity is present when the influence of one's views is so strong that opposed arguments will not even be considered. Senator Gary Hart's opposition to the restoration and refitting of the battleship New Jersey was certainly influenced by his prior views on the particular strengths and weaknesses of the U.S. Navy, but his opposition did not lack objectivity. The opinion of a spokesman for independent truckers on an increase in the federal gasoline tax, on the other hand, probably is a nonobjective, biased one. The extent of the independent truckers' personal stake in the matter would make it difficult for their spokesman to look upon the issues without a degree of blinding bias.

The eight and ninth questions pertain to empirical evidence. Although a debater citing the results of an empirical study is not obligated to know the very last details of the study's methodology, that methodology can be challenged or questioned by an opponent. It can be challenged if the opponent *knows and can prove* that the methodology is flawed; it can be questioned if the conclusions are so unusual or so contrary to expectations as to raise suspicions in an objective listener. (If a debater is going to offer such empirical evidence, he or she would be well advised to look into the study carefully and know how its conclusions were reached.) The flaws of studies usually deal with one of four elements: the size of the sample; the representativeness of the sample; the adequacy of the controls; and the freedom from bias.

Suppose a system of government-funded health maintenance organizations (HMOs) was being advocated by an affirmative team, and they cited a study done of two groups of employees at a large state university as proving the superiority of employer-paid HMOs to traditional employer-paid health insurance. The group that chose HMOs ended up with a higher rate of improved health at a year's end than the group that chose to stay with traditional health insurance. Where's the flaw in the study? The size of each group was sufficiently large, and each group had representatives from a wide range of employee types—i.e. maintenance, clerical, faculty, administrative—roughly parallel to categories found in society at large. The employees did not know that they were being studied, so the person conducting the research could not have biased the experiment by injecting a pro-HMO bias which might have "psyched" HMO participants to seek out preventive medical care more frequently in order to "win" the contest. The flaw is found in the absence of adequate controls. Since the employees chose their group, nothing stood in the way of all the health-conscious people choosing HMOs or all the workers who were indifferent to health care sticking with the traditional health insurance. You should examine all evidence drawn from empirical research in a similar manner.

The results of empirical research are often presented in statistical terms. Statistics can be misused in countless ways: there are books several hundred pages long discussing "how to lie with statistics." You should be particularly alert to three misuses: (1) falsely claiming significance; (2) using percentages when the raw data are weak; (3) making comparisons without appropriately adjusting the data. Let's consider these misuses one by one.

(1) Falsely claiming significance. "Significance," as noted in Chapter 3, is a technical term in statistics. If, let's say, federal grants lead to a Gross National Product increase of 5 percent and a reduction in corporate income tax rates lead to a Gross National Product increase of 7¼ percent, the difference between the economic stimulation might well be shown to be due to factors other than the different policies. If so, the difference in stimulation between the two policies is said to lack significance. The question of statistical significance is far too complex to discuss here; as a debater who is trying to refute arguments using statistics, you need to know that relatively small differences are *probably not* statistically significant and that policy decisions should not be based on such differences.

(2) Using percentages when the raw data are weak. Let's say you are debating a team that is arguing that periodic examinations for public high school teachers will improve the quality of education. Let's say this team presents statistical evidence drawn from a county system in rural New York state. Once an examination system was adopted by this school system, the number of students going on to college increased from 80 to 140 over a five-year period. The numbers are not going to impress too many listeners, so the team presents the raw data in a percentage: "The number of students going on to college increased 75% percent over a five-year period." (The raw data could also be presented and misrepresented

by saying, "The number going on to college almost doubled.") As a debater engaging in refutation, be dubious of percentages. If a piece of statistical evidence sounds too good and uses percentages, press the team offering the evidence for the raw data.

(3) Making comparisons without appropriately modifying the data. If one compares dollar amounts across the years, an adjustment has to be made for inflation. For example, the average starting salary for a college teacher was approximately $9,000 in 1970; in 1983, it is $15,000. The raw data suggests that college faculty are much better off in 1983 than in 1970. Not so. Once the latter figure is adjusted for inflation, the *decline* in real starting salary is evident. Furthermore, a comparison between 43,000 American families in New York City who have incomes under the national poverty level of $6,200 and 182,000 American families in Appalachia who have incomes under that level would be a fallacious one. Why? Because $6,200 is indeed a poverty income in New York City, but only a low income in some parts of West Virginia and Kentucky. An adjustment in the definition of "poverty income" is necessary as you move from urban areas with a high cost of living to rural areas with a typically lower cost of living.

The tenth and final question to ask of evidence deals with the relevance of both opinion evidence and empirical evidence. That times change is a cliché with a fair amount of truth to it. Opinions voiced or studies made several years back may no longer be relevant. Many debaters claim that evidence more than a couple of years old is "no good"; therefore, they do not record such evidence and they tell judges to throw it out if opponents dare to offer it. These debaters are not completely correct in their assumption; much "old" evidence is indeed irrelevant and weak, but some "old" evidence is very relevant and therefore strong. Whether a piece of evidence is relevant or not depends on whether times have indeed changed in the area under discussion. For example, commentary on the politics of Arab nations dated in the mid-1970s would probably be suspect now. Many Arab nations are far friendlier to the United States now than in 1975; there are numerous rifts in what may have seemed like a fairly unified "Arab world" front in 1975, and the economic situation has changed thanks to conservation of petroleum and the worldwide recession in the early 1980s. However, commentary on racism in South Africa from 1975 might still be relevant, since the internal politics (according to most observers) have not changed significantly since the mid-1970s. In the field of domestic affairs, there have been significant changes in election financing procedures since the early 1970s, but little new labor legislation. In the areas often under discussion in value debate, again, the relevance of an "old" piece of evidence depends upon the particular area under discussion. The rights afforded an accused criminal have changed little since 1970; on the other hand, the rights of journalists to maintain confidentiality have been challenged, and the use of the insanity defense has increased. The work ethic has come into question as researchers have said more and more about "workaholism," whereas the same fundamental questions are being raised now as in 1970 concerning prayer in school, sex education, abortion, and forced busing to achieve racial integration. Debaters should know the area or areas they will be discussing and know whether recent changes have made "old" evidence irrelevant.

7. Challenge the Logic

The last available strategy that the general heuristic for refutation (Figure 6.1) offers you is to challenge the logic. As with challenging the evidence, there are several ways to accomplish this task. The heuristic presents ten questions you should ask of an argument's logic.

The first question should alert you to the logical fallacies of appeals to pity and anger. There is nothing necessarily wrong with such appeals, but they, by themselves, do not warrant the acceptance of the argument. If a debater has appealed to the listener's pity while presenting evidence on the extent and horrors of poverty in urban slums, that is acceptable; however, if there is little or no solid evidence and if "sob stories" make up the bulk of the presentation, then the argument is logically shaky.

The second question should alert you to the logical fallacy known as *argumentum ad hominem*. Instead of arguing against an argument, a speaker will attack the character of the person making the argument or—more commonly in debating—the source he or she has quoted. No matter what you think of former President Richard M. Nixon's political behavior, he is a qualified source on many foreign affairs issues—for example, on China. Saying that Nixon was almost impeached is *not* a logical way of refuting his authoritative statement that China is ready to embrace American culture and technology and willing to pay certain political prices to warm the U.S. government to a new American-Chinese relationship.

The third question should alert you to the logical fallacy known as *argumentum ad populum* or "bandwagoning." This fallacy is the "everybody believes" fallacy. A debater who is arguing that the Soviet Union is a threat to world peace cannot simply say, "Everyone is aware of the threat that the U.S.S.R. poses." Evidence must be offered; an audience should not be "bandwagoned" into accepting a position just because "everybody" does.

The fourth question should alert you to another logical fallacy: faulty particularization. To every general statement, there is an exception. Don't let an opponent get away with applying a generalization *too quickly* to a particular instance. Ask yourself if the particular instance might be the exceptional one. For example, many will argue that inflation is bad. Although generally true, the statement is *not* true in the case of federal revenue collecting. Thanks to antiquated tax brackets, the federal government gets a higher and higher percentage of your income as you creep from a 20 percent tax bracket to a 25 percent bracket to a 30 percent bracket. Your buying power does not increase because the rise in salary is nothing but inflation; as your income rises, however, you pay the federal government an increasingly higher percentage of your income. As long as these old tax brackets are in force, inflation will benefit, not harm, federal revenues.

The fifth question should alert you to a logical problem known as false dilemma. Someone committing this fallacy suggests that there are two courses of action and argues that, since course "x" is horrible, course "y" ought to be taken. For example, a debater might argue that we either improve our land-based nuclear weapons or build a new and better fleet of bombers. Since the land-based missiles cannot be made invulnerable to a first-strike knockout, the debater would continue, the United States should expand its plans for the B-1 and Stealth bombers. Are land-based missiles and new bombers the only choices? No. The U.S. submarine fleet could be improved and expanded, and cruise missiles could be deployed on land, on sea, and in the air. The debater has set up a false dilemma.

The sixth question should alert you to the use of an analogy as proof. Hitler committed this fallacy with horrible results in his anti-Jewish propaganda. Hitler said that since dogs do not mate with cats, it is not natural for the superior Aryan Germans to mate with the inferior Jews, and, furthermore, just as the result of a dog-cat mating would be a weak, freakish creature, so would the offspring of an Aryan-Jewish sexual relationship. To prevent just such relationships, Hitler decided to exterminate the Jews. What was wrong with Hitler's logic? He tried to apply what is true of two separate species to two races of the same species. Two races of human beings may be analogous in some ways to cats and dogs — e.g., the races do tend to fight like cats and dogs at times; however, two races are *not logically similar* to two species.

Another example. Let's say a debate team was arguing that capital punishment is a deterrent for murder. The team might say that, just as fear of spanking deters a little boy from stealing a piece of candy before dinner, fear of execution deters a potential murderer from killing. There are, however, many striking differences between a little boy and a potential adult murderer. The little boy may, in some way, be analogous to the potential murderer, but they are not logically similar. A logical argument cannot be premised on an analogy.

The last four questions deal with the complex area of causality. Persuasive writers and speakers are frequently guilty of logical errors in this area. One common error is to mistake a sequential relationship for a causal one. Just because two events occur closely related in time does not mean that the first is the cause of the second. Peace precedes war; war precedes peace. Does the proximity in time mean peace causes war and, contradictorily, war causes peace? Consider the debater who argues that deregulation of the aviation industry is the cause of an increase in airplane accidents because the second followed the first. That debater may be correct in his understanding of the commercial aviation industry; however, as long as the proximity in time of the two events is his sole evidence, the argument is logically flawed.

The second common error is to misrepresent a sufficient cause as a necessary cause. A sufficient cause is a force or event that will probably have certain results; a necessary cause is a force or event that *must* be present for certain results to happen. The distinction is an important one. Let's consider the subject of intoxication. The existence of a wild fraternity party on campus is a sufficient cause of intoxication; the ingestion of large quantities of alcohol is a necessary cause. This illustration is a rather simple one. Let's consider the public policy problem posed by the decaying streets and bridges in many older American cities. A debater might argue that the problem is caused by heavy truck traffic and propose restrictions on truck traffic in large cities. Is heavy truck traffic a sufficient or a necessary cause? It probably does cause the problem, but the problem could exist, heavy truck traffic or not. In other words, the cause is not necessary for the problem to exist; it is only a sufficient cause. The distinction is important in a debate because of the stock issue of solvency. If a cause of a problem is argued—explicitly or implicitly—to be a necessary one and if the plan eliminates the cause, the plan is solvent. If the cause is really only a sufficient cause, however, the plan will not necessarily solve the problem. Banning heavy truck traffic on city streets would not solve the problem of decaying streets and bridges since there are several other causes of the problem—climate, chemicals used to melt ice and snow, and age.

A third common error in causal reasoning is to confuse cause and effect. This error sounds difficult to make; after all, a cause is a cause and an effect is an effect. Right? Wrong. Consider an argument for American military intervention in Central America on the grounds that, in the absence of U.S. counterintervention, Cuban subversion will lead to the spreading of a Marxist ideology. The Marxist ideology, however, may be spreading for other reasons, e.g., poverty amidst luxurious living by the privileged few, and this ideology may be opening doors for Cuban activity. If the alleged cause is really the effect (i.e., if a Marxist ideology is leading to Cuban interference rather than Cuban interference leading to a spreading Marxist ideology), then American intervention supposedly directed against the cause would really be action against the effect. As a result, the proposed solution would be, at best, symptomatic (rather than addressing the cause) and, at worst, a sign to the poor natives that the United States supports the privileged few. The policy of American intervention to counter Cuba could then actually encourage indigenous Marxism and thereby help Cuba.

A fourth common error in causal reasoning is to mistake correlation for causation. This error is frequently made by debaters who are new to such matters as statistics and experimental design. Let's say you are discussing environmental protection. You hear the argument that tests have shown that water pollution in the Monongahela River has increased at the same rate as industrialization in the several Western Pennsylvania counties that comprise the Pittsburgh Standard Metropolitan Statistical Area (SMSA). The person offering the argument suggests that, since industrial growth there and in most SMSAs has stagnated, water pollution will not get worse. Implicit in his or her argument is the assumption that industrialization was the cause of water pollution, but the evidence only pointed to a direct correlation. Perhaps the real cause *of both* was the increase in population incident to industrialization and the resulting increase in sewage entering the river; perhaps, despite a decline in industrial activity, population

122   *Debating*

growth will continue because of significant increases in white collar and service jobs in the region. If the real cause was population growth and it is continuing, the decline in industrial activity will not be paralleled by a decline in water pollution or even maintenance of the status quo. Mistaking a correlation for a causal relationship led to someone's incorrectly optimistic forecast for water pollution in Western Pennsylvania.

An Example of the Heuristic's Use

The general heuristic I have just finished presenting is just that, a heuristic, not a list of ways you can challenge an argument for reference at your leisure. You should use this heuristic to help you discover what you might say in refutation of an argument as you are debating.

Let's say an affirmative team has argued that U.S. military salaries are too low to attract qualified technical personnel. Use Figure 6.1 and consider the seven strategies listed there; under strategies six and seven, consider the several different types of evidentiary or logical problems. This consideration might have led you to the following list of possibilities:

2. Salaries are indeed low; however, salaries are only part of the generous compensation package the military offers.
3. The affirmative assumes that money will necessarily lead to sufficient manpower. This assumption may be false given the danger of and the restrictions of one's freedom in military service.
4. Let's hear some evidence indicting the total compensation the military offers— i.e., salary *plus* the costs of housing, food, medical care, post-service education, etc.
6b. The affirmative, in talking about the salary which technical personnel would receive in the Army, is only talking about a part of the compensation they would get.
6g. One of the quotations used by the affirmative was from a technical worker in the Army who says he won't re-enlist unless salaries are increased. He is a biased source since he has a personal interest in increased salaries.
6h. The affirmative also cites a study in which a group of Army technicians in Virginia were offered a salary $3,000 higher than a group in California if they would re-enlist. More of the Virginia workers re-enlisted than the California workers. The study is flawed because the groups were not equal in technical aptitude, marital status, and commitment to the military.
6i. The difference in retention rate in that study, twelve percent, was not statistically significant.
7a. The affirmative's appeal to our patriotism was an irrelevant emotional appeal.
7c. The affirmative cannot simply claim that everyone knows that the U.S. Army is having a difficult time recruiting.

7d. Even if the Army is having a difficult time in general (due, perhaps, to many people's fear of combat), this does not necessarily mean that the Army is having a difficult time recruiting technicians (who rarely see combat).
7h. A low salary is a sufficient cause of one's not joining the military, but not a necessary cause. Therefore, the affirmative cannot guarantee that more money will necessarily mean more recruits.

From nothing to say, you now have eleven arguments. You need to combine, delete, and select, and then you need to wrap your arguments up in a nicely organized package. You will not be *attacking, ignoring,* or *reading*; rather, you will be thinking and clashing:

The affirmative argues that the United States military is having a difficult time attracting qualified technical personnel. I have three responses.

First, the affirmative evidence is flawed: they quote a biased source, a U.S. Army technician, saying he would require more money to re-enlist; then they cite a weak study in which more members of a group getting more money opted to re-enlist than among a group getting $3,000 less. The study is flawed because (a) it did not control the two groups for technical aptitude, marital status, and commitment to the military and (b) the difference in retention, twelve percent, is not statistically significant.

Second, the affirmative talks only about salary, but military technicians receive a generous compensation package including housing, food, and education after they leave the military. Let's hear some evidence indicting compensation.

Third, the affirmative assumes money is the cause of the alleged recruiting problem. Money may be a factor, but it is not the sole cause. Other factors—fear of combat and lack of freedom, for example—may also be hurting recruiting. These other factors will still affect recruiting even if the affirmative raises salary levels. Therefore, the affirmative team cannot guarantee us that they will solve the problem they have presented.

Exercises: Challenging Arguments I

Use the general heuristic for refutation to discover ways to challenge the following arguments:

1. The First Amendment's protection of free speech covers pornography. We may not like it, but to preserve our right to express ourselves without fear of governmental interference or suppression, we must tolerate pornography.
2. NATO land forces, even if tripled, could do little to stop a massive Soviet assault. Therefore, special tactical weapons, perhaps nuclear ones, are necessary to slow down or stop such an advance.
3. The salaries of sports stars may seem high; according to Ed Garvey, President of the N.F.L. Players' Association, however, the salaries are *far* short of the players' market value.
4. High school teachers do the best job they can given the conditions which exist in most American high schools today—violence, apathy, absenteeism, and minimal parental support or encouragement.

5. Crime is lower in states where capital punishment is a reality than in states where capital punishment is either illegal or not practiced. There are thirteen percent fewer murders *per capita* in Utah than in Pennsylvania.
6. Computer crime—e.g., switching money into one's bank account by gaining illicit access to the bank's computer—cannot be stopped by federal regulations that would insist on uniform technical safeguards throughout the computer industry. According to the president of IBM, uniform safeguards would make the criminal's job easier, not more difficult.
7. Television-watching is thwarting the development of analytical skills in children. A clinical study of twenty children revealed that television stimulated the brain's right hemisphere, which helps one see information as a whole, but not the left, which helps one see the parts which make up the whole.
8. The Soviet Union would not allow Cuba to leave its sphere of influence if Cuba wanted to. They did not allow Hungary, Czechoslovakia, and Afghanistan to escape; they aren't allowing Poland to escape, either.

Topoi for Argumentation

When trying to follow the fifth strategy on the general heuristic, denying and offering counteranalysis or counterevidence, beginning debaters sometimes find it difficult to come up with the necessary counters. Help is available in the rhetorics of old—those of Aristotle and Cicero written in ancient Greece and Rome. These rhetoricians—as well as others since—outlined the places where arguments might be found. The Greek word for places is *topoi*. If you are seeking a counterargument, you can use an updated version of the classical *topoi* to help you discover the possibilities.

Kinds of Definitions

The first *topos*, or place to look for an argument, is in definitions. There are two kinds of definitions; each can provide you with an argument.

You can define something by placing it in a category and then differentiating it from other members of that category. This kind of definition is called a *genus + differentia* definition. Consider the following definitions:

Abortion is the willful murder of an unborn child.

A college education is the instruction of the human mind in modes of thinking characteristic of the different academic disciplines.

Self-determination is a human right of all peoples that they must be allowed to exercise without restraint.

Subversion is any nonmilitary attempt to undermine or overthrow a government.

These definitions are *not* facts; contrary to common belief, no definitions are facts. The ones in dictionaries are simply records of how a word is used, and they can and do change as usage changes. That these dictionary definitions are records does give them a factual quality, but definitions need not be records and need not have this factual quality. Definitions are statements which limit the meaning of a term: they can limit in the usual way or they can limit in a way that is debatable.

The four definitions above are debatable; nonetheless, they are powerful statements because they *seem* definitive. If an opponent accepts these statements, he or she will be in considerable trouble. Once someone grants that the act of abortion is a type of murder, the argument is practically over; once someone grants the above definition of a college education, he or she would have a difficult time arguing that all students should not study a science. The third definition, the one on self-determination, could be used to argue that CIA involvement in Nicaragua is *not* a violation of this right since the Marxist government there was not freely chosen by the people. The fourth definition, the one of subversion, could be used to argue that all U.S. propaganda efforts, including Radio Free Europe, are examples of subversion and objectionable as such.

The second kind of definition involves establishing the end or goal of something. (Aristotle's term for it is the "final effect"—the effect to which all things point.) Consider the following definitions:

The goal of a college education is to prepare young men and women for the working world.
The end of international trade is the increased prosperity of American citizens.
The goal of our penal system is to rehabilitate those who have violated the law.
The goal of professional athletes is to entertain the masses.

Again, these definitions are not facts; they are debatable attempts to establish meaning. They could be used as a powerful springboard for, respectively, the argument that computer science be required of all students at "x" college, that trade with Japan be curtailed, that poor prison conditions be improved, and that baseball players be paid as much as television, motion picture, and recording stars are paid.

Similarities and Differences

The second *topos* is found in the similarities and differences between things. As I mentioned earlier, comparing human races and animal species or comparing the capital punishment of adult criminals to the spanking of little boys is not logical. However, two things can be sufficiently similar for a comparison to be a logically valid basis for an argument. Comparing U.S. involvement in El Salvador in the 1980s to U.S. involvement in Vietnam in the 1970s could be the basis for an argument against or for more U.S. military aid to the Central American nation. Comparing sports stars to movie stars could be the basis for an argument in favor of higher salaries for professional athletes.

Differences between things that might seem similar can also provide a logical springboard for an argument. The Florida East Coast Railway and the Seaboard Coast Line were, in the mid-1970s, comparable railroads. The one was profitable; the other nearly bankrupt. The difference—it might be argued—is to be found in the fact that the Seaboard Coast Line had unionized employees whereas the Florida East Coast had kicked the unions out, with the permission of the federal courts. The difference between the financial standing of the Seaboard Coast Line and that of the Florida East Coast might be used as the basis for an antiunion argument.

Causes and Consequences

The third *topos* is to be found in the causes and consequences of things. What has gotten us to the point we are now at? Where will we go if nothing changes? These questions can take us to possible argumentation.

Consider the problems of hard-core unemployment. What are its causes? Poor educational environment at home; poor schools in the slums; demoralization. What are some of the consequences if this unemployment continues? Its continuation would lead to deeper and deeper poverty; it could lead to violence in areas where unemployment is high. Citing the causes could lead a persuasive speaker to a call for generous federal aid for education in areas of chronic high unemployment. Citing the consequences could lead the speaker to a call for federal jobs programs to prevent the harms of poverty and urban violence.

An Example of the Topoi's *Use as A Heuristic*

These three *topoi* can be used to generate arguments for or against. Let's say an affirmative team has argued for a flat-rate income tax. Under such a system, every taxpayer would pay 15% of his or her income to the federal government; there would be no deductions and no loopholes. You may want to argue against such a tax. Using the *topoi* as a heuristic, you might come up with the following possible counterarguments:

Definition by genus + differentia
Taxation is a citizen's or resident's *fair contribution* to the operations of his or her government.
Definition by end
The goal of taxation is to garner sufficient revenue without unduly burdening any group of taxpayers.
Similarities
The flat-rate income tax is much like the sales tax in its regressive quality and unfairly burdensome impact on the lower and middle classes.

Differences
The flat-rate tax, unlike the progressive income tax we currently have, will take a higher percentage of the income of those who need money to live and a lower percentage of the income of the rich.

Causes
The cause of the current revenue shortfall is the existence of numerous loopholes the rich can slide through to avoid paying a fair amount of tax. Let's get rid of these loopholes rather than change to a flat-rate tax.

Consequences
If the United States were to adopt a flat-rate tax, it would (A) bankrupt many lower- and middle-class Americans and (B) destroy the home housing industry.

Using the *topoi* as a heuristic gives you plenty to say. Premising your counterargument on taxation being a *fair* method of garnering revenue, not just a method, you can argue that a flat-rate tax (A) is inferior to the present progressive tax, (B) is much like the sales tax in its regressive qualities, (C) does not address the cause of the present revenue shortfall, and (D) will lead to serious disadvantages.

Exercises: Generating Arguments

Use the *topoi* as a heuristic to generate arguments against the following statements:

1. One should be allowed to sunbathe in the nude on public beaches.
2. White-collar criminals should be treated just like any other class of criminals.
3. Teenage workers should be given a wage lower than adult workers, if doing so allows employers to hire more teenagers.
4. The drinking age should be 21 across the entire nation.
5. Prayer in school should indeed be banned.
6. We should build a new and bigger ocean-to-ocean canal in Costa Rica.
7. If Quebec tries to secede from Canada, the United States should adopt a hands-off policy.
8. School districts should be required to bus students so that all schools are racially mixed.

More on Analyzing the Logic of Arguments

Another strategy listed on the general heuristic for refutation that poses difficulties for many beginners is the last one: "challenge their logic." In the next three subsections of this chapter, I will offer you three very different ways of analyzing the logic of an argument. The first way is a recent approach, pioneered by noted logician-rhetorician Stephen Toulmin and his many disciples. The second is a very traditional method, one promoted by the work during the past twenty years by Ohio State University rhetorician Edward P. J. Corbett. The third method is a common approach in applied logic texts to seeing how arguments connect and the implications of those connections.

Analyzing the Structure of Arguments

Logician-rhetorician Toulmin examined arguments in a wide variety of fields— law, business, science, social science, art. He found that, despite disciplinary differences, all arguments had six ingredients. First, there is the argument or *claim* that is being made; second, there is the evidence or *grounds* upon which the claim is based. Those are the two obvious ingredients. Third, there is the *warrant*. The warrant is the rule of reasoning in the particular field which justifies the jump from grounds to claim. Fourth, there is the *backing* the warrant has. Fifth, there is the *modality*—the degree of certainty suggested for the claim; and, sixth, there are the *rebuttals*—the announced exceptions to the claim.[1]

Consider two very different arguments: one in the field of medicine, the other in the field of civil law. Let's say someone goes to the doctor at the college

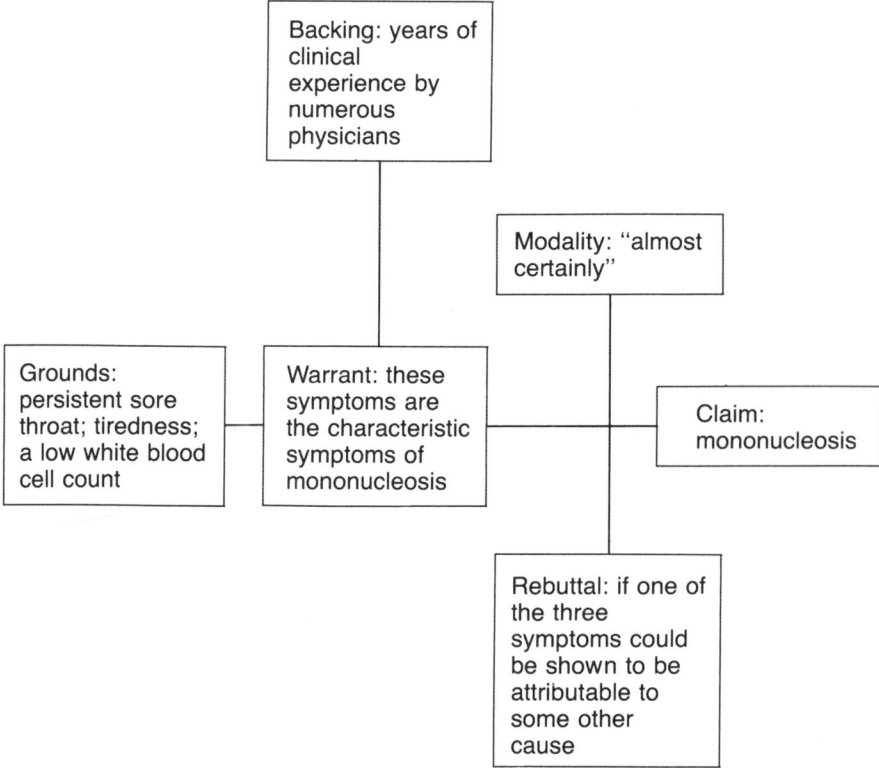

Figure 6.2 An example of the Toulmin analysis of an argument.

health clinic. Based on the symptoms or grounds of a persistent sore throat, tiredness, and a low white blood cell count, the doctor claims the problem is mononucleosis. The warrant for this jump from grounds to claim is the belief that these symptoms are indeed the characteristic symptoms of "mono." Years of clinical experience by numerous physicians provide the backing for this warrant. The doctor says that this person "almost certainly" has "mono": the modality is contained in the doctor's phrase "almost certainly." The doctor, if pressed, might say that his diagnosis might be questioned only if one of the three symptoms could be shown to be attributable to some other cause. In that qualification is the rebuttal. If you look back to the previous chapter, Figure 5.3 presents the Toulmin schematic for an argument. Figure 6.2 fills in the blocks with this medical argument.

Let's say a newspaper is being sued by a politician for libel. The newspaper had claimed, in a story, that this politician was connected with some suspect massage parlors in the city in which the newspaper is published. The politician's lawyer would claim that the politician was libeled; the grounds would be the text of the newspaper story. The warrant would be the libel law; the backing for it would be the many statutes and court decisions which have established that law. The lawyer would claim that the newspaper is guilty without a doubt. The modality is implicit in the phrase "without a doubt." The lawyer would admit that his claim would not be valid if the newspaper could prove the truth of the statement. That is the rebuttal. Figure 6.3 fills in the blocks with this legal argument.

In a debate, arguments will rarely if ever be presented in such a way that these six ingredients are immediately evident. You need to analyze the arguments you hear into these six elements. Then, you can look for some of the characteristic logical problems this kind of analysis often reveals.

The Existence of a Warrant. Many jumps between grounds and claim will be totally unwarranted in a debate. You may not be sure how the opposing team got from its evidence to its conclusion; if cross-examined, that team may not know how it got there. The claim may be that the United States is in grave danger; the grounds may be the small number of troops we have compared to the Soviet Union. The claim may be that the U.S. economy is in bad shape; the grounds may be high inflation. There are ways to get from these grounds to these claims. However, if a team does not understand what warrants their argument, they do not understand why their evidence proves their point and probably have no right offering the argument. Asking a team why their evidence proves their point will reveal their lack of understanding of what they are arguing and should weaken their case for or against the resolution considerably.

The Validity of the Warrant. In the two examples just discussed, the warrants could be stated as "Troop strength is a time-honored measure of defensive capability in discussions of military preparedness" in the first case and "High

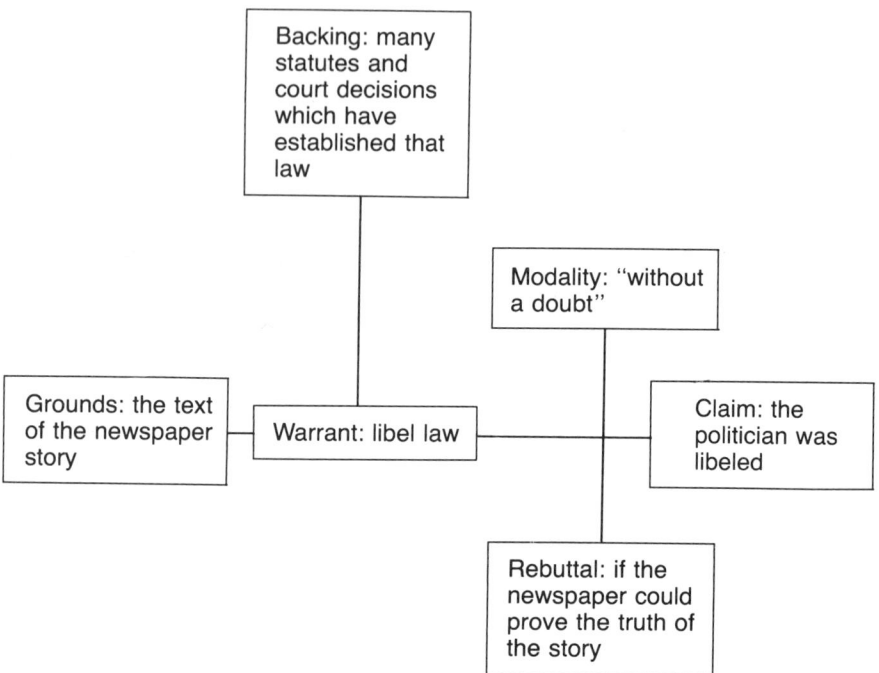

Figure 6.3 An example of the Toulmin analysis of an argument.

inflation is a mark of an economy that is out of control" in the second. Are these warrants valid? What backing can be offered for them? Perhaps troop strength is an irrelevant measure in our nuclear age; perhaps high inflation is simply an unfortunate side effect of a booming economy. When warrants are clearly established rules of reasoning—e.g., in meteorology, a clash between hot air and higher cold air usually means precipitation—the request for the warrant's backing usually leads both parties in a discussion to an understanding of an offered argument. However, when warrants are theoretical statements, as in the two cases above, the request for the warrant's backing may well lead to extensive debating over the validity of the backing and thus the validity of the warrant. Debaters should remember that, if the warrant is invalid, the whole argument is invalid.

There are three other ways in which a warrant can be invalid. First, if the grounds are opinion evidence, then the warrant—i.e., the authority's credentials—may be invalid if the credentials are inadequate. Those credentials may be inadequate if they are not in the right area or field, are not substantial, or are not given. A scholar in sociology may not have an appropriate background to speak authoritatively concerning economics. A scarcely published assistant professor of political science may not have a sufficiently substantial background to speak authoritatively concerning the politics of the Middle East. A name without any credentials at all attached to it is worthless as a source because his or her claim cannot be warranted.

Second, if the grounds are empirical evidence, then the warrant—i.e., the study's worth—may be inadequate if the study's design, controls, or objectivity can be called into question.

Third, if the grounds are documented facts, then the warrant—i.e., the ability to generalize from sufficient facts—may be invalid if the warrant seems to require more than the grounds provide. For example, let's say a debate team is arguing for wage and price controls. Let's say they claim that wages are skyrocketing, and they offer as grounds data from three industries. The warrant is a common sense statement: if the majority of workers' wages have gone up significantly, then wages can be said to be skyrocketing. This warrant requires the majority (or something reasonably close to it), and the grounds in this case do not meet the requirement. Therefore, the warrant does not permit the leap from grounds to claim, and it is not valid. Another example. Let's say the debate is over the value of the United Nations. One team says that the United Nations is a Soviet puppet because the Soviet Union can control the votes of so many nations. The warrant is, again, a commonsense statement about the amount of data necessary for the claim to be valid. It might be stated this way: "If the Soviet Union controls a sufficient number of votes so that it always get its way, then the United Nations could correctly be called a Soviet puppet." Since the grounds do not offer the requisite number of votes, the warrant cannot validly justify the jump to the claim.

Hidden Modalities. The modality of an argument is very important because it contains the degree of certainty being claimed for the argument. Many debaters honestly give an argument the correct modality when initially presenting it, but then, in summarizing it or defending it, they hide the modality if it is not one which comes close to one hundred percent certainty. They do this out of enthusiasm for their argument and out of fear an opponent will jump on "most probably" and harp on the argument's supposed weakness.

A debater who is looking closely at an argument should try to pinpoint the modality of an opponent's argument. If the argument's modality is expressed by phrases like "possibly could" or "perhaps will" or "may result in," the debater has the right to point to the relatively low certainty we have that the argument is valid, especially if the debater offering the argument is claiming a higher degree of certainty. The debater should stress that policy changes or prepolicy decisions should *not* be based on low-certainty claims. However, a debater should not rant and rave when the modality is contained in phrases like "most probably will" or "*in all* likelihood will." These phrases reflect a relatively high degree of certainty, and a relatively high degree of certainty is all that can be realistically expected. This modality is the best one because, first, in debating you are often dealing with intelligent predictions and, second, in all discussions of public issues, you are in a realm, like all human realms, where mathematical certainty is simply not a possibility.

Hidden Rebuttals. The admitted conditions under which an argument is invalid are important because, if these conditions can be shown to exist, the entire argument can be thrown out. For example, if someone is arguing that the United States should build a new strategic bomber unless it would jeopardize disarmament talks with the Soviet Union, you could beat the argument—no matter how strong the grounds—by showing that the building plans would indeed jeopardize the disarmament process. Quite often debaters, in cross-examination, will volunteer the conditions under which their argument falls; sometimes, the opinion evidence they offer will point to the rebuttals.

A debater should try to find out what rebuttals an opponent will acknowledge as valid. Furthermore, a debater should think of rebuttals on his or her own, suggest them to the judge, and demonstrate that the conditions specified in these rebuttals exist. For example, let's say a debater argues that government-funded health care will lead to inferior care. That debater's opponent might suggest that this could happen unless (a) stringent safeguards are adopted to prevent the quality of care from declining, and (b) doctors are given a strong role in the design and administration of the program. Then, the opponent might show that both of these conditions will be met by the policy he or she is advocating and that, therefore, the objection falls.

An Example of the Toulmin Analysis. The analytical procedure I have outlined has two steps: first, you must isolate the six elements of the argument; second, you need to see if the argument exhibits any of the usual logical problems. Let's use the procedure as a heuristic to find challenges to the argument.

A debater argues that, according to international economist Jeremy Rifkin, the world is rapidly exhausting its mineral and petroleum resources (claim). Rifkin cites objective data. The grounds are, thus, Rifkin's expert opinion supported by data. The warrant is Rifkin's strength as a source: the person voicing the argument could cite Rifkin's degrees, publications, and honors to provide backing for the warrant. In Rifkin's words, the modality is "most probably." Neither Rifkin nor the debater admit any rebuttals.

Let's look for the logical problems. Is there a warrant? Yes, Rifkin's credentials are given and the debater suggests that someone with such credentials is qualified to offer authoritative commentary in this field. Is the warrant valid? Rifkin certainly is an authority; however, despite his credentials, he is well-known as a radical-thinking intellectual. Perhaps his objectivity can be questioned, and the warrant is not as valid as it first seemed. Is the modality hidden? No. Rifkin is rather sure of his conclusions. Are there hidden rebuttals, or put another way, are there conditions you can suggest which would make Rifkin's conclusion invalid or questionable? Here is where the argument may be weakest. You could suggest that Rifkin's argument weakens if open ocean sources of minerals and petroleum could be tapped and if new sources were discovered. Then you could show that the technology *now* exists for open-ocean exploration and extraction and that several new sources have been very recently discovered—in the United States and elsewhere.

Exercises: Challenging Arguments II

Analyze the following arguments using the Toulmin method. Look for the common logical problems.

1. Observers of Soviet government and foreign policy tell us that now is probably the best time to press the Russians for concessions in arms reduction negotiations.
2. If the winter weather is severe during the upcoming decade, the city of Pittsburgh may find itself with only three safe bridges out of the downtown area rather than the present seven.
3. The number of abortions performed daily in the United States will continue to rise unless the federal government stops paying for them as if they were tonsilectomies or wart removals.
4. Test drillings in the Atlantic Ocean have not encouraged oil company executives. The United States' reserves of petroleum seem to be as limited as commentators in the early 1970s suggested.
5. According to the president of the Teamsters, truckers pay more than their fair share of road-use fees and taxes.
6. Government officials in Libya have reported CIA activities in that nation.
7. Red China will never renounce its claim to the island of Taiwan.
8. Unless Libyan leader Muammar Kaddafi is stopped in Chad, he will engage in more and more "adventures." France and the United States should reflect on Hitler's actions as he was left unimpeded.
9. The tax base has declined in real dollars in Philadelphia, New York, and Baltimore, according to the reports of the governments of these cities. Clearly, American cities are sailing into dire financial straits.
10. According to Supreme Court decisions, the freedom of speech guaranteed by the First Amendment is not an absolute right. If the exercise is harmful, then the right can be limited. Therefore, the freedom of religious groups to solicit funds can be constitutionally limited.

Expanding Enthymemes

Traditional logic books, as many of you may know, do not discuss argumentation in Toulmin's terms of claim, grounds, warrant, etc. A more traditional approach is taken, one centering on the way arguments are combined into the syllogism. A syllogism looks something like this:

All men are mortal.
Socrates is a man.
Therefore, Socrates is mortal.

It consists of three propositions; the first two are called premises, and the final one is called the conclusion.

In a debate or in any discussion, you will rarely find people offering syllogisms. Rather, they will be offering what are known as *enthymemes*. Enthymemes are informal syllogisms; they contain or imply the three propositions of a syllogism, however, they are presented in the flow of regular discourse, not "1; 2; therefore, 3." Rhetoricians have, since antiquity, recognized that the use of enthymemes dominates all but the most formal human discussions. Therefore, they have given their students practice in recognizing enthymemes and expanding them into full syllogisms. Why would one want to expand an enthymeme into a syllogism? So that the enthymeme's *full* logic can be seen and examined for flaws that are only noticeable if the argument is expanded into a syllogism.[2]

Consider the following argument: the Soviet Union will not attack Western Europe because of its fear of U.S. nuclear retaliation. The argument is an enthymeme. If expanded into a syllogism, the argument would look like this:

Fear of nuclear retaliation deters aggression.
The U.S.S.R. fears U.S. nuclear retaliation.
Therefore, the U.S.S.R. will not act aggressively toward Western Europe.

When the enthymeme is translated into a syllogism, avenues for refutation can be more readily seen. No matter what kind of syllogism you are dealing with (more on different kinds in a minute), you will want to question the validity of each premise. Treat each premise as a separate argument. Use the general heuristic for refutation to discover how it might be challenged; analyze it using the Toulmin method to discover any flaws in logic that it may possess. You would want to challenge the premises above on a number of counts. For example, an assumption hidden behind the initial premise may be a definition of aggression as "blatant use of force." Recognizing this assumption, you might argue that fear deters only the blatant acts, not the more subtle ones which the Soviet Union and its client states are notorious for. Another example. The second premise's warrant may require far more examples than the one (the Cuban missile crisis of 1962) that the person making the argument has offered. Since the grounds do not meet the requirement of the warrant, the argument can be said to be unwarranted.

When you deal just with the enthymeme, you quite often do not realize quite what the premises are, for they are a bit or totally hidden. When you restate an enthymeme as a syllogism, the premises become evident, and, if they are weak in any way, you can challenge them. Consider the common argument that the United States should cut taxes to encourage savings and investments. When that enthymeme is translated into a syllogism, a premise totally hidden in the argument comes into the open:

All means of increasing the money in the hands of the public will encourage savings and investment.
A tax cut will increase the money.
Therefore, a tax cut will encourage savings and investment.

The first premise, hidden in the enthymeme, demands scrutiny. Do all economists support that principle? Are there conditions under which the principle is invalid—i.e., are there, in Toulmin's terms, rebuttals?

All syllogisms have premises; therefore, no matter what kind of syllogism you are scrutinizing, you should look closely at the premises. Other possible problems will vary from one type of syllogism to another.

Questions to Ask of Categorical Syllogisms. All of the syllogisms we have looked at thus far have been categorical syllogisms. The first premise in a categorical syllogism establishes a characteristic about a class or category, the second premise establishes that a particular person or thing or event belongs in that category, and the conclusion argues that the particular person or thing or event possesses the characteristic of the category. "All men are mortal" establishes that the characteristic of mortality belongs to the category of men, "Socrates is a man" establishes that Socrates belongs in the category of men, and "Socrates is mortal" argues that Socrates possesses the characteristic of mortality.

Quite a few logical problems are common in arguments which take the form of categorical syllogisms. You should look for them. First, the syllogism may be guilty of equivocation. Equivocation occurs when the term common to the two premises means slightly different things in the different premises. Consider the following argument:

Full employment is the goal of the United States economy.
Since the proposal only reduces unemployment to 5.4 percent, it does not achieve full employment.
Therefore, the proposal does not meet the goal.

The crucial term is "full employment." The first premise uses the term in its strict economic sense. In this sense, full employment is theorized to be somewhere between five and six percent unemployment. The second premise uses the term in an everyday sense—i.e., everyone working. The difference in the term's meaning between the first premise and the second invalidates the conclusion.

Second, the syllogism may have an "undistributed" middle term. The middle term is the term which appears in the premises but not in the conclusion, i.e., the category. It is said to be undistributed in the following two syllogisms:

All murders are heinous crimes.
All abortions are heinous crimes.
Therefore, all abortions are murders.

Education is vital to the future of the United States.
Computer literacy is also vital to the future of the United States.
Therefore, computer literacy should be a goal of education.

In the first case, murders are placed in a large category; then abortions are placed in the same large category. We do not know, however, whether murders and abortions occupy different, overlapping, or the same parts of that large category. The parts of the category have yet to be distributed. Therefore, logicians say that the middle or category term is undistributed. The same is true in the second case: education is placed somewhere in the huge category of things vital to the future of the United States, and computer literacy is also placed somewhere in that category. However, the space in that category has not yet been assigned, or distributed. Unless the nonmiddle terms in both arguments occupy the same space within the middle term, or unless the second nonmiddle term occupies space contained within the first, we do not have a valid argument.

Third, the categorical syllogism may exhibit what logicians call "illicit process." This ominous-sounding problem occurs when the conclusion is either more general or more definite than the premises warrant. Look at the two following syllogisms:

Some corrupt labor unions can be prosecuted under a 1963 federal law.
The Widget Makers' Union is corrupt.
Therefore, it can be prosecuted under the 1963 law.

Many famous journalists will do anything to get a story.
John Jones is a famous journalist.
Therefore, he will certainly do anything necessary to get a story.

The initial premise in both cases ascribes a particular quality to some, but not all, members of a class. The conclusions assume that *all* members have been given the characteristic. As a result of this faulty assumption, the arguments present invalid conclusions.

Fourth, the categorical syllogism may get tangled up in negative premises. Look at the following two similar syllogisms:

Federal courts cannot have original jurisdiction over violations of state law.
Racial discrimination is not a violation of state law.
Therefore, federal courts have jurisdiction over cases of racial discrimination.

Federal courts cannot have original jurisdiction over violations of state law.
Murder is a violation of state law.
Therefore, state courts have original jurisdiction over cases of murder.

Both of these arguments may seem valid, but, as presented, they are illogical and therefore invalid. The first argument establishes a characteristic of the category "violations of state law"; the argument then establishes that racial discrimination is not a member of this category. We do not know anything about nonmembers: the characteristic, "no original federal jurisdiction," may be true of all, some, or none of them. We suspect it is the last—*none*, however, without knowing that, we cannot draw the conclusion. The second argument establishes the same characteristic of the same category; then, it establishes that murder is a member of the category. So far, so good. The conclusion could be drawn that "federal courts cannot have original jurisdiction over cases of murder," but the conclusion that "state courts have original jurisdiction" is unjustified. The argument simply does not tell us enough to permit us to logically draw that conclusion.

To avoid the tangles these two syllogisms exhibit, remember two fundamentals of categorical syllogistic reasoning: first, no valid conclusion whatsoever can be drawn from two negative premises; second, no affirmative conclusion can be validly drawn if either of the two premises are negative. So, when constructing an argument, watch out for negative premises, and, when refuting an argument, look closely at any syllogism containing a negative premise or negative premises.

Questions to Ask of Disjunctive Syllogisms. A second type of syllogism is the disjunctive syllogism:

Either the federal government has to provide incentives to encourage college students to go into mathematics teaching or school districts must pay mathematics teachers significantly better.
School districts will not pay significantly better.
Therefore, the federal government must provide incentives.

The first premise in a disjunctive syllogism is an either-or statement, the second premise denies one of the two alternatives, and the conclusion argues for the other alternative. The pattern is a far easier one to grasp than that of the categorical syllogism.

One problem more than any other tends to flaw the disjunctive syllogism: often, the first premise sets up a false dilemma. In the syllogism above, are the two choices mentioned in the initial premise the only two possibilities? Perhaps teachers in other fields could be trained at someone's expense to teach their subject area *and* mathematics. Perhaps private industry, which is so concerned with the inadequacy of mathematics education, can devise some sort of incentive system.

Questions to Ask of Hypothetical Syllogisms. A third type of syllogism is the hypothetical. The following are two examples:

If nuclear power development continues, the safety of millions is in jeopardy.
Nuclear power development shows no sign of slowing.
Therefore, the safety of millions is in jeopardy.
If the President claims national security is in danger, he can commit U.S. troops without prior congressional approval.
The President will claim national security is in danger if Soviet, Cuban, and Nicaraguan aid to leftist forces in El Salvador increases.
Therefore, he will be able to commit U.S. troops to El Salvador without seeking prior congressional approval.

Again, the syllogism has two premises and a conclusion. The first premise sets up a condition and a consequent: if the condition is met, then the consequent follows. The second premise affirms the condition, and the conclusion affirms the consequent. This syllogism embodies a fairly simple logical pattern.

Two problems are common in reasoning using hypothetical syllogisms. Both problems occur when a debater does not follow the pattern. For example, what if the second premise affirmed the consequent. Would it be logical to infer that the condition was met? No, but some debaters will try to argue as follows:

Arab nations have said they'd back down from their oil price demands only if the United States changed its pro-Israel stance significantly. The lower oil prices mean that the United States has weakened its support of Israel.

Expanded into syllogistic form, this enthymeme would have the following form:

If the United States changes its pro-Israel stance significantly, then Arab nations will lower their oil price demands.
Arab nations have lowered their oil price demands.
Therefore, the United States must have changed its pro-Israel stance significantly.

The second premise affirms the consequent, and the conclusion argues that the affirmation of the consequent affirms the condition. This reasoning is fallacious *except* when the condition is an "if and only if" condition. Such exclusive conditions are, however, very rare in public policy discussions where numerous human factors make such exclusivity or definitiveness impossible.

The other problem with the hypothetical syllogism occurs when the second premise denies the condition and the conclusion denies the consequent, as in the following:

If the federal gasoline tax were defined as a percentage of the price of gasoline, not as a fixed dollar amount, then the federal government would have enough money to maintain the national highway system.
Congress, however, will not pass such a tax.
Therefore, the government will not have enough money to do the job.

The reasoning is flawed because there may well be other avenues open to the federal government to obtain the necessary funds for highway maintenance. The reasoning would hold only under an "if and only if" condition.

Exercises: Challenging Arguments III

Expand the following enthymemes into syllogisms; then, examine the syllogisms for weak premises and other logical problems.

1. Either we send our children to school twelve months a year, eight hours a day, as the Soviets do, *or* we surrender the future to the Soviets. Since no one seems to support more intensive education—not school boards, not teachers, not voters, certainly not children—I say we're already waving the white flag.

2. Nations must defend themselves against their enemies. Japan is certainly the American automobile industry's enemy. The United States should recognize this fact and adopt defensive measures such as quotas and duties.
3. Religious leaders said years ago that sex education would lead to promiscuity among the school-aged. Promiscuity is rampant; sex education must have caused it. Those religious leaders were right!
4. Several members of Congress told former President Carter that if he cut funds to boondoggle water projects in their districts or states, they would vote against him on key economic legislation. The record shows they voted against the President when this legislation came up. He must have put a stop to those wasteful water projects.
5. Public Broadcasting System programs are always superior to the regular network offerings. "Hill Street Blues" is an NBC show; it must be a waste of time to watch it.
6. The Supreme Court is supposed to protect constitutional rights. A woman's "right to regulate her body" is not a constitutional one. Therefore, the Supreme Court should not deal with any cases that talk about this right.
7. The courts have yet to decide if a company is responsible for the damage done by its waste products, if those products are disposed of in accordance with existing law. If the courts decide against industry, many companies will go bankrupt; if they decide for industry, many Americans will suffer financial ruin since the equity they had in their homes will disappear overnight. Given the conservative orientation of the Supreme Court at present, a proindustry decision is inevitable. Therefore, the total ruin of innocent Americans is imminent.
8. Conscientious objectors to military service should offer the nation some peaceful alternative service.
9. Men and women are equal. Therefore, they should share equally in the responsibilities of citizenship, including the responsibility to defend the nation in armed conflict.
10. Federal programs which are wasteful should, of course, be abolished. The space program is not wasteful: it brings the United States glory and it provides valuable information to science. Therefore, it should be continued.

Charting the Structure of Argumentation

Enthymemes and their implied syllogisms tie a number of arguments together in small packages. The packages argumentation comes in are usually larger. Consider an affirmative case where many arguments are tied together to justify a particular policy or a particular prepolicy value judgment. Quite often, understanding the interconnections among arguments is valuable. For example, if one argument in a cluster of six offered by an opponent is so interconnected to the others that its defeat would defeat all, wouldn't you want to have *that* information?

Applied logicians speak about there being four possible kinds of connections between arguments. Each of these kinds of connections can be diagrammed so as to make the relationship clear.

Serial Structure.   First, arguments may be related serially. If a debater is trying to prove that the President's sending aid to Guatemala over the objections of Congress will lead to difficulties for the President, the argument would probably be serial in structure:

[1] If the President ignores Congressional opposition and gives military assistance, [2] he will alienate several key members of Congress [3] who will, in turn, block tax legislation the President feels is crucial to economic recovery.

The three arguments, indicated by the superscripts at their beginnings, follow one after the other. Diagrammed, the serial structure of the argument would look like the following:

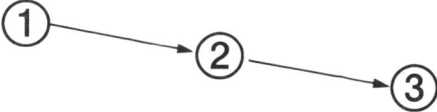

Divergent Structure.   Second, two arguments may both flow from a preceding argument. In this case, the structure is said to be divergent. If a debater is arguing that [1] FBI wiretapping of suspected subversives will lead to [2] no increase in national security as well as [3] a chilling effect on all intellectual exchanges on political matters, the argument would have the following divergent structure:

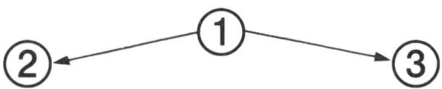

Linked Structure.   Third, two (or more) arguments may be linked together so that a subsequent argument flows from a combination of the arguments, not any one separately. If a debater argues that [1] an increase in defense spending coupled with [2] no cuts in domestic programs will lead to [3] a significant amount of inflation, he or she will be using a linked structure:

Convergent Structure. Fourth, two (or more) arguments may converge to prove a point. In this case, as opposed to the linked structure, each converging argument could independently serve as proof of the point; however, the convergence of two or more separate arguments makes the proof more certain. If a debater argued that [1] high wages to airline personnel and [2] the high cost of jet fuel are causing [3] ticket prices to go up, he or she is using a convergent structure:

Once the use of a particular structure is discovered, the debater whose job it is to challenge the argument should be alert to each structure's weakness. An argument with a serial structure can be defeated if *any* link is beaten. An argument with a divergent structure can be beaten if the situation which leads to all the others is shown not to exist—in the case above, if the FBI can be shown to be not engaging in wiretapping or if the argument that the FBI is engaging in the wiretapping of suspected subversives can be called into doubt. An argument in a linked structure can be beaten if any one of the linked arguments is defeated. An argument in a convergent structure can be *weakened* if one of the converging arguments is beaten; it can be beaten only if all converging arguments are defeated, *or* if the supposed convergent structure can be argued to really be a linked structure.

An Example of Charting. Let's consider a sample argument. It will be a relatively brief one used by a debater discussing the right to privacy:

[1] In order to be considered for credit—whether it be at a local store or a state-wide bank, [2] you have to waive your right to privacy. [3] You can maintain that right; however, [4] to do so, you must give up all hope of engaging in a normal commercial life and [5] lose out on the necessities, conveniences, and luxuries available to other Americans with comparable financial means.

Arguments (1) and (2) are related to each other serially; so are arguments (3), (4), and (5). What is the relationship between the strings of arguments beginning with (2) and (3)? The debater's words suggest that they are *two* choices and, furthermore, that the choice is unfair. Let's label this last implicit argument (6), and complete our charting of the overall argument:

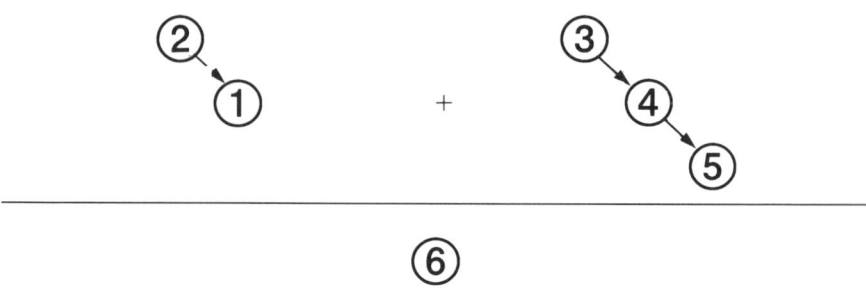

Seeing this structure provides the debater attempting to refute with a strategy: beat either string, and beat the chosen string by beating any link. In other words, if the debater defeats argument (4), the whole argument falls!

The reasons for charting should, I hope, be obvious. Arguments in prose lack the sharp clarity of arguments that have been diagrammed. The logical structure becomes evident, and, as it becomes evident, so do avenues to refute the argument.

Exercises: Challenging Arguments IV

Analyze the structure of the following arguments. With the argument's chart before you, pinpoint places where the argument seems especially vulnerable.

1. Jobs programs, if they are not coupled with strong government and news publicity on the work's necessity, tend to demoralize the workers who take the positions.
2. Developers who convert apartment buildings into condominiums are often acting irresponsibly: they make "a killing" and, at the same time, lose nothing when the building begins to deteriorate with age. Buyers see their investment turn sour and have no legal recourse as long as the developer provides minimal maintenance. The problem is worsened by the fact that the majority of the residents are elderly and unwilling or financially unable to seek redress in court.
3. The minerals buried in the open ocean are resources belonging to the entire world. Therefore, the technologically advanced nations should not be allowed to mine these resources unless they are willing to provide financial compensation to the undeveloped nations. If the developed nations go ahead and mine without providing compensation, then the undeveloped nations would be justified in taking all necessary action, including terrorism, against the offenders.
4. The newspapers must be free to seek the truth. The courts have undermined that freedom by requiring reporters to reveal their sources and to pay fines or spend days in jail if they will not. These actions will cause reporters to be careful in what they write and sources to be reluctant to speak to reporters who pledge confidentiality. Truth will suffer and, with it, our nation.

5. The expected increase in the price of gasoline between now and 1995 will reverse employment patterns which developed in the 1960s and 1970s. People will now move closer to their place of work. This trend will result in the revival of the residential areas close to business districts; this trend will also result in the development of work place-living place complexes in surburbia. Both of these trends will combine to weaken the "old" suburbs, which are already showing signs of becoming the slums of the future.

After reading and studying Chapter 6, you know:

- that, when confronting an argument, you can (1) concede the point, (2) concede the point with qualifications, (3) challenge assumptions underlying the argument, (4) ask for evidence of a specific kind, (5) deny the argument and offer a counterargument, (6) challenge the evidence—in ten different ways, or (7) challenge the logic—in ten different ways;
- how to use the classical *topoi* to generate possible counterarguments;
- how to analyze the logic of argumentation by:
    —using the method recommended by rhetorician-logician Stephen Toulmin and dividing an argument into its claim, grounds, warrant, backing, modality, and rebuttals and then looking for certain common flaws;
    —expanding enthymemes into categorical, hypothetical or disjunctive syllogisms and then looking for certain common flaws;
    —charting the structure of a large argument, relating the component arguments in the large argument to each other in one of four possible ways.

Notes

1. See Stephen Toulmin et al., *An Introduction to Reasoning*, New York: Macmillan, 1979.
2. See Edward P. J. Corbett, *Classical Rhetoric for the Modern Student*, 2nd ed., New York: Oxford University Press, 1971, pp. 56-72.

CHAPTER 7

The Negative Task I

In this chapter, you will learn:

- how to adopt three conventional negative strategies for challenging an affirmative case and follow them in refuting the standard types of affirmative cases in policy debate;
- how to offer a counterplan in policy debate;
- how to respond to the net benefits and alternative justifications approaches in policy debate;
- how to refute the affirmative case for the three different kinds of value resolutions;
- what observations properly are and what the common observations of topicality and justification are.

The fundamental skill required of debaters who oppose the adoption of the resolution is *thinking*. Chapter 6 introduced you to several heuristics to help you engage in precisely the kind of thinking necessary when you take the negative side in a debate. With those heuristics available to you, with plenty of practice using them before you enter competition, and with a small amount of thinking time before you speak, you should be able to come up with plenty of intelligent arguments to offer in response to the affirmative case.

You could expand an enthymeme the affirmative team has offered into a full syllogism and show the judge how an unvoiced premise—a hidden assumption—is invalid and crucial. Or you could examine an affirmative contention in the manner logician-rhetorician Stephen Toulmin recommends and discover that the *warrant* which allegedly justifies the jump from evidence or *grounds* to the *claim* is inadequate. You could show the judge this logical weakness and easily convince him or her that the entire affirmative contention falls. Or you could challenge the affirmative team's evidence in a variety of ways. Or you could deny the affirmative contention and offer a counterstatement based on the *topos* of "definition—genus + differentia."

Having studied Chapter 6, you have plenty of options. Many negative debaters simply stand up and hesitantly say "No" or "Prove it." Or they repeat the same stock challenges in debate after debate rather than specifically addressing the affirmative case. You, however, have many thoughtful, relevant arguments to present. Do, however, remember to present them fully—so that the judge understands your reasoning completely. Also remember to relate them to the specific affirmative case you are refuting.

Armed with all these arguments, are you ready to debate on the negative? Not yet. Debating is not just affirmative argument and negative refutation. Just as there were rules and procedures governing the structuring of the affirmative case, there are rules and procedures governing the negative team's task. Chapter 4, "The Affirmative Case," should have indicated to you how new theories and strategies are constantly being introduced into the art of debating and are affecting these rules and procedures. Well, there are even more innovations—and controversies—when we turn to the negative task. So be attentive!

The Negative Team as Policy Advocates: Judicial versus Legislative Paradigms

The history of debating has never been written. The records of the earliest intercollegiate debates in this country *seem* to indicate that they were modelled on criminal trials. Perhaps the use by many students of debating as prelaw preparation dictated or encouraged the use of this model.

In a criminal trial, the defendant is accused. The prosecutor tries to prove the indictment valid and calls for conviction and punishment: the defense attorney tries to refute the indictment. If he or she can cast any doubt on the accusation—by challenging logic, by questioning the evidence, by offering a counterexplanation of the facts of the case, then the defendant is declared by judge or jury to be "not guilty." A debate is similar: the affirmative accuses the status quo and calls for the adoption of a specific plan to solve the problem with the status quo; the negative team tries to refute the indictment. If the negative can cast any doubt on that indictment, the status quo is declared to be unimpeached and the change the affirmative has proposed is not justified. Like the defendant in a criminal trial, the status quo is presumed innocent unless proven guilty beyond a reasonable doubt.

The analogy between debate and criminal prosecution has long served as a paradigm, i.e., a theoretical model. Your student government probably has the U.S. federal government–or a simplified version of it—as its paradigm. Most scientific research follows an established theoretical model known as "the scientific method"; this method is scientific research's paradigm. Scientists, student legislators, and debaters refer to their paradigm when explaining what they do and why they do it; they also refer to their paradigm when evaluating new ideas.

Many recently suggested innovations do not fit the time-honored judicial paradigm for debating. Rather than reject these new ideas, however, many in debating have called for a new paradigm. Debating deals, they argue, with public policy, and public policy is rarely made in the courtroom. The authentic setting for public policy debate is the legislature; therefore, a better paradigm for debating than the criminal trial would be the legislative process.

If debating embraces this new paradigm, what then? Well, in legislative assemblies, there is no presumption in favor of the innocence of the status quo. There may be a presumption against unnecessary or unwarranted change, but this presumption is far easier for a policy advocate to overcome than the "beyond a shadow of a doubt" presumption protecting the status quo under the judicial paradigm. If there is a shift to the legislative paradigm, then the affirmative team's job of advocating the resolution will be easier. Also, in legislative assemblies, opponents of a proposed policy rarely get away with simply refuting. The colleagues of legislators—and their constituents—want to know what these opposing legislators advocate, not simply what they object to. Opponents of proposed legislation usually must opt for *some* policy alternative, even if it is the continuation of the present policy. If there is a shift to the legislative paradigm in debating, then the negative team will find certain traditional strategies no longer viable. The next sections of this chapter should make the strategic consequences of this paradigm shift clear.

Comparable to a paradigm shift is the shift many debaters have made from policy resolutions to value resolutions. Debaters discussing the second kind of resolution are advocating judgments which may eventually lead to action or policy. Deciding which is of greater value, environmental protection or energy availability, will lead one to embrace one sort of policy as opposed to another sort. Deciding if a foreign aid policy that would further the respect for human rights is desirable or not will lead one very quickly to embrace a certain sort of policy. However, the affirming or denying of a value judgment is not a policy decision. Therefore, for value debate, some nonpolicy-oriented paradigm seems necessary. No such paradigm yet exists. What exists are modifications of the strategies and procedures used in policy debate.

More on negative strategies for debating value resolutions much later in this chapter. First, let's look at the standard negative strategies which have evolved through the years in policy resolution debate.

Going "Straight Negative"; Defending the Status Quo

Going "straight negative" is at present an unpopular negative strategy in policy debate. If you were to adopt this once very popular strategy in a particular debate, you would simply refute all the contentions the affirmative had offered. You might show problems with the affirmative team's discussion of causality; you might probe their arguments for *modalities* and *rebuttals* that might not have been obvious to the judge at first hearing. Your point in all this refutation would be to demonstrate that the affirmative had not made its case for the adoption of the resolution. If you followed this "straight negative" strategy, you would be totally in line with the traditional judicial paradigm.

If the judge strongly believes that the judicial paradigm is a poor model *or* if the affirmative strongly insists that you offer some alternative policy, then you will find the "straight negative" strategy awkward. It will be awkward because you will spend almost as much time defending your paradigm and your strategy as you will arguing against the affirmative case. Therefore, when the judge strongly believes in the legislative paradigm or when the affirmative team strongly pushes you to accept it, you would probably be better off abandoning the "straight negative" strategy. If you abandon it, you have several options. You can adopt three fairly traditional strategies that *both* paradigms seem to permit: 1) defending the status quo; 2) defending the status quo with minor repairs; 3) offering a traditional counterplan. You can also become as fervent in support of the legislative paradigm as some affirmative teams are, and opt for some newer strategies which have evolved as more and more coaches and debaters have made this paradigm shift (more on these newer strategies later in this chapter).

The first and most traditional of the three strategies possible under both paradigms is defense of the status quo. Because it is as traditional as the "straight negative" strategy, it shares much with it. Therefore, I will discuss the two strategies together.

Before I discuss how to use these two strategies to counter the standard affirmative case structures presented in Chapter 4, let me explain precisely what it means to defend the status quo.

The affirmative team always presents a problem. The problem can be of different kinds. The status quo could be harming the poor, or the status quo could be inefficient, or the status quo could be failing to meet important foreign policy goals. The affirmative may never use the word "problem." No matter: the affirmative always presents—explicitly or implicitly—some problem as a justification for a new policy. Even when the affirmative team argues that their proposed policy has certain benefits, they are implying that the status quo is flawed because it fails to produce these benefits. That flaw and that failure are a problem.

When the negative team opts to defend the status quo, it argues that the status quo either does not have or can solve the problem. The defense of the status quo is usually not the entirety of the negative team's position; usually, a negative team will mix elements of the "straight negative" strategy with the defense of the status quo. In this case, the negative stance sounds like one of the following:

Contrary to what the affirmative team says, the status quo is not flawed. Let's look at the evidence they used to support their claim.

The affirmative team has not demonstrated that there is a problem. However, if there were a problem, then the status quo could solve it.

These statements reflect a combination of the "straight negative" and the "defense of the status quo" stances. How do you, a negative debater, take these stances in particular debates? Well, let's look at the standard affirmative case structures and see how you would challenge each kind of case.

Challenging the "Needs Case"

Just as you will have to generate telling refutation round after round, you will have to confront the standard case structures round after round. What you should do in response to them will become very obvious to you after considerable practice. Right now, you need heuristics to help you ask the important questions, just as you needed heuristics to aid you in generating refutation. Figure 7.1 is a heuristic for refuting the "Needs Case." It focuses on the three obligations an affirmative team using this case has. That affirmative team must demonstrate that there exists a significant problem; so you, the negative debater, question the problem's existence and significance. That affirmative team must demonstrate that the problem brings about serious harms; so you question the harms: Do they stem from the problem? Are they indeed serious? Are they mitigated by any benefits? That particular affirmative team must demonstrate that the status quo cannot solve the problem—that the problem is inherent in the status quo; so you question whether the affirmative's examination of the status quo is accurate. *Significance, Harms, Inherency*: these are your three focal points when objecting to the "Needs Case." The heuristic offers subquestions under the three focal questions. These subquestions are very important. Consider the following negative arguments:

1. The affirmative has not shown us a serious harm.
2. The affirmative has not shown us a compelling harm. They must quantify the harm they point to.
3. The affirmative has not shown us a compelling harm. They tried to quantify it. However, the amount of money they said the nation lost, although it *sounds* large, equals only 1.3 percent of federal spending. If we are to accept the risk of adopting an untried policy, we need a more compelling reason than this rather small loss.

Which argument is the most telling? The third, of course. Many beginning debaters offer the first—in debate after debate; many slightly more experienced debaters realize (through experience) that simply asking the affirmative for quantification of its harm can lead to negative wins if the affirmative team then fails to quantify it and offer the second—in debate after debate. Using this heuristic, you should be able to generate arguments as fully developed as the third. Of course, the arguments will develop along different lines in confrontation with different "Needs Cases." The quantification of the harm will not be a relevant or important issue in every confrontation.

Given a "Needs Case," you should ask:
1. Is the problem significant?
   a. Does it affect a large number of people?
   b. Are the cited examples numerically significant?
2. Are the harms compelling?
   a. Do they necessarily stem from the problem?
   b. If quantifiable, have they been suitably quantified?
   c. Does the quantification strike you as significant?
      i. In relation to total federal spending?
      ii. In relation to Exxon profits?
      iii. In relation to the number of lives lost in traffic accidents?
   d. If not quantifiable, have a sufficient number of authorities testified to the harms' significance?
   e. Are the harms mitigated by any benefits?
3. Can the status quo solve the problem?
   a. What laws stand in the solution's way?
   b. What decision-making structures stand in the solution's way?
   c. What attitudes stand in the solution's way? Are these attitudes held by those who might solve the problem?
   d. Could these barriers be easily overcome?
      i. By "education"?
      ii. By political pressure?
      iii. By *minor* changes in procedure or law?

Figure 7.1 Heuristic for refuting the "Needs Case."

Before we move on and discuss how to respond to the "Comparative Advantages Case," let's use this heuristic for refuting the "Needs Case" once together.

Let's say the affirmative case talks about the increasing costs of postsecondary education for the children in an average American family. The heuristic's use might give you the following answers:

1. Yes. Over forty-five percent of American high school graduates go on to college; seventy-eight percent of these are from middle- or lower-class families.
2. The alleged harms do stem from the high cost; however, the affirmative team has not quantified the harm. They have said how much college costs, but *not* how paying the bill harms the family's finances. And, even if there were some harm, it would be mitigated by the tangible and intangible benefits the student gains.
3. The status quo could solve the problem if loan programs and other federal government aid are maintained at the present level. The present administration and Congress are, according to the affirmative, opposed to maintaining these programs, *but* the affirmative has not shown the firmness of these attitudes in the face of political pressure from the families of college-bound children. This pressure will exist if the affirmative is correct about the cost of college causing serious financial problems.

Before I formulated the answer to the focal question, I looked at and studied the subquestions. Not all were relevant in this case. Some were not only relevant but fruitful—pointing to how the affirmative case ought to be attacked. (2b), (2e), and (3d) proved especially fruitful.

If you were to launch assaults growing out of the heuristic's first and second questions, you could be either going "straight negative" or defending the status quo. Negative debaters taking either stance could offer all the lines of argumentation suggested by the subquestions under (1) and (2). However, when it comes to focal question (3), the two negative stances part company: debaters taking the "straight negative" stance would phrase their argument one way; debaters defending the status quo another. The rare "straight negative" debater simply argues that the affirmative team *has not demonstrated* that the status quo is incapable of solving the problem. The negative debater who is defending the status quo, on the other hand, argues that the status quo *can solve* the problem. The difference might seem trivial to you, but the distinction is worth keeping in mind, for the second position, although far stronger, requires evidence on the negative team's part whereas the first simply requires forceful analyzing, questioning, and challenging.

Challenging the "Comparative Advantages Case"

As you discovered in Chapter 3, the "Comparative Advantages Case" places demands on the affirmative different from those that stem from the "Needs Case." A negative team, if called upon to debate a "Comparative Advantages Case," must adjust to these differences. Figure 7.2 is a heuristic for refuting the "Comparative Advantages" affirmative. If you use it, you will be forcing the affirmative team to meet the particular responsibilities they shouldered when they selected their case structure.

When presenting a "Comparative Advantages Case," the affirmative must, rather obviously, present advantages. Some plans will be advantageous because they solve a specifically stated problem; others because they perform better (i.e., overcome an adminstrative problem). Both of these types of advantage—solving an explicitly stated problem or overcoming inefficiency—imply that a problem exists. Under focal question (1), you question that problem. You question the problem implicit in *each* advantage! Has the affirmative demonstrated that such a problem exists? Is the status quo problem-ridden, as the affirmative claims? (The difference in phrasing between these two questions is the difference between the "straight negative" and the "defense of the status quo" stances.) The negative should also ask if each problem is significant. Keep in mind that the problem may not be as significant as the problems discussed in a "Needs Case" and still be a valid starting point for a "Comparative Advantages Case."

Under the *very* important second focal question, you question every advantage's significance, topicality, and uniqueness. All advantages must be demonstrably significant: push the affirmative team to make this demonstration. All advantages

Given a "Comparative Advantages Case," you should ask:
1. Is there a problem?
   a. Has the affirmative demonstrated that a problem exists? Has the affirmative demonstrated that the status quo is problem-ridden or inefficient?
   b. Is the problem/inefficiency significant?
      i. Does it affect a large number of people?
      ii. Does it cost a large amount of money?
      iii. Are the cited examples numerically significant?
2. For each advantage:
   a. Is the advantage *significant*? Can the difference between the affirmative plan and the status quo or negative policy be quantified?
   b. Does the advantage flow from the adoption of the resolution? Is it *topical*?
   c. Is the advantage *unique* to the affirmative plan? Could the status quo claim the advantage in equal measure?
3. Are the advantages *independent*? If not, how are they related to each other and to the plan? Is one advantage a "keystone," upon which all of the others depend?

Figure 7.2 Heuristic for refuting the "Comparative Advantages Case."

must stem from the adoption of the resolution. If the advantage (e.g., a fairer taxation system) could be gained by adopting a plank of the affirmative plan (e.g., funding by federal income tax revenue rather than by state sales tax revenue) without adopting the resolution (e.g., the upgrading of secondary education in the United States), then the advantage is extratopical and the negative can concede it without wavering from its insistence that the resolution be rejected. All advantages must stem from the adoption of the resolution *and not* from the maintenance of the status quo. If the advantage (e.g., a stronger civil defense system) could also be obtained under the status quo, then the advantage is *not unique* to the affirmative plan. Only unique advantages justify the adoption of the resolution. There are two ways to voice this uniqueness argument: (1) "The affirmative has not shown why the status quo cannot gain the advantage" or "The affirmative's arguments designed to show why the status quo cannot gain the advantage are flawed" (in specific ways, which you would specify), *or* (2) "The status quo *can* gain the advantage; therefore, it is not unique to the affirmative plan." The difference between the two approaches is the difference—again— between the "straight negative" strategy and the "defense of the status quo" strategy. The second, although the stronger position, does require more evidence on the part of the negative speaker.

One other focal question is listed on the heuristic for refuting the "Comparative Advantages Case." Affirmative teams using the "Comparative Advantages Case" usually claim that their four advantages are "independent." They make this claim for a strategic reason: if the advantages are indeed independent, then the affirmative only has to win one to justify the adoption of the resolution and win the debate. Is the affirmative's claim always accurate? No—often, the word "independent" is just tossed into the presentation of the advantages in the first affirmative's constructive speech because the writer heard it used in debates and feels it makes his or her presentation sound more impressive. So, by all means, ask yourself if the advantages are indeed independent. The best way to ask yourself the question is to examine the structure of the cluster of arguments the affirmative has offered under the rubric "Advantages." Examine it using the charting procedure we discussed in Chapter 6.

Is the cluster of arguments a divergent structure? This is the question you should ask. Be especially careful of the following two common structures. In all cases, P is the affirmative plan and 1, 2, 3, and 4 are the four advantages.

Case One: P→1→2→3→4

Case Two: P→1 and $\frac{P + 1}{2}$ and $\frac{P + 1}{3}$ and $\frac{P + 1}{4}$

In Case One, the advantages are not independent. The first advantage flows from the adoption of the plan, but the second flows from the first advantage and the third flows from the second advantage and the fourth flows from the third advantage. To defeat *all* advantages, the negative needs only defeat the first.

In Case Two, the advantages are again not independent. The first advantage flows from the plan, but all of the others flow from a necessary combination of the plan and the first advantage. To defeat *all* advantages, the negative needs only defeat the first. The negative, however, would be wise in both cases to challenge all four advantages, just in case the judge does not accept your analysis of the advantages' argumentative structure.

If the advantages are indeed independent, the structure would be a divergent one:

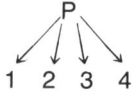

Many advantages claimed to be independent are not, so check the affirmative's claims by examining their argument's structure.

The heuristic for challenging the "Comparative Advantages Case" compels you to focus on the crucial issues in a debate which the affirmative begins by offering such a case. Of the three focal questions, the second is the most crucial. By choosing the "Comparative Advantages Case" structure, the affirmative team has decided to make their claim of an advantage over the status quo *the* big issue. Make sure you devote most of your time to the advantages they have offered, their significance, topicality, and uniqueness.

Challenging the "Goals Case"

The "Goals Case" is fairly rare. It is, however, a good strategic choice for an affirmative team for the several reasons discussed in Chapter 4. Another reason is that many negative debaters do not know how to challenge it well.

If you are confronted with a "Goals Case," remember that it has three equally important parts: the goals, the evaluation of the status quo, and the evaluation of the affirmative plan. Figure 7.3, another heuristic, helps you focus on these three parts.

If any of the three parts is most important, it is the first. The affirmative states the goal or goals a particular policy should meet. The U.S. defense policy should meet certain goals; so should the federal programs designed to assure that every American receives his minimal nutritional needs every day. These goals set up the entire debate, and a shrewd affirmative team chooses the goals strategically so that the debate starts off and remains on strong affirmative ground. Therefore, the negative team *must* question them. The subquestions under focal question (1) should help you in this questioning.

You look for *False Goals*, *Trivial Goals*, and *Ignored Goals*. An affirmative team might try to tell you that they can set the goals just as they define the resolution's key terms. If they argue this, they very seriously misunderstand

---

Given a "Goals Case" ask:

1. Are the goals valid ones?
    a. Are some claimed goals not really goals?
    b. Are some claimed goals not particularly important goals?
    c. Are genuine goals ignored?
        i. Does the status quo meet these goals?
        ii. Does the affirmative plan?
    d. How are the given goals weighted? Be careful: the weighting may be implicit.
        i. Do you agree with the weighting?
        ii. How does a more accurate weighting affect the case's indictment of the status quo?
2. Is the evaluation of the status quo an accurate one?
    a. Has the status quo always failed to meet the goals? If not, has it failed in enough cases to warrant a change?
    b. Has the failure been the result of some force or variable which will equally affect the proposed plan?
    c. Are the goals more ideals than attainable realities?
3. Is the evaluation of the affirmative plan a believable one?
    a. Is the logic linking plan to goal valid? Strong?
    b. Is the evidence supporting the affirmative prediction strong? Sufficient?
    c. Do extratopical planks in the plan lead to the meeting of the goals?

Figure 7.3 Heuristic for refuting the "Goals Case."

their responsibilities: the goals are *the core* of a debate which a "Goals Case" kicks off and they *are subject to challenge*.

Besides looking for goals that are not goals, goals that are unimportant, and goals that were not mentioned, you must question the weighting assigned the affirmative's goals if the affirmative presents a set of goals. Perhaps the affirmative signalled this weighting by phrases such as "most important" and "still more crucial"; perhaps the weighting is implicit in their ordering of the goals, with the last and first most prominent and, therefore, most significant. Does the affirmative's weighting seem fair? Consider the following goals for a privately sponsored and funded retirement plan a company is considering:

1. Give the employees a voice in the investment of employee-contributed retirement funds;
2. Pass retirement benefits on to heirs if the employee dies before retirement age;
3. Provide an annual retirement income equal to eighty percent of the employee's income before retirement;
4. Cost the company as little as possible;
5. Provide activities for the retired employee.

No signals were given by the affirmative team in listing these goals 1-2-3-4-5, yet the ordering of the goals suggests that providing postretirement activities and giving a voice in the investing of the pension funds are very important.

How can this *implicit* weighting affect the evaluation of the status quo or the plan? Let's assign weights to the goals, 5 to (5); 4 to (1); 2 to (2), (3), and (4). These weights are in keeping with the rhetorical principle of Nestorian order discussed in Chapter 4. Let's assign points, 1 through 5, to two different retirement plans. The first is a very lucrative, but rather traditional plan. It gives employees no voice at all: 1 point; it passes benefits to heirs with limitations: 3 points; it provides a retirement income equal to eighty-two percent of that before retirement: 5 points; it costs the company relatively little: 4 points; it provides no organized activities for the post-retirement period: 1 point. Total: 14 without weighting; 33 with. The second is a newer model. It gives the employees control over pension fund investments: 5 points; it passes benefits to heirs with very few limitations: 3 points; it provides an income equal to fifty-eight percent of one's present income: 1 point; it costs the company a fair amount: 2 points; and it provides low-cost, fully guided tours on a monthly basis for retirees: 5 points. Total: 16 without weighting; 57 with. The selected criteria themselves tilt the evaluation in favor of the second, more innovative plan; however, when the implicit weighting is considered, the extent of the evaluation's proinnovation bias is seen. Is the second plan nearly twice as good as the first? Most people would question whether it is even better. The third criterion is far more important, in most people's minds, than the implicit weighting suggests.

If you accept the affirmative goals and their weighting, you could be in serious trouble in the debate. Look for false goals, trivial goals, and ignored goals, and question the weighting when more than one goal is offered.

After spending some time questioning the goals, question the two evaluations the affirmative team has offered. First, the affirmative must evaluate the status quo in terms of the goals it has established. The heuristic offers you three important subquestions to ask of this evaluation. Has the status quo always failed to meet the goal? If not, has it failed enough times to warrant a change? Has the failure been the result of some force, perhaps the economy, in the face of which both the status quo and plan are equally baffled? Is the goal an unrealistic ideal or something genuinely unattainable?

The difference between the "straight negative" stance and the "defense of the status quo" stance in response to a "goals case" is small, but important. Whereas the "straight negative"—in response to the first subquestion—would argue that the affirmative had not demonstrated the failure of the status quo, the negative debater defending the status quo would argue that it had not failed.

The second evaluation the affirmation must offer is of their plan. Again, the affirmative marches one-by-one past the goal(s). The heuristic offers you questions to ask of this evaluation.

One strategic problem could arise in a debate if you follow my advice. *If* you have challenged the affirmative's goal(s), do you then attack their evaluation as it was presented? If you do, you might seem to be contradicting yourself—rejecting the goals only to turn around and talk about them. What should you do? Answer: force the affirmative team to debate on your grounds.

Let's say the affirmative offers you six goals for a college curriculum. Let's say you reject #2 as false and #1 as trivial; let's say you believe that another goal—let's call it #7—must be included and that the correct weighting isn't 6-1-2-3-4-5, as the affirmative implies, but 7-3-4-5-6. What do you do?

You say that you are dismissing #2 and #1 and refer to your previous arguments against those goals; then you treat the remaining goals and #7 in *your* order. Introduce the evaluation versus the first goal you want to discuss with a "very important"; introduce the evaluation versus the middle goals with "in addition"; and introduce the evaluation versus the last goal you want to discuss with "and most crucially." If the affirmative tries to return the debate to their list of goals (as they should try to), you return it at first opportunity to yours.

Defending the Status Quo with Repairs

When you adopt the traditional "straight negative" strategy, you simply point out inadequacies in the affirmative argumentation. When you choose to defend the status quo, you insist, as a counterargument to the affirmative's argument, that the status quo is successful, not flawed. These two strategies are similar, as we have seen, because the second usually incorporates the first.

That second strategy's counterargument, however, is not the easiest to uphold, for rarely is the status quo without *some* defect. Not all defects, however, mandate that a policy be scrapped: slightly defective policies can be repaired, just as cars with a leaking radiator can be repaired. In recognition of the possibility of repairing rather than scrapping the status quo, more and more negative teams in the 1960s and 1970s opted to defend the status quo with minor repairs.

This strategy, possible under both judicial and legislative paradigms, begins with an admission that the status quo, as it operates, does pose a problem. Usually, the problem is minimized as much as possible. To take care of this minimal problem (the negative team would argue), the affirmative plan is not necessary; only minor repairs to the status quo are.

What is a *minor* repair? There is no definite answer to this troublesome question. I would offer the following guidelines: a repair is minor if (1) the change is in how a program operates, not in its purpose; (2) the status quo seems capable of having its machinery so repaired with relative ease; (3) adopting the repair is not equivalent to adopting the resolution. If, for example, the affirmative argued that revenue sharing is needed to combat rural poverty and that all the stipulations surrounding present antipoverty grants tie them to urban areas, then the negative team might say that the problem is merely a technical one and propose that the present grants be consolidated and revised so as to have fewer "strings," strings which seem to tie them to urban areas. The repair the negative proposes is in the operation of the federal antipoverty program; the repair does not set up new goals (the goal is still to fight poverty) or new programs. The status quo features many block grants similar to the one the negative suggests. Since "few strings" block grants are part of the status quo, the repair can be argued to be an easily made one. And the repair does not inadvertently adopt a system of revenue sharing and, thereby, inadvertently adopt the resolution.

Be careful when using the "repairs" strategy. Do not, in other words, go with *just* it. Why? Because an affirmative team might convince a sympathetic judge that your repair is substantial enough to really be a counterplan (for which there are special rules). A good strategy would mix the three strategies discussed thus far:

Rural poverty is a minor problem resulting in few tangible harms (straight negative), harms which the status-quo's antipoverty programs can and are taking care of (defense of the status quo). But *if* these programs were impeded from fully doing their job by stipulations, then we could easily repair the status quo by converting them into a single, "few strings" block grant.

Exercises: Refuting the Affirmative Case

Identify the case structure the affirmative is using in the following situations. Based on that identification, select the correct heuristic and plan your negative strategy. The heuristics in Chapter 6 might also prove helpful.

1. Strikes in basic industries (fuel, minerals, rubber, transportation) harm the economy. Collective bargaining and federal mediation do not solve the problem: they offer no guarantee of settlement and they allow harms to continue. Therefore, we need a law declaring strikes illegal and establishing compulsory arbitration.
2. The cost of medical care is soaring. The present system of private insurance and federally funded programs encourages inflated bills because doctors and hospitals are paid on the basis of services rendered. A system of regional Health Maintenance Organizations, however, would hold down costs and provide a better guarantee of care for all. An annual fee would entitle citizens to all necessary care. The HMO physician would receive an annual fee from the HMO for treating each patient, a fee which is the same for all patients, regardless of how much or how little care they receive.
3. The United Nations is designed to promote peace and to improve the living conditions of mankind. Since it does neither, the United States should withdraw from it and form a new international organization made up of only those nations willing to sign a very strict pledge of nonaggression, nonintervention, and international cooperation.
4. The United States Navy has for decades relied on wooden hull minesweepers; however, helicopters are superior. They are safer, more economical, and better adapted to sweeping the newer types of mines. Therefore, the United States should scrap its minesweeper fleet and build large numbers of helicopters.

The Traditional Counterplan

Thus far, three negative strategies have been discussed: (1) going "straight negative"; (2) defending the status quo; (3) defending the status quo with minor repairs. The first, in its purest form, is possible only under the judicial paradigm; the other two are possible under both paradigms. And, as we have seen, the three are quite often combined in practice.

A fourth strategy—a traditional one—is to offer a counterplan. It is a permissible strategy under either paradigm. Traditionally, teams choosing this stance or strategy have had to make sure their counterplan met two tests.

Nontopicality

The negative team's plan, first, must *not* be topical. If it is topical, then *both* the affirmative and the negative teams are calling for the resolution's adoption. They disagree concerning the form in which it should be adopted; but, nonetheless, they agree that it should be adopted. When this situation occurs, the judge is really listening to *two* affirmative teams and therefore can automatically vote for "the affirmative."

Competitiveness

The negative team cannot, however, present any old nontopical counterplan. If the topic is "Resolved: That a system of compulsory arbitration for labor-management disputes in the public sector be established," and if the affirmative argues how harmful strikes by public employees are and therefore establishes a nongovernmental agency composed of members of organized labor, government, and corporate America to arbitrate labor-management disputes, the negative *cannot*, according to most debate theorists, say that we would do better to give more economic aid to the Third World. The negative could, however, advocate a plan outlawing strikes by public employees.

Why? Because the counterplan and the affirmative plan must be mutually exclusive for all practical purposes: both cannot be adopted. If we did outlaw strikes by public employees, we would eliminate the harmful strikes the affirmative has pointed to, thereby making the affirmative's arbitration board unnecessary. True, Congress could technically adopt both the counterplan and the affirmative plan, but Congress would have no reason to, for the affirmative plan would have no *raison d'être*, no problem to solve. The two plans are, for all intents and purposes, mutually exclusive: you either have the one or the other. On the other hand, if we did give extra aid to the Third World, we could still adopt the affirmative plan. And the reason for adopting it would still exist.

More often than not, the traditional counterplan competes with the affirmative plan because the counterplan solves the affirmative's problem. Therefore, the majority of teams offering a traditional counterplan concede the affirmative's rationale for change. This concession makes the offering of a traditional counterplan a very risky strategy.

You need not, however, concede to the affirmative its rationale for change. You could shrewdly concede one part and claim that another part is incorrect. For example, if the topic were "Resolved: that the United States adopt a system of wage and price controls," and if the affirmative did just that, arguing that the harms of inflation caused by high wages and prices mandated such action, the negative might concede the harms of inflation but deny the affirmative's causal analysis. Perhaps, the negative might argue, the true cause is excess profits, as companies raise their margins in anticipation of an economic slowdown. Based on the negative's causal analysis, the negative offers a counterplan imposing a stiff federal tax on excess profits. Since the counterplan would, according to the negative team, solve the problem the affirmative has outlined, it is competitive. If the negative makes only a partial concession such as this one, the traditional counterplan strategy is not as risky.

Innovative Approaches to the Counterplan

Recently, the counterplan strategy has provoked a great deal of discussion, and the theory behind it has been questioned.

Why all these new thoughts? There are many reasons. Perhaps the strongest one is the growing popularity of the legislative paradigm with its insistence that the negative do more than refute, that the negative offer a policy. Couple with this the problems negative teams have faced trying to defend the status quo (problems which led to the repairs strategy), *and* couple these two reasons with the problematic question of what is a minor repair, and you have a good idea of the competitive conditions which have made the counterplan prominent again and subject to considerable rethinking.

A Redefinition of Competitiveness

Traditional counterplan theory virtually requires that the negative team concede part or all of the affirmative rationale for change. This traditional requirement grew out of a very narrow interpretation of "competitiveness." As it was defined above, to be competitive, a counterplan need only preclude the adoption of the affirmative plan. Consider the following situation: If there is only a finite amount of money available for scientific research and if the affirmative advocates spending ninety percent of it on cancer research, would a counterplan advocating that fifty percent of the finite sum be spent on solar energy research be competitive? If "competitiveness" is interpreted in the *very* traditional, narrow manner, no; however, if "competitiveness" is interpreted more broadly, yes. The two plans do indeed preclude each other.

Theorists often speak about the redefinition of "competitiveness." Actually, it has not been redefined by most. In rethinking the concept, most are simply escaping from an imprisoning, narrow interpretation of the concept. The "escape" has taken many forms—some of them far-fetched. Two of the most common nontraditional counterplan types are discussed below. Then, some *more* radical counterplan theory is briefly presented.

Negative "Needs" Contentions?

In the brief example above, the affirmative and negative teams are clearly talking about two different issues: the affirmative team is discussing cancer research; the negative, solar energy research. The two teams might agree on some very general statements about the importance of federally funded scientific research, but that is the extent of it.

To win the debate, the negative must convince the judge that the finite money should be spent on solar energy. Two approaches should be taken: first, the negative should try to deny or minimize the need for federal money for cancer research; second, the negative should present the need for money for solar energy research. The negative should, in other words, present its own "needs" contentions. Finite money is not the only jumping-off point for separate negative "needs" contentions. However, it is a major one.

Beware. Many judges will reject a counterplan which relies solely on limited funds for its competitiveness. They feel that such a counterplan leads to negative "needs" contentions and that such contentions lead to debates where there is very little clashing. Some judges, however, will accept such a counterplan because the resulting debate does indeed mirror actual policymaking very accurately. In the real world, there often are competing needs and competing programs chasing limited funds. Another word of warning: the affirmative can win the entire debate *if* they deny your fundamental premise and demonstrate that money is available. This possible affirmative counterargument makes this particular jumping-off point for a counterplan risky in my judgment.

Using up all the money is not, however, the only "new" way in which a counterplan can be competitive. Let's say the affirmative reforms the welfare system by granting some, but not all, services to alien workers who enter the United States on an "as needed" basis. The negative might turn around and offer as a counterplan *severe* restrictions on work visas. The negative *need not* deny either the affirmative argument that these aliens need some social services or the affirmative argument that they are not entitled to all. The negative could present its own "needs" contentions concerning the effect of employment of large numbers of such workers on U.S. unemployment, the effect on wages in areas where such alien workers dominate, and the effect on the local and state budgets in these areas. The counterplan is competitive in this case, *not* because it solves the affirmative's problem, *not* because it exhausts available funds, *but* because it removes most of the alien workers the affirmative plan provides services for and thus the need for the services.

Generic Counterplans

Generic counterplans are, by definition, usable round after round, regardless (to a large extent) of what the affirmative team is arguing. Most of these counterplans grow out of the resolution's terms; some grow out of the debate process itself.

If, for example, the resolution calls for *federal* action to achieve quality secondary education, a generic counterplan might admit the problem and call for state and/or local action. The counterplan is both nontopical insofar as the action is not federal and competitive insofar as it solves the problem the affirmative outlines. What the counterplan does is focus the entire debate on the question of federal versus state and/or local action.

A similar example would involve a resolution calling for United States action to preserve Third World independence. A generic counterplan might call for U.N. action or NATO action or even Soviet action.

Another similar example would involve a resolution calling for guaranteed health care for all U.S. citizens. A generic counterplan might call for such a program for the poor only or for the aged only or for those under age twenty-one only.

The affirmative, the negative insists, must defend all the terms of the resolution. Those generic counterplans which stem from the resolution focus the debate on one key term. Such counterplans, which can be prepared well in advance, are extensions of the justification observations we will discuss a bit later in this chapter.

Generic counterplans growing out of the debate process itself are more controversial than the ones just discussed. For example, there is the "studies counterplan." The affirmative team in a debate is required to guarantee that the action prescribed in the resolution be taken. The affirmative can phase action in, but the affirmative cannot predicate action on the results of future studies. Arguing that the affirmative is premature in adopting the resolution, the "studies counterplan" negative advocates more studies and may even specify the exact kinds of studies or the research methodology necessary. Since the negative does not argue for the adoption of the resolution, this counterplan is nontopical; since the adoption of the affirmative plan would make the studies counterplan superfluous, this counterplan is competitive.

Another generic counterplan which grows out of the debate process itself is the "referendum counterplan." The affirmative team in a debate is, once again, required to *guarantee* the adoption of a plan embodying the resolution. The affirmative cannot call for a referendum and have that vote decide whether or not the action will be taken. So, the negative, arguing that the affirmative is undemocratic, advocates a referendum. Since the negative does not *necessarily* call for the adoption of the resolution, this counterplan is nontopical; since the adoption of the affirmative plan would make the referendum pointless, this counterplan is competitive.

These kinds of counterplans are highly controversial. Many judges object to them *on principle* because they are based on inherent flaws of the debate process (from which the affirmative cannot escape), not flaws in the affirmative argumentation. Picking on flaws or limitations over which the affirmative has no control strikes many judges as unfair. So, use such counterplans with a great deal of caution *if at all*.

Challenging the Innovative "Alternative Justifications" Case

Whether it endures into the 1990s or not, you might run across an affirmative team in the 1980s offering an "Alternative Justifications Case." As you learned in Chapter 4, this case is really several cases wrapped up in one. The affirmative offers, let's say, four rationales and plans, fully prepared to zero in on one or two depending upon the negative's response. Since the affirmative needs to win only one to justify the adoption of the resolution, this dropping of parts of the case does not, in theory, weaken the case the affirmative presents.

What do you do on the negative? You are faced with a strategic challenge. You almost have to the play the affirmative's game—and play it better.

Many judges will readily reject the "Alternative Justifications Case" if the negative challenges its validity. These are judges who feel that tricks designed simply to help one win have no place in academic debate. So, your first strategy should be to offer an observation on the affirmative's invalidity. Note how it is a trick, how it is unfair to the negative team, and how it is contrary to the purposes of competitive debate on public policy issues. Then, challenge each case, and try to spend an equal amount of time on each justification for change. If you are better prepared to debate one, don't reveal it; if you are weakly prepared on another, try not to show it. Force the affirmative team to choose the case they will emphasize without knowing your strength and your weakness. For each case, point out *everything* the affirmative team *must* prove *with good evidence* to satisfy you and the judge. Make the affirmative's task seem as impossible as can be; put your opponents on the defensive. The affirmative could not have developed their four or five or six cases as well as they could have developed a single one: point out *all* that they did not do and must do. When the affirmative team finally chooses its ground, respond by recalling *all* of their obligations, especially those pertinent to this ground. And, after the affirmative team has opted for one case, don't drop the challenge you made to the legitimacy of their approach. What the affirmative has essentially done is postpone *real* discussion until a late point in the debate. The result is insufficient time to develop arguments. Point out to the judge that this postponing is unfair and contrary to debate's purposes; also argue that the resolution should not be adopted with the arguments for and against it still in an embryonic state.

The approach you take to each case should emphasize all that the affirmative must do. This emphasis is compatible with the "straight negative" defense of the status quo, and defense of the status quo with repairs strategies we discussed earlier in this chapter.

Could you offer a counterplan? Yes, but it must be competitive with *all* of the affirmative plans. Such a counterplan would be very difficult to devise on the spot; you might have to offer a generic counterplan. Or you *could* offer as many counterplans as there are plans—a counterplan for each affirmative plan. The result would be a *reductio ad absurdum* of the "Alternative Justifications Case." Most judges would delight at such a debate, but discourage its repetition. If you have really got a debate "to kill," you *might* try to outfox the affirmative by offering multiple counterplans as a deliberate (i.e., announced to the judge) attempt to show how contrary to the purposes of debate the "Alternate Justifications Case" is.

Defending a Negative Policy in a "Net Benefits" Debate

Just as a debate in which the affirmative presents a "Needs Case" and the negative goes "straight negative" is the purest embodiment of the judicial paradigm, so a "Net Benefits" debate is the purest embodiment of the legislative paradigm. In such a debate, both teams agree with the assumption that policies are dynamic systems, not static entities. Just as the status quo is a dynamic policy system directing the course of inevitable change, so is the affirmative's proposed new policy. Recognizing that the status quo has no "engraved in marble" status, affirmative teams and judges are not going to grant any presumption in its favor. A negative team will not be able to win a debate by saying that the affirmative's charges against the status quo are shaky or even by demonstrating that the status quo can solve the problem the affirmative has outlined. The negative must show that the status quo is a better policy system than the policy system the affirmative has advocated. The negative must, in other words, defend as a superior policy, the status quo, the status quo with repairs, or a counterplan. The strategic advantage is greatest if the negative chooses to defend the status quo with or without repairs because, in a "Net Benefits" debate, *some* presumption is placed against new policies, since we are necessarily less certain about the positive and negative effects of new policies than we are about the effects of existing policies.

The negative strategies in a "Net Benefits" debate are pretty much the same as in all the other debates we have discussed thus far in this chapter. Although the negative cannot go "straight negative," the negative can combine the "straight negative" strategy with a defense of the status quo, a defense of the status quo with repairs, or the advocacy of a counterplan. All of the advice offered thus far is relevant.

To be successful, however, a negative team should *conceive* of a "Net Benefits" debate differently. Much of the theory behind the "Net Benefits" approach is borrowed from systems analysis. In systems analysis, decisions are made using the following formula for comparing benefits–costs ratios. In this formula, "A" stands for the policy system advocated by the affirmative; "N" for the policy system advocated by the negative:

(Benefits of A) (Certainty) − (Costs of A) (Certainty)
<or>
(Benefits of N) (Certainty) − (Costs of N) (Certainty)

If the inequality favors A, the affirmative team wins: it offers a superior benefits–costs ratio; if the inequality favors the negative, it wins: it offers a superior benefits–costs ratio. All statements concerning benefits and costs are predictive: they deal with the future. The predictive nature of these statements is taken into consideration, however, when the benefits and costs are quantified. The quantification of either a benefit or a cost is the product of its value and its certainty or probability. In other words, a significant but unlikely advantage would be worth less than a less significant but very likely advantage; this is where presumption against new policies enters into the debate.

Let's say an affirmative policy forbidding the proliferation of nuclear technology might lead to peace in the world. This benefit or advantage is valuable—let's say 10 out of 10—but unlikely—let's say 2 out of 10. Its quantification would be 20. The negative policy is the status quo—proliferation with many controls. It will in the future improve the quality of life for millions by providing electrical power; in fact, the policy is already achieving that end. The benefit is significant—7 out of 10—and likely—8 out of 10: a total of 56. And 56 is far higher than 20.

Debates in this mode *do not* become numbers games. No one actually talks in terms of 56 and 20. The formulae and computations are important to recall, however, in formulating a negative strategy for this kind of debate. That strategy would have four parts; for each part, the negative team would have two goals.

First, the negative must show that the affirmative policy's benefits are low. Goal one: show that the claimed benefits are not significant; goal two: show that they are not likely to result. Remember also to question the benefits' topicality and uniqueness, just as you would if debating a conventional "Comparative Advantages Case." These benefits must, according to the rules of debate, stem from the adoption of the resolution—i.e., be topical. These benefits also must not be possible under the negative team's policy, for, if they were, the benefits would cancel each other out in the formula we looked at a moment ago. The benefits must be unique to the affirmative policy.

Second, the negative must show that the affirmative policy's costs are high. Goal one: show how high they will be; goal two: show that these costs are likely to result. In other words, maximize both the significance and the probability.

Third, the negative must show that *its* policy's benefits are high. Goal one: show how high they are; goal two: show how probable they are. If you are defending the status quo, the second goal should be fairly easy to meet, for you are not predicting but rather reporting what already exists.

Finally, the negative must show that its policy's costs are low. Goal one: show how low they are; goal two: show how predictable these low costs are.

To an uniniated observer, a "Net Benefits" debate looks very much like a more traditional debate in which the affirmative offers a "Comparative Advantages Case." If the assumptions underlying this new approach to debating are understood, then how the debate differs from the traditional debate should be clear and the need for different negative strategies should be apparent. If the theory seems fuzzy, keep thinking about it *and* keep the formula on page 163 very much in mind when you debate a team that insists on a "Net Benefits" format.

Still Newer Ground for Counterplans

The "new" counterplans we have already discussed are possible under both the judicial and the legislative paradigms, although the increased popularity of the legislative paradigm has made counterplans of all types much more common than they once were. The legislative paradigm in its purity is seen in the "Net Benefits" debate, where both teams offer policy systems which are compared. This kind of debate would seem to be the ideal situation for the explosion of the counterplan. It has been. This explosion within the context of the "net benefits" debate, with its emphasis on evaluative formulae, has not only led to numerous counterplans but also pushed many theorists to *truly* redefine "competitiveness."

"Competitiveness" has meant either solving the problem specified by the affirmative team (if defined narrowly) or making the adoption of the affirmative plan impossible or pointless (if defined broadly). If "competitiveness" is defined *still more broadly*, within the context of a comparison of policy systems, another possible counterplan strategy arises. Traditionally, if the affirmative team can advocate the adoption of both its plan and the counterplan, then it wins the debate, for no arguments against the affirmative case stand and no counterpolicy precludes the affirmative plan. But, what if the adoption of both, although possible, is less desirable than the adoption of the counterplan alone? Within the context of a "Net Benefits" debate, such a counterplan would be considered competitive by many. Not only would the benefits of the counterplan less its costs exceed the benefits of the affirmative plan less its costs, *but* the benefits of the counterplan less its costs would exceed the benefits of affirmative plan and counterplan together less their costs. This situation would occur because of the interaction of affirmative plan and negative counterplan as a single policy system.

Could this strange-sounding situation *really* occur in real policymaking? Yes. Let's say the problem area under discussion is urban transportation. The affirmative, defending the resolution that the federal government should subsidize urban rapid transit, advocates large federal grants. The negative offers a nontopical counterplan: federally financed development of industry-residence complexes on the city's periphery. Both could be adopted: the one does not preclude the other. The negative, however, could argue that the peripheral working-living complexes would have a better cost-benefit ratio than the rapid rail systems and, furthermore, because (1) the peripheral complexes would hurt the downtown area that the rapid transit would focus on and be designed to revive and (2) the availability of rapid transit downtown would inhibit the development and growth of peripheral complexes, the peripheral complexes *alone* would have a better benefit-cost ratio than the rapid transit and peripheral complexes *together*. Since this situation could really occur, many theorists and judges recommend that the argument for a competitive counterplan based on its superiority to plan and counterplan *combined* be granted.

Value Debate

Recall the three kinds of value resolution discussed in Chapter 4—Pre-New Policy or PNP, Pre-Present Policy Choice or 3PC, and Pre-Present Policy Rejection or 3PR. For each kind of proposition, the negative team has several strategic options. They are listed in Figure 7.4. If you examine this list, you will notice that some strategies are appropriate for all three kinds of resolutions. We will discuss those strategies first; then we will consider the strategies that are available only in certain cases.

Given a PNP Resolution—e.g., Disarmament is desirable—you can:
1. Challenge the affirmative's definitive contention;
2. Challenge the affirmative's indictment of present policy;
3. Defend the present policy;
4. Defend the present policy with minor repairs;
5. Offer and defend a counterdesignative contention which points to a policy different from both the present policy and the policy the affirmative is pointing to;
6. Challenge the affirmative's evaluation of a new policy.

Given a 3PC Resolution—e.g., Environmental protection is more important than energy exploration—you can:
1. Challenge the affirmative's definitive contention
2. Challenge the affirmative's indictment of the alternative policy;
3. Defend the alternative policy;
4. Defend the alternative policy with minor repairs;
5. Challenge the resolution by claiming it poses a false dilemma and offer a counterdesignative contention claiming the two policies together are superior to either one alone;
6. Challenge the resolution by claiming it poses a false dilemma and offer a counterdesignative contention claiming another action is more valuable than either specified in the resolution;
7. Challenge the affirmative's evaluation of a new policy.

Given a 3PR Resolution—e.g., Schools have failed—you can:
1. Challenge the affirmative's definitive contention;
2. Challenge the affirmative's indictment of present policy;
3. Defend the present policy;
4. Defend the present policy with minor repairs.

Figure 7.4 Negative Strategies in Value Debate.

Challenge the Definitive Contention

The negative team should always consider this strategy, since the value the affirmative case has defined is the drive wheel which makes the case go. For example, if the affirmative argues for disarmament on the basis that "Life is desirable," you might want to say that things are not so simple and that, "Whereas life with freedom is desirable, life under the constraints of a dictatorial government is not; therefore, the United States should fight to the death to preserve the former."

Ask the following questions of the definitive contention: (1) Is the claimed value truly valuable? (2) Is the claimed value perhaps not as simple as the affirmative suggests? (3) Are there values which, you can argue, are superior?

Consider a resolution advocating a foreign policy with a human rights orientation. Let us say the affirmative team argues that the United States' image is of supreme value in designing the nation's foreign policy. Is image *really* valuable in the hard, cold sphere of international relations? Perhaps image is important, but perhaps an image of morality must be coupled with an image of strength if the morality is to matter. Perhaps the affirmative's reasoning is, therefore, too simple. Are national security, democracy, and self-determination more valuable than morality?

Challenge the Affirmative Indictment;
Defend the Present or Alternative Policy

Whether the affirmative case indicts the present policy as when advocating that court-imposed restraints on police be lifted or indicts an alternate policy as when arguing for anti-inflation measures rather then proemployment measures, the case indicts. If the case is an adapted goals case, then (1) ask if the problem exists, (2) ask if it is serious, and (3) ask if the problem is structurally or attitudinally inherent in the indicted policy.

Consider an affirmative case which argues that our criminal justice system overprotects criminals. Let's say the affirmative team says "justice" is the value they will defend and that following present procedures does not promote justice. You might, in refuting this case, argue along the following lines. First, you might argue that, although some guilty individuals are perhaps overprotected, the system protects thousands of innocent individuals who fall under the suspicion of law enforcement officers, and, therefore, the system does more good than harm and *does not present a problem*. Then, second, you might argue that the guilty criminals who are set free because their rights were infringed upon are very small in number and declining and, therefore, insignificant. Then, third, you might argue that the problem was not with the court-imposed rules but, rather, with the way the courts were later interpreting them. Since the courts nationwide are now in the hands of more conservative jurists, the interpretation of the rules will now be such that the rules will no longer present a problem. The inherent attitudinal barriers which existed years ago have been overcome, you might argue.

If the case is an adapted comparative advantages case, then the indictment will be buried in the claim/s of advantage. The affirmative will be emphasizing that a particular course of action is more valuable than either the status quo in the case of PNP resolutions or an alternative policy in the case of 3PC resolutions. As a negative debater, your job is to minimize the difference. You can accomplish this task by arguing that the problem the affirmative has pointed to either (a) does not exist or (b) does not exist to the extent claimed or (c) exists but is mitigated by benefits. You should also try to minimize the difference by challenging the claim that the action the affirmative points to is better. More on that later.

Consider the resolution "That increasing salaries is a method of improving education superior to constructing new facilities." Let's say the affirmative defines "a well-disciplined mind" as valuable and tries to show that higher salaries will mean better teachers and that better teachers will mean better education and that better education will mean more well-disciplined minds, whereas better facilities will not help improve minds at all. The negative approach would probably use some of the following arguments. These arguments match the approaches, (A), (B), and (C), just identified:

A. New facilities are not being built anymore. The little money being appropriated for education is not being funnelled into buildings and the like. No problem.
B. Some facilities are not educationally valuable, but most are. Most help train minds.
C. Building better facilities is educationally sound. They create a better educational environment; furthermore, they make possible educational opportunities in areas such as computer science, industrial arts, and athletics. These benefits outweigh any problem.

If you challenged the affirmative's definitive contention by arguing that the operative value in the debate should be something other than what had been pointed to by the affirmative, you should do one more thing in responding to the affirmative's indictment of the present or alternate policy. You should evaluate the present or alternate policy in terms of this "something other." For example, if you feel that "well-disciplined minds" are less important than "community pride," you might have argued that the success of a school is to be measured by the extent it contributes positively to a community's image of itself. Based on this superior value, you might argue, building new facilities makes sense since these facilities will boost civic pride.

Defend the Present or Alternative Policy with Minor Repairs

Consider the two affirmative cases just discussed. The first indicts the present criminal justice system for not promoting justice; the second indicts a policy of building new educational facilities. As was demonstrated above, both indictments can be challenged by a mixture of questioning the indictment's validity and defending the present or a stated alternative policy. If that present or stated alternative policy does not perfectly promote the established value, you could suggest that only small modifications are necessary to make the policy valuable. For example, you might suggest that police procedures be updated so that they are in line with the letter and the tone of the most recent Supreme Court decisions. Or you might suggest that all states adopt a so-called "Taj Mahal" law designed to prevent the construction of educational facilities that are not educationally justified.

The same guidelines should govern minor repairs in value debate as minor repairs in policy debate: (1) The repair should be in the operation, not the purpose, of an existing policy system or the stated alternative policy system; (2) The repair should be easily made; (3) Adopting the repair should not be the equivalent or near-equivalent of adopting the resolution. Police procedures are written so as to conform to judicial standards. By bringing police procedures in line with recent court decisions, you are not changing the purpose of police procedures, only updating police operations. Such updating occurs anyway: you are simply speeding it up—a relatively easy action to take. You are not admitting the resolution's indictment of present procedures; rather, you are showing that present procedures, with just minor dickering, can be freed from accusation.

A similar argument could be made for a bill requiring all educational construction to be justified in terms of instructional improvement. Certainly, instructional improvement has been the goal of such construction all along. Since so-called "Taj Mahal" bills, designed to put an end to costly, educationally indefensible building, do already exist in many states, they are already a part of the status quo and you are merely extending existing procedures. The repair is, therefore, an easy one: the status quo is already part of the way there. And you are *not* admitting the affirmative's indictment of the status quo; rather, you are arguing that present construction, with a small repair in some states, can be freed from indictment.

Challenge the Affirmative's Evaluation of Its Chosen Action

Since 3PR resolutions indict without suggesting specific lines along which public policy should proceed, an affirmative team debating a 3PR resolution will not be defending a particular policy orientation. Therefore, this strategy—challenge the evaluation of that policy—will not be available to you. When the affirmative is defending a PNP or 3PC resolution, however, it will be a strategy you ought to pursue.

If the affirmative team has offered a modified goals case, then the affirmative is saying that the action it is pointing to *is* valuable. If the affirmative team, has offered a modified comparative advantages case, then the affirmative team is saying that the action is *more* valuable than either the present policy or an alternative identified in the resolution. Three questions suggest three ways a negative debater might challenge either of these claims: (1) is the action as valuable as the affirmative claims?; (2) does the action promote whatever is opposed to the defined value rather than or while promoting that value?; (3) does the action have unforseen negative consequences? Consider the case focusing on the allegedly excessive rights of the accused. The affirmative is advocating a lessening of these rights so that justice is better served. Is such an action truly in the service of justice? What if innocent people are coerced into false confessions? What if these confessions hold up in court? These scared, innocent men and women would be in prison, their lives ruined. Does the action the affirmative advocates serve justice or injustice or a confused muddle of both? Might the action lead not only to the injustice of innocent men and women suffering but to more and more police brutality as law enforcement officers make up for lost time and clear up the streets now that the handcuffs of the accused rights are no longer restraining them?

Again, what should you do about the value you may have argued is superior to the value the affirmative team offered in its definitive contention? You should show how the action the affirmative team's pre-policy judgments points to measures up against your value. In the case above, let's say the affirmative defined "safety" as valuable; you might have countered with "human rights." If you did, you would want, in responding to the affirmative's evaluation of its action, to consider how a policy which removes many of the restraints imposed on police by the Warren Court protects the "human rights" of accused criminals. You should try to show that the action the affirmative is pointing to in its second designative contention measures up poorly to the value you are arguing is superior to the value the affirmative has selected to defend.

Offer and Defend a Counterdesignative Contention

The remaining three strategies listed in Figure 7.4 all call upon the negative team to offer a counterdesignative contention.

If you are debating a PNP resolution such as "Unilateral disarmament is desirable," you might want to *neither* defend the present arms race nor agree with the affirmative that unilateral disarmament is the course to be taken. You might want to argue that bilateral mutual disarmament is a far more desirable course to take than either the arms race or unilateral disarmament. To make the debate a manageable affair, you would be wise to concede or qualify the definitive contention; however, nothing prevents you from defining "desirability" your own way and rejecting the course of action the affirmative advocates—unilateral disarmament—because it fails to be desirable in your way and advocate your course of action—mutual disarmament—because it succeeds.

If you are debating a 3PC resolution such as "Raising teachers' salaries is more conducive to better education than building new facilities," you may feel you are faced with a false dilemma—in the sense that there are other options other than the two announced in the resolution. If you feel this way, you might want to offer a counterdesignative contention, arguing that hiring more personnel (thereby making closer contact between teacher and student possible) is more conducive to better education than either the course of action the affirmative has indicted—building—or the course of action the affirmative has pointed to—raising salaries. As with the unilateral disarmament resolution, you could complicate the debate by objecting to the definitive contention and offering your own sense of what "better education" is. You would then argue for your counterdesignative contention in terms of that sense.

Counterdesignative contentions are much like counterplans in policy debate. (Of course, they are *not* plans but, rather, generally stated policy directions.) The two rules that govern counterplans are also applicable to counterdesignative contentions. First, the counterdesignative contention must be nontopical—that is, if the judge accepts your counter, he or she cannot be also affirming the value judgment of the resolution. Second, the counterdesignative contention must be competitive—that is, your counterdesignative contention and the course of action the affirmative is advocating cannot *both* be accepted. Consider the two counters outlined above. The judge cannot accept both unilateral disarmament and bilateral mutual disarmament since they are contradictory; the judge cannot opt for higher salaries and more personnel, given the implicit assumption of a finite amount of money.

Exercises: Refuting the Affirmative Case in Value Debate

Consider the following value debate cases. Determine what kind of resolution you are dealing with, review the negative strategies that are available to you, and figure out how you would execute each strategy.

1. *Resolved: That the right to privacy is paramount.*
   The affirmative team argues that the pursuit of happiness is man's ultimate goal. If man feels under observation, paranoia builds. This paranoia prevents happiness from being reached. Present law enforcement and credit-recording techniques put man under observation, promote paranoia, and deny happiness.
2. *Resolved: That the government has the moral obligation to provide for the elderly.*
   The affirmative argues that a society must fulfill its obligations to be a moral society. Abandoning or failing to adequately fund Social Security would then represent an immoral failure to treat the elderly as they deserve. Social Security then must be *improved*.
3. *Resolved: That employing Americans to do work for the country's good is more desirable than paying them unemployment compensation.*
   The affirmative argues that working in and of itself has value; therefore, unemployment compensation is bad and jobs programs are desirable.
4. *Resolved: That an American foreign policy designed to assist the Third World is a moral necessity.*
   The affirmative argues that we should strive to eliminate world hunger, disease, and poverty. American foreign policy has traditionally emphasized national security and international dominance, not the satisfaction of global human needs. American foreign policy ought to reorient itself.

Observations

All I have said about refutation in Chapter 6 and debating against the adoption of the resolution in this chapter suggests that the negative task is *clashing*. The affirmative says something, and you respond to that something. Clashing is a major negative responsibility, for by clashing, you make it absolutely clear where and how you and the affirmative team differ. Sometimes, however, you will want to lead off your review and refutation of the affirmative case with observations.

Many negative debaters misuse observations. They offer six minutes of them and then briefly review the affirmative case without really clashing much. This imbalance is a sign of a poor debater. Observations should make up no more than twenty percent of a negative speech, and you should have a good reason for offering an argument as an observation rather than as a counterargument to a specific affirmative contention. There are three good reasons.

Anchors

Sometimes you will want to begin your presentation with an argument to which you plan to refer throughout your presentation. For example, if your defense of the status quo is strong and will come up again and again, you might want to offer as an observation

> Marie and I believe that, if there is a problem, the status quo can solve it. Let me elaborate briefly.

If your offering of repairs is central,

> Marie and I believe that the status quo can be repaired very easily to take care of the very small difficulty the affirmative has shown. We do not need to adopt the major policy change the affirmative plan embodies; all we need to do is . . .

Oftentimes, an observation as an anchor—unlike the two just presented—has nothing to do with the negative strategy or philosophy *per se*. For example, if the major problem with the affirmative case is its illogic, then the following anchor might be useful:

> The affirmative case *sounds* good; however, if it is examined closely, its illogic is apparent. I intend to show you, as I review the affirmative case, how the logic breaks down upon close examination.

A similar anchor could be used in the common situation where the affirmative evidence is suspect.

When debating a value resolution, you might want to isolate the basis for the negative's objection to the affirmative's definitive contention so that you can readily refer to it again and again as you refute the affirmative case:

> The affirmative team has tried to focus this morning's debate on the value of peace. The philosophy of the affirmative is admirable, but naive. Marie and I are going to be more realistic, more worldly-wise and talk about security-through-power as our nation's foreign policy goal.

Orphan Arguments

Not all of the arguments you will want to offer as a negative debater will neatly fit the affirmative case structure. Sometimes, in fact, the affirmative writes its contentions so that good negative arguments will not quite fit.

For example, let's say the affirmative team is advocating increased federal money for commuter railroads. The best case structure would probably be "Comparative Advantages," since the affirmative wants to emphasize how it provides better for urban mass transportation. The case might read as follows:

1. Urban mass transportation is a problem:
   A. Highways are inadequate;
   B. Local governments do not have enough money to build rail systems.
   Plan: Federal money for construction (with mandatory guidelines on construction and service quality) and federal subsidies for fifty percent of the operating costs through the year 2010.
2. Advantages:
   A. Affirmative plan will provide better urban mass transportation;
   B. Affirmative plan will permit local government to use more of its funds to improve its business district, roads, etc.;
   C. Affirmative plan will unclog city highways.

Let's say you recognize the very high costs of rapid rail transit and wish to suggest that there are, within the status quo, low-cost alternatives. In other words, you want to offer one or several low-cost repairs. Where do you tie them in? You *could* tie them to (1A), saying, "Highways are not the only thing the status quo has to offer." However, this crucial argument might get lost there because it only indirectly clashes. The argument really does not have a home, a place where it can spread out into all of its substructure. An observation may be in order. Framing the argument as an observation will emphasize it, and framing it will make it easy for you to return to it later in the debate.

Out-of-Order for Emphasis

Let's consider that affirmative case again. Let's say you have examined (2C)—the third advantage—using the general heuristic for refutation in Chapter 6. The advantage is unclogged highways; the evidence should prove the superiority of the proposed mass transportation system if that system is going to attract customers and help clear the highways. But superior in what way? Faster? Cleaner? More convenient? Let's say the superiority is to be found in speed. And let's say that rides on the system will prove expensive despite subsidies. The evidence points to the advantage only if we can *assume* that speed is more important to potential customers than cost. Is this assumption valid?

Look at (2A)—the first advantage. Will the proposed system be better *if* citizens do not use it because they value money more than time? No. *If* the affirmative assumption about the importance of speed is not valid, then two of the three advantages (related to each other serially) fall. You might want to make this point (with evidence, if possible, demonstrating the importance of cost to the commuter) when you refute the claimed advantage. *Or* you might want to emphasize the argument, since it knocks out two thirds of the affirmative's rationale for the adoption of the resolution, by presenting it as an observation. If you do present it as an observation, refer to it when you refute the advantages. The relationship between the observation and the advantages may be obvious *to you*; however, never assume that the judge sees the debate precisely as you do. You see it from the inside; the uninvolved judge sees it from the outside.

Two Common, Related Observations

Two observations are so often offered in policy debate that they require separate treatment. They require separate treatment *together* because they are easily confused with each other by beginning debaters.

Topicality

An affirmative case must embody the resolution. A judge's affirmative vote must be a vote *for* the resolution. If it is, then the case is topical. If the judge can, in theory, accept the affirmative case without accepting the resolution, then the case is not topical.

The affirmative team *must* present a topical case. If the affirmative case can be proven nontopical, then the negative team can, in theory, accept the affirmative case and claim that *no* rationale for the resolution's adoption has been presented and, therefore, it should *not* be adopted. In other words, if the negative can demonstrate that the affirmative case is not topical, then the negative can automatically *win* the debate. No wonder many negative teams offer a topicality observation. They might get lucky.

In addition to the many situations in which the negative (unfortunately) tosses out the topicality observation "just in case," there are three common situations which frequently occur in which topicality *should* be an issue: (1) when the case is blatantly not topical; (2) when the case's topicality hinges on a tricky or disputable definition of a term; (3) when the case *indirectly* embodies the resolution. Let's look briefly at an example of each situation.

Let's say the topic is "Resolved: That the federal government should curtail the power of labor unions in the United States." Let's say the affirmative proposes to strip the United Mine Workers of some of its power. This proposal is blatantly nontopical because the topic or resolution clearly requires action against unions, not a single union.

Let's say the topic is "Resolved: That the information-gathering activities of government agencies should be significantly curtailed." Let's say the affirmative defines "government agencies" as "any operations managed and/or funded by any level of government" and then proposes to enact controls on the scientific research at state universities because the research (which, of course, involves information gathering) may be dangerous to community health. Did the framers of the resolution have state universities in mind when they said "government agencies"? Probably not. The affirmative stretches the meaning of the phrase to include universities by defining it very broadly. The negative team would base its nontopicality observation on a challenge to that definition. According to the rules of academic debating, that definition challenge *must* be voiced in the first negative speech.

Let's say the topic is "Resolved: That the power of the President should be significantly increased." Would a plan limiting U.S. Presidents to a single six-year term be topical? Yes, an affirmative team might argue. It would free a President from reelection worries and give him or her a bit more time to bring policies to fruition. A President could do what was necessary, public opinion be damned, and be confident that a policy's success or failure would be known before the term expired. More power would be acquired, maybe, *but* acquired indirectly. The negative might be able to challenge this *indirect* adoption of the resolution. Judges *tend* to accept indirect plans as long as the steps between the plan and the resolution are few and tightly logical. If you choose to challenge the topicality of an indirect affirmative case, then you would be wise, in making your observation, to stress that the steps are many and the logic linking step to step is loose. You could *also* argue that plans must *directly* implement the resolution in case the judge is a strict constructionist.

One final point about the topicality observation: It is subject to debate. The affirmative will respond, and you must respond to their response. Do not just repeat your initial argument; respond specifically to what they say.

Justification

The justification observation is fairly new. Its development parallels the development of the generic counterplan. Both are based on the assumption that an affirmative case must justify *all* the terms of the resolution.

An example should make the observation's basis clear. Let's say the topic is "Resolved: That the federal government should guarantee adequate health care for all U.S. citizens." Let's say the affirmative team argues that the poor do not receive adequate care and, for that reason, calls for the adoption of the resolution. The negative justification observation would probably have two thrusts: (1) the affirmative has not justified federal action; (2) the affirmative has not justified a plan covering all citizens. An affirmative case, in other words, can be "resolutional" or "topical" without the affirmative team's having justified the resolution. An affirmative team—according to some (but not all) theorists—must justify all the major terms in the resolution it is supporting.

Most of the comments in this chapter, you will discover as you actually compete, pertain to the first negative speaker's task. This emphasis in Chapter 7 is due to the traditional bipartite division of the affirmative case in policy debate into rationale for change and plan and the corresponding bipartite division of the negative task. Traditionally, the first negative speaker challenges the rationale for change while the second negative takes on the plan. In value debate, although there exists no comparable division of the affirmative case and, therefore, no comparable justification for a two-part negative task, such a divided task exists. The first negative speaker challenges the case that has been offered; the second negative speaker does other jobs. The next chapter, which continues our discussion of the negative task, emphasizes the plan attacks and the other jobs. It also discusses several general matters of interest to *both* members of a negative debate team.

After reading and studying Chapter 7, you know:

- how to go "straight negative" *or* defend the status quo *or* defend the status quo with minor repairs and refute the needs case, both versions of the comparative advantages case, and the goals case;
- what the traditional counterplan is and how innovative approaches to the counterplan have been developed by broadening the definition of "competitiveness," focusing on specific terms in the debate resolution, and focusing on the rules of debate;
- how to respond strategically to the net benefits and alternative justifications approaches in policy debate;
- to refute the affirmative case in value debate by using some or all of the following strategies:
    —challenge the definitive contention;
    —challenge the affirmative indictment;
    —defend the present or alternative policy;
    —defend the present or alternative policy with minor repairs;
    —challenge the affirmative's evaluation of its chosen action;
    —offer and defend a counterdesignative contention;
- that observations properly serve as anchors, as places for orphan arguments, and as spots for arguments presented out-of-order for emphasis *and* what the common observations of topicality and justification mean and how they are used.

CHAPTER 8
The Negative Task II

In this chapter, you will learn:

- about the conventional negative division of labor and the conditions under which it might be violated;
- how to challenge the affirmative plan in policy debate;
- how to structure your plan attacks in policy debate;
- what options are open to the second negative debater in value debate;
- the different kinds of briefs you might prepare;
- how to handle some special problems you might face when you are on the negative side of the proposition.

Successful negative debaters are good thinkers. The affirmative team members can prepare a great deal in advance of competition and, as a result, know what they will say in response to the majority of arguments a negative team might offer. (The way to prepare, by the way, might be to play negative team against your own case using the procedures outlined in the preceding two chapters and in this chapter.) The negative debaters, on the other hand, will be successful to the extent that they think during the actual debate. After reading and studying Chapter 7, the first negative debater should be ready. This chapter focuses on what the second negative speaker should do.

The Negative Division of Labor

As in previous chapters, I intend to proceed in a historical manner—discussing the debating of policy resolutions first, and then the more recent debating of value resolutions. In the older kind of debating, there has been for a long time

177

a well-defined division of labor between the two negative debaters. In the newer form of debating, a division of labor is in the process of evolving.

The Conventional

An affirmative case that supports a policy resolution contains both a rationale for change and a plan. The rationale for change, no matter what form it takes, is referred to in debate jargon as "the case." The plan is referred to as "the plan." (This use of "the case" to mean half of the affirmative case may strike you as confusing, but, once you start debating, you will quickly get used to the two contradictory uses of the word "case.") The first negative addresses "the case"; the second negative, the plan. Generally speaking, the first negative presents a few observations and then systematically refutes the affirmative's argumentation, or offers a counterplan and tries to demonstrate its superiority to the affirmative plan. Again, generally speaking, the second negative offers three kinds of arguments against affirmative plan—workability arguments, solvency arguments, and disadvantages of the plan. If the negative team has offered a counterplan, then the second negative will defend the counterplan as well as indicting the affirmative plan. This chapter should help the second negative do these jobs. Before I talk specifically about these jobs, let me first talk about the circumstances under which first and second negative speakers might want to exchange tasks.

Reversed for Strategic Reasons

Three situations may arise in which negative speakers might wish to reverse roles.

In Response to "Squirrels." "Squirrels" are unusual affirmative cases. They have been nicknamed "squirrels" because they may represent rather fuzzy interpretations of the terms of the debate resolution and/or because they are somewhat crazy or "nutty" ways of approaching or affirming the resolution. In some areas of the country, "squirrels" are common and coaches and judges are not at all resistant to them; in other areas of the country, "squirrels" are not as common because some coaches and judges are not particularly fond of them. An affirmative team offers a "squirrel" to gain a strategic advantage over the negative team. Since the negative team has never heard the "squirrel" before, they have no prepared arguments. They also have no or little evidence to use in refuting the case.

The common characteristics of "squirrels" *might* justify a reversal of first and second negative roles. The "case" is usually flawed and, if a debater can study it sufficiently, he or she can usually find the flaw and kill the "squirrel"; also, some prepared plan attacks—with evidence—are usually applicable. Since the debater attacking the plan has something to say, that speaker might want to go first and indict the plan, giving his or her partner the extra time to study the case and find the flaw(s). The speaker indicting the case would not, of course, be prohibited from also offering arguments against the specific plan.

This reversal could be handled in one of two ways: the designated first negative speaker could simply do his or her partner's usual job, and vice versa, or the negative team members could announce to the judge that they will not be speaking in the designated order but the reverse order. The judge might be slightly miffed since the ballot will have to be doctored a bit, but this slight annoyance should be easily overcome if the role reversal strikes the judge as strategically justified.

In Response to a Strong Case. If the case an affirmative team offers is very difficult to refute, the negative might want to focus the debate on plan attacks, especially if the plan seems vulnerable. Whatever is discussed by the first negative speaker necessarily gets more attention because the issues enter the debate earlier and can be discussed in more speeches. Therefore, if you want the plan attacks to be *the focus* of the debate, you might consider offering them in the initial negative stand and saving the arguments against the affirmative's rationale for change until the second negative stand.

You might want to make this switch at times when the case contentions are soundly reasoned and well-evidenced, or very obviously true. You might want to make this switch when you are surprised by a different, although non-"squirrel," case.

The switch has another strategic advantage. You force the second affirmative speaker, who is used to defending the case, to defend the plan; you force the first affirmative, who is used to defending the plan in his or her rebuttal, to defend the case. Trying to put the affirmative team in this predicament is viewed by many judges as unfair trickery; so switch only when there is sufficient justification for it and offer that justification to the judge if the judge seems to disapprove.

The affirmative team has offered, as its case, a number of virtual truisms together with several arguments that we, in an attempt to be reasonable, must concede. The affirmative plan, on the other hand, is seriously flawed. In order to focus this debate on that plan, I (the first negative) will indict that plan. My partner will examine the case a bit and then further indict the plan.

An alternative to switching in such a situation would be to have the first negative speaker indict "the case" and then offer what are called "case-side plan attacks." The second negative then would add to the list of plan attacks in his or her constructive speech.

To Avoid Late Turnarounds. The word "turnaround" is misused by many debaters. A turnaround is achieved when the absolute opposite of the negative's claimed disadvantage is proven by the affirmative team. *The opposite* would be that their plan will not lead to dire results; *the absolute opposite* would be that their plan will not only not lead to the dire results but will lead to positive results in the area the negative has specified. For example, let's say the negative argues that a plan will lead to damaging inflation. The opposite would simply be that the plan will not lead to inflation; the absolute opposite or turnaround would be that the plan will not only not lead to inflation but will lower inflation. The turnaround gives the affirmative team another advantage to claim for its plan. It is a cheap advantage too because the negative team, in arguing how significant the disadvantage was, has granted the significance of the advantage. As I mentioned earlier when discussing independent advantages and turnarounds in Chapter 4, some debate theorists and judges argue that a turnaround is an independent justification for casting an affirmative ballot.

Turnarounds are usually achieved rather late in a debate, because disadvantages do not enter the round until the second negative constructive speech. Negative teams often find their arguments against a plan being turned on them at times when they have very little or even no time to respond. This uncomfortable situation could justify a reversal of negative roles. The disadvantages of the plan would be on the floor early in the debate, and, if the affirmative team was going to try to turn one or more around into an independent justification for the resolution, the affirmative would be compelled to do it early enough in the round for the negative team to have the opportunity to respond to it at length.

Again, reversing roles puts the affirmative team in an awkward position, and, as a result, some judges will look with disfavor on a team that reverses roles unless that reversal seems justified. If you are switching to avoid late turnarounds, you may want to justify your switch in terms of either (a) the tendency in your league or region to try to turn around almost every disadvantage or (b) a particular opponent's tendency to try to turn around any and all disadvantages. In justifying your switch in this way, make sure your judge knows enough to accept your assessment of the league's, region's, or an opposing team's tendencies.

Challenging the Affirmative Plan

Figure 8.1 is a heuristic you can use to help you to devise objections to the affirmative plan. These objections typically fall into the three categories of workability, solvency, and disadvantages. The heuristic is divided into corresponding categories.

Workability

The general question you ask under the rubric of workability is, "Are the plan's 'nuts and bolts' satisfactory?" The heuristic gives you five questions to ask of a particular plan.

Let's apply the questions to a particular plan. Let's say the affirmative team advocates that the United States build nuclear power plants throughout the nation. Does the administrative machinery exist to make this energy plan work? Is there a status quo agency that could do the job? Does the affirmative team establish

Heuristic for Challenging the Affirmative Plan

Workability: Are the plan's "nuts and bolts" satisfactory?
1. Does the administrative machinery exist (in the status quo or in the plan) to make the plan work?
2. Is there sufficient funding?
    - How much will the plan cost?
    - How will the necessary money be obtained?
    - Is the financing feasible?
3. Are the necessary raw materials and other supplies readily available?
4. Can plan mandates, if controversial, be enforced?

Note: To the extent that a workability argument points to an insurmountable barrier, the workability argument is also a solvency argument.

Solvency: Does the plan solve the problem? Accrue the advantages? Meet the goals?
1. Are all necessary provisions included in the plan?
2. Can the necessary causal links between the plan and the solution/the advantages/the goals be demonstrated?
3. Will opposed forces block solution?—e.g., administrators, bureaucrats, the bureaucracy itself, lobbyists, those adversely affected by the plan

Disadvantages: Will the plan's adoption cause serious problems?
1. How will the plan affect the economy?
2. How will the plan affect important social programs?
3. How will the plan affect specific socioeconomic groups?
4. How will the plan affect the quality of life, the standard of living?
5. How will the plan affect the environment?
6. How will the plan affect domestic tranquility?
7. How will the plan affect international peace?

Note: For each problem identified, ask, what is the short-term impact *and* what is the long-term impact?

Figure 8.1   Heuristic for challenging the affirmative plan.

an agency? If there is neither a status quo agency nor a new agency, the affirmative may have a policy but no means to carry it out. In the case of building nuclear power plants, the policy could have been implemented by the U.S. Department of Energy, but President Reagan has abolished it. In the absence of either a status quo agency set up to handle such matters as nuclear power or an affirmative-established agency, the plan is in trouble.

Is the funding sufficient? The plan will typically contain a funding plank. This particular case funds its construction program "through a 'vice tax' on cigarettes and liquor and an additional five-cent tax on gasoline." Ask the affirmative team how much its program would cost, and how much revenue its tax package will garner. If the first figure is higher than the second, the affirmative has a workability problem. If the affirmative team refuses to answer your question, (a) appeal to the judge, saying you cannot assess the plan's workability if you are not given specifics and (b) make your own reasonable guesses and argue accordingly.

Some plans require raw materials or other supplies to be workable. Are these available? For example, it would be pointless to spend huge sums of money to build nuclear power plants if uranium fuel were not going to be available at a reasonable price for the foreseeable future. Ask about the requisite materials.

Many plans require specialized personnel—are the needed men and women available? To build a network of nuclear power plants, engineers and construction workers would be necessary. No problem. To operate the network, highly trained specialists in nuclear physics would be necessary—especially if public safety were to be assured. Are they available?

Finally, many plans require enforcement. The specific plan under discussion probably does not, but a plan curtailing union violence, a plan prohibiting CIA activity, and a plan forbidding sexual harassment do. Has the affirmative plan provided for enforcement? If the affirmative has not, then they are relying upon status quo enforcement. You might be able to show problems with enforcement of existing laws and regulations; and you might find in the affirmative team's own reasoning and evidence support for this argument. If the affirmative team has provided enforcement mechanisms in their plan, examine them closely.

Solvency

The general question for solvency is: does the plan solve the problem the affirmative has detailed, if the affirmative case is a "Needs Case" or a modified "Comparative Advantages Case"; does the plan accrue the claimed advantages, if the affirmative case is a pure "Comparative Advantages Case"; does the plan meet the goal(s), if the affirmative case is a "Goals Case." The second negative debater should try to argue that the plan does not solve the problem or accrue the advantages or meet the goal(s). The arguments the second negative speaker will offer can be called solvency arguments. In the first case, they are also known as "PMN's" (*P*lan does not *M*eet *N*eeds); in the second case, they are also known as "PMA's" (*P*lan does not *M*eet *A*dvantages); in the third case, they have no jargony, semi-grammatical nickname.

To help you find solvency arguments, the heuristic (Figure 8.1) offers you three questions to ask of plans. Let's ask them of a plan which freezes wages and prices at their present level.

Are all necessary provisions included in the plan to permit it to solve the problem of inflation? Yes. But let's say the affirmative was claiming to restore incentive to workers because, under the plan, pay raises would be worth working for, as opposed to automatic cost-of-living increases which only allow the workers to keep up with inflation. To accrue this advantage, the affirmative would have to have provisions in its plan allowing raises in pay for merit. Without clear and workable provisions, the affirmative's solvency is questionable.

The second negative speaker should also examine the affirmative argumentation very closely to see if all the necessary causal links between the plan and the solution, advantages, or goal(s) are present. Three causal problems are frequent.

First, many affirmative teams assume that removing the cause necessarily removes the effect. For example, U.S. pressure may well have caused Fidel Castro to get closer and closer to the Soviet Union; however, adopting a conciliatory policy toward Cuba cannot guarantee that Castro will move away from Russia. He may not want to, and he may not be able to since Cuba is now so economically dependent on the Soviet Union.

Second, many affirmative teams assume that if their plan leads to the first link in a chain, they can safely assume all the other links. Will a jobs program reduce the potential for violence in poor sections of America's cities? Maybe. But all the affirmative plan necessarily guarantees is that jobs will be available to those who are presently unemployed. Will these citizens take the jobs? Will being employed at a menial job change their attitudes toward society, the wealthy members of it, and the government?

Third, many affirmative teams assume that a one cause-one effect relationship exists when, actually, there are two or more causes. Is lack of employment *the* cause of frustration among America's urban poor? Perhaps racial injustice is also a cause. Is the federal deficit *the* cause of investors' lacking sufficient confidence in the American economy to make long-term capital investments? Perhaps the absence of protection from foreign trade or fears concerning the scarcity of petroleum are also causes. To the extent that there are causes besides the one the affirmative plan attempts to solve, the affirmative has solvency problems.

Finally, the second negative debater should ask if opposed forces will prevent the plan from being solvent. Perhaps those forces will act to prevent the plan from solving the problem, being advantageous, or meeting the goal(s). If the affirmative's goal is to reduce the federal budget deficit and the plan is to reduce the size of the federal bureaucracy, might not members of that bureaucracy decrease their productivity in order to justify its present size? If the affirmative wants to stop the President from ordering covert operations in Latin America, he might use all the special privileges he has and every cloak of secrecy government has developed to get around the prohibition.

When offering the kind of solvency argument suggested by this last question, negative debaters should remember that the affirmative's fiat power (discussed in Chapter 2) allows the affirmative to assume that its plan will be given the necessary legislative consents. Therefore, a negative team member could not argue that the National Rifle Association will lobby so vigorously that Congress will not pass the affirmative's gun control law or that the Democrats will not have enough votes in the Senate to get the affirmative's national health care program enacted. When the second negative debater talks about forces preventing the plan from being solvent, the negative speaker must be referring to the operation of forces *after* the plan is in force.

When offering this kind of solvency argument, the second negative is obligated to demonstrate the existence of three ingredients. The blocking or circumventing force must be shown to have a *motive* for its antiplan actions. When the affirmative has demonstrated that attitudes prevent the status quo from meeting a need, accruing an advantage, or meeting a goal, the second negative's job is half done. Attitudinal inherency tends to concede to the second negative at least some motive to circumvent or block. The circumventing or blocking force must also be shown to have available to it a *mechanism* for its antiplan actions. The President's "state secrets" privilege may be a mechanism which would permit him to order CIA activities in violation of law with impunity; unions might be able to get around an antistrike law by encouraging a sick-out, encouraging a slow-down, or even encouraging a wildcat strike. Loopholes in the affirmative's law give unions several mechanisms. Finally, the circumventing or blocking force must also be shown to have demonstrated a propensity for its antiplan actions. If the negative is arguing that businesses will get around election-financing laws restricting the size of contributions to candidates for federal office by having employees give company money in their own names, the negative must be able to show where companies have shown their willingness to act in this manner or a comparably "shady" manner.

Solvency arguments can be either partial or absolute. This distinction is important, for, when you are on the negative side, you will want to stress any absolute solvency arguments you believe you have. A partial solvency argument minimizes the amount of solvency an affirmative plan has. The negative should try to specify how much solvency the argument removes—a bit, a fair amount, a lot—with reasoning and/or evidence. An absolute solvency argument totally negates solvency. If a solvency argument is indeed absolute, explain why and offer evidence, if you can, to demonstrate the absoluteness. For example, if the affirmative plan prohibits grants of immunity to witnesses who may have committed felonies, district attorneys and lawyers for these prospective witnesses may use plea-bargaining to achieve the same results—good and bad—of immunity grants. The solvency problem would be absolute; if district attorneys have a motive to circumvent, they can use the mechanism of plea-bargaining whenever they want. They can use it to the same extent they used grants of immunity.

Disadvantages

The general question to ask in order to generate disadvantages is "Will the plan's adoption cause serious problems?" The seven questions listed in the heuristic for plans are designed to suggest possibilities. The list is not exhaustive.

Let's return to the affirmative plan to build a network of nuclear power plants. Ask the seven listed questions of this plan. They might lead you to the following arguments:

1. The plan will increase deficit spending and discourage investment in American business, thereby damaging the economy.
2. Since Congress does not wish to have a huge deficit, when the money goes to the plan, money will be drained from important social programs.
3. Cutting these social programs will especially hurt the poor. Also, since the plants will displace many rural poor, the plan will doubly hurt the poor.

4. The plan will provide a reliable source of energy, but the energy will be expensive. The consumer will be spending a considerably larger chunk of his or her income on energy, leaving a smaller amount of money for other needs. The consumer's quality of life will decline.
5. The plan will raise the temperature of bodies of water used in cooling the reactors, thereby altering the ecosystem significantly. The plan will also create significant waste disposal problems which will, in future years, endanger all life near disposal sites.
6. The displaced rural poor will riot; those in areas near disposal sites will violently protest.
7. Nuclear materials could be stolen by terrorist groups unless the plan's security provisions are excellent. If terrorists acquire materials, international peace could be significantly disrupted.

Consider a plan calling for no more arms sales to nations who violate fundamental human rights. The heuristic questions might lead you to the following arguments:

1. The plan will hurt U.S. arms manufacturers; the plan will create additional unemployment in this industry as well as related others.
2. U.S. arms sales act as a controlling force, giving the United States leverage. We give arms, for example, to prompt social reform. Under the plan, social reform will suffer.
3. The decline in social reform in interdicted nations will adversely affect the poor and, in some nations, minority groups.
4. The absence of U.S. arms will decrease the interdicted nation's sense of security. This decrease will lead to paranoia; the paranoia will lead to more policing and repression. Life will no longer be as free, with the fear of "Big Brother" always poisoning it.
5. Not applicable.
6. Unemployment in arms and related industries may cause some domestic uneasiness.
7. The weakness of interdicted nations will invite hostile neighbors to invade them. These invasions will lead to regional warfare.

For every possible disadvantage, you should ask what is its short-term impact and what is its long-term impact. Disadvantages must have an impact in order to be strong reasons for rejecting an affirmative plan, especially if the affirmative proves the plan to be significantly advantageous. In the first list of possible disadvantages we generated, look at number (4). What is the short-term impact? Fewer luxuries; more modest meals; more modest vacation trips. What is the long-term impact? Less revenue for manufacturers of the goods and the providers of the services consumers will have to forego and resulting harms to the entire economy as bankruptcies occur and people lose jobs. In the second list of possible disadvantages we generated, look at number (7). What is the short-term impact?

Regional war with destruction and death. What is the long-term impact? A broader war, perhaps involving the superpowers, perhaps involving nuclear weaponry.

Structuring Plan Attacks

In academic debate, you will be expected to structure your plan attacks. Just saying what the disadvantage is and why it is bad will not be adequate. So that you, your opponents, and your judge understand how the plan presents difficulties, you show everyone the plan attack's logic by structuring it. Structure is *not* just a list of five points which somehow, if put together, equal a workability problem, a solvency problem, or a disadvantage. *Structure mirrors the plan attack's logic.*

For a workability argument, you might want to consider the following three-step model. First, specify what the plan must have to work; second, show that it does not have what is necessary; third, tell the judge that the result of the plan's insufficiency is either the partial or absolute lack of solvency. Let's say the affirmative plan calls for the federal government to set up health maintenance organizations so that all Americans can, for a minimal fee, be guaranteed quality health care. As a negative debater who has researched HMOs, you would know that some existing HMOs have had trouble attracting top-notch physicians. Knowing this, you could offer the following workability argument and structure it as suggested:

Workability Argument 1: Not Enough Quality Physicians:
A. To guarantee quality health care, affirmative plan must guarantee that top-notch physicians will work for HMOs;
B. HMOs will not attract top-notch physicians;
C. Therefore, the affirmative cannot guarantee quality health care.

Most solvency arguments should be structured in much the same way: first, specify what the affirmative plan must do to solve the problem, accrue the advantage, or meet the goal; second, show what will prevent the affirmative from doing it; and third, tell the judge that the result is either partial or absolute lack of solvency. Consider a plan which forbids U.S. covert activities directed against the Marxist government in Cuba. The claimed advantage is the eventual moderation of that regime. As a negative debater, you would probably doubt that Cuba would become moderate. You could voice your doubt in the following solvency argument:

P.M.A. 1: Cuba Will Not Turn Moderate:
A. To be solvent, the affirmative plan must guarantee that Cuba will turn away from the Soviet Union;
B. Cuba will not turn away because:
  i. Cuba is economically dependent on Russia;
  ii. The Soviet Union does not allow its satellites to steer a free course (e.g. Hungary, Czechoslovakia, Afghanistan, Poland);

iii. Castro needs anti-Yankee propaganda to divert Cuban attention from the nation's economic ills;
C. Affirmative case is, therefore, absolutely not solvent.

Circumvention arguments have, as already suggested, their special logic. The argument's structure should mirror this logic: first, motive; second, mechanism; third, propensity; fourth, impact, that being either the partial or the absolute lack of solvency. Let's say the affirmative plan passes a national Right-to-Work law. Such a law would make the requirement of union membership to hold a job illegal. One might argue that unions, who would very vehemently oppose such a law, might try to circumvent the law by subtly coercing workers to join. The circumvention argument should be structured along the following lines:

P.M.A. 2: Union Coercion Will Prevent Workers from Having a Right to Work:
A. Motive. Unions need members to gain power and money;
B. Mechanism. Unions can use numerous subtle means to coerce new workers to join the unions;
C. Propensity. Unions have used high-pressured tactics in the past to increase membership, to make strikes total, etc.;
D. Impact. To the extent these tactics are undertaken, the right to work will not exist and the plan will be absolutely *not* solvent.

Disadvantages should be structured in three steps: first, indicate what the affirmative plan does; second, indicate what the results of this action will be; third, indicate the impact(s) of these results. Let's consider an affirmative plan which calls for federal control over all potable water resources with a new agency then regulating the distribution of water to industrial and domestic users. Objecting to this plan, the second negative debater might raise the following disadvantage:

Disadvantage 1: Federal Control of Water Will Hurt Domestic Users:
A. The affirmative plan gives control of water distribution to industrial and domestic users to a federal agency;
B. Federal regulation in and of itself will increase the cost by thirty percent;
C. In addition, federal regulation will favor industrial users, resulting in an additional increase in cost of ninety percent to domestic users;
D. As a result, domestic users will be paying 120 percent more for water under the affirmative plan;
E. Short-term impact: significantly reduced standard of living for domestic consumers.
F. Long-term impact: reduced consumer spending will stall economic growth.

Subpoint A presents the first step; subpoints B, C, and D present the second step; subpoint E and F present the third step. As you can see, there is no one-to-one correspondence between the subpoints and the logical steps in the disadvantage's development. The second and third steps (and occasionally the first) will in many cases require several points if they are to be clearly presented.

"Meatball" Disadvantages

Let's consider one more disadvantage. A particular affirmative plan's enforcement mechanisms are very severe. The plan calls for a freeze on technology transfer to Communist nations and declares violations of the plan treasonous. The negative team *might* come up with the following disadvantage:

Disadvantage 2: Affirmative Enforcement Will Lead to Domestic Violations of Human Rights:
A. The affirmative plan declares violations treasonous;
B. Treason is a capital offense;
C. The affirmative punishment is therefore cruel and unusual punishment and therefore unconstitutional;
D. Affirmative, however, has fiat power and can assume a Constitutional Amendment;
E. A get-tough attitude toward crime and criminals exists today;
F. In absence of Constitutional protection against "cruel and unusual punishment," this get-tough attitude will lead to such punishments for crime;
G. Impact. Such punishments will violate the human rights of criminals;
H. Impact. Such punishments will create a police-state mentality which will repress the human rights of noncriminal citizens.

Subpoints A and B correspond to the first step: they simply explain what the affirmative plan does. Subpoints C, D, E, and F explain the results of the affirmative's action; subpoints G and H explain the short- and long-term impacts.

This disadvantage may strike you as being a bit absurd. If it does, you are responding correctly. Despite its logical structure, it is *not* the kind of disadvantage you should be offering if you think debating should be a serious discussion of important issues. Generally speaking, when the number of subpoints gets this high, you are in danger of leaving genuine public policy discussion and offering what some critics have called "meatball disadvantages." Sometimes the public policies under discussion are so complex that many logical steps are absolutely necessary to demonstrate how the policy will result in serious problems. So, the number of subpoints it takes to make the second step is not *necessarily* an indication of your having left public policy debate and entered a "twilight zone" of mere game-playing. However, when the number gets high, be suspicious.

Two more symptoms of "meatball disadvantages" are present in this disadvantage. One is seen in subpoint D. Oftentimes, a "meatball disadvantage" will cite what the affirmative is bound to do as a result of debate rules or theory and use it as one of the links in building the disadvantage. The other is seen in subpoint H. "Meatball disadvantages" often claim exaggerated impacts: a police state, dead Third World babies, nuclear war, a melted polar icecap.

So, if the number of subpoints or causal links is high, if a rule or procedure of debate is part of the chain of reasoning, *or* if the impact(s) seem exaggerated, *beware*. These symptoms do not always mean you have abandoned serious public policy discussion; after all, ill-conceived policies can result in dire consequences, including nuclear war, and public policies do sometimes initiate a chain of effects.

However, the presence of these symptoms should make you suspicious. Also, ask yourself if a member of Congress would ever think to raise the objection you are thinking of raising. If you cannot imagine hearing the objection voiced in the Senate or the House of Representatives, you may be on the verge of offering a "meatball disadvantage."

Exercises: Challenging Plans

Use the heuristic for plans to generate workability arguments, solvency arguments, and disadvantages for the following plans. Structure those arguments according to the suggestions in this chapter.

1. The resolution is "That United States intelligence gathering be significantly curtailed"; the plan bans the FBI from investigating political dissenters, enforces the ban by establishing a special prosecutor within the Department of Justice, and funds the operation of this prosecutor through a "vice tax" on tobacco and alcohol.
2. The resolution is "That Presidential control of United States foreign policy be significantly curtailed"; the plan requires detailed accounting to Congress, in advance, of all defense expenditures. The Department of Defense (which is an executive department under the President) has too much control, the affirmative argues, when large lump sums are appropriated which the Pentagon spends as it pleases.
3. The resolution is "That the United States should adopt a comprehensive program to control water resources"; the case identifies the significant threats to water resources as industrial pollution and nuclear energy production. Therefore, the plan sets up a new federal agency to set and enforce standards for emissions into waterways and to approve nuclear power plant cooling procedures in advance of construction. The agency will issue licenses; without a license, a company cannot operate or a plant cannot be built. The agency will be staffed as necessary and funded through the closing of selected tax loopholes.
4. The resolution is "That the United States military be significantly strengthened"; the plan calls for increasing military pay significantly so as to increase the number of qualified men and women in the armed forces. Funding will be through the best optimal mix of closing selected tax loopholes, a five percent increase in the corporate tax rate, a "vice tax" on tobacco and alcohol, and cuts in federal expenditures.

Value Debate and the Second Negative Speaker

All of the comments thus far in this chapter assume that the second negative speaker will concentrate his or her attention on the policy or plan the affirmative team chooses to offer. Value resolutions are, however, prepolicy; therefore, there is no specific plan or policy to attack when debating such resolutions.

In earlier chapters, I have emphasized that the theory underlying the debating of value resolutions is evolving and I have tried to offer some safe, but nonetheless substantial guidelines. My concluding warning to all participants in value debate in Chapter 4 was to be alert to changes in theory and practice because they will be rapidly occurring. For the second negative debater, I must repeat that warning and underscore it: because second negative debaters cannot do what their counterparts in policy debate do because there is no plan in value debate, numerous approaches to that speaker position in value debate have been tried and more will be tried in the years to come.

I would suggest that what should be done will vary depending on the kind of value resolution under debate. If it is a PNP resolution (for example, "Resolved: That unilateral disarmament is desirable"), the affirmative is defending value statements which, if accepted, would lead one to draft a particular kind of policy. The second negative seems to have three options: (1) extending his or her partner's argumentation; (2) citing the disadvantages of *the kind* of policy the affirmative is suggesting; or (3) objecting to pursuing the value(s) the affirmative team is defending. The difference between the second and third strategies is subtle. A disadvantage would be, "A policy like the one the affirmative is validating would lead to Soviet adventurism"; a value objection would be, "Basing foreign policy on promoting peace will lead to nonpeaceful actions by nations not sharing the affirmative's values." The first is a more practical objection; the second is broader, more philosophical. Any of these three approaches could be taken. However, debaters should be aware that taking the first approach *could* lead to repetition and monotony, especially among beginning debaters and at a season's start. Furthermore, debaters should be aware that taking the second approach will offend some judges who do not want the debating of value resolutions to resemble the debating of policy resolutions.

If the value resolution is a 3PC resolution (for example, "Resolved: That environmental protection is more desirable than energy exploration"), the affirmative is defending value statements which, if accepted, would lead one to draft a particular kind of policy. Thus, the same options are available to a second negative debater when a 3PC resolution is under discussion as when a PNP resolution is being debated. The same cautions apply. If the value resolution is a 3PR resolution (for example, "Resolved: That America's schools have failed"), the situation is very different. The affirmative is defending value statements which do not clearly or directly imply a specific policy. The resolution is indeed prepolicy; however, it is far more "pre" than typical PNP or 3PC resolutions. As a result, the second negative speaker is denied the second option discussed above. Thus, he or she must either extend the arguments offered in the first negative speech and offer more arguments of the same kind *or* cite the disadvantages of acting upon the value(s) the affirmative team is defending (in other words, offer what are often called "value objections"). For example, let's say the affirmative team criticizes American education for not providing students with a sufficient moral basis for adult life. A second negative might try to list and explain the problems that might develop if morality were emphasized in education. Such an emphasis would lead to—a second negative debater might argue—(1) a further deterioration in instruction in science and technology and (2) cultural discrimination, since the morals of the majority culture would be taught and those of other cultures ignored or demeaned.

If the second negative offers either these kinds of value objections or more policy-oriented disadvantages, the arguments should be structured along the lines suggested earlier in this chapter for disadvantages in policy debate. First, announce what the affirmative team does; second, explain the consequences; third, announce the impact of these consequences. Following this three-step pattern, you would structure the value objections above as follows:

Objection 1: Emphasizing morality will lead to a further deterioration in instruction in science and technology:
A. The affirmative wants to teach morality;
B. Teaching morality means less time for vital subjects, such as science and technology. Given state requirements in certain subject areas and in basic skills such as writing and computation, it is the more advanced science and technology courses that will suffer;
C. As a result, the United States will fall behind the Soviets, the West Germans, and the Japanese; our national security and our economic health will be in danger.

Objection 2: Emphasizing morality will lead to cultural discrimination:
A. The affirmative wants to put morality into the classroom;
B. The morality taught will certainly be that of the majority culture;
C. The result is discrimination, which is in and of itself bad, but may also produce discontent on the part of cultural minorities and cultural racism on the part of majority students.

Let me offer two pieces of advice on structuring such objections in debates on value resolutions. First, avoid going beyond A, B, and C. Excessive structuring is one of the faults of policy-oriented debating those who have turned to value-oriented debate often cite. If you structure your arguments beyond A, B, and C, you may be offending your judge. Second, avoid both the words "impact" and "massive." The words are suggestive of policy-oriented debate and its excesses; furthermore, absurd impacts, such as nuclear war, the melting of the polar icecap, and millions suffering from starvation, are among the characteristics of many policy debates that annoy coaches/judges who have abandoned policy-oriented debating and have embraced value-oriented debating as an alternative.

Briefs

To what extent can you or should you prepare negative arguments in advance of competition? Many debaters will write out, complete with evidence, arguments they will offer if the affirmative team does such-and-such. Many affirmative

NICARAGUA

Topicality
1. Is the affirmative prohibiting *all* forms of military intervention? If not, argue that the affirmative is not meeting the parameter.
2. Is the affirmative largely talking about the CIA? If so, argue that the CIA is paramilitary and civilian, not military. Therefore, the affirmative is not talking about "military intervention."
3. Is the affirmative talking about U.S. intervention into Nicaragua or U.S. support for Hondurans or guerrillas based in Honduras who themselves intervene into Nicaragua. If the latter, the affirmative is not talking about "United States military intervention."

Justification
4. If the affirmative is prohibiting all forms of military intervention, they must justify the broad prohibition, not just parts of it.

Problem, Significance
5. Argue that U.S. intervention into Nicaragua is justified because:
    a) Nicaragua is an ideological enemy to freedom;
    b) Nicaragua violates human rights;
    c) Nicaragua exports revolution;
    d) Nicaragua is functioning as a Soviet or Cuban proxy;
    e) Only military pressure on Nicaragua will force the government to pursue a moderate course.
6. Does U.S. aid to antigovernment forces lead to benefits which outweigh any possible problems? See #5 for possible benefits.
7. If the affirmative argues that U.S. intervention into Nicaragua violates Nicaragua's right to self-determination, argue that the present government was not chosen by the people and that an overthrow of the present government is necessary so that the people can exercise their right to self-determination.

Causality
8. Is U.S. pressure the *only* cause of the military buildup in Nicaragua? Suggest others. To the extent there are others, affirmative solvency is questionable.
9. Is the Nicaraguan buildup the *only* cause of the arms race in Central America? Suggest others. To the extent there are others, affirmative solvency is questionable.
10. Is U.S. pressure the *only* cause of the Nicaraguan rush to the Soviet Union? Suggest other causes. To the extent there are others, the affirmative's solvency is questionable.

Inherency
11. The Reagan Administration has recently made peaceful overtures toward the Nicaraguan government; therefore, U.S. policy is not inherently interventionist or hostile.
12. Several treaties, etc., already exist which outlaw what the affirmative claims the United States is doing. There is no need for the affirmative prohibition since prohibitions already exist.

Solvency
13. Will eliminating U.S. pressure on Nicaragua necessarily lead to either a reduction in the military buildup there or a reduction in the arms race? Removing the initial cause does not necessarily lead to the elimination of the problem. Use dominoes analogy.
14. If the affirmative argues (in response to #12) that these treaties have been violated again and again, ask what stops the U.S. from violating the affirmative's law or treaty.
15. Will eliminating U.S. pressure on Nicaragua necessarily lead to a reversal of its Soviet drift? Perhaps the Soviet Union "owns" Nicaragua now. Remember that eliminating the initial cause does not necessarily lead to the elimination of the problem.

Disadvantages
16. Honduras will fall, then El Salvador.

Figure 8.2   Sample case brief.

cases are predictable, and for these, preprepared negative arguments are useful. These arguments, in written form, are referred to as "briefs."

There are three kinds of briefs you might want to prepare during the competitive season. First of all, you will find "case briefs" useful; they list the arguments you *might* want to offer against a specific type of affirmative case. For example, if the resolution concerns military intervention, a popular case may focus on CIA activities directed against the Marxist government in Nicaragua. You could brainstorm using the appropriate heuristics in Chapters 7 and 8 and come up with a "case brief" such as that given in Figure 8.2. In an actual debate, you would pull arguments from the brief and apply them to the *particular* contentions of the *particular* affirmative case you are refuting. You should not simply read the brief, for some arguments on it will be inapplicable to the particular version of the case you are refuting and your failure to follow the organization of the affirmative case will blunt considerably the impact of your arguments and will probably muddle the debate.

Second, you will find "generic briefs" useful. The first negative debater may wish to begin his or her speech with a general philosophical observation—an observation applicable to any case which affirms the resolution. For example, a resolution calls for federal control of all water resources. A possible "generic brief" for the first negative might be one that argues that such federal control violates the states' constitutional rights. The second negative debater may want to prepare some general, almost-always-applicable disadvantages or value objections. A "generic brief" would save this debater time during the actual debate, for he or she would not have to prepare this argument from scratch in every debate. Figure 8.3 is such a "generic brief."

Third, you will find "argument-specific briefs" or "blocks" useful. These outline preprepared negative (or affirmative) arguments to respond to specific

Disadvantage: Plan Will Prevent Necessary Emergency Intervention.
A. Plan prohibits all U.S. military intervention;
B. A number of possible emergency situations would warrant U.S. military intervention:
    i. The seizure of the American embassy;
    ii. A threat to the lives and property of U.S. citizens;
    iii. a Cuban missile crisis-like situation;
    iv. *gross* violations of human rights;
    v. a natural disaster;
    vi. significant U.S.-bound drug traffic;
    vii. a cut-off of vital resources (oil, minerals, coffee);
C. Our inability to intervene would have significant costs.

Figure 8.3 Sample generic brief.

The Soviet Union Is Not Expansionistic:
A. Soviet doctrine calls for economic and ideological conquest, not military conquest.
   See Weatherspoon, #100
   Marx, #100
   Lenin, #100
   Stalin, #100
   Khrushchev, #100
   Brezhnev, #100
   New York Times on Andropov, #100
B. The Soviet Union has never acted aggressively against a nation not already within its sphere of influence.
   On Hungary, see Dickinson, #101
   On Czechoslovakia, see Dickinson, #101
   On Afghanistan, see Myers, #101
   On Poland, see *Christian Science Monitor*, #101
C. And, even if the Soviet Union wished to act aggressively, her economy would not permit her to.
   See *Washington Post*, #102
   Myers, #102
   Anderson, #102

Figure 8.4 Sample argument-specific brief.

arguments. Figure 8.4 is a brief prepared to counter the specific argument that the Soviet Union is expansionist. This sample makes references to the evidence the debater would use to support the outlined arguments. The brief could have been prepared with the evidence typed on it.

In theory, negative teams could prepare "argument-specific briefs" for over a thousand affirmative arguments. The wisdom of spending a great amount of time writing such briefs is, however, questionable. The time would probably be better spent on other debate-preparation activities or simply on other activities, such as studying or sleeping. You would be wise to reserve "argument-specific briefs" or "blocks" for the most usual or the most difficult to handle arguments.

Briefs are overused and misused in debate today. The result of overuse is unthinking debate. Some debaters panic if they do not have a brief to read: they cannot think of refutation on their own. Some debaters misapply briefs: they do not think about what their opponents are saying and *then* decide if the brief is applicable or not; rather, they just read. Some debaters read briefs their coach or teammates have prepared without really understanding the briefs. Some debaters read applicable briefs but they lazily do not think much about the specific case they are confronting, and therefore fail to see a telling argument they could voice against it.

This overuse and misuse has weakened debating as a thinking activity, and has turned off many faculty members and prospective debaters who view the activity as the maniacal preparation of hundreds of plastic-covered briefs (also called "slicksheets") rather than disciplined, quick thinking. Briefs have a place in debating; they can help debaters perform more efficiently, and preparing briefs is educational. However, they are not a substitute for thinking, but rather a store of previous insights. Use briefs then, but be careful not to let them replace or dull your mind's very important on-the-spot work.

Some Special Negative Problems

The affirmative team can be relatively sure of how a debate will go. It chooses the ground and knows the negative will respond in one of several ways. If the affirmative team is well-prepared for competition, it should know how to handle all of these ways. Every now and again, a negative team will do something surprising, but the affirmative can usually count on not being thrown horribly off its established course.

The negative team, on the other hand, can run into some unusual situations. Four, in particular, should be mentioned.

Dealing with "Squirrels"

A "squirrel," as noted earlier, is an unusual affirmative case—one that represents a fuzzy, nutty interpretation of the resolution. Consider the resolution "That all United States military intervention into the internal affairs of any foreign nation or nations in the western hemisphere should be prohibited." Would an affirmative case talking about U.S. citizens sending money to the Irish Republican Army surprise you if you were a negative debater? What about the following cases: potential U.S. military involvement in Poland; U.S. coercion of the Colombian government to send Colombian troops into the northeastern section of that nation to stop drug traffic to the United States; banning U.S. intervention in the prospective civil war between Quebec and the rest of Canada.

Each of these cases is a "squirrel" and ought to surprise you. The Irish Republican Army case uses a strict geographical definition of "western hemisphere," rather than the more common definition which would exclude the parts of Europe (and Africa) that just happen to be west of the Greenwich Meridian. This case is fuzzy, squirrel-like. The Poland case interprets "any foreign nation or nations in the western hemisphere" to mean that an affirmative case can legitimately deal with *either* any foreign nation in the whole world *or* two or more nations in the western hemisphere. This case is also fuzzy. The Colombia case is based on the argument that, if we force a nation to use its troops, then that use of troops constitutes *de facto* U.S. military intervention. This third case is also fuzzy. Unlike the other three, the Canada case is *not* based on any unusual reading of the resolution, but it is a "squirrel" nonetheless. Why? Because when one thinks of U.S. military intervention, Canada is one of the last nations which would come to mind. And even then, most would dismiss the thought given how unlikely U.S. military action would be in the event Quebec tried to secede and form an independent nation.

How should you handle "squirrels"? First, don't panic. "Squirrels" win because they produce panic (especially among nonthinking debaters who do not have any briefs on the case), not because they are good cases. Every now and then, a "squirrel" is also a good case, but solidity and "squirrelness" rarely coincide. If you remain calm, you can probably find some crucial weakness in the "squirrel" that stands before you. The weakness, more often than not, is either in the area of topicality or the area of significance. Review what Chapter 7 says about topicality challenges. Also review what that chapter says about the affirmative's obligation to establish the existence of a significant problem by showing either a significant harm resulting from that problem, or significant advantages in solving the problem better than the present policy or doing a significantly better job of meeting a goal or goals than the present policy. The first three "squirrels" mentioned above are beatable on topicality; the second of those—i.e., Poland—and the fourth case—i.e., Canada—can be beaten by arguing that there is no likelihood of U.S. military intervention and therefore no significant problem.

Some negative debaters like to "cry foul" when they are confronted by a "squirrel." Many judges are sympathetic, and a few judges will give an affirmative team a loss if they offer a "squirrel" case. However, most judges expect the negative team to debate the case and beat it. The complaint that "the 'squirrel' is unfair because I didn't have time to prepare briefs on it" will fall on many deaf ears. It is the lament of a debater who does not understand that good debating is characterized by on-the-spot thinking, not the reading of "slicksheets." In a fairly recent National Debate Tournament championship round, the affirmative team surprised the negative by using a brand-new case. The negative team cried foul, arguing before a large audience that it was unfair of the affirmative to "run" a new case, because they (the negative) had not had the opportunity to prepare briefs in response to it in advance. The judging panel's 6-1 decision in favor of the affirmative team and the panel members' remarks made it clear to the negative team (and all readers) that their complaint was without merit. So, if you complain that a "squirrel" is unfair, base your complaint on its fuzziness or craziness, not on your inability to prepare briefs in advance. And don't stop there: use your mind and find the flaw or flaws.

One other strategy is available to you, although not in all regions or leagues. If the affirmative's case is, in your judgment, a really far-fetched interpretation of the resolution, you could argue (a) that the affirmative case scarcely embodies the resolution. Since (b) the judge at the end of the debate must decide whether or not to accept that resolution, (c) the affirmative has given him or her no basis upon which to accept or reject the resolution. Therefore, you offer what are known as counterwarrants. You present several *reasonable* interpretations of the resolution and refute them, arguing that you have provided the judge with a firm basis upon which to pass judgment—a negative judgment—on the resolution. Some debate theorists suggest the offering of counterwarrants as a viable negative strategy when the affirmative case is either far-fetched or too limited; many coaches and judges reject the suggestion because it allows the negative team to set up straw men and then burn them and because it tends to minimize clash. *If* you are in a league or region where the debating climate is suitable for counterwarrants, you *might* profitably combine the offering of counterwarrants with indictments of the affirmative case's topicality and significance.

Debating and Unorthodox Affirmative Teams

What is an "unorthodox" team? The answer depends, of course, on what is orthodox or standard. If you are debating in a region or league where experimentation in affirmative cases is common or where new debate theory is being tried out or created, very little would be "unorthodox." Except, perhaps, an affirmative team who chooses to use the half-serious, half-comic Parliamentary style. Such an unorthodox approach would not only pose problems in a wide-open district or league; it would be unorthodox and pose problems in a conservative district or league. In the conservative area, some of the more recent approaches to debate would also strike a negative team as unorthodox. The alternative justifications case, for example, would probably throw beginning debaters in a conservative area for a loop. That case structure has been around long enough so that its possible use can be anticipated and, as in Chapter 7, prepared for. But you would bother to prepare only if you did indeed anticipate it. Also, out there somewhere, there are debaters and coaches devising approaches even more radical (or at least newer) than the alternative justifications case.

When debating a team that uses the unorthodox Parliamentary style, which often emphasizes wit at the expense of substance, you have three choices. First, you can stand up and tell your judge and your opponents that their style is inappropriate and you intend to be absolutely serious. This choice tends to stop the debate for all intents and purposes and puts the judge in the awkward position of judging *not* what goes on during the particular debate but what should be going on at the tournament. I don't recommend making this first choice. Second, you can play the affirmative's game and try to match their wit and irreverence. Making this choice will usually put you at a disadvantage, for your opponents, who chose the Parliamentary style, may well be masters of it and you may be relatively inexperienced at it. Therefore I don't recommend making this second choice. Third, you can steer a middle course: you can try to treat the issues humorously *and* seriously. I recall vividly an intercollegiate debate I was involved in as a freshman at a major varsity tournament. The resolution required the affirmative to significantly curtail the foreign policy powers of the President. An affirmative team from a Canadian university offered, in Parliamentary style, a plan that called for Canada to take over the direction of U.S. foreign policy because, they argued, the United States was stuck in Freud's "anal stage" of development and had made a mess of things. My partner and I chose to treat their proposal both seriously and flippantly, and the judge, a coach at one of the nation's best debating schools, commended us for keeping the debate pleasant and giving her serious, substantive reasons for rejecting the outlandish proposal. I recommend making this third choice.

When debating a team that is doing something theoretically bizarre (from your point of view), you again have three choices. First, you can scream "unfair" and argue that "they can't do that." Taking this course stops debate and puts the judge in the awkward position of deciding *not* who won the particular debate but what should and should not be allowed in debating. Some judges relish this position; however, most would prefer to make a decision based on issues, not their views on theory. Also, if you put the judge in this position, the decision could just as easily go against you as for you. When you take this first course, you tend to lose control of your destiny. Second, you could try to grasp the theoretical underpinnings of the new approach and respond accordingly. Time is, however, limited, and you may not come to a complete understanding of the approach until well into the debate—too late to win. Third, you can try to relate what the affirmative team is doing to the theory of debate you know and debate the affirmative accordingly.

Let's say the affirmative team offers a new twist on the alternative justifications case: the team offers two cases and says it will defend the first, but if the negative team seems to be defeating the first, it will then switch to the second and defend it. You should argue that you have two cases before you, and you should attack both *from the very start* and insist that the affirmative defend both *from the very start*. Let's say the affirmative team argues that there is no such thing as a static status quo, that the status quo is properly defined as a dynamic policy system, and that the policy system is already heading toward the adoption of the resolution. Therefore, in defending the resolution, the affirmative advocates staying with present policy and demands that the negative must justify a change in policy to win. You should argue either that the affirmative has misunderstood the direction of present policy and has, as a result, misdefined the system's direction or that the resolution calls for immediate action and that the long-term course of present policy is irrelevant. Either way you end up demanding that the affirmative team justify a policy—one which is either different from the status quo in kind or at least different from the status quo in its immediate effect. You, in other words, try to force the affirmative team to do what it traditionally does. There is no guarantee, of course, that the affirmative will do what you want them to do, but even if the affirmative refuses to move off its radical ground an inch, you have succeeded in giving the judge something substantive to decide the debate on— in the first instance, your attacks on both affirmative cases; in the second, either your view of present policy or your indictment of the affirmative for failing to justify an immediate change in policy.

Debating Underprepared Affirmative Teams

Sometimes an affirmative team will have embraced more sophisticated theories than you know or immediately understand: this situation poses a problem for the negative team. So does the opposite situation, the situation in which the affirmative team does not seem to be aware of or in control of debate theory. The team may not understand key concepts such as inherency or the extratopicality of an advantage. Worse, the team may not know exactly what is expected of each speaker.

What should you do when debating such an affirmative team? Believe it or not, it is *not* difficult to lose to such a team. You can lose if you (a) become so confident of your victory that you neglect to really debate, (b) act superior and lecture your opponents on their obligations and thereby prompt the judge to be overly sympathetic toward them, or (c) get so frustrated and/or flustered that your arguments lose their clarity or coherence or impact. You need to guard against these three responses. First, take your underprepared opponents seriously. Second, although you should make it clear what an affirmative team must do to justify the resolution's adoption and although you should make the judge understand precisely how the particular affirmative team does not meet its obligations, you should not lecture them. Be polite. Make their failures clear without implicitly and explicitly calling them "stupid" or any adjective like "stupid." Third, stay calm. And plan your speeches so that they project an air of calmness. You can project this air by organizing your speeches clearly, speaking a bit more slowly than usual, and using the beginnings and endings of your speeches to best effect by highlighting at these points the inadequacies of the affirmative team's defense of the resolution. At the beginning, you can offer your overview of the debate as it has progressed; at the end, you can summarize the reasons why the judge should reject the affirmative case and thus the resolution.

Debating a Poorly Organized Affirmative Case

Cases can be poorly organized in two different directions. At one extreme, the case may be a string of arguments among which there is no clear logical connection. If you stand back from such a case, you can probably see what its logic is, but the organization does not help convey it. At the other extreme, the case may be overorganized with subpoints and sub-subpoints and sub-sub-subpoints. Overorganization is difficult to deal with because it distracts the listener's attention from the case's content by calling excessive attention to the mechanics of structure — i.e., whether you are now listening to (1), (A), (ii), (b), or (1), (A), (iii), (a). A negative team would be well-advised *not* to follow either of these weak organizations, for, if the team does, the entire debate will either seem to lack logic or will quickly become rather fuzzy in even the best judge's mind. As a negative debater, you want the judge to see the problems with the logic or the inadequacy of some of the links in the affirmative's overall argument; you also want the debate's issues clear, for, in a fuzzy debate, a judge's decision will depend excessively on his or her perception rather than clearly defined affirmative and negative positions.

Thus, if an affirmative case is weakly organized, you ought to rearrange it for the affirmative. Tell the judge that you intend to refute the affirmative contentions in a logical order; tell the judge that you will first consider what the affirmative labeled contention (3) and then you'll consider contention (1), contention (2), the second half of contention (4), and the first half of contention (4). Stick to your order in later speeches, even if the affirmative team insists on proceeding in an illogical manner. At least, the negative speeches will keep the case's logic and its logical problems in the judge's mind.

If an affirmative case is overorganized, engage in "grouping." Let's say the affirmative team offers a contention and develops it with four subpoints and develops the subpoints with three, two, four, and three sub-subpoints respectively. You should, at least, consider grouping the sub-subpoints together and responding to them as if they were a single point. You might even consider grouping two or more of the subpoints together and responding to them as if they were a single argument. Just make sure you make your procedure clear to the judge. Begin your refutation of a particular contention by telling the judge to "group the (A) and (B) subpoints"; begin your refutation of a particular subpoint by telling the judge to "group all the points under (B) together."

You should now know what the affirmative team does in a debate and what the negative team does in response. You should know the basics as well as some of the more advanced strategies. You probably now have some idea as to how the entire debate would proceed, but, if you've never seen an actual debate, the idea is probably a bit fuzzy. The next chapter looks at the entire debate and helps you handle its dynamics.

After reading and studying Chapter 8, you know:

- what the conventional negative division of labor is in policy debate and how it might be violated (1) in response to "squirrels," (2) in response to a strong case, and (3) to avoid late turnarounds;
- how to devise workability arguments, solvency arguments, and disadvantages against the affirmative plan in policy debate;
- how to structure these kinds of plan attacks so that the structure reflects the attack's logic;
- that the second negative speaker in value debate may (1) extend the arguments his or her partner voiced against the affirmative case, (2) offer disadvantages of the kind of policy the affirmative case implies, or (3) offer broader objections to acting upon the value/s the affirmative team is defending;
- what "case briefs," "generic briefs," "argument-specific briefs" are and how to use them properly;
- how to:
    —deal with "squirrels";
    —debate unorthodox affirmative teams;
    —debate underprepared affirmative teams;
    —debate against a poorly organized affirmative case.

CHAPTER 9

The Entire Debate

In this chapter, you will learn:

- how a debate is organized;
- what each speaker does in a conventional policy debate;
- how to modify these speaker duties in a number of special situations;
- what each speaker does in a value debate;
- how to plan for the toughest rebuttals;
- how to keep a flow sheet in policy and value debate;
- how different types of judges judge.

Debating is, in some senses, a game: as such, it has its rules and its procedures. The preceding chapters have introduced you to some of these, but not to the game in its entirety. This chapter steps back from particular arguments or particular affirmative cases and looks at the entire debate.

An Overview

Debate and other speech activities are often referred to as "forensics." The person who is teaching or coaching you may have the title "Director of Forensics." Most people, thanks to the popular television show "Quincy" are used to hearing the term "forensics" in conjunction with medicine and, therefore, may well wonder what debaters have to do with autopsies and the like. Well, debaters do dissect arguments, but it is not in debaters' skill at cutting and probing that the connection between debating and "Quincy" lies.

Aristotle is one of the earliest rhetoricians: he made a systematic study of the art of persuasion in the fifth century B. C. Among the many analyses he offered was his division of persuasive speeches into three types: speeches suitable for the law-making process, which he termed *deliberative oratory*; speeches suitable for ceremonial occasions, which he termed *epideictic oratory*; and speeches suitable for the courtroom setting, which he termed *forensic oratory*. Forensic medicine, you see, is medicine pertinent to judical proceedings; similarly, debate and other speech activities were originally seen as communications activities pertinent to judicial proceedings.

I mention the origin of the word "forensics" at this time for a reason. Although debaters may see themselves as engaging in a kind of speech activity similar to what goes on in the Congress or some other policymaking forum, in the beginning, debate was conceived of as more judicial than legislative, more forensic than deliberative. The procedures were set back in the beginning, and, as a result, the procedures have a judicial tinge.

Imagine the status quo as a criminal defendant. The affirmative team indicts the status quo, trying to find it guilty beyond a reasonable doubt; the negative team defends the status quo and/or tries to demonstrate the flaws in the affirmative's case, thereby creating doubt as to the validity of the accusation. Trials are divided into two parts: (1) the opening remarks followed by the presentation of the evidence which makes the lawyer's case—either against or for the accused; (2) the summations. A debate is similarly structured: there are constructive speeches in which the cases for and against are built; then there are rebuttals. Debates could, in theory, be between individuals, between teams of two, between teams of three, etc. Although all but the most unwieldy formats have been tried, the settled format for almost all debates has a team of two people on the one side, a team of two on the other. Given this format, each team needs two constructive speeches and two rebuttals if everyone is to deliver each kind of speech.

Since the affirmative team accuses the status quo, the affirmative team must speak first. To maximize the exchange of views, constructive speeches alternate:

First Affirmative Constructive Speech
First Negative Constructive Speech
Second Affirmative Constructive Speech
Second Negative Constructive Speech

In both a courtroom and in a debate (traditionally conceived), there is a strong presumption for the accused: the accused must be shown to be guilty beyond a reasonable doubt to be convicted. This presumption of innocence was made a part of the American judicial system by our forefathers to insure the protection of individual rights and it, therefore, seems just and necessary. In the context of debating, the comparable presumption of the innocence of the status quo seems a bit unfair: the affirmative has a tremendous burden to overcome, and only a debate ballot, not someone's reputation or life, is at stake. The unfairness is mitigated a bit by the affirmative team's being able to choose the nature and the structure of the accusation or case against the status quo. Still, the affirmative has quite a burden. Therefore, to compensate for this burden, the affirmative team is given the last rebuttal speech. To maximize the exchange of views within the rebuttal period, rebuttals alternate:

First Negative Rebuttal
First Affirmative Rebuttal
Second Negative Rebuttal
Second Affirmative Rebuttal

In most high school debates, the constructive speeches are eight minutes long, the rebuttals four; in most college policy debates, the constructive speeches are ten, the rebuttals five; in most college value debates, the constructive speeches are eight, the rebuttals four.

If you list the four constructive speeches and then the four rebuttals together, you will see that the negative team has a solid twelve or fifteen minutes of speaking time at the core of the debate. This is called the *negative block*, and, according to most observers of debate, if the negative has not established a lead by the end of this block, an affirmative victory is almost a foregone conclusion. Once upon a time, there was a mandatory recess or break between constructive speeches and rebuttals, but no more.

The only things that can interrupt the negative block are cross-examination and preparation time. In the vast majority of high school and college debates, there is a period of cross-examination (usually three minutes long) after each constructive speech. (More on cross-examination in Chapter 10.) In the overwhelming majority of high school and college debates, each team is allotted a set amount of time for preparation during the debate. Ten minutes is usual. How a team spends its preparation time is important. Negative teams try to spend it at two points in the debate: (1) before the first negative constructive speech to get a firm grasp of the particular affirmative case and decide upon an effective negative strategy; (2) before the second negative rebuttal to make that last negative presentation as good as possible. Few negative teams choose to spend preparation time between the second negative constructive speech and the first negative rebuttal since spending time at that point provides the first affirmative rebuttalist with extra preparation time. Affirmative teams tend to spend their allotted preparation time at three points: (1) before the second affirmative constructive speech, especially if the first negative debater has taken an unusual approach, such as a counterplan, in his or her constructive speech; (2) before the very demanding first affirmative rebuttal; and (3) before the important second affirmative rebuttal.

Case Side, Plan Side

In one very important way, a debate is *not* like a criminal court trial. In a trial, the prosecutor make a case against the defendant—that's it. In a debate, the affirmative team makes a case against the status quo, but then offers a specific policy or plan to address the problem which the status quo has. Because of this important difference between judicial proceedings and debates, many have stopped viewing debate within a judicial paradigm and have chosen to view debate within a legislative paradigm. Some implications of this paradigm shift for negative teams were discussed in Chapter 7. No matter what paradigm you accept today, you must understand that the origin of the rules and procedures of debate is found within the judicial paradigm. Given this origin, one can understand why, not too many years ago, the case against the status quo was *very* important and the specific affirmative plan of less importance. As the paradigm shift from judicial to legislative has taken place, the plan has acquired equal importance with the case. In fact, many debaters and a few coaches would probably argue that the plan is more important today than the case. As the plan rose in prominence in actual debates, the negative speakers—and, as a result, the affirmative speakers—became either "case side" or "plan side" specialists.

Figure 9.1 reviews the structure of a competitive debate, noting each speaker's "case-side" or "plan-side" responsibilities. In many ways, the first negative and the second affirmative carry on their own debate over the indictment of the status quo while the second negative and the first affirmative carry on their own debate over the plan. Overspecialization can, however, be a mistake, for, as you will notice as you examine Figure 9.1, the first affirmative rebuttalist and the two summary rebuttalists (second negative and second affirmative) are expected to address themselves to both the affirmative case and the affirmative plan.

In value debate, there may or may not be a division comparable to the case side versus plan side division in policy debate. If the second negative constructive speaker chooses to simply extend on his or her partner's arguments, then there is only a case side in the debate. If the second negative constructive speaker chooses to offer either disadvantages or value objections, then there is what is called a case side/off-case side division.

Modifications

The procedures outlined in Figure 9.1 are the usual ones. However, there are some unusual circumstances which may well pop up. These unusual circumstances require modifications in the usual speech-by-speech procedures.

When an "Alternative Justifications Case" Is Presented

If the affirmative team who offered multiple justifications for adopting the resolution intended to debate all of them throughout the debate, then the procedures would be the same in this situation as in the usual situation where there is one rationale for change and one plan—except each speaker would have the enormous task of attacking or defending three or four cases or plans. However, when an affirmative team goes the "alternative justifications" route, the team usually expects to give

1st Affirmative Constructive Speech	1st Negative Constructive Speech	2nd Affirmative Constructive Speech	2nd Negative Constructive Speech
Presents Affirmative Case and Plan	Offers Observations Refutes Affirmative Case	Responds to Observations Defends Affirmative Case	Offers Workability Arguments Offers Solvency Arguments Offers Disadvantages
1st Negative Rebuttal	1st Affirmative Rebuttal	2nd Negative Rebuttal	2nd Affirmative Rebuttal
Defends Observations Made in 1st Negative Constructive Speech Refutes Affirmative Case	Refutes Workability Arguments Refutes Solvency Arguments Refutes Disadvantages Refutes Observations Made in 1st Negative Constructive Speech and Defended in 1st Negative Rebuttal Defends Affirmative Case	Defends Workability Arguments Defends Solvency Arguments Defends Disadvantages Defends Observations Made in 1st Negative Constructive Speech and Defended in 1st Negative Rebuttal Refutes Affirmative Case	Refutes Observations Made in 1st Negative Constructive Speech and Defended in 2nd Negative Rebuttal Defends Affirmative Case Refutes Workability Arguments Refutes Solvency Arguments Refutes Disadvantages

Figure 9.1 The structure of a debate.

up on some of its justifications and concentrate on others, depending on what the first negative constructive speech sounds like. The shrewd negative team will not permit the affirmative team to get away with this dumping. As a result, every negative speech, after the affirmative team has made its choice(s), should (1) attack this "alternative justifications" strategy as unfair and unproductive (see Chapter 7); (2) insist that the affirmative team, since it chose to offer multiple justifications, must win or lose based on all, not the one or two it finally selects; (3) attack the rationales and plans of any dropped cases. This cluster of arguments should be planned so as to take no more than three minutes of the second negative constructive speech and no more than one minute of the negative rebuttals. Why? The cluster may well strike a responsive note in the minds of some judges but leave others cold. These others buy the "alternative justifications" strategy and expect the negative team to meet the affirmative head-on. To meet the affirmative head-on and thereby meet the expectations of these judges, the second negative constructive speech should focus on the remaining plan/s; the first negative rebuttal should focus on the remaining justification(s); and the second negative rebuttalist should focus on both the remaining plan(s) and rationale(s). The bulk of the negative speeches should be devoted to this head-on argumentation.

In a "Net Benefits" Debate

In a "Net Benefits" debate, the negative team will defend a policy system, either the status quo, the status quo with repairs, or a counterplan. The negative team will try to minimize the affirmative advantages and stress the affirmative disadvantages; the negative team will also try to stress its policy's advantages and minimize its policy's disadvantages. The affirmative team will try to do the opposite on all four counts. If the policy system the negative chooses to defend is the status quo (with or without repairs), the procedures will only be slightly different from the usual ones.

The first negative constructive speech will zero in on the claimed advantages, denying them; this speech will also deny or minimize any alleged problems with the status quo. This speech *may* go farther and present the benefits of the status quo and a few of the proposed plan's disadvantages. The second affirmative constructive speech responds directly to the first negative: it argues that the affirmative plan is advantageous; it argues that the status quo is indeed disadvantageous; if appropriate, it argues that the status quo does not have the claimed advantages or benefits; and if appropriate, it argues that the affirmative plan is not disadvantageous. The second negative constructive speech concentrates on the affirmative plan and tries to show how it will not be advantageous as claimed and how it will lead to disadvantageous consequences. The second negative constructive speech may then emphasize the advantages of the status quo and refute any claims that the status quo has problems.

The first negative rebuttalist responds to the second affirmative constructive speech. Therefore, this rebuttal will emphasize the affirmative's lack of compelling advantage and the freedom of the status quo from serious problems. The first affirmative rebuttalist responds to the second negative constructive speech. Therefore, this rebuttal will emphasize the plan's ability to accrue its claimed advantages and the plan's freedom from disadvantages. This rebuttal should also briefly refute the alleged advantages of the status quo and briefly argue that the status quo does indeed have problems. The summary rebuttalists have to cover all four bases: (1) the status quo's disadvantages or problems; (2) the status quo's advantages or benefits; (3) the affirmative plan's advantages; (4) the affirmative plan's disadvantages. The order in which each speaker covers these four bases will depend on the particular debate.

One other issue will often arise in a "Net Benefits" debate, the question of certainty. "Net Benefits" debates are based, as Chapters 4 and 7 explained, on a simplified version of systems analysis. Systems analysis compares two systems—in this case, policy systems—assigning no presumption per se to either system.

However, the higher the degree of certainty of a claimed benefit or problem, the more weight the claim is assigned. Since the status quo is in operation, its problems and benefits are more certain. Therefore, there is greater certainty that the status quo has certain benefits and certain problems. This higher degree of certainty gives both teams a kind of presumption: we are rather certain about the affirmative's claims that the status quo has problems; we are also rather certain about the negative's claims that the status quo has advantages to offer. Debaters alert to the question of certainty and how it functions in a "Net Benefits" debate will emphasize the certainty of status quo problems (if on the affirmative) and status quo benefits (if on the negative). Alert debaters will also try to maximize the certainty of the claimed affirmative plan advantages (if on the affirmative) and disadvantages (if on the negative). How does one accomplish this latter goal? There are at least two ways: first, one can show that the benefits (if affirmative) or disadvantages (if negative) accrued when the policy was tried elsewhere—on a smaller scale, in another nation, at an earlier time; second, one can keep the causal links few and well evidenced.

Figure 9.2 presents the structure of a "Net Benefits" debate if the negative team chooses the status quo as its policy system. If the negative team chooses the status quo with minor repairs as its policy system, the structure would be the same except the first negative constructive speaker would have to outline the repairs and show that they would take care of any and all problems; subsequent affirmative speakers would argue (a) that the repairs are not repairs and (b) the repairs, if they were repairs, would not address the problems; and subsequent negative speakers would argue the opposite.

When a Counterplan Is Presented

Figure 9.3 presents the structure of a debate if the negative team chooses to present a counterplan. In such a debate, the first negative speaker addresses the affirmative team's rationale for change: (1) he or she may grant its validity; (2) he or she may qualify it in some way—for example, saying that the affirmative team has not analyzed the situation as completely as they should have and therefore has not discovered the true cause of the problem; (3) he or she may argue that there is a more compelling rationale for a policy change than the one the affirmative team presented. After addressing the affirmative rationale for change, the first negative speaker offers the counterplan—in as much detail as the affirmative plan (See Chapter 4). Next, the first negative speaker argues that the counterplan is superior to the plan. If the negative has chosen either the first or the second approach outlined above, then he or she will likely argue that the counterplan solves the agreed-upon problem better. "Better" here means three things: (a) more completely; (b) with additional advantages; (c) without the disadvantages of the affirmative plan. If the negative has chosen the third approach outlined above, then the negative speaker will likely argue that the counterplan is the better policy option. "Better" *here* can mean several different things: (a)

1st Affirmative Constructive Speech	1st Negative Constructive Speech	2nd Affirmative Constructive Speech	2nd Negative Constructive Speech
Presents Affirmative Case and Plan	Denies Advantages of Affirmative Plan Denies Problems of Status Quo Argues Advantages of Status Quo (optional) Argues Disadvantages of Affirmative Plan (optional)	Defends Advantages of Affirmative Plan Defends Problems of Status Quo Denies Advantages of Status Quo (if 1st Negative argues Advantages) Denies Disadvantages of Affirmative Plan (if 1st Negative argues Disadvantages)	Presents/Adds to Advantages of Status Quo Presents/Adds to Disadvantages of Affirmative Plan
1st Negative Rebuttal	1st Affirmative Rebuttal	2nd Negative Rebuttal	2nd Affirmative Rebuttal
Denies Advantages of Affirmative Plan Denies Problems of Status Quo Defends Advantages of Status Quo Offered in 1st Negative Constructive Speech Defends Disadvantages of Affirmative Plan Offered in 1st Negative Constructive Speech	Denies Advantages of Status Quo (both those argued by 1st Negative and those argued by 2nd Negative) Denies Disadvantages of Affirmative Plan (both those argued by 1st Negative and those argued by 2nd Negative) Defends Advantages of Affirmative Plan Defends Problems of Status Quo	Defends Advantages of Status Quo (all of them) Defends Disadvantages of Affirmative Plan (all of them) Denies Advantages of Affirmative Plan Denies Problems of Status Quo	Defends Advantages of Affirmative Plan Defends Problems of Status Quo Denies Advantages of Status Quo (all of them) Denies Disadvantages of Affirmative Plan (all of them)

Figure 9.2 The structure of a "Net Benefits" debate.

1st Affirmative Constructive Speech	1st Negative Constructive Speech	2nd Affirmative Constructive Speech	2nd Negative Constructive Speech
Presents Affirmative Case and Plan	Addresses Affirmative Case Offers Counterplan Argues Counterplan is Superior to Plan	Argues Counterplan is Topical and Noncompetitive Responds to 1st Negative Comments on Case Denies Superiority of Counterplan to Plan Presents Disadvantages of Counterplan	Argues Counterplan is Nontopical and Competitive Reestablishes Negative Position on Affirmative Case Argues Counterplan is Superior to Plan Refutes Disadvantages of Counterplan
1st Negative Rebuttal	1st Affirmative Rebuttal	2nd Negative Rebuttal	2nd Affirmative Rebuttal
Argues Counterplan is Nontopical and Competitive Repeats Negative Position on Affirmative Case Continues Arguing that Counterplan is Superior to Plan	Argues Counterplan is Topical and Noncompetitive Responds to Negative Position on Affirmative Case Denies Superiority of Counterplan to Plan Reestablishes Disadvantages of Counterplan	Argues Counterplan is Nontopical and Competitive Reestablishes Negative Position on Affirmative Case Argues Counterplan is Superior to Plan Denies Disadvantages of Counterplan	Argues Counterplan is Topical and Noncompetitive Reestablishes Affirmative Position on Case Denies Superiority of Counterplan to Plan Reestablishes Disadvantages of Counterplan

Figure 9.3 The structure of a counterplan debate.

the affirmative plan cannot solve the affirmative problem; (b) the counterplan does solve the serious problem the negative has pointed to; (c) the counterplan solves a more important problem than the one the affirmative plan either solves or tries to solve; (d) the counterplan accrues a number of advantages; (e) the plan accrues a number of disadvantages. Since a counterplan must be nontopical and competitive (see Chapter 7), the first negative speaker may be well-advised to offer arguments that the counterplan is nontopical and competitive, perhaps offering these arguments as a conclusion.

The second affirmative constructive speaker and both affirmative rebuttalists pretty much follow the same pattern. First, the affirmative team tries to show that the counterplan is topical; second, the affirmative tries to show that the counterplan is not competitive using whatever standard of competitiveness the negative team has chosen or using an affirmative standard. The affirmative does these jobs first because either can automatically lead to an affirmative win. If the counterplan is topical, there are two teams in the room affirming the resolution and the judge can, at that point, give the ballot to "the affirmative." If the counterplan is not competitive, then there is no reason *not* to adopt the affirmative plan, and the judge has no choice but to adopt it.

What the affirmative team does after arguing the topicality and noncompetitiveness of the counterplan depends on what strategy the negative has adopted. If the negative has chosen to grant—with or without qualifications—the affirmative's rationale for change, then the affirmative speakers should (1) reestablish the affirmative understanding of the problem, (2) argue that the affirmative plan addresses the problem better than the counterplan, (3) argue that any claimed additional advantages of the counterplan either do not accrue or are not significant or are not unique to the counterplan (i.e. are common to plan and counterplan), (4) argue that any claimed disadvantages of the affirmative plan either do not accrue or are not significant or are not unique to the plan (i.e. are common to plan and counterplan), and (5) argue that the counterplan will result in significant, unique disadvantages.

If the negative team has chosen to establish a different problem area and address it, then the affirmative speakers should (1) reestablish the affirmative rationale for change, (2) argue that the affirmative plan does solve the affirmative problem, (3) deny the argued disadvantages of the affirmative plan or show they are insignificant or not unique to the affirmative plan, (4) deny or minimize the negative rationale for change, (5) argue that the counterplan does not solve the problem the negative has raised, (6) deny the argued advantages of the counterplan or show they are insignificant or not unique to the counterplan, and (7) argue that the counterplan results in significant, unique disadvantages. The affirmative might also want—as an extension of (4)—to argue that even if the counterplan does solve the problem the negative team has offered, the affirmative plan solves a more serious problem and is, therefore, preferable as a policy.

The second negative constructive speaker and both negative rebuttalists will proceed in the same manner as the second affirmative constructive speaker, arguing the opposite view, of course.

The order in which the issues other than topicality and competitiveness should be addressed by all affirmative and negative speakers, after the first negative constructive speaker, will vary a bit from debate to debate. In a few minutes, I will discuss flow sheeting. The way a debate's arguments are generally recorded (i.e., flow sheeted) by competitors and judges suggests that the order listed above and on Figure 9.3 is probably the best bet. Of course, if you wanted to strongly emphasize one of the five, six, seven, or eight arguments, you would do well to pull it out of line and address it first.

In Value Debate

Value debate derives many of its patterns and practices from policy debate. For example, the overall pattern for value debate is not unlike that for the most usual kind of policy debate. If you simply replace the plan attacks and the responses to them with the two different types of "off-case" arguments (disadvantages of the kind of policy the affirmative prepolicy judgment implies and objections to acting upon the value/s embraced by the affirmative) and the responses to them, you will have modified the general pattern presented at the beginning of this chapter and in Figure 9.1 into the more usual value debate pattern.

If you are embarking upon a career in value debate, you should keep in mind that its practices and patterns are still evolving. Since value debate is in many fundamental ways different from policy debate, perhaps modeling procedures on policy debate procedures is a mistake; perhaps value debate will soon make some radical departures from those of policy debate. Be alert to the possibility of such departures. But, until such new courses are navigated, the simple modification just presented of the basic pattern for policy debate should be your guide in most instances.

One common instance in which this modification will not work as a guide in when the second negative constructive speaker decides *not* to present "off-case" arguments but simply extend his or her partner's argumentation, perhaps adding to it. In this instance there will be nothing like "case side" and "plan" or "off-case side"; rather, each and every speaker—four constructive speakers and four rebuttalists—will go over the same territory, territory charted by the contentions in the first affirmative constructive speech.

A rare instance in which this modification will not work as a guide is when the first negative constructive speaker offers a counterdesignative contention. In such an instance, the debate will resemble a counterplan debate. The tasks each speaker in such a debate should undertake are outlined in Figure 9.4. If the negative team concedes the definitive contention and bases the choice between designative contention and counterdesignative contention on the value/s the affirmative presented in the first constructive speech, then the first two tasks listed can be ignored.

Planning Rebuttals

Let's return to the usual policy debate procedures and the four rebuttal speeches in their usual form. The first negative rebuttal is rather easy to conceive of: the rebuttalist responds to the second affirmative constructive speech; since that speech was, to a large extent, a response to what the first negative debater said in his or her constructive speech, the first negative rebuttalist will to a large extent be rebuilding his or her original positions against the affirmative rationale for change. The first affirmative rebuttal is also rather easy to conceive of; however, that conception can be mind-boggling. That rebuttal, therefore, merits some special attention. The remaining two rebuttals are summaries—first the

Task	1AC	1NC	2AC	2NC	1NR	1AR	2NR	2AR
Argues for Definitive Contention	Yes		Yes			Yes		Yes
Argues against Definitive Contention		Yes		Yes*	Yes		Yes	
Argues for Designative Contention(s)	Yes		Yes			Yes		Yes
Argues against Designative Contention		Yes		Yes*	Yes		Yes	
Argues for Disadvantages of or Value Objections to Designative Contention(s)				Yes			Yes	
Argues against Disadvantages of or Value Objections to Designative Contention(s)						Yes		Yes
Argues for Counterdesignative Contention		Yes		Yes	Yes*		Yes	
Argues against Counterdesignative Contention			Yes			Yes		Yes
Argues that Counterdesignative Contention is Topical and Noncompetitive			Yes			Yes		Yes
Argues that Counterdesignative Contention is Nontopical and Competitive				Yes	Yes*		Yes	
Argues for Disadvantages of or Value Objections to Counterdesignative Contention			Yes			Yes		Yes
Argues against Disadvantages of or Value Objections to Counterdesignative Contention				Yes	Yes*		Yes	

* if time allows

Figure 9.4 The jobs of the different speakers in a value debate in which a counterdesignative contention is offered.

second negative and then the second affirmative must review their team's position in the debate which is quickly coming to an end. These rebuttals are important and, therefore, merit some close attention.

The Tough Rebuttal: The First Affirmative's

The first affirmative rebuttalist must respond to twelve to fifteen minutes of negative speaking, the negative block. The workability and solvency arguments initiated in the second negative constructive speech *must* be answered by the first affirmative rebuttalist; if not, these arguments will sink the affirmative plan. The disadvantages voiced by the second negative constructive speaker *must* be answered by the first affirmative rebuttalist; if not, these arguments will sink the affirmative plan. The arguments offered against the affirmative rationale for change in the first negative rebuttal must also be answered; if not, that rationale is in danger *at best*. That's lot to do in four or five minutes! Some preparation in advance and some guided thinking on the spot can help the first affirmative rebuttalist do the job.

Rebuttal Sheets. Most debate teams use a particular affirmative case for a long period of time. It is developed carefully so that it will endure—with revisions. Only if it has major flaws is it scrapped. Because affirmative cases have a certain longevity, affirmative teams after a while know what will be argued against it. The first several times the team presents the case, they are often surprised; after that, surprises are few and far between. An affirmative team would be able to list, if they wanted to, all of the likely arguments against their rationale for change and plan. They would also be able to preplan responses for the second affirmative constructive speaker to use against likely arguments against "the case." (These preplanned responses are often called "affirmative blocks" and will be discussed shortly.) Similarly, they would be able to preplan responses for the first affirmative rebuttalist to use against likely workability arguments, solvency arguments, and disadvantages. Figure 9.5 is an excerpt from just such a rebuttal sheet. The first column lists likely negative arguments; the second column lists numerous *brief* affirmative responses from which the rebuttalist could choose. Rebuttal sheets have two advantages: first, they save thinking time at a point in the debate when the preparing speaker needs all the thinking time he or she can get; second, they save speaking time (because the responses are brief, to-the-point) in a speech where time is *extremely* short.

Challenging Plan Attacks: A Heuristic. In devising rebuttal sheets and in thinking about unexpected plan attacks, you will find the heuristic in Figure 9.6 useful. It is based on an analysis of the three kinds of plan attacks into three parts: initial premise, links, and impact. Generally speaking, a first affirmative rebuttalist can defeat a plan attack quickly by defeating any of these parts.

If 2NC argues	Respond
Plan will not reduce Marxist influence in Nicaragua.	Case-side evidence shows 1. Sandinista government wants good relations with the United States; 2. Sandinista government wants the assistance of the American government and American corporations in setting up industry.
Plan will not reduce Soviet influence/ presence in Nicaragua because Soviets will not "free" Nicaragua from their camp.	Soviets are there only to counterbalance American anti-Nicaraguan actions; being there is straining the Soviet economy.
Plan will not stop anti-Sandinista forces from fighting.	1. Plan will stop them eventually because they are presently dependent on the United States for arms; 2. In the meantime, or if they receive arms from another source, their activities will not be associated with the United States and, therefore, Nicaraguan-American relations will improve and Soviet influence will wane.

The United States will secretly channel weaponry to anti-Sandinistas through Honduran government.	1. Under Plank III of plan, such a transfer would be illegal:
	  A. American officials would be guilty of treason; therefore, they would not have motive to circumvent;
	  B. Honduran government would lose U.S. military and economic assistance; therefore, the Honduran government would not have a motive to help the U.S. circumvent.
	Possible Preempt—"secrets" do come to light thanks to careful Congressional oversight and investigative reporting; *Fear of* secret operations coming to light will deter circumvention given the harshness of affirmative enforcement.

Figure 9.5 Excerpt from a rebuttal sheet.

Let's consider three different plan attacks—all in response to a plan abolishing the Central Intelligence Agency. Argument 1 is a workability argument: it argues that the affirmative team will not be able to fund the pensions it promises dismissed operatives. Argument 2 is a solvency argument: it argues that military intelligence will simply assume the role and projects of the CIA, thereby denying the affirmative its claimed diplomatic advantage. Argument 3 is a disadvantage:

it argues that the absence of vital intelligence gathering will undermine U.S. security.

The three guide questions for workability arguments focus your attention on initial premise, links, and impact. Ask three questions of Argument 1 above. The questions should lead you to see that the argument is beatable because its initial premise is wrong and its impact is overstated. Since the affirmative plan dismantles the CIA, money that would ordinarily be used to fund CIA operations would be available to fund pensions—more than enough money. And, even if

Workability Arguments:
    Premise—Is what the negative claims to be necessary for the plan to work truly necessary?
        Could something/someone else do the job?
    Link—Does the plan indeed fail to provide what the negative assumes it fails to provide?
        Does the plan provide a substitute?
        Can the plan, using status quo mechanisms, acquire what is seemingly lacking or a substitute for it?
    Impact—Does the plan's inadequacy mean absolute nonsolvency or just a minor administrative problem?
        Has the negative team specified how much of a problem the plan's inadequacy will pose?

Solvency Arguments:
    Premise—Does the plan need what the negative says it needs to be solvent?
        Can a substitute be found, either in the plan or in the status quo?
    Link—Is the problem the negative points to true?
        Can the problem be solved using plan or status quo mechanisms?
    Impact—Is the plan absolutely or just a tiny bit nonsolvent?
        Has the negative team specified how much of a solvency problem the affirmative allegedly has?

Disadvantages:
    Premise—Is the statement the negative makes concerning what the plan does accurate?
    Link—Is the negative discussion of causality strong?
        • Has the negative mistaken a chronological relationship for a causal one?
        • Has the negative mistaken a correlation for causation?
        • Has the negative mistaken a sufficient cause for a necessary cause?
    Can the plan or the status quo solve the problem anywhere along the way?
    Is the problem at the end of the causal chain truly likely or a far-fetched possibility?
    Impact—Is the impact truly significant?
        Is the impact mitigated by any benefits? If so, what is the net impact of the disadvantage?

Figure 9.6 Heuristic for challenging plan attacks.

pension money were not available, its unavailability would not mean that the affirmative plan will not stop CIA activities which cause diplomatic problems for the United States *unless* the negative team can show that unpensioned CIA operatives will, on their own, engage in a significant number of subversive activities (life-threatening activities) and that these activities will be associated with the U.S. government by foreign nations.

Solvency arguments are, as Chapter 8 noted, of three kinds: arguments that point to a missing ingredient in the affirmative plan; arguments that question the affirmative team's causal analysis; and arguments that point out ways the plan's intent can be circumvented. The first two types have to be addressed head-on. If the negative points to a missing ingredient, the affirmative team must be prepared to show that either it is not missing or it is not necessary. If the negative team cites an alternate cause of the problem that the affirmative plan must and does not take care of, the affirmative must be prepared to show that the alternative cause is not a cause or that the alternative cause does not have to be addressed for the problem to be solved. If the negative argues that the cause-effect relationship is not reversible, the affirmative team must be prepared to prove reversibility. If the negative team argues that the affirmative plan will indeed have an initial effect but that this effect will not lead to further effects, effects the affirmative depends on for solvency, the affirmative team must be prepared to prove that the initial effect will have the second effect, and so on. The third type of solvency argument can be analyzed into initial premise, links, and impact, the initial premise being the agent's *motive* for circumvention, the crucial links being the *propensity* of the agent to circumvent (or block) and the existence of a *mechanism* which the agent could use, and the impact being either absolute or partial insolvency. The heuristic (Figure 9.6) focuses the first affirmative rebuttalist's attention on these crucial elements.

In the case of Argument 2 above, it would be difficult for the first affirmative rebuttalist to question the motive; however, has military intelligence shown the propensity to violate federal law and be guilty of treason? Does military intelligence have the necessary facilities, etc., to engage in the kinds of covert activities the CIA is being faulted for? Even if military intelligence might be able to engage in some covert actions, do these actions negate solvency or just slightly detract from it?

Disadvantages can also be analyzed into initial premise, links, and impact. Again, Figure 9.6 should help. Argument 3 above has, as its initial premise, that the affirmative team abolishes the CIA. True. The impact is a threat to national security. This impact is valid only if the link in the disadvantage is valid. The link argues that abolishing the CIA means an end to vital intelligence-gathering. Is this link valid? Not necessarily. The first affirmative rebuttalist could successfully argue that satellites can now gather all the vital intelligence the United States needs.

There is one other way a disadvantage could be handled by a first affirmative rebuttalist: the rebuttalist could turn the disadvantage around. Let's say the negative team argues that the affirmative plan to withdraw U.S. troops from Western Europe will reduce the security of West Germany. A shrewd first affirmative rebuttalist might argue that, right now, with a strong U.S. presence, West Germany is in danger of a nuclear strike, whereas, under the plan, West Germany would be in danger of only a conventional assault. This reduction in the level of the threat under the plan allows the affirmative to claim that, rather than a disadvantage in the area of West German security, the affirmative team actually has an advantage. This "turnaround" can be argued to be an independent justification for affirming the resolution.

Exercises: Challenging Plan Attacks

Use the heuristic (Figure 9.6) to argue against the following plan attacks:

1. The affirmative proposes federal regulating of the construction and operation of coal slurry pipelines:
   A. The affirmative lacks sufficient manpower to regulate all the possible sites;
   B. The affirmative will bankrupt the principal carrier of coal to the coal ports of Hampton Roads, Virginia; St. Louis, Missouri; and New Orleans, Louisiana—the railroads;
   C. Sabotage of pipelines by irate residents (who don't like the intrusion into their community) and railroad workers will prevent pipelines from doing their job.
2. The affirmative proposes a ban on U.S. arms sales to Israel until Israel withdraws from the West Bank:
   A. The affirmative plan will endanger Israeli security;
   B. Since Israel can get arms elsewhere, the affirmative plan will not lead to either a Palestinian homeland or peace;
   C. The affirmative will cause the United States to lose allies, since nations will see that the United States expects to dictate internal policies if a nation accepts U.S. arms.
3. The affirmative proposes import restrictions on certain goods from Japan:
   A. The affirmative will not help American manufacturers since the real cause of the problem is quality control and high costs in American plants;
   B. The affirmative will damage U.S.-Japanese relations;
   C. The affirmative will invite other nations to enact similar import restrictions directed against U.S. goods.
4. The affirmative proposes a federal agency to regulate computer technology so as to insure the security of data:
   A. Bureaucracy moves too slowly to keep up with the fast-paced changes in computer technology; as a result, the federal agency will not be able to do the job;
   B. Computer companies, to gain a market advantage over competitors, will disguise new procedures and technologies as old and thereby circumvent government regulations;

C. The affirmative will actually increase the chance of criminal access to computer-stored data by making numerous procedures uniform.

Responding to the Spread. The first affirmative rebuttalist also must learn how to group plan attacks together. This skill of grouping is vital when the second negative speaker tries to "spread" the first affirmative rebuttalist by offering numerous workability arguments, solvency arguments, and disadvantages. Consider the following situation. The affirmative team has proposed that the corporate income tax be abolished so as to encourage industrial growth through investment. The second negative debater offers the following solvency arguments and disadvantages:

Solvency

1. American businesses are scared of a recession; given extra money, they will not invest it.
2. "Smart money" right now goes into overseas investment; therefore, the plan will not help the U.S. economy because the extra money will leave the country.
3. The extra money will not be plowed back; rather, it will be paid out as dividends to investors, who will hoard the money.

Disadvantages

1. The plan will place an extra tax burden on middle-class Americans.
2. Middle-class Americans, their available capital decreased, will not be able to purchase homes; as a result, the housing construction industry will collapse.
3. Middle-class Americans, without money to spend, will not consume as many finished goods; therefore, there will be a recession.
4. With the tax base lower, the government will have to cut the social services it provides; this cut will hurt the poor.
5. If extra money is plowed into the economy, it will increase the risk of a major depression since the American and the global market can no longer support a "boom" economy.
6. Absence of a corporate income tax will result in fewer U.S. government records on corporate activities; the result is less supervision and more potential for improper, illegal conduct.
7. Money would go to support Republican Party-oriented Political Action Committees (PACs); this extra funding would damage the Democratic Party, the two-party system, and democratic government in the United States.

Three solvency arguments and seven disadvantages do not constitute a *very* thin spread; nonetheless, the first affirmative rebuttalist will be spread fairly thinly if he or she is to respond to all of these plan attacks and then return to "case side." One solution to the problem is to speak very rapidly, but I would advise against this solution since extreme rapidity can significantly reduce comprehension. The better solution is to group arguments.

Look at the three solvency arguments. Implicit in all three is the assumption that corporations will not reinvest the money the plan gives them. If the affirmative team can show that corporations will reinvest the money in the United States, then the affirmative can beat all three solvency arguments. The shrewd first affirmative rebuttalist has the crucial proof and proceeds as follows:

Group all three solvency arguments together. They all assume that U.S. corporations will not reinvest the extra money in the U.S. They *will* invest for two good reasons. First, they . . .

Now, look at disadvantages (1), (2), and (3). They all assume that the personal income tax will have to be increased in order to make up for the shortfall in revenue when the corporate tax is abolished. If the affirmative team could argue that savings in federal programs could compensate for the shortfall, then the affirmative could beat all three advantages. Group and refute.

Look at disadvantage (7). This plan attack, like all three solvency arguments, assumes that the freed money will not be reinvested in the United States. Therefore, this disadvantage can be defeated by a quick cross-application of the responses to the three solvency arguments.

What a quick examination of the plan attacks should show a shrewd debater is that rather than ten arguments to refute, he or she has five, with the fifth one taking only a few seconds. Grouping (and looking for the possibility of cross-applying responses to solvency arguments as responses to disadvantages) helps make a formidable task a very manageable one.

Exercise: Grouping Plan Attacks

Your plan calls for the nationalization of rail transportation. The second negative speaker tries to "spread you" by offering the following plan attacks. How would you group them in order to make your task manageable?

Workability Arguments

1. The different rail networks would have to be connected at a considerable expense.
2. The federal government lacks the expertise in the Department of Transportation to run a railroad system.
3. The federal government would have to assume sizeable existing deficits and pay considerable sums for the upgrading and maintenance of existing track mileage and equipment.

Solvency Arguments

1. Federal management never works: e.g., it didn't work for AMTRAK. Therefore, federal management of all railroads will not make railroads a viable mode of transportation for goods.

2. Railway labor, disliking federal employment with its no-strike law, will slow down, causing the federally run railroad to be inefficient.
3. Shippers will go with more reliable truck transport; if the government lowers the cost to attract shippers, the Teamsters will vandalize rail lines.
4. Railroads have too bad a reputation as an inefficient hauler in some areas for the federal railroad to overcome.

Disadvantages

1. Nationalization will end competition among rail carriers; without competition, high rates, poor service, and no incentive for improvement will ensue.
2. Nationalization will lead to socialism: once you open the door. . .
3. Nationalization will lead to labor unrest: workers in other unions will fear the nationalization of their industry.
4. Nationalization, as a possible bailout, will remove the incentive to address problems on the parts of numerous corporations.
5. Nationalization will lead to additional government regulation in the transportation industry; regulation will lead to reduced competition.

The Tough Rebuttal in Value Debate

The first affirmative rebuttal is usually the tough speech in value debate as in policy debate. Just as the first affirmative rebuttalist in policy debate must cover all the plan attacks voiced in the second negative constructive speech *and* get back to attacks against "the case" that the first negative rebuttalist has just reviewed, the first affirmative rebuttalist in value debate usually must cover all the "off-case" arguments the second negative voiced *and* get back to attacks against the case which the first negative rebuttalist has just reviewed. Since delivery is typically slower in value debate, because the negative block is twelve minutes long (not fifteen), and because "spreading" one's opponent is discouraged in value debate, the first affirmative rebuttalist's task in value debate is not quite as difficult as the parallel task in policy debate. It is tough, nonetheless. Unless the second negative constructive speaker chooses to simply extend on what his or her partner has said, the first affirmative rebuttalist is going to have a lot of ground to cover.

In Chapter 8, we considered two different kinds of "off-case" arguments. The first type is similar to plan disadvantages: the second negative asks what would happen if the kind of policy the affirmative team seems to be pointing to is adopted. The second type is more philosophical: the second negative asks what would happen if the value the affirmative is defending becomes operative.

In responding to "off-case" arguments, the first affirmative rebuttalist needs — just like his or her policy debate counterpart — to plan and think. Rebuttal sheets should be the product of planning. "Off-case" arguments should be anticipated and responses should be charted out in advance of actual competition. Heuristic thinking should be used during the round to help the rebuttalist come quickly to terms with unanticipated "off-case" arguments.

Like disadvantages in policy debate, these "off-case" arguments can be divided into three parts: initial premise, links, and impact. Let's say the value resolution calls upon the affirmative team to defend the desirability of free speech and the affirmative team chooses to define "desirable" in terms of promoting the free and productive exchange of ideas. The second negative constructive speech might present the following "off-case" arguments: (1) free speech can lead to violence; (2) free speech allows so many ideas to fly around that the result is entropy, not action; and (3) free speech gives dangerous dissident forces a chance to grow. Let's examine them one by one.

The premise for the first is that free speech means *irresponsibly* free speech. The United States Supreme Court, in discussing the First Amendment's declaration of our freedom of speech, has not hesitated to allow restrictions on certain irresponsible speech acts—for example, yelling "Fire" in a crowded movie theatre. Speech that would incite violence would fall in the same irresponsible category. Since the affirmative team is defending the Constitutional right, as it has been defined by the Supreme Court, the value objection does not apply.

The link in the second "off-case" objection is weak. Do many ideas *necessarily* lead to inaction? Only if there is no effective decision-making process in operation. Since we can assume most viable institutions are viable because of their ability to make decisions, we can assume that entropic inaction will be a very rare result of an idea glut, a result confined to the few ineffective institutions.

The third "off-case" argument has an impact that can be challenged. The growth of dissident groups—it could be argued—keeps America strong. These groups and their ideas force the United States to address its problems rather than rest on its laurels.

When faced with unanticipated "off-case" arguments, you should think in terms of premise, links, and impacts. If you do, you will almost always pinpoint a possible weakness in the argument you are confronted with. When faced with many arguments, follow the advice given to the first affirmative rebuttalist in policy debate: group and refute.

The Summary Rebuttals

The concluding speeches in a debate are very important: they represent the negative team's and the affirmative team's last opportunity to make the case against or for the resolution. Two weaknesses often mar these two speeches. First, the concluding speakers often drop crucial arguments against or for the resolution. Some judges will simply ignore those arguments and *not* make them a deciding factor in their decision. Other judges will allow such arguments to play a part in the decision; however, the arguments' impact on the decision will be considerably blunted. Either way, the dropped arguments hurt. Second, the concluding speakers often try to cover everything. As a result, none of the arguments is treated with the requisite depth; they are all given the superficial treatment inevitable when you must zoom on to more arguments.

Before the summary rebuttals, both teams must think. What are the crucial arguments in the particular debate? The first negative should indicate where he or she believes the case is most vulnerable; the second negative debater should decide which plan attacks (in policy debate) or "off-case" arguments (in value debate) he or she believes will most likely damage the affirmative team's position. The first affirmative debater should indicate where he or she believes the plan is in danger (in policy debate) or which "off-case" arguments he or she believes represent the strongest challenge to the affirmative's stance (in value debate). The second affirmative debater should decide where he or she believes the rationale for change or the case for a particular value judgment is in danger.

Both the negative and the affirmative teams, if they think a few minutes, will have before them a list of arguments they know they must cover. For each, they will want to (a) establish firmly their position and (b) refute the opponents' position as it has been extended throughout the debate—through the first affirmative rebuttal for the second negative rebuttal; through the second negative rebuttal for the second affirmative rebuttal. Both tasks must be undertaken. Doing (b), but not (a) can leave the team's position fuzzy in the debate—something particularly dangerous for the affirmative team. Doing (a), but not (b) can leave the team open to criticism for being merely repetitive and nonresponsive. OK; you now have a list of arguments and you know how you plan to reestablish your position on each issue and refute the last-offered argument/s of your opponents. How should you organize your summary rebuttal?

You should proceed down either "case side" or "plan side" and then down the other. You might want to briefly comment on arguments other than those you intend to stress as you go; however, you will want to strongly emphasize the arguments that you and your partner have identified as crucial in the particular debate. Emphasis means *saying more*, *spending more time*, and *using the resources of oral communication* (e.g., repeating key phrases, changing volume and pitch, using strong gestures).

As you plan and deliver the summary rebuttal, try to envision yourself as the prosecutor or the defense attorney. Even if you do not accept a judicial paradigm for debating, visualizing yourself as prosecutor or defender will help you keep the nature of your job in mind. You're not just another speaker; rather, you're responsible for summing up—in the most convincing manner possible—the negative or the affirmative position in the debate. Is the status quo guilty as charged? Your last rebuttal in a policy debate should lead the judge to a definite, full answer to that question. Is a particular value judgment—one upon which much hinges—to be accepted as valid? Your last rebuttal in a value debate should lead the judge to a definite, full answer to that question.

Flow Sheets

Debates, as you have certainly gathered by now, are a complex network of arguments, refutations, and defenses. When you debate, you are responsible for knowing everything that has been said by the preceding speakers; you are responsible for comprehending this complex network. You therefore need to listen carefully and take good notes.

Once upon a time, debaters took notes in any old way. Over the years, a systematic method of note-taking has evolved. It is called *flow sheeting*. During a debate, all four debaters and the judge use a flow sheet to keep track of the arguments, refutations, and defenses.

There are several related ways to "flow" a debate. I will be presenting one to you. Feel free to adapt it to your "style"; listen to your instructor or coach when he or she advocates some variation of the basic method I will be describing. The art of "flowing" a debate is still evolving, and your coach—or you—may see a way of improving that art and making it a more effective way of recording what goes on during a debate.

Take a sheet of paper—preferably a 14" × 8½" legal pad sheet, turn it sideways, and divide side one into eight vertical columns. This will be "case side." In column (1), you will record the affirmative rationale for change; in column (2), what the first negative constructive speech says about "the case"; in column (3), what the second affirmative constructive speech says about "the case"; etc., all the way through the second affirmative rebuttal. Figure 9.7 offers you a partially filled-in example of the "case side" of a flow sheet. You will see that, by examining it, you can trace the development of a particular argument throughout the entire debate.

Now turn the sheet of paper over. (You many want to line it up so that it is longer than it is wide.) If you are in a policy debate, make five vertical columns. In column (1), you will record the affirmative plan; in column (2), you will record the second negative constructive speech's plan attacks; in column (3), you will record the first affirmative rebuttalist's responses; in column (4), you will record what the second negative rebuttalist has to say about the plan; in column (5), you will record what the second affirmative rebuttalist has to say. Figure 9.8 offers you an example—again, partially filled-in—of the "plan side" of a flow sheet in a policy debate.

If you are in a value debate, you will need only four columns. In column (1), you will record the second negative constructive's "off-case" arguments; in column (2), the first affirmative rebuttalist's responses; in column (3), the second negative rebuttalist's responses; in column (4), the second affirmative rebuttalist's responses. If the second negative constructive speaker chooses not to offer "off-case" arguments, you will not even need this flip side of the flow sheet.

This basic pattern should suffice in almost all value debates and most policy debates. The most usual situation in which this pattern must be supplemented in policy debate is when the negative team offers a counterplan. Then, you will want to use two flow sheets at once. The second will have eight columns on one side; here you flow the arguments on the counterplan's nontopicality and competitiveness; the advantages the negative team claims the counterplan has (which may include solving a more serious problem than the one the affirmative

1) The railroads are important A) Most fuel-efficient mode of transport B) Necessary for some heavy goods (which cannot go via truck)	Trucks got better mpg than trains	but train carries 100x as much freight per ton. trains for better — ICC didn't respond		granted by negative →
2) The railroads are in serious financial trouble	Quite a few railroads are doing well now e.g. Conrail, CSX	Only a few	Few show railroads are on rebound evidence suggests Conrail much improved	but few shows status-quo is solving problem	Only a few problem not denied not as near to bankruptcy as before, but still "in red"	Majority are in serious trouble Few being helped by exceptional circumstances
3) Work rules imposed on railroads by strong unions have caused financial problems A) Crew size B) Freight districts C) Work day definition	large crews necessary for safety — knowledge of tracks etc, needed for safety alertness necessary for safety	Thanks to govt. subsidies (listed in financial reports as revenue) Thanks to virtual coal-shipping monopoly only in heavy/urban areas not by entire crew 100 mis./3 hrs a day is certainly nd.work/day	necessary nonetheless — off reduces crew size ∴ safety problem Needed by brakeman too	not necessarily — it up to management Freight districts make sense	management, given the railroads financial state, will cut ∴ safety in danger not w/modern technology and highly-trained engineers work day is ult. more absurdity
4) Arbitration procedures under National Railway Act for work rules are borne by pro-union	A) govt. can use NRA procedure to impose settlement on unions; govt. could ∴ change work rules if govt wanted to ∴ no inherency B) e.g of FEC proves no inherency	Neg misunderstands — Procedure for wages different from procedures for work rules Work rules slay the same unless unions agree to change!	Under NRA, govt can impose settlement; ∴ can solve problem	No they can't — railroads are union shop by federal law	Under NRA, work rules cannot be changed by govt. (quotes law)
5) Taking work rules out of contract and putting them under management's control will solve problem e.g. Florida East Coast RR	affirmative is stuck in inherency / solvency dilemma	FEC, because it engages in no inter-state commerce, was able to de-unionize FEC a unique case ∴ solvent and inherent both	Other railroads can follow FEC e.g. dilemma still stands	FEC not covered by law but all others are	FEC covered by law, IF FEC can slip around law, so can others FEC never crosses state line — no other major railroad can say that

Figure 9.7 Case-side of a flow sheet.

	PMN			
I) Work rules removed from union contract; authority given solely to management (w/ OSHA supervision)	1) RR's will strike over other matters (but work rules will be real issue)	Once work rules are raised in negotiations, unions in violation of law	Unions will not mention, just imply, to get around the law	If railroads stand fast, unions will have to mention work rules or never get what they want
II) Strikes over work rules illegal	2) RR workers will slow-down and sick-out	Once work rules enter discussion, unions in violation of law	Unions will never explicitly mention work rules, just hint it's been done before in similar instances	If railroads stand fast, unions will have to mention work rules or never get what they want, not in railroad industry
III) Enforcement: fines and prison sentences	**DA**			
IV) Aff. speeches establish legislative intent	1) Truckers will be angered A) aff. costs trucks business B) truckers won't like that C) impact - violence	A) Truckers can team up with railroads in piggyback operations B) Good for truckers C) ∴ No violence	Truckers like things the way they are, will reject new ideas	2NR didn't respond specifically to 1AR reasoning
	2) RR safety problems A) aff. allows financially troubled management to call shots B) safety will be sacrificed C) Accidents, etc.	OSHA oversees ∴ no safety problems	Prove OSHA's effectiveness	Evidence on OSHA's effectiveness
	3) Workers exploited A) aff. removes union power B) power necessary to protest C) w/o power, no protection and exploitation	Not applied to this specific affirmative case		2NR dropped this DA

Figure 9.8 Plan-side of a flow sheet.

has chosen to speak about); and the negative team's argument that the counterplan solves the affirmative problem or accrues the affirmative advantage/s or meets the affirmative goal/s (if this argument is offered). You begin flowing in column (2) with the first negative constructive speech; you leave column (1) totally blank. Why have it at all? Many debaters like to line up this side of the counterplan flow sheet with the case-side of the regular flow sheet: if both have eight columns, then the different speeches will align perfectly.

The counterplan flow sheet's opposite side will be longer than it is wide and will have six columns. The first column will contain the attacks the second affirmative constructive speaker offers against the counterplan. The succeeding columns will "flow" what the succeeding five speeches say concerning these counterplan attacks.

One other modification will be necessary when the negative team offers a counterplan. The plan side of the original flow sheet may have to be modified so that it has eight columns. This modification is necessary since many (not all) counterplanning first negative constructive speakers will offer disadvantages of the affirmative plan as part of their rationale for their alternative policy.

Flow sheeting is not immediately mastered by a beginning debater, so, if your earliest flow sheets start off clear and fade into fuzziness, don't worry. Do, however, make a concerted effort to master flow sheeting. "Flow" all debates you hear—practice debates, debates your teammates are in. The skill is *absolutely* necessary if you are to keep track of the complexities of argumentation during a debate, and you cannot succeed as a debater unless you are able to keep track of the cross-fire of argument and counterargument and counter-counterargument.

Judging Criteria

The major complaint debaters have during and after competition is about the judging. Unfortunately, at times the complaints are valid—especially on the high school level where many judges lack the requisite understanding of debating to do a good job. More often than not, the complaints are invalid. The complaints are quite frequently the result of either the debater's distorted perspective or the debater's lack of understanding concerning judging philosophies. The perspective problem is easy to understand if you consider the debater's situation. Debaters necessarily view things from the perspective of competitors fiercely caught up in the complexities and energy of an actual debate and the dynamics of a debate season. In an actual debate, debaters themselves know what they mean, how their arguments are logically put together, and how their arguments relate to other arguments in the debate; however, often, they do not convey meaning, logic, and connection to the judge. They think they do, but what they are actually doing is assuming that what is clear to them is clear to the judge sitting in the back of the room. The judge, however, has not shared the thinking process—whether the thinking took place then and there or in practice days before the actual debate; therefore, he or she will not always see things as the debater does. Debaters then must be very alert to their audience's situation: make a special effort to convey your meaning clearly; make a special effort to convey the logic of your arguments; and make a special effort to show the judge where a particular argument applies and how. You will be aided in accomplishing these three goals if you try to be explicit, use substructure which reflects the logical development of an argument, and always tell the judge what you're doing before you do it ("I'm refuting . . .) and what the effect of your argument is ("Without evidence on . . . , the affirmative contention must fall."). In doing all of these things, you will be escaping your distorted perspective and trying to enter the audience's more objective perspective.

A solution to the philosophical problem requires three ingredients: first, an understanding of the basic judging philosophies; second, knowledge of the philosophies which the judges you will debate before hold; and third, a willingness to adapt to your audience. You will have to commit yourself to the third; you will have to do some investigation—perhaps in your debate program's files—to acquire the second. This text will help you with the first.

The Stock Issues Judge

The stock issues judge expects the affirmative team to jump many hurdles. This judge asks

- Is the affirmative case *topical*?
- Is the affirmative's need, advantage(s), or failure to meet a goal(s) *significant*?
- Is the problem the affirmative has identified *inherent*; are the advantages unique?
- Is the plan *workable*?
- Does the plan *solve* the problem or accrue the advantage(s) or meet the goal(s)?
- Is the plan free from significant *disadvantages*?

The first five questions correspond to the stock issues discussed in Chapter 4. The last question reflects the growing importance of disadvantages in the minds of all judges.

If the affirmative case prompts a "Yes" response from the judge at the debate's end, then the judge casts an affirmative ballot. If, however, the negative team manages to bring the judge to the point where he or she cannot answer any single question with a firm "Yes," then the judge casts a negative ballot. This kind of judge usually has a pronounced negative inclination. This kind of judge will frequently have a rather low toleration for counterplans since counterplans will compel him or her to abandon this judging procedure (which assumes the negative team is supporting the status quo—with or without repairs—or going "straight negative") or modify it significantly.

The Policymaking Judge

This judge weighs the policy the affirmative team asks him or her to adopt against the policy the negative team chooses to defend—the status quo, the status quo with minor repairs, or a counterplan. In such a comparison, advantages and disadvantages play a major role. The affirmative wants to show that its policy is more advantageous than disadvantageous and that the negative policy is more disadvantageous than advantageous; the negative team wants to show that its policy is more advantageous than disadvantageous and that the affirmative policy is more disadvantageous than advantageous. This emphasis tends to make the second negative constructive speech *the* one this judge listens to most intently, whereas the stock issues judge tends to see the first negative constructive speech and the second negative constructive speech as equally important since each usually focuses on three of six questions he or she is asking.

The policymaking judge will, of course, listen to arguments other than advantages and disadvantages and apply them as follows. Workability and solvency arguments will be seen as minimizing (if not negating) the claimed advantages. Significance arguments will also be seen as minimizing the claimed affirmative advantages. Negative inherency or uniqueness arguments, if accepted, can obliterate the distinction between the affirmative policy and the negative policy. If the negative team has chosen to defend the status quo, winning an inherency or uniqueness argument can lead to a virtually automatic negative victory since both change and no change lead to the same advantage/s, in which case no change is the preferred policy.

Nontopicality arguments voiced against the affirmative plan or topicality or noncompetitiveness arguments voiced against a negative counterplan are, in the eyes of many policymaking judges, preliminary arguments. If the negative demonstrates that the affirmative case is not topical or if the affirmative demonstrates that the counterplan is either topical or noncompetitive, the debate essentially stops. In order for an affirmative case to be considered, it must be topical; in order for a negative counterplan to be considered, it must be nontopical and competitive. Other policymaking judges feel that voting on these procedural issues unfairly decides the contest on account of technical considerations, not arguments, and will not decide a debate based solely on the nontopicality of a plan or the topicality or noncompetitiveness of a counterplan.

The policymaking judge tends to vote as frequently affirmative as negative since he or she tends to grant a lesser degree of presumption to the negative side. The policymaking judge tends to be much more open to counterplans than the stock issues judge. Some policymaking judges, especially younger judges, tend to be unreceptive to the "Needs Case" structure since it doesn't give them advantages *per se* to consider.

The Issues Judge in Value Debate

The stock issues are not as clearly defined in value debate as in policy debate. This lack of clear definition is due to the relative newness of debate on value resolutions.

The issue judge in value debate seems to be asking the affirmative team to (1) define and defend a definite value (against alternatives, if they are raised); (2) show that the value judgment the resolution embodies is in line with this value; and (3) show that objections to accepting or acting upon the judgment the resolution embodies are invalid. The second request is the complex one, for the precise burden placed in the affirmative will vary significantly among the various kinds of value resolutions. For example, in cases where the resolution affirms the value of a new policy orientation (e.g., unilateral disarmament is desirable), the affirmative team will be expected to demonstrate that the present policy cannot be similarly valuable. In demonstrating this, the affirmative team would be proving that the present policy inherently cannot be valuable. Thus, inherency, one of the issues most often associated with policy debate, can come into play in some value debates. (Some of the other terms associated with policy debate, significance, solvency, and disadvantages, can be related to the above requests (1), (2), and (3) respectively.)

The Skills Judge

The skills judge is a possibility in either policy or value debate; however, given the nature of the objections which led to the development of value debate in the early 1970s, the skills judge is likely to be more common in value debate than in policy debate. The skills judge is also common in high school debating.

The skills judge is very concerned about how effective a communicator you are. This kind of judge will raise such matters as delivery, eye contact, gestures, poise, and wit in making his or her decision.

The *pure* skills judge is rare. Even when a speech teacher is thrust into a debate, he or she usually understands that a debate is not *just* an oratorical contest. Some judges, however, so strongly weigh communications skills in their decisions that they make a decision opposite to that of a judge who is concerned only with the issues being raised. Their ballots often say—explicitly or implicitly— that even though team X won the arguments, team Y gets the decision because the members of team Y were the more successful communicators and debate is, after all, an activity designed to foster excellence in oral communication.

Adjusting to the Judge

Audience adaptation is one of the fundamentals of rhetoric and debaters need to learn to adapt just as much as writers of sales messages must learn to adapt their pitch to the particular audience who will hear or see the message. Such writers do not adapt based on guesses; rather, they adapt after considerable research into the nature of their audience. Debaters, in adapting to judges, should learn from the example of the advertising writers. Don't adapt based on your guesses as to what the judge likes or dislikes; do some research. Most regular debate judges have had to, at one point or another, write a judging philosophy. Your debate program may have kept philosophies written a while back on file. Your coach has read and studied many ballots penned by most of the judges you will face. Ask your coach for his or her assessment of a particular judge's philosophy. Many judges will be more than willing to "talk debate" with you during the course of a tournament; some will be willing to answer questions concerning their judging philosophy right before you debate with them as judge. Interview your prospective judges to the extent possible.

When you find out enough information about a particular judge, adapt accordingly. If you cannot find out enough information, you are best to pursue a moderate course. Adjusting radically on the basis of minimal information can lead to mistakes and losses. And, once you've "figured a judge out," be prepared to adjust your assessment periodically. Debate theory and practices change from year to year; anyone, like a debate coach, who hears *many* debates each year and reads, hears, and participates in discussions of theory and practice, will be almost constantly refining and revising his or her philosophy. Be alert to the possibility of this kind of refining and revising.

One procedural aspect of almost all debates has not been fully discussed: after each constructive speech, a period of cross-examination ensues. The next chapter discusses this often unnecessarily scary time during a debate when speakers debate person-to-person.

After reading and studying Chapter 9, you know:

- that a debate has four constructive speeches, followed by four rebuttals;
- that each speaker in a conventional policy debate has specific duties;
- how these duties change (1) when an alternative justifications case is presented, (2) in a net benefits debate, and (3) when a counterplan is presented;
- that the speaker duties in value debate are quite similar to those in a conventional policy debate except (1) when the second negative speaker chooses to *not* offer disadvantages or value objections and (2) when the negative team chooses to offer and defend a counterdesignative contention;
- how to plan for
    —the first affirmative rebuttal in policy debate by preparing rebuttal sheets, using heuristics, and grouping plan attacks;

—the first affirmative rebuttal in value debate by using these same techniques;
   —the summary rebuttals;
- how to flow conventional policy debates, policy debates featuring a counterplan, and value debates;
- how the stock issues judge in policy debate, the policymaking judge in policy debate, the issues judge in value debate, and the skills judge differ.

CHAPTER 10

Cross-examination

In this chapter, you will learn:

- some things you *should not* do in cross-examination;
- four general uses of cross-examination;
- special strategic goals for all of the cross-examination periods;
- how to make admissions gained in cross-examination count;
- how to prepare for cross-examination;
- what *ethos* is and how cross-examination can build or destroy it.

Cross-examination need not scare you. Yes, you will be on the spot. But, if you know your stuff—how to ask and what to answer, being on the spot means having a chance to shine, a chance to strengthen your position in the debate. The key then is knowing your stuff. This chapter should help.

Some Don'ts

Three common mistakes cause many cross-examination periods to be something other than what they should be. One mistake is the questioner's; one is the person questioned; one could be either debater's fault.

The questioner *is not* a courtroom attorney interrogating a witness. The questioner should not demand "Yes" or "No" responses; the questioner certainly should not pace back and forth like a television courtroom attorney. Rather than think of himself or herself as an interrogating attorney, the questioning debater should conceive of himself or herself as an interviewer. As such, the questioning debater's job is to gain information and probe for weaknesses in the case the questioned has offered. This gaining and probing should be done politely. You should try to be on friendly terms with your opponents; you should be firm without being overly aggressive.

The person questioned should not be evasive. Questions should be answered directly; information should be provided upon request if at all possible. Now, no one expects a cornered debater to admit that his or her case has a damning weakness: trying to escape from a corner is not evasion, but rather self-defense. But some debaters treat every question as a threat and try to avoid it rather than handle it head-on. For the most part, you should want to handle questions head-on: it provides you with an important opportunity to clarify and strengthen your position in the eyes of the judge.

Neither the questioner nor the questioned should offer an extended argument. The questioner should not speak for thirty seconds and then say, "Don't you agree?" Similarly, the questioned should not take advantage of an opening and launch into a thirty-second or longer argument. Cross-examination is for exchange, for dialogue, *not* for little speeches. Save the thirty-second or longer arguments for constructive speeches or rebuttals.

Procedural Matters

Cross-examination periods follow each constructive speech. Usually, these periods will each be three minutes in length. The speaker remains at the front of the room after his or her speech, perhaps moving a little to one side of the podium or desk or table. The questioner stands beside the speaker, probably a little to the other side of the podium or desk or table. Both speaker and questioner face the judge, occasionally looking at each other. This procedure is rigid; it may strike you as unnatural not to face the person you're speaking to, and it is. Remember that, in origin, debating is an oratorical performance addressed to an audience. It is the audience you stand before and the audience whom you face and speak to. You may well find that debaters in your league or district do not observe these formal conventions anymore. If so, then certainly adopt the degree of informality which seems the average. But even if you end up face-to-face with your opponent, remember that you have an audience out there too—an important audience since it is, or contains, the judge.

Who should question whom? There is only one rule: both team members must question; one cannot do all the questioning for a team. The answer to the question is finally a matter of strategy. The speaker can be questioned by the debater who will speak next: the first affirmative by the first negative; the first negative by the second affirmative; the second affirmative by the second negative; the second negative by the first affirmative. This strategy, although not unusual in the 1960s and early 1970s, is rare today. Its advantage is that it gives the questioner the opportunity to set up the refutation that will immediately follow in his or her speech. The alternative is for the speaker to be questioned by the opposing debater who is "at leisure" at that particular moment, not frantically preparing for an impending speech. Following this alternative strategy, the second negative would cross-examine the first affirmative; the first affirmative would cross-examine the first negative; the first negative would cross-examine the second affirmative and the second affirmative would cross-examine the second negative. This scheme gives the debater who must speak next more time to prepare; therefore, it is the scheme preferred by most debaters. However, it usually does not result in as effective use of cross-examination responses in subsequent speeches as the first scheme.

The Uses of Cross-examination

Some debaters see the cross-examination period as providing three extra minutes of preparation time for the seated debater who must speak next. These debaters just use up the time so as to help their seated partners. This use of the time is a waste of the time. Cross-examination time should be used, not occupied. I will outline four different uses of this time.

To Clarify

In a debate, it is important that matters be clear. Use the cross-examination period to clarify things that are fuzzy. Ask your opponent to explain an argument he or she has just offered. Ask your opponent to repeat plan planks you did not get down because of the speed at which they were presented or your being busy doing something else at the precise moment the plan plank was presented. Ask your opponent to clarify his or her stance. For example, if the first negative constructive speaker offhandedly mentions the possibility of some other policy solving the problem you have specified but solving it better, you might want to ask whether the negative team is indeed offering a counterplan. For example, if the affirmative team's demonstration of inherency seems fuzzy to you, you might want to ask if the claimed inherency is indeed only an attitudinal inherency, as it seems.

Many beginning debaters are afraid to ask for clarification for two reasons— both bad ones. First, they fear they are giving the opposition a chance to clear something up that, if left fuzzy, would be helpful to their own cause. This reason is bad because fuzzy argumentation, plans, and stances very easily become messy and get out of *all* the debaters' control. The judge has to intervene to an extent that he or she may not want to and make some sense of matters. This intervention can be to the detriment of the team that offered the fuzzy argument *or* it can be to the detriment of the team that failed to seek clarification and then respond. The judge, in other words, may throw the unclear argument out *or* the judge may make sense out of it and fault you for not responding to it. And there is no sure way of knowing which way a given judge will handle the mess. To maintain control of your fate during a debate, seek clarification. Second, they fear they will look stupid. On the contrary, a debater seeking clarification will strike a judge as smart—smart enough to realize that confusion benefits no one.

To Challenge Evidence

Evidence is, more often than not, presented fairly rapidly in a debate. As a result, certain things about the evidence may not be clear—the date, the source, the source's credentials. These matters can be clarified in cross-examination. Other aspects of evidence, however, should be scrutinized carefully in a debate. The context of a particular piece of evidence might well be questioned, especially if the quotation is in any way cut, if the quotation is rather brief, or if the quotation seems to begin in the middle of an argument. Ask:

In what context does so-and-so offer this comment?
What was cut out of this statement at this point?
What preceded this comment in the original?
What followed this comment in the original?

The reasoning behind a quoted statement also might well be questioned. Sometimes you will be attempting to discredit a piece of vague, conclusionary evidence by indicating that the reasoning behind it isn't known; sometimes you will be searching for weak spots in the reasoning to challenge. In many cases, rather than reasoning *per se*, a study or studies will be the basis upon which a conclusion rests. Then, you may want to inquire about the methodology employed in the study. Several common flaws in the methodology of empirical studies are considered in Chapters 3 and 6.

When you are challenging evidence, do not expect the opposition to crumble before your onslaught. Yes, objectively, you may have succeeded in doing considerable damage to the evidence your opponents used to substantiate an argument; you cannot, however, in the competitive atmosphere of a debate, expect them to yield. Assume that the judge realizes that damage has been done to the evidence and don't press and press for unlikely concessions. Just use (or have your partner use) the information you gained to challenge the evidence when you (or your partner) speak.

To Challenge Reasoning

Evidence isn't everything. Arguments can be well-supported merely by reasoning. A debater who uses reasoning should be questioned closely. Very likely, under cross-examination, you can expose an assumption in the argument which you can question. Ask:

Aren't you assuming _____?
How did you get from _____ to _____?

Many instances of reasoning in a debate will involve the thorny question of causality. Causality is a complex issue: it has been the subject of much philosophical writing through the centuries. For the purposes of debating, you should focus on three points in the causal statement "X causes Y." First, is X the sole cause, or one of many causes, and, if there are several causes, is X a sufficient cause or a necessary cause? (See Chapter 6 for a discussion of these types of causes.) Second, is Y the only effect: maybe there's a Z which mitigates Y. Third, is the alleged relationship reversible: will removing X lead to the removal of Y? To get at the logical problems these questions suggest, ask:

Is X the only thing causing Y?
Does X alone cause Y or are other ingredients necessary?
Isn't W just as major a cause of Y as X?
Doesn't X have other effects besides Y?
If X is removed, will Y necessarily end?

To Sustain Argumentation

The affirmative team must pull most if its arguments through in a debate; the negative team is interested in sustaining many of its arguments. To help you pull through or sustain arguments, you can do two things in cross-examination. First, you can point out to the judge arguments that your opponents didn't respond to; second, you can set up your responses to counterarguments that were offered. To draw the judge's attention to arguments not responded to, ask:

Did you respond to _____?
What did you argue in response to _____?

Be careful not to give your opponent a chance to voice a response then and there. *Do not ask*, "What is your response to _____?"

To set up your responses, you can do a number of things. Consider the following two examples.

Example one: Let's say your team has argued that welfare fraud is widespread; let's also say the negative team has argued that recent procedural changes have minimized the problem significantly. You intend to point to very recent data on welfare cheating, data postdating the procedural changes, and you intend to infer from the existence of this data that the changes have not been as effective as your opponents have claimed. Ask your opponents, "If I show you that fraud is still a problem months after these procedural changes you've spoken of, will you grant that those changes have not solved the problem?" Very few opponents will give you a simple "Yes" response; most will qualify the "Yes" in some way or another, and some will argue then and there that the changes will take time to have their effect. The precise response is in many ways irrelevant; no matter what your opponents say, you have set up your response in the judge's mind.

Example two: Let's say your team has argued that genetic engineering experiments are dangerous and the negative team has challenged the significance of the danger. You intend to argue, with evidence, that continued experimentation may lead to disease epidemics twenty times worse than the bubonic plague epidemics of the Middle Ages and Renaissance and to an average life expectancy reduced by fifteen years. Ask your opponent, "Would an epidemic twenty times worse than the bubonic plague epidemics of the Middle Ages be significant?" "Would a reduction in the average life expectancy by fifteen years be significant?" Your opponent will again rarely cooperate and simply say "Yes." Regardless of the voiced qualifications, the very questions and the obvious seriousness of the consequences you mention will have set up your response in the judge's mind.

Special Goals for Questioners

All cross-examination periods can be used to clarify, to challenge evidence, to challenge reasoning, and to sustain argumentation. Each cross-examination period is, however, different—because of its place in the overall debate. Its place gives it special potential in the rebuilding or defeating of the affirmative case. Let's consider each cross-examination session.

Questioning the First Affirmative

Most first affirmative constructive speeches *sound* good: time has gone into their preparation. The judge is usually—due to this preparation and polish—swayed toward the affirmative side of the proposition at the end of the initial speech. The negative needs to recall to the judge *all* the tasks the affirmative must accomplish before its rationale for a new policy or its value judgment can be accepted. The negative team can accomplish this task and put the affirmative team on the defensive when cross-examining the first affirmative constructive speaker. That the affirmative's goal or value is superior to alternative goals or values X, Y, and Z should be questioned. That the problem is *the* cause of claimed harms should be questioned. The significance of harms and advantages should be questioned; quantification should be requested. That the problem cannot be solved using presently existing means should be questioned. The solvency of the affirmative policy should be questioned: sound evidence attesting to or suggesting the plan's ability to solve the problem, accrue the advantages, or meet the goal/s should be requested. Alternative evaluations of policy types should be suggested.

The negative team's goals are to initiate doubt in the judge's mind *and* to set hurdles for the affirmative team to surmount. Questions such as the following help accomplish these special goals:

- Why is privacy more important than due process?
- Why is the promotion of global human rights more important than national security?

- Isn't archaic American technology as much a cause of the U.S. industrial decline as Japanese competition?
- How many needless deaths will your proposed health care plan save?
- How much revenue are large northern cities losing because of industrial flight to the Sun Belt?
- Couldn't improved administration of welfare solve the problem you're talking about?
- Won't the Stealth bomber currently under development solve the strategic defense weakness you're talking about?
- Can you prove that the deployment of the neutron bomb in Western Europe will deter the U.S.S.R. from launching a conventional assault?
- Can you prove that ending the CIA's anti-Sandinista operations will lead to a weakening of Soviet-Nicaraguan ties?
- Wouldn't restrictions on solicitations by religious groups seem less desirable if we valued freedom of speech more than the right to get to an airline counter quickly?

An important part of the task-setting goal of this cross-examination is to pair each question of the kind above with a request for additional information. Consider the following exchange:

Questioner: Won't the Stealth bombers currently under development solve the strategic defense weakness you're talking about?
First Affirmative: No.
Questioner: Why not?
First Affirmative: Because the masking technology used in these bombers will be penetrable by the time the first plane flies.
Questioner: I hope your partner will prove that claim with evidence in his or her constructive speech.

The first affirmative may have been bluffing in offering his or her response to the question. Whether the negative ultimately wins the particular argument implicit in the question or not, the negative has succeeded in tying up some of the second affirmative constructive speaker's time.

Consider another exchange illustrating the same strategy on the part of the questioner:

Questioner: How much revenue is Philadelphia losing because of industrial flight to the Sun Belt?
First Affirmative: As my source indicated in my speech, "a substantial amount."
Questioner: How much is "a substantial amount"?
First Affirmative: I don't know precisely.
Questioner: I hope then that your partner can precisely quantify the alleged harm.

The first affirmative speaker would have a difficult time beating the strategy in the second instance. In the first instance, the quick first affirmative would add

First Affirmative: If your partner makes that argument *with evidence* in his next speech, my partner will gladly respond.

Questioning the First Negative

After the first negative constructive speech is over, the judge may be in a kind of fog. This fog is a result of the barrage of arguments and challenges he or she has just heard. Most of this argumentation should be in direct response to the arguments the first affirmative constructive speech offered; only a few of the arguments voiced in the first negative constructive speech should represent lines of argumentation not tied to the first affirmative constructive speech. However, in many debates, especially those involving beginners, the balance is closer to half and half—half clearly clashing with a first affirmative argument and half not. As a result, the judge's perspective on the debate begins to become fuzzy. Given this incipient fogginess, the affirmative team member cross-examining the first negative speaker should consider re-establishing the affirmative case structure as a primary objective. Three questions will be useful in re-establishing the affirmative case structure:

- You argued _____. Which affirmative contention was that argument a response to?
- What did you argue in response to the _____ contention in the affirmative case?
- You offered no response to our _____ advantage. Is that correct?

A good affirmative strategy for cross-examining the first negative is to proceed through the affirmative's case structure, asking these kinds of questions as well as the ones that clarify, challenge evidence, challenge reasoning, and help sustain arguments. A questioner who chooses this multifaceted strategy needs, however, to maintain firm control of the cross-examination period and an eye on the clock.

Questioning the Second Affirmative

The cross-examination period which follows the second affirmative constructive speech comes at the crossroads in most debates: the debate's emphasis is about ready to shift from the case to the plan attacks or the "off-case" arguments. The cross-examination period therefore looks in both directions: back to the case, and forward to the plan attacks or "off-case" arguments the second negative constructive speech will offer.

Some questioning time ought to be used to establish the extent to which the second affirmative constructive speech (1) failed to do what was requested, (2) did not respond to first negative argumentation, and (3) responded inadequately to first negative argumentation. Questions such as the following would indicate to the judge that the second affirmative speaker has not been successful in turning the tide toward the affirmative on "case side":

(1) Did you quantify the amount of revenue lost by Philadelphia, as your partner said you would?

Did you prove that the Stealth bomber's masking technology will be outdated by 1990?
(2) Did you respond to the first negative argument that the American automotive industry is being hurt by a technological failure, not unfair foreign competition?
(3) Was _____ your only response to the argument that the real cause of the decline in educational quality is to be found in the family, not in the school? What did you argue in response to the argument that the Soviet Union is not overtly aggressive? (To be asked only when you know the response, know it is weak, and want to expose that weakness.)

Some questioning time should also be used to set up plan attacks or "off-case" arguments. You can try to get the second affirmative (who is not as familiar with the "plan side" or "off-case side" as his or her partner) to grant you key links in these arguments, the severity of the impacts of the disadvantages, or the severity of the results of basing action on a particular value or pursuing a general policy line.

Suppose you are debating a team that is defending the proposition that the federal government should use general revenue to bail out the near-bankrupt social security system. One of the disadvantages you or your partner plan to offer has as a crucial link the assertion that increased federal spending fuels inflation and has as its impact significantly reduced spending power for middle- and working-class Americans and a resulting slowdown in the production of consumer goods. To get the second affirmative to concede the link, you might ask, "Does increased federal spending fuel inflation?" or, more subtly, "Your plan will increase federal spending. What will the economic results of such an increase be?" To get the second affirmative to concede the impact, you might ask, "Would reduced spending power for the working and middle classes hurt these people" and then follow the question up with, "Would a reduction in consumer spending have an adverse effect on the manufacturers of consumer goods?"

Let's look at another example—this one from value debate. Let's say the affirmative team is arguing for the value statement that the right to life of the unborn baby is more important than a woman's right to control her body. A second negative debater may well wish to argue that a policy premised on such a value judgment would lead to large numbers of abused children. A key link in this "off-case" argument or value objection would be that unwanted children will be unloved; the impact is the psychological and physical damage child abuse causes. To get the second affirmative to concede the link, you might ask, "Why are children unwanted?" After the second affirmative responds that children are unwanted because the child would interfere with a woman's professional or social life, ask, "Wouldn't the child then be resented and unloved if the mother were compelled by law to bear the child?" To get the second affirmative to concede the impact, you might ask, "Is a battered baby—battered to, perhaps, the point where brain damage is a possibility—a serious problem?" or "Is it mentally healthful for hundreds or thousands of children and young teenagers to have an abnormal need for love and feel compelled to go to any lengths to win that love?"

When you are cross-examining, remember that your real goal is to convince the judge, not your opponents. So, even if your opponents refuse to make crucial admissions or concessions, you may still be having a successful cross-examination period, for the judge may be understanding and accepting the positions you are trying to advance. Such a judge will be very receptive when the plan attacks or "off-case" arguments are advanced in the second negative constructive speech.

Questioning the Second Negative

The second negative constructive speech is the one that makes the first affirmative rebuttalist's life miserable. Therefore, when cross-examining the second negative, the questioner should try to help the first affirmative rebuttalist out. The questioner can help out in three ways: (1) by beating inapplicable plan attacks or "off-case" arguments; (2) by pointing out common assumptions or impacts among the separate arguments the second negative advanced (thereby helping the first affirmative rebuttalist group arguments); and (3) by setting up turnarounds.

Some plan attacks will be based on an inadequate understanding of the affirmative plan. Once the plan is correctly understood, the plan attack vanishes. In cross-examination, a questioner can ask, "Are you aware that our plan _____?" After the second negative is informed as to the plan's provisions, then a questioner can ask, "In view of this provision of the plan, isn't your argument that _____ irrelevant?"

Plans are fairly elaborate in policy debate; plans are virtually nonexistent in value debate. However, implicit in many affirmative cases in value debate is the advocacy of a general kind of policy. Many "off-case" arguments are objections to this general policy direction. Given its intentional vagueness, misunderstandings of it tend to be more fundamental and less related to the presence or absence of specific provisions. The line of questioning which an affirmative debater might use to expose this kind of misunderstanding would be similar to the following:

Questioner: You argue that placing a high value on privacy will lead to an increase in subversive activity?
Second Negative: Yes.
Questioner: Now tell me. Does saying that privacy is more important than other things, such as domestic tranquility, mean that domestic tranquility is unimportant?
Second Negative: Well, no.
Questioner: So the affirmative position could well be that privacy should take precedence over domestic tranquility, not that privacy should dictate all policy decisions and domestic tranquility none?
Second Negative: I don't understand.
Questioner: Would a policy which tries to balance the need for privacy and the need for domestic tranquility, giving the former a bit of an edge, be at odds with the affirmative position in this debate?

Second Negative: Well, no.
Questioner: Then the FBI will not necessarily be totally stripped of all information on dissidents as you claim if privacy rights are judged foremost?

At this point, the second negative would start arguing that valuing privacy would lead to a stripped FBI, even if domestic tranquility were not totally ignored. At this point, you should change the course of cross-examination, for you have made your point: the second negative was making an incorrect assumption and basing an "off-case" argument on it.

Pointing out common assumptions and impacts will not get rid of plan attacks or "off-case" arguments; however, it will help the first affirmative rebuttalist group arguments, and grouping is almost always an advantage since it frees time for the sustaining of other arguments. The questions to ask to achieve this goal are rather straightforward:

- Doesn't disadvantage (2) assume _____? Doesn't disadvantage (3) assume the same thing? If that assumption is false, then both disadvantages fall, right?
- Doesn't your second "off-case" argument assume _____? Doesn't your fourth one assume the exact same thing? If this assumption falls, then don't both arguments?
- The impact of advantage (1) is _____, right? The impact of advantage (4) is also _____, right? If that impact is not significant, then both disadvantages fall, right?

The last part of each question serves two purposes: first, it sets up the rebuttalist's argument in the judge's mind; second, it deflects the questioned debater's attention away from the grouping. In other words, he or she will be so ready to argue that the assumption is valid or the impact is significant that he or she will let the grouping stand.

Setting up turnarounds in cross-examination saves the first affirmative rebuttalist some valuable time. The kind of questioning sequence to follow would be similar to the following:

Questioner: You argue in disadvantage (3) that the affirmative plan will cause a recession because it will reduce consumer spending, correct?
Second Negative: Yes.
Questioner: Why is this so?
Second Negative: Because the increase in inflation caused by the increase in federal spending will reduce the value of paychecks. It's simple economics.
Questioner: So, you're saying each consumer will have in effect less money to spend?
Second Negative: Exactly.
Questioner: What if the affirmative plan results also in significantly increased employment? Won't the affirmative plan increase the number of consumers and thereby, according to your own logic, cause economic growth, not recession?

At this point, the second negative will naturally begin to balk: if he or she is smart, the word "turnaround" has flashed through his or her mind. The balking is largely irrelevant, for you've already set up the turnaround for the first affirmative rebuttalist. You've saved that rebuttalist some valuable time by providing the judge with a good preview of the argument's outline. Now the judge needs only a review, not a step-by-step presentation. The rebuttalist can say:

Disadvantage (3). The negative argues that our plan will lead to a recession. On the contrary, our plan will lead to economic growth. Why? As the second negative admitted in cross-examination, the key to the disadvantage is the level of consumer spending. As was noted then, rather than decrease consumer spending, we will be increasing it significantly by increasing employment significantly.

What would follow would be an explanation and proof of the claim that the plan will increase employment and then the affirmative claim that the disadvantage has been turned into an advantage and now represents an independent justification for voting affirmative in the debate.

Applying an Opponent's Responses in the Speeches That Follow

The excerpt from a first affirmative rebuttal above illustrates an important principle of cross-examination and debating: you must *apply* the concessions, admissions, etc., you gain in cross-examination for them to count.

All judges pay attention to cross-examination; some judges even flow cross-examination. Very few judges will apply what you gain as a cross-examiner for you. If a second negative debater admits in cross-examination that half of his or her "off-case" arguments or disadvantages are inapplicable, the first affirmative rebuttalist must apply the admission to the appropriate arguments to beat them. If a second affirmative admits that certain impacts would indeed be serious, the second negative must apply the admission if he or she is going to argue that his or her disadvantages have a significant impact by the affirmative's own admission.

Related to the requirement that debaters apply what they found out during cross-examination is the question of whether or not admissions, concessions, and comments made during cross-examination should be binding. Whereas almost all agree that cross-examination responses must be applied to count in a debate, debate coaches do not agree on the question of whether or not cross-examination is binding.

Those who argue that cross-examination should not be binding argue that responses are sometimes offered without sufficient thought, that questions are often misunderstood and answered in ways that are unintentionally damaging, and that a more experienced debater should not be allowed to win a debate by intimidating and/or browbeating a less experienced debater during cross-examination. Those who argue that cross-examination should be binding respond that to allow retraction encourages careless behavior during cross-examination: if debaters know that they will not be held accountable, they need not think. Furthermore, those who argue that cross-examination should be binding argue that to allow retraction is unfair to the competitors. Would it be fair, when a second negative debater had made damaging admissions when being cross-examined and the first affirmative rebuttalist used those admissions to refute the second negative's plan attacks, if the second negative were to say in his or her rebuttal that he or she was retracting those admissions, and that the plan objections still stood since their substance had not yet been touched?

I obviously cannot resolve the controversy here. Debaters should be aware that a large number of judges believe that cross-examination is binding and act accordingly. Acting accordingly would mean thinking when being interrogated; acting accordingly would mean pleading "I don't know" or "I'm not sure" when you either don't know for certain or are being pushed into a response by an overaggressive opponent. Acting accordingly would mean *not* trying to get out of a tight spot by claiming that "cross-examination isn't binding." Debaters should also be aware that some judges believe that cross-examination is not necessarily binding and act accordingly. Acting accordingly would mean pleading confusion or even intimidation to escape from under the onus of a damaging response. Acting accordingly would mean not just responding "he can't do that" when an opponent tries to retract a cross-examination response that has been applied to his or her disfavor, but (a) screaming "foul" *and explaining* why a retraction is unfair and (b) challenging the position the opponent has retreated to head-on.

Preparation for Cross-examination

Cross-examination is usually one of the last parts of a debate a team will practice and prepare for. Everything else—the case, blocks to defend it, briefs on popular cases, preplanned plan attacks—seems to take precedence. Cross-examination should not be shunted off to last place in the tournament preparation regimen, as it so often is.

The questioner can prepare question-answer trees which should guide him or her in pursuing some standard lines of argumentation during cross-examination. Figure 10.1 is a brief example of a question-answer tree. Such an aid is probably more valuable in the preparation than in actual competition: in preparation, such a tree helps you think matters through; in actual competition, such a tree *could* cause you to stall when your opponent doesn't offer a response you planned on or offers a response you must reflect on for a few seconds before deciding along which branch of the tree it will take you. If you are sure you will not be too tied to question-answer trees during an actual debate, go ahead and write up a few on some of the issues that come up again and again. Writing them up would be a very good collaborative activity.

The better preparation is actual practice. Cross-examine your partner; cross-examine your teammates concerning their affirmative cases; cross-examine your coach. As you practice, strive for clarity, brevity, efficiency, and politeness. Strive to make your questions immediately clear to your audience—that is, your opponent and your judge. Also strive to make your questions brief by forcing

Q: Where, specifically, is the U.S.S.R. threatening the U.S.?

A: In Western Europe.
A: In the Third World.
A: In Central America.
A: In the U.S., through nuclear weapons.

Q: What is the nature of this threat?
Q: Is this a direct threat involving Soviet troops?
Q: Is this a direct threat involving Soviet troops?
Q: Doesn't the U.S. threaten the U.S.S.R. in just the same way?

A: A troop buildup in Eastern Europe.
A: Yes.
A: No. The U.S.S.R. uses proxies.
A: Yes.
A: No. The U.S.S.R. uses proxies.
A: Yes.
A: No.

Q: The troops are there then to threat Western Europe?
Q: Where?
Q: Where have they proved successful?
Q: Where?
Q: Where have they proved successful?
Q: Then why be so alarmed if we've met the threat already?
Q: Why not?

A: Yes.
A: ———
A: ———
A: ———
A: ———
A: Because nuclear war is more and more likely?
A: Because the U.S. is peaceful?

Q: Couldn't the situation in Poland have something to do with the increase in troops?
Q: Soviet troops are involved in the fighting?
Q: Why did they succeed?
Q: Soviet troops are involved in the fighting?
Q: Why did they succeed?
Q: So it is your team's goal to prevent war? If so, then why are you advocating a military buildup?
Q: But aren't we the only nation that has ever used nuclear weapons?

Figure 10.1 Sample question-answer tree.

yourself to get to the point and state it succinctly. Strive to be as efficient as possible. Efficiency can be defined in terms of coverage. As questioner, you will probably want to cover many arguments. So don't let yourself get bogged down. If a particular line of questioning is getting nowhere, change to another line. Opponents will often try to prevent you from being efficient by answering at too great a length—with detailed explanations and examples. You need to take charge and indicate that your question has been answered—"Thank you, you've answered my question."—after your opponent has had a chance to respond and *briefly* explain his or her response. Finally, strive to be polite. More on being polite later.

You also need to prepare for being questioned, especially when you're on the affirmative. On the affirmative side of the proposition, you will be setting the debate's tone by offering a case for the adoption of the resolution. You should, after a tournament or two, be able to anticipate almost all questions you will be asked; even before the first tournament, you should be able to anticipate many of the questions. For these anticipated questions, you might want to prepare a two-column question and answer brief. In column one, list the anticipated question; in column two, list the answer/s. This brief is especially useful for beginning debaters and debaters who are defending a particular affirmative case the first time. This brief should be studied in advance. I strongly discourage searching through it while being cross-examined; such behavior is unprofessional, and it makes it look as if you cannot think on your own two feet.

As with questioning, the best preparation for being questioned is practice being questioned. Ask your partner, teammates, or coach to cross-examine you. As they do, strive to be *brief but full* in your responses. Also, and very important, constantly ask yourself where your questioner is trying to take you; what your questioner is trying to set up. If you are thinking along these lines, you will very rarely make costly admissions. Also, like your questioner, be polite. The antagonistic questioner can lose speaker points because he or she lacks style and grace; if the debater who is being questioned is antagonistic, not only can he or she lose points but this debater can lose credibility. Antagonistic responses— ranging from evasiveness to rudeness to anger—make it look like the debater has something to hide.

Cross-examination and *Ethos*: A Brief Word

The next chapter will discuss some aspects of argumentation that have nothing to do with logic and evidence. These dimensions, alogical dimensions, are important in debate as long as we conceive of the activity as one which involves human beings and human communication. One of the most important alogical aspects of argumentation discussed in Chapter 11 is that of *ethos*. The term goes back to Aristotle's *Rhetoric*. There he says man makes three kinds of arguments: *logos* or logical argumentation; *pathos* or emotional argumentation; and *ethos* or argumentation based on the character you project. If you come across as sincere, honest, truth-seeking, etc., you are making an ethical argument for your position; if you come across as deceptive, evasive, overly competitive, etc., you are inadvertently making an ethical argument *against* your position.

As the next chapter will note, throughout a debate you are making ethical arguments for or against your position. When you are cross-examined or when you cross-examine, the possibility of making a positive or negative ethical appeal is heightened. I earlier urged you to be polite, and I suggested that impolite behavior could cost you points. Overaggressive questioning or evasive responding and other behavior that causes judges' faces to turn sour may cost you points not just because the judges see themselves as defenders of a code of etiquette. These actions cost points because they result in your argumentation lacking the impact it ought to have. A good argument presented by a debater with a strong *ethos* may well be rated by a judge as twice as effective as the same argument presented by a debater with a negative *ethos*. The difference is not the result of conscious choice on the part of the judge: he or she may be totally unaware of it. The response is rooted in human psychology. It operates in Presidential campaigns, in debates, in all situations involving human communication. Debaters should be aware of the *ethos* they project, especially during cross-examination periods. Timidity, evasiveness, cockiness, and bullying can weaken your arguments; assurance, straightforwardness, modesty, and masterfulness can strengthen your arguments by adding a strong dose of ethical appeal to them. Debaters need to be concerned with the impressions they give and to practice giving ones that improve their chances of success.

After reading and studying Chapter 10, you know:

- that the questioner should *not* act like a courtroom attorney, that the questioned should *not* be evasive, and that neither should offer extended arguments;
- that cross-examination should be used
    —to clarify;
    —to challenge evidence;
    —to challenge reasoning;
    —to sustain argumentation;
- that the questioner in each cross-examination period should have one or more strategic goals:
    —the debater cross-examining the first affirmative speaker should try to initiate doubt in the judge's mind and to set tasks for the affirmative team;
    —the debater cross-examining the first negative speaker should try to reestablish the affirmative case structure;
    —the debater cross-examining the second affirmative speaker should try to (1) expose what that speaker *did not do* and (2) set up plan attacks or "off-case" arguments;

—the debater cross-examining the second negative speaker should help the first affirmative rebuttalist *quickly* deal with plan attacks or "off-case" arguments;
- that admissions gained in cross-examination must be applied in the speeches that follow;
- how to prepare question-answer trees and that practice is essential;
- that *ethos* is the appeal you make based on the character you project and that during cross-examination you should strive to project a positive *ethos*.

CHAPTER 11
Alogical Argumentation

In this chapter, you will learn:

- what ethical appeal is;
- what pathetic appeal is;
- how forms, large and small, have their own persuasive power.

Debating is a persuasive activity: you are not trying to make marks on an unthinking, unfeeling slate; rather, you are trying to persuade an audience, a judge. Recognizing this as your goal should lead to the recognition that more is involved in debating than simply "having the best arguments." There are some important *human* dimensions of debating which you ought to consider.

Let me first mention the human dimension which most coaches wish were *not* present in debating: politics. Some judges will have motives for voting for a particular team that have nothing to do with the actual debate: perhaps the coach of your opponents is a "good buddy" of the judge; perhaps your loss will enhance the judge's team's chances; perhaps your opponents come from a "name school" whereas you come from a lesser-known school. To the extent these motives consciously affect decisions, they are totally reprehensible. Most educators involved in debating would find any of these motives for making a decision so and condemn the judge who judges politically. There are, however, a few bad apples out there. To say otherwise would be to deceive you. In addition—and this fact is important to realize—some judges will have these motives without realizing it and these motives will *unconsciously* enter into the decision in close debates.

Hearing that politics sometimes enter into the picture should not turn you off to debating. Rather, hearing this bad news should alert you to the fact that debating involves human beings—some of whom are less noble than they'd perhaps like to be. Judging is frequently a subject of student complaints, particularly prejudiced judging. Usually, the accusation is unfounded: debaters are seeking an excuse; debaters don't want to say "we blew it." Sometimes, however, there is some basis to the complaint.

You need to be aware of these dimensions of debating as human communication, dimensions which can cause problems. *More important*, you need to be aware of some other dimensions of debating as communication, the three kinds of appeals people often make when persuading: ethical appeals, pathetic appeals, and formal appeals. These appeals work because we are human and respond—consciously and unconsciously—to things other than logic. Because these appeals are not logical but do not violate logic, I call them alogical appeals.

Ethical Appeal

The first kind of alogical appeal, ethical appeal, has long been recognized—at least in theory. Aristotle defined this dimension as the persuasive appeal speakers and writers make through their personality or character, through their projected selves. In the *Rhetoric*, he stresses its importance: "It is not true, as some writers on the art [of rhetoric] maintain, that the probity of the speaker contributes nothing to his persuasiveness; on the contrary, we might affirm that his *ethos* is the most potent of all the means to persuasion."[1] This *ethos*, Aristotle notes, is created by the discourse itself. A judge's opinion of debaters when he or she walks into the classroom—an opinion largely based on their personal appearance, their friendliness, and the amount of reference material they have before them—will certainly predispose him toward being persuaded or away from being persuaded. However, the speeches themselves will either sustain or destroy this preliminary opinion of the speakers' characters, and the *ethos* which the discourse itself creates will become dominant. This *ethos* is rich in persuasive power.

Let me show you the power of ethical appeal in a kind of communication where it is a bit easier to recognize. Consider the following two business letters, which appear in the third edition of the very popular *Written Communication in Business* by the late Robert L. Shurter. The first is a collection letter, the second is a sales letter:

When we permitted you to have the privilege of a 90-day account with us, it was with the definite understanding that you were to pay all bills in three installments over a three-month period.

Now we find that you have paid only the first month's portion on that new refrigerator and that interest at 1½ percent per month is piling up on your balance, which is now $320.64 but will be larger a month from now.

To help you with dividing, you owe us $160.32 this month and again next month *if* you send us a check right now. If you don't, we will reluctantly keep adding interest charges. Why not pay now?[2]

A bore, Mrs. Jones, is a person who is here today and here tomorrow.

But tomorrow, you can be a different person by subscribing to *Facts Illustrated*, the magazine for people who know.

Your conversation will be brighter, your understanding of events deeper, and your interest in life greater, if you spend two hours each week reading this tautly edited, brilliantly illustrated magazine for the cognoscenti.

Just sign the enclosed card. We'll bill you for $21.95. And you'll be off and running with all the facts and all the background you need.[3]

Neither letter works, because the *ethos* is condescending in the first case and insulting in the second. The bill collector's sound argument for paying one's debts and the salesman's pitch for *Facts Illustrated* will fall on deaf ears—ears deafened because of the persuasive writer's inept use of a powerful alogical resource. The bill collector and his company "permitted" the delinquent debtor "the privilege" of an account; the collector condescendingly assumes the debtor cannot divide $320.64 by two. The word that comes to mind to describe this collector is indeed "condescending." Will that *ethos* or projected self aid persuasion? The salesman practically calls Mrs. Jones a "bore," and implies that her conversation is dull, her understanding shallow, and her interest in life small; and, in a horribly inept metaphor, compares her to a racehorse. The word for this persuader's *ethos*? "Insulting." Will this *ethos* or projected self aid persuasion and drum up business for *Facts Illustrated*? Only if Mrs. Jones neurotically fears that she is indeed a bore!

These two persuasive writers are not making an ethical appeal to their readers. They are ignoring a powerful alogical resource in human argumentation. In debate, that same resource is also often ignored.

What should your *ethos* be in a debate? You should project honesty, sincerity, humility, and amicability. If you are to come across as honest, you must offer full citations for all the evidence you read and you must be careful not to stretch evidence beyond the point of believability. You also must, in cross-examination, seem willing to answer all questions directly and succinctly. Furthermore, you must be careful not to misrepresent in any way your opponent's position. To come across as sincere, you must seem to believe your arguments. You must also seem genuinely interested in getting to the truth of things—whether or not a particular policy is a good idea; whether or not a particular value judgment is valid. To come across as humble, you must—within reason—admit your limitations. if you don't know the answer to a question posed in cross-examination, admit it; if you've called an argument into question rather than "beating it cold," admit it. Any ground you lose because you humbly admit limitations will be made up by the ground your *ethos* gains you. To come across as amicable, be friendly to the judge and your opponents—when speaking, when listening, when setting up or packing up. Wit during a debate and smiling during a debate also project an amicable *ethos*.

Your *ethos* should *not* be dishonest, insincere, cocky, and unfriendly. One instance of misrepresentation, too-obvious game-playing, arrogant dismissals of opponents' arguments, or rudeness can destroy a debater's *ethos*—just one instance. Keep in mind that building an *ethos* requires time; destroying it requires only one blunder.

Pathetic Appeal

Most logic textbooks list "appeal to pity" and similar appeals under the rubric "fallacies." In doing so, these textbooks make a fundamental error: they assume that all argumentation should, if at all possible, be strictly rational, strictly logical. Does this assumption make sense? I would argue it does not because argumentation assumes a human audience and a human audience has an emotional side as well as a rational side. To pretend that this emotional side plays no role in decision making is absurd. Whether the decision is to buy a house which looks like one's childhood home *or* to provide federal money for drugs to aid diseases which are so rare that the drugs do not provide pharmaceutical companies with a sufficient profit motive to produce them *or* to unilaterally freeze the number of nuclear warheads at the present level, emotions are part of it. Sentimentality, pity, fear, and numerous other human emotions play important roles in human argumentation. I would argue that the role that emotion plays in "real-world" human decision making and argumentation justifies a similar role for it in the simulated decision-making-through-argumentation of debating.

I cannot think of a situation where sentimentality would come into play in a debate; I can, however, think of numerous situations into which pity and fear would enter. Add to these two emotions anger, and you probably have the three emotions most relevant to argumentation in a debate.

Where would pity come into play? Most probably when the affirmative tries to establish that a significant problem exists, one giving rise to harms. Rural poverty in the mountains of Appalachia is pitiable; so is the plight of teenage boys and girls who must turn to pornography and prostitution in order to survive; so are the numerous unwanted, unloved babies born in the United States every year. And the list goes on. A debater should *not* feel reluctant to make a pathetic appeal in cases such as these where a pathetic appeal is appropriate.

Where would fear come into play? Many affirmative cases are premised on fear—fear of an erosion of American freedoms, fear of nuclear war, fear of the economic collapse of this nation. Similarly, many disadvantages and "off-case" arguments play off the audience's fear. If the disadvantages of stopping U.S. military aid to El Salvador is a security threat to the United States along its southern border, that disadvantage plays on the audience's fear of insecurity and fear of Communism. If the argued effect of government controls on scientific research is a slowdown in vital research and discovery, that disadvantage plays on the audience's fear of disease and, ultimately, death. A debater should *not* feel reluctant to make a pathetic appeal in order to strengthen the impact of such arguments.

Where would anger come into play? Usually when the affirmative argues that injustice is being done or that problems are not being addressed for political or bureaucratic reasons. Perhaps the human rights of black Americans in certain parts of the United States are *still* being violated with impunity. Those who know turn their heads; those who complain are ostracized or beaten or worse. Perhaps millions of dollars of federal money could be rechanneled from pointless pork-barrel projects to needed social services *if* political considerations did not govern the appropriations process in Washington, D.C. Perhaps extra money to upgrade the water and sewage systems of America's older cities is available *if* the needy cities meet numerous conditions, fill numerous forms, pledge numerous actions, and wait and wait and wait and wait. A debater should *not* feel reluctant to make a pathetic appeal—to express his or her justified anger—in noting these situations and arguing against them.

Pathos has a place, but it must be—for the sake of intelligent decision or judgment making—subservient to *logos*. Many teachers of argumentation advise students to get rid of pathetic appeals entirely; they advise them in this manner because they are afraid that, once the door is open to emotion-laden argumentation, more and more such argumentation will come rushing in (because it's relatively easy to make emotional appeals). The better advice is to use pathetic appeals in recognition of the human audience you are trying to persuade, but to use pathetic appeals sparingly in recognition of that audience's desire to be as rational and logical as possible in making decisions.

Formal Appeal

Another alogical dimension of argumentation is suggested by American rhetorician Kenneth Burke in *A Rhetoric of Motives*. He tells his readers that " . . . many purely formal patterns can readily awaken an attitude of collaborative expectancy in us."[4] These forms can be organizational patterns. When, for example, a speaker or writer is rising to his crucial argument in support of increased defense spending, his rise to climax invites our participation. Our participation, in turn, lends persuasive power to his climactic argument. The last argument's logical worth is somewhat irrelevant: we *feel* persuaded because we have collaborated in its articulation. These forms which seduce us and sway us need not be on as large a scale as the organization of an argument. The forms "which awaken an attitude of collaborative expectancy" can be constructed of sentences or clauses or phrases.

Here is a small-scale example of the scheme of climax described above: the example is from John F. Kennedy's Inaugural Address. Early in the address, Kennedy leads us up the parallel rungs of an emotional ladder when he declares, "Let every nation know, whether it wishes us well or ill, that we shall pay any price, bear any burden, meet any hardships, support any friend, oppose any foe to assure the survival and success of liberty."[5] Even on the wings of patriotic fervor, we should not soar into global military commitments. That Kennedy was directing our nation's course toward such commitments—toward Vietnam—is lost in the quick assent we still give his argument. That we give such an assent is a product of Kennedy's deft use of the rhetorical schemes listed and illustrated in the rhetoric of old. These rhetorics identified and recommended the use of schemes because the authors knew that, as Burke observes, " . . . a yielding to the form prepares for assent to the matter identified with it." The listener or reader, Burke continues, is "drawn to the form, not in his capacity as partisan, but because of some 'universal' appeal in it."[6] This formal appeal is totally alogical, and incredibly powerful.

Consider the following excerpt from an address made by the then Senator Hubert H. Humphrey. He was addressing the 1964 Democratic National Convention, accepting its nomination as his party's vice-presidential candidate:

The temporary spokesman of the Republican party—yes, temporary Republican spokesman—is not only out of tune with the great majority of his countrymen, he is even out of step with his own party.
In the last three and a half years most Democrats and Republicans have agreed on the great decisions our nation has made. But not the Republican spokesman. Not Senator Goldwater. He's been facing backwards against the mainstream of American history.
Most Democrats and most Republicans in the United States Senate, for example, voted for the nuclear test-ban treaty but not the temporary Republican spokesman.
Most Democrats and Republicans in the Senate voted for an $11.5 billion tax cut for American citizens and American business but not Senator Goldwater.
Most Democrats and Republicans in the Senate—in fact four-fifths of the members of his own party—voted for the Civil Rights Act, but not Senator Goldwater.
Most Democrats and Republicans in the Senate voted for the establishment of a United States Arms Control and Disarmament Agency that seeks to slow down the nuclear arms race among nations, but not the temporary Republican spokesman.
Most Democrats and most Republicans in the Senate voted last year for an expanded medical-education program, but not Senator Goldwater!
Most Democrats and most Republicans in the Senate voted for the National Defense Education Act, but not the temporary Republican spokesman.[7]

A witness to this part, and the succeeding minutes, of this address would have experienced the power of the rhetorical scheme of epistrophe, the repetition of the same word or phrase or sentence at the end of several increments of discourse. Approximately at the midpoint of Senator Humphrey's criticism of Senator Goldwater, he no longer said "but not Senator Goldwater" alone; the packed Convention Hall in Atlantic City, New Jersey, said the phrase with him. Approximately two-thirds of the way through the criticism, he no longer said the repeated phrase at all; the audience alone announced, "but not Senator Goldwater." At that point, Humphrey could have voiced any indictment against Goldwater and the audience would have responded "but not Senator Goldwater." The audience was so swayed by the rhetorical scheme that the logical, rational content of Humphrey's argument became irrelevant. If Humphrey had announced that most Democrats and most Republicans love puppy dogs, the audience would have dutifully repeated, "but not Senator Goldwater."

The power of that particular use of a rhetorical scheme evidently lingers in the minds of the Democratic Party hierarchy, for, at the 1980 Democratic National Convention, both Humphrey's protégé, then Vice-President Walter F. Mondale, and (to a lesser extent) Senator Edward M. Kennedy echoed Humphrey's use of epistrophe in issuing their rallying calls against Ronald Reagan. Debaters should be alerted to the alogical persuasive power rhetorical schemes such as epistrophe have, so that they can be as alert to it as Humphrey, Mondale, and Kennedy.

Climax and epistrophe are, of course, not the only formal patterns. There are hundreds—all with funny names supplied either by classical rhetoricians such as Cicero or by Renaissance English rhetoricians such as George Puttenham in his *The Arte of English Poesie* and Henry Peacham in his *Garden of Eloquence*. Mentioning a few of the most useful schemes and their effect on an audience should help debaters add this alogical dimension to their argumentation. The other five I want to briefly mention are anaphora, antithesis, anadiplosis, polysyndeton, and asyndeton.

Climax and epistrophe invite participation and, through participation, assent. So does anaphora. Consider Winston Churchill's famous words to the British House of Commons on 4 June 1940: "We shall fight on the beaches, we shall fight on the landing-grounds, we shall fight in the fields and in the streets, we shall fight in the hills."[8] Churchill repeats "we shall fight" at the beginning of a series of clauses. This repetition at the beginning of a series of grammatical units is anaphora. Like Hubert H. Humphrey's repetition of "but not Senator Goldwater" at the end of units, this repetition at the beginning invites participation and assent.

Antithesis calls the auditor's attention to contrasts or oppositions. Consider the following excerpt from an article in *America* authored by civil rights activists Jesse E. Hobson and Martin E. Robbins. Those of you who know Charles Dickens' *A Tale of Two Cities* will recognize their debt to the famous beginning of this novel:

It is the best of times, yet the worst of times: we live in unparalleled prosperity, yet have starvation; modern science can perform miracles to save lives, yet we have war; we balance ourselves delicately on the moon, yet destroy the delicate balance of the earth. Young people search for meaning in life, yet are confused, demoralized, frustrated.[9]

Hobson and Rollins set up a series of contrasts between what is good about our society and what is bad. These contrasts are emphasized by the "x yet y" structure they use. "But" or "however" or "nevertheless" could be used in this structure in place of "yet," and the effect on the audience would be essentially the same.

Anadiplosis emphasizes a chronological or causal sequence by using the last word in the first item of a sequence as the first word in the next, etc. An example should help make the scheme clear to you. The National Security Advisor to former President Jimmy Carter, Zbigniew K. Brzezinski, wrote in *The Permanent Purge, Politics in Soviet Totalitarianism* that, "Having power makes it [totalitarian leadership] isolated; isolation breeds suspicion and fear; suspicion and fear breed violence."[10] Brzezinski uses this scheme to emphasize the causal progression he believes lies behind Soviet foreign policy.

Polysyndeton emphasizes connection by repeating conjunctions where the repetition is grammatically uncalled for. Let's say that you are a second negative debater in a policy debate. You presented several disadvantages that you claim the affirmative plan will lead to in your constructive speech; in your rebuttal, you want to emphasize that the affirmative's plan will lead not to one, not to two, not to three, but to four horrible disadvantages. You could use polysyndeton to help you accomplish this rhetorical goal:

The affirmative plan calls for wage controls. Such a plan will lead to hardship among the poor *and* a reduction in morale among the middle class *and* increased government interference *and* the weakening of the entire American economy.

The opposite of polysyndeton is asyndeton. When you use this scheme, you omit conjunctions, even when they are required according to the conventions of English grammar. The effect of this scheme is either an emphasis on a close connection or a sense of an infinite progression. Lincoln's "of the people, by the people, for the people" is an example of asyndeton: the use of the scheme emphasizes how closely connected the phrases descriptive of American government are. If a debater, on the other hand, were to say that, "This affirmative lacks topicality, significance, inherency, solvency," the omission of the final conjunction would suggest that the case's problems continue on, that the list has not ended yet, that there's more—perhaps infinitely more—to be said in criticism of the affirmative's position.

The examples I have offered of these formal schemes should suggest to you times when they are useful. They are useful at times in a speech when you want to be emphatic; they are particularly useful when you are summarizing a particular argument, an entire speech, or an entire debate.

When you use formal schemes in a debate, keep in mind two principles. First, they are not interchangeable flourishes of style. Their use certainly makes you sound more eloquent; however, on top of eloquence, each scheme has a particular rhetorical effect. Climax, epistrophe, and anaphora invite participation; participation aids persuasion. Antithesis emphasizes contrasts: if a contrast is at the core of your argument, the use of antithesis will aid persuasion. Anadiplosis emphasizes chronological or causal sequence: if such a sequence is important in your argument, the use of anadiplosis will aid persuasion. Polysyndeton emphasizes connections, and asyndeton can also emphasize connection. If a strong connection between, let's say, organized crime, labor unions, and certain politicians is an important part of argument, these two schemes can emphasize it and aid persuasion. Asyndeton can also suggest a continuing, perhaps never-ending sequence. If you want your audience to believe that such a sequence is going to result if a particular course is followed, or a sequential course is being pursued now, asyndeton may be a formal scheme which will alogically aid persuasion.

Second, alogical formal appeals should not be used *in lieu* of sound logical argumentation supported with evidence. They should be a supplement; they should be a method for adding force, adding extra persuasiveness.

Rhetorical schemes are examples of formal appeal on a small scale. According to Kenneth Burke, following any form that the audience discerns and feels comfortable with will enhance persuasiveness. This large-scale formal appeal can be made when you carefully organize your constructive speeches and rebuttals. If you carefully organize what you have to say, if you adequately preview your organization, if you make clear transitions in your speech, if you review where you've been at the end, you'll find your audience with you the entire way. He or she could actually predict your next few steps accurately. When the audience gets to this point, they can be genuinely said to participate in the making of the speech with you. If they are participating in this manner, then your argumentation is certainly going to be alogically enhanced. To an extent, *your* arguments will feel like shared arguments to your audience and will therefore be granted more power.

Speech teachers and writing teachers (perhaps all teachers) counsel students to be organized. The advice is given not just because these teachers are obsessed with neatness and order, or because these teachers want you to be considerate of your listeners or readers. The advice is also given because these teachers have intuited or know that good organization in and of itself makes a powerful alogical appeal which can sway a reader or listener when an argument is close.

After reading and studying Chapter 11, you know:

- that ethical appeal is the persuasive appeal you make when you come across to your audience as honest, sincere, humble, and amicable;
- that pathetic appeal is the persuasive appeal you make when you appeal to emotions such as pity, fear, and anger, *and* that such an appeal can be appropriate;
- that rhetorical schemes such as climax, epistrophe, anaphora, antithesis, anadiplosis, polysyndeton, and asyndeton, as well as a clear, well-conceived organization can enhance your arguments' persuasive power.

Notes

1. Lane Cooper, ed., *The Rhetoric of Aristotle*, Englewood Cliffs, New Jersey: Prentice-Hall, 1932, p. 9.
2. Robert L. Shurter, *Written Communication in Business*, 3rd ed., New York: McGraw-Hill, 1971, p. 234.
3. Shurter, p. 260.
4. Kenneth Burke, *A Rhetoric of Motives*, 1950; rpt. Berkeley: University of California Press, 1969, p. 58.
5. Houston Peterson, ed., *A Treasury of the World's Great Speeches*, 2nd ed., New York: Simon and Schuster, 1965, p. 832.
6. Burke, p. 58.
7. *The New York Times*, 28 August 1964, p. 12.
8. Edward P. J. Corbett, *Classical Rhetoric for the Modern Student*, 2nd. ed., New York: Oxford University Press, 1971, p. 472.
9. Corbett, p. 465.
10. Corbett, p. 476.

CHAPTER 12
Delivery

In this chapter, you will learn:

- how to make rapid delivery effective delivery;
- how to reduce your rate of speaking a bit without reducing content;
- how jargon and shorthand should and should not be used in debating;
- a few small points to be aware of as you speak.

Human Communication or Information Processing

Delivery is—you may be surprised to hear—a controversial aspect of debating. Once upon a time, debating was viewed by participants and supervising faculty members as an oratorical activity. Argumentation was, of course, important: style without substance could not win; however, style was expected or at least encouraged. Debate became increasingly competitive as the years went by. Negative teams offered more and more and more arguments; affirmative teams felt obliged to cover each negative argument with several responses. As both teams did more and more, the time limits remained where they were. As a result, debaters began speaking at increasingly more rapid rates. They also began using lots of debate jargon (which helped them abbreviate some arguments) and shorthand (which helped them abbreviate even more). These developments, which have occurred over many years, have turned debating into an activity that at times seems scarcely oratorical.

Not all faculty members are comfortable with the present state of affairs. In fact, I would suggest to you that the overwhelming majority of coaches would like to see delivery emphasized more. The pressure to "motor mouth," as it's called, arises out of the normal human desire to win. Beginning debaters imitate the behavior they see more experienced debaters engaging in and winning with; these more experienced debaters imitate the behavior they see champion debaters practicing and winning with; these champion debaters imitate the behavior of previous champions and usually try to do them one or two better. No one in this chain dares slow down—for fear of jeopardizing their winning form. The words of protesting coaches are either ignored or mocked. In many cases, judges who complain about rapid delivery, excessive jargon, and too much shorthand are criticized as mentally slow, uninformed, and anachronistically concerned about communication. Quite a few coaches and judges give way under the mocking and criticizing and cease making the case for good delivery.

As you begin your career as a debater, you need to consider the role of delivery in debate. The passionate desire for victory aside, there may be some justification for rapid delivery, etc., *if* you conceive of debate solely as information processing. The goal in information processing is to achieve the optimal combination of rate and effectiveness. Rate should increase as long as effectiveness—i.e., the ability of opponents and judges to transcribe what is said—does not decrease. Given the skill most opponents develop and most judges possess in flowing rapidly delivered, jargon-ridden speeches, rate can be rapid and optimal. With this rapid rate, more information enters into the decision-making process; the more information entered, the better-informed and therefore the better the decision.

If, on the other hand, you conceive of debate as human argumentation—by humans, for humans—then you will find a number of flaws in this justification for rapid delivery and other departures from good public speaking practices. First, human beings are not information-processing machines. They do not chew up information and then request, "More data please." Rather, they digest—that is, they reflect on, evaluate, and assemble information with other information; then they test the logic of the particular "assembly." This human action requires time; in addition, it requires that debaters develop arguments, not just pour forth five or six or seven discrete, undeveloped lines of argumentation. Second, human beings respond to appeals other than logical ones. As I just noted, human beings are persuaded by fully developed logical arguments, not one-liners. Furthermore, as Chapter 11 showed, human beings are persuaded by *ethos* and *pathos* and forms both large and small. These important alogical dimensions of argumentation are totally lost when debaters "motor mouth" their way through speeches.

So . . . *you must decide* what debating is. Is it information processing or human argumentation? If you choose the former, most of what this chapter offers will be of little interest to you. If you choose the latter, this chapter should help you improve your delivery. This chapter is realistic too. It does not pretend that the developments of the past fifteen years will vanish as soon as you decide to value your delivery and to work on it. This chapter assumes that rapid delivery, jargon, and shorthand will be part of debating for years to come and advises you on how to improve your delivery *within this context.*

Conceiving of the Speech as a Whole

A first step toward better delivery is conceiving of each speech you give not as a collection of separate arguments but as a whole. As a whole, a speech has a strategic organization.

Organization means a readily discernible order. As you begin, as you are proceeding, and when you conclude, the judge should know where you've been, where you're at, and where you're going. "Strategic" means, in the case of competitive debate, that you recognize and merge the principle of Nestorian order (discussed in Chapter 4), the expectation that you proceed along certain general lines, and the realistic fact that quite frequently debaters spend too much time on the early things they say and must rush through the late. The principle of Nestorian order dictates that the most important material go last in a spoken or a written argument and the second most important material go first. As you recall, this principle is based on the fact that an audience remembers what is said last, what is said first, and what is said in between *in that order*. The audience expectations are established by the different speaker roles that have evolved through the years. For example, the second affirmative constructive speech is expected to begin with responses to any and all first negative constructive speech observations and then to proceed through the affirmative case (as presented in the first affirmative constructive speech) and respond to all first negative responses to the arguments in that case. The realistic fact dictates that you not put crucial items at the very end of your planned organization because you may not get to these.

These three strategic considerations—Nestorian order, audience expectations, and practicality—may well seem contradictory. Nestorian order dictates putting your crucial argument at a speech's end, something practicality advises against. And the audiences's expectations seem to give you little freedom to choose a strategy at all. Actually, you *can* reconcile these considerations and devise an effective organizational strategy.

Consider the following situation. You are the second negative rebuttalist. Your job, therefore, is to summarize the entire debate from the point of view of the negative team. The proposition is a proposition of value which affirms that a strong economy is preferable to a strong defense. The negative team's position boils down to the following five arguments:

1. The affirmative criterion (in its definitive contention) of value—survival—is correct; however, there is an important distinction to be made between immediate survival and long-range survival. The latter is dependent on the former; therefore, the true criterion should be immediate survival, not simply survival.
2. If evaluated based on this better-understood criterion, a strong defense is much more valuable than the affirmative claims.
3. If evaluated based on this better-understood criterion, a strong economy is not as valuable as the affirmative claims.

4. If a policy were based on the affirmative's value judgment, then our allies would lose faith in United States defense commitments. The impact would be the virtual neutralization of Western Europe and Japan.
5. If a policy were based on the affirmative's value judgment, then we would lose friends around the globe, *and* this loss of friends would mean a loss of trading partners. Without these trading partners, any economic recovery would be short-lived.

The principle of Nestorian order would dictate that the two strongest arguments go last and first. Argument (1) is obviously crucial. Let's say the the first affirmative rebuttalist has mishandled argument (5), and, therefore, you want to stress it. Arguments (1) and (5) then should be ones you want to stress. Expectations would have you proceed case-"off case" or "off case"-case (1-2-3-4-5 or 4-5-1-2-3). The realistic fear of slighting things toward the end of a speech would dictate that you end with neither (1) nor (5).

If you try to merge these three principles, you might well end up with the following order: 1-2-3-5-4. You would have one of your crucial arguments, (1), in an emphatic position. The other crucial argument, (5), may well seem lost in the middle; however, since you do not anticipate having a great deal of time to devote to (4), the second-to-last position is more emphatic than it looks. So, you are somewhat in line with the principle of Nestorian order. You would almost be doing what the audience expects. If you just make it clear to your audience that you will be treating your two "off-case" arguments in reverse order, you should be sufficiently in line with expectations for the audience to follow you with ease. You would finally be responsive to what reality teaches you: you would *not* be planning to drive home crucial argument (5) at the rebuttal's very end when time may be very short. You have made sure arguments (1) and (5) will receive sufficient attention.

Consider another situation. You are the first affirmative rebuttalist in a policy debate. You and your partner have advocated a federal agency to regulate the computer industry. You have argued that federal control will result in four independent advantages: (1) better control of computer-related crime; (2) increased compatibility of technology and improved communications; (3) encouraged and directed technological development; (4) quicker application of computer advances in defense. Implicit in each advantage is some sort of problem. The negative team has chosen to defend *laissez-faire* capitalism and has responded to advantage (1) that computer crime is not a significant problem, to advantage (2) that compatibility is presently increasing due to market forces, to advantage (3) that government control will inhibit, not stimulate development, and to advantage (4) that there is no inherent barrier preventing the kind of research and communications that would be necessary to keep the Pentagon abreast of computer developments. The negative has also chosen to run an elaborate solvency argument based on the gross inefficiency of government regulatory efforts and two fairly brief disadvantages, the first being that government regulation will lead to large numbers of reincorporations as multinational corporations titularly headquartered outside the United States and an associated loss in corporate tax revenue; the second being that government supervision will eliminate corporate secrecy, thereby reducing the incentive to be innovative and decreasing the American edge over foreign manufacturers. Let's number these plan-side arguments (5), (6), and (7) for the sake of the following discussion of strategic organization.

The second negative speaker has just presented the plan attacks; the first negative rebuttalist has just emphasized the negative response to the third and fourth advantages. Following the principle of Nestorian order, you would then want to stress your responses to the solvency argument (5), your defense of (3) and (4), and your responses to the disadvantages (6) and (7). The best order to proceed in would then be 3-4-6-7-1-2-5. The audience, however, will most probably expect 5-6-7-1-2-3-4 (plan side, case side) or 1-2-3-4-5-6-7 (case side, plan side). Wild variations from either of these orders would cause the audience some problems unless the first affirmative rebuttalist made every step clear.

The practical recognition that time will probably be short at the rebuttal's end dictates *not* treating (5) or (3) or (4) or (6) or (7) last. The best order then would probably be 5-6-7-3-4-1-2. You would be allowing yourself time where you need it and want it, relegating the advantages you are less worried about until the rushed end. The two most crucial areas of debate—the solvency argument (5) and the two strongly challenged advantages, (3) and (4)—would be handled at the speech's beginning and almost at the speech's end. Therefore, you're pretty much in line with the principle of Nestorian order. You would, finally, be giving the audience pretty much what they would expect. The only twist would be the treating of advantages (3) and (4) before advantages (1) and (2). If you simply tell the audience, "I'll be dealing with advantage (3) and advantage (4) before I turn to advantages (1) and (2)," they will be able to follow you.

The first step in viewing your speeches as wholes is to choose a strategically effective organization. The second step is to adequately preview and guide and review. Toward the speech's beginning, you should say something like the following:

I will respond to the second negative's solvency argument. Then I'll refute the disadvantages; then I'll go to case-side and defend advantage 3, advantage 4, advantage 1, and advantage 2—in that order.

At transitional points in the speech, you should say something like the following:

Contrary to what the second negative claims, we are solvent. The claimed disadvantages are also flawed. Let's consider them.

We then carry two significant independent advantages—increased development and quicker application to defense. We also accrue two more advantages, ones the negative has not substantially challenged since the first negative constructive speech.

At the end of the speech—in, perhaps, the last ten seconds, you should say something like the following:

I have shown you that the affirmative is indeed solvent; I've shown you that neither disadvantage applies to the affirmative case; and I've shown you that adopting the plan will accrue four significant independent advantages. Therefore, you should vote affirmative.

The principle these previews, guides, and reviews illustrate is an elementary one: "tell them what you're going to do, do it, and tell them you've done it." This kind of *very* explicit organization may well strike you as excessive, especially if you are more familiar with written argumentation and communication than spoken argumentation and communication. It is necessary in debate because, first, debate is oral argumentation and an audience has to "get it" the first time when listening to an oral presentation; and second, debate is fairly rapid oral argumentation and the speed, even if controlled, makes "getting it" more difficult and explicitness more important.

First-Time-Final Strategies for Speaking

Conceiving of your speeches as wholes will help your reader follow you, even if you find yourself talking at a rate that is faster than you would like it to be. Keeping what are called "first-time-final" strategies in mind will also help.

"First-time-final" strategies have been developed by researchers in the field of written composition. The major emphasis in the teaching of writing these days is on the writing process, especially on the necessity and different phases of revision a piece of writing should go through. This emphasis is fine *if* it is assumed that all writers have the leisure to revise and revise and revise. If a paper is due at 8 A.M. in a history class and it's now 11 P.M. the night before, the possibility of repeated revision is minimized. Now, in this instance, the writer can be faulted for waiting until the last hours, for not allowing sufficient time for repeated, careful revision. However, consider the frequent instance in business when, at 10 A.M. the boss requests a brief report (two or three or four pages) and wants it on his desk by 4 P.M. Here, no one really can be faulted, not even the boss, for the pressures of business may be dictating the pace, not his decisions.

To handle situations such as this one in business—and also, by extension, the situation of the procrastinating student—researchers in business writing have devised several strategies to use when you know your draft is likely to be, with only a bit of polishing, your final draft. Thus, the term "first-time-final" for these strategies. These strategies are based on cognitive psychology—i.e., what goes on in the mind of the writer and the mind of the reader—and have been validated through careful studies. These strategies are applicable to oral communication where your first draft has to be your final one.

"First-time-final" strategy number one: choose a straightforward organization. Subtle organizational strategies in writing or speaking require careful revising; anything extremely out-of-the-ordinary or *far* removed from first-second-third-fourth in writing or in speaking requires careful revising. You cannot revise your speeches; you cannot say, "Scrap that first two minutes, pretend that what I just said I saved until later, and let me fill in the gaps I left with the following insertions." Therefore, avoid the subtle, the extraordinary, the extreme departures from first-second-third-fourth. Stick to the straightforward to assure maximum communication.

"First-time-final" strategy number two: make your organization explicit. We touched on this principle earlier. Preview your organization, provide a large number of guideposts along the way, review where you've been at the end. Use numbers and letters to signal transition from one point to another, to thrust the key lines in your argumentation forward, and to indicate relationships among your arguments. Again, you may feel you are being overly explicit, especially if you believe you are a good writer. Keep in mind two principles: first, what may be absolutely clear in your mind will *not* be immediately clear to your audience and, since you automatically, unconsciously supply all the links and clarifying explanations, you will not be able to understand the audience's confusion for some time; second, spoken communication is different from written communication—an audience listening to a speech cannot reread or slow things down. Explicitness helps your audience follow your train of thought.

"First-time-final" strategy number three: rely heavily on concrete examples. Concrete examples are more immediately comprehensible (and also more memorable) than complex reasoning. Your argumentation, to be valid, requires that reasoning; add to it examples when you can. Consider the difference between the following two versions of the same argument:

Version 1
Even if contributions to political action committees (PACs) are made voluntary, union members will still be coerced. There are numerous coercive methods the union hierarchy can use. As so-and-so says in the May 1983 *Labor Relations Quarterly*, "Union leaders will garner the funds necessary to sustain union political activities even if mandatory contributions are declared illegal on Constitutional grounds."

Version 2
Even if contributions to union PACs are made voluntary, union members will still be coerced. There are numerous coercive methods the union hierarchy can use: these range from peer pressure to a stern-looking union officer standing next to the box into which pledges are to be deposited to slashed tires. A friendly union official might even approach a reluctant union member and, within ear-shot of other workers, graciously offer to save the member the trouble and take his or her pledge card to the contribution box for him or her. As so-and-so says in the May 1983 *Labor Relations Quarterly*, "Union leaders will garner the funds necessary to sustain union political activities even if mandatory contributions are declared illegal on Constitutional grounds."

The second version is just a bit longer. It is also far easier for a listener to grasp and remember. The examples add to the persuasiveness of the argument and are well worth the few extra sentences.

"First-time-final" strategy number four: avoid long, elaborately structured sentences. Such sentences may well cause you, as speaker, to get tangled up: you may forget, part of the way through such a sentence, where it began and where you were going. You can use such sentences effectively when you have the opportunity to revise them, to fine-tune them. When you are speaking extemporaneously, you do not have this opportunity. Furthermore, in spoken communication, these kinds of sentences can put a strain on the memory of your audience. Only so many separate pieces of information can be juggled in the short-term memory at once. An elaborately structured sentence tends to give the listener several discrete pieces of information at once without giving the listener the principles based on which they can be "batched" until the sentence's end. The results of taxing the short-term memory this way are the loss of one or more of the pieces of information (since a listener cannot reread) and the resultant inability to connect the information in the way desired. The better way to proceed is to use a simple sentence, presenting and connecting or "batching" a few pieces of information, and then to use another simple sentence, presenting more information, batching it, and connecting this batch to the first batch. This way, you keep the short-term memory working with a smaller number of units.

Rate

We have talked about two general ways to improve your performance as a debater-speaker. If you conceive of each speech you give as a whole and if you use "first-time-final" strategies, you will enhance your performance. Whether you go fast and use jargon and shorthand or whether you go more slowly and avoid jargon and shorthand, you will enhance your performance. Now, it's time to return to the questions of rate, jargon, and other forms of debate shorthand.

How rapidly should you speak? If you think of debating as information processing, not communication, then the question is answered with, "as rapidly as possible without losing the madly scribbling opponents and the madly scribbling judge." If you think of debating as an activity involving communication, then the question is best answered with two boundaries and one ideal:

boundary one: not so slow that you fail to fulfill your responsibilities;

boundary two: not so fast that someone standing out in the corridor listening to the debate wonders what central nervous system stimulant you're on;

ideal: at a rapid conversational rate.

In a value debate, you will find it easier to achieve this ideal, for the faculty members who have embraced value debate as an alternative to policy debate have had, as one of their motives, the desire to make debating more communicative. In policy debate, you may find it difficult to achieve this ideal because the first boundary will, in many debates, seem very close to the second. If you want to fulfill your responsibilities and still sound like a human being, here is some advice.

Let a Clear Organization Save You Time

If you are proceeding in a way that is clear to the listener, you will then *not* have to spend large amounts of time explaining what's what. A good organization, replete with a good preview, succinct guideposts, and a good review, will remove the necessity of long-winded, time-wasting explanations designed solely to make sure the listener and you are on the same track. Following the advice I offered earlier in this chapter on conceiving of your speeches as wholes and using "first-time-final" strategies may have struck you then as time-consuming. Actually, following that advice concerning organization will *save you time*.

Don't Say Everything

Many debaters feel compelled to respond to an argument with anything and everything they can think of. The probable motivation is the hope that opponents will fail to respond to one or two of their fifteen responses and they can then stand up, pull the dropped argument across the flow sheet, and triumphantly declare themselves the winner. Debaters who proceed in this manner often make three mistakes: first, they contradict themselves within the list of fifteen responses; second, they fail to develop their arguments, making all of them *far* less persuasive than they might be; third, they mistakenly assume that all arguments are equal when, in an intelligent judge's eyes, they aren't. As a result of this last mistake, debaters often "pull across" an argument and feel triumphant while the judge is musing, "So what? Big deal."

It is far better to select the strongest arguments you've got and develop them fully. Heeding this advice will lead to better argumentation and, thus, better debating; heeding this advice will also result in a more manageable rate of delivery, especially in the rebuttals where speakers will not have to cover so much ground.

Group Arguments

Whenever possible, group arguments together and respond to them *en masse*. This advice, as I noted in Chapter 10, is especially useful, if not vital, to the first affirmative rebuttalist. But all debaters should heed it. If the first negative constructive speaker in a policy debate suggests that there are six (count 'em) mechanisms in the status quo to solve the problem the affirmative team has presented and they can be refuted with pretty much the same arguments, the second affirmative constructive speaker should group them and refute them all at once. Similarly, if the first negative constructive speaker in a value debate suggests that due process, national security, knowledge, and fiscal security are all more valuable than privacy, the state the affirmative team has defended as "most desirable," and these alternative values can be refuted in pretty much the same way, the second affirmative constructive speaker should group them together and refute them all at once. Heeding this advice should lead to more focused and, thus, fuller and better discussion of issues; heeding this advice will also help you keep the rate of delivery near the ideal.

Zero In

Many debaters, perhaps blinded by the mechanics of flow sheeting, feel compelled to respond to everything. There is room in debating for intelligent selection. In fact, some of the most exciting debates are ones in which both teams are making strategic selections. As first negative constructive speaker, do you have to respond—somehow—to every subpoint of every point in the affirmative case? Wouldn't the debate be better if you pinpointed the areas in which you think the case is to be beaten and zeroed in on these? As second negative constructive speaker in a policy debate, do you have to bring up every imaginable solvency problem and every conceivable disadvantage? Wouldn't the debate be better if you offered only those that you felt were *really* problems? As a summary rebuttalist, wouldn't the debate be better if you zeroed in on the issues you are convinced will win the debate for your team? Trying to cover everything leads to shallow debating and to extremely rapid delivery; zeroing in should improve debating and help keep delivery near the ideal presented earlier.

Cut Back on Verbosity

Verbosity, by definition, is excessive words. People who are verbose use twenty words when ten would do. Debaters are quite often verbose. Debaters' verbosity usually takes two forms: first, many debaters make the same argument several different ways; second, many debaters unnecessarily lengthen their sentences with impressive-sounding but time-wasting phrases. You should try to overcome both of these tendencies.

Since the first instance of verbosity is caused by debaters' desire to make their arguments absolutely clear to the judge, you should strive to make your initial statement of the argument as clear and as full as possible. You should get in the habit of speaking directly to the judge. The judge's reaction should tell you whether you succeeded or not in making that initial statement clear and full. If the judge is with you, proceed; don't restate the argument. If the judge looks puzzled, then you should clarify your position—not so much by restating it in different words as by explaining what you mean, step by step. For example, let's say you are responding to an alleged disadvantage of your plan: that your proposed reduction in American forces in Western Europe will cause unemployment. You say, "No. No net increase because funds will go to domestic projects." The judge looks puzzled. You could say, "Likely real location of defense funds will negate possible problems"; then you could say, "The shift in funding from defense to domestic will mean no net increase in unemployment." The judge may still look puzzled, since all you've done is restate. Try to offer the best initial statement of the argument: "The shift in spending from defense to domestic projects will create jobs; therefore, there will be no net increase in unemployment." If the judge looks puzzled, offer, as a step-by-step explanation, "Yes, the plan will result in present soldiers being unemployed; however, the money now spent on troops in Western Europe will be reallocated to domestic projects and these domestic projects will employ many Americans. Therefore, the plan will result in no *net* increase in unemployment."

The second instance of verbosity must be fought by, first, a realization that bureaucratese, legalese, and businessese add words, *not* sophistication, to a speech and, second, an effort to remove such words from your speeches. Consider the following passage; look especially at the italicized words and phrases:

Restricting the ability of the American *journalistic corps* to *engage in investigative reporting* during *primary elections* will lead to other restraints upon the freedom of the press. These restraints will seriously impair information flow from the *governmental sector* to the public via the press. The results will be serious. First, during *adjudication*, valuable *data* may not be available to attorneys, thus *impeding judicial processes* and possibly causing *unjust outcomes*. Second, during *electoral processes, decision making* may be impaired by *the inadequacy of the information upon which votes are being cast*. Injustice and poor decision making are difficult to quantify *costwise*. They are qualitative disadvantages. In considering them, you should realize how fundamental justice and good democratic decision making are to the American system of government. If these values are *allowed to be demoted*, then *in the very near future*, we will see further inroads into *basic fundamental* Constitutional freedoms.

Consider the words and phrases one by one:

- journalistic corps—inflated way of saying "journalists."
- engage in investigative reporting—inflated and technically inaccurate way of saying "report."
- primary elections—two words for one; say "primaries."
- governmental sector—inflated way of saying "government."
- adjudication—fancy way of saying "trials."
- data—inflated and technically inaccurate synonym for "information."
- impeding judicial processes—vague and inflated way of saying—I think—"slowing trials."
- unjust outcomes—stiff way of saying "unjust results."
- electoral processes—inflated way of saying "elections."
- decision making—inflated way of saying "voting."
- the inadequacy of the information upon which votes are being cast—long-winded way of saying "because of inadequate information."
- costwise—an awkward coinage that isn't even necessary.
- allowed to be demoted—long-winded way of saying "demoted."
- in the very near future—five words for one; say "soon."
- basic fundamental—redundant; use one word or the other.

If you revised the passage as suggested above, you would end up with:

Restricting the ability of American journalists to report during primaries will lead to other restraints upon the freedom of the press. These restraints will seriously impair information flow from the government to the public via the press. The results will be serious. First, during trials, valuable information may not be available to attorneys, thus slowing trials and possibly causing unjust results. Second, during elections, voting may be impaired because of inadequate information. Injustice and poor decision making are difficult to quantify. They are qualitative disadvantages. In considering them, you should realize how fundamental justice and good democratic decision making are to the American system of government. If these values are demoted, then soon we will see further inroads into fundamental Constitutional freedoms.

The edited version is twenty-six words briefer. That probably means it would take you something like fifteen seconds less to deliver the edited version than the original. Fifteen seconds might not sound like much, but if you can cut fifteen seconds out of every minute's worth of argumentation, you have saved two full minutes or more in a constructive speech and a minute or more in a rebuttal.

If you cut back on the two types of verbosity discussed here, you will find yourself with extra time in a debate. You can do two things with that extra time: first, you could fill it with *more* argumentation; second, you could slow down a bit and let your present material fill out the time. I hope you will do the latter and make debating an activity featuring human communication, not motor-mouthing.

Jargon and Shorthand

Jargon is a pejorative term for the special language of a particular field. Football has its jargon—"blitz," "power-I," "nickel-defense;" so does computer science—"byte," "string," "CRT." These special languages have been given a pejorative name for a very simple reason: specialists quite frequently use these languages with audiences who do not understand the terms. Either these specialists have forgotten to analyze their audience or they are trying to impress by using their special lingo.

There is nothing wrong with using debating jargon such as "topicality," "inherency," "turnaround," "impact," "competitiveness," etc., as long as you remember two principles. First, for jargon to be a communicative specialized language, you, your opponents, and your judge must understand it. If you are really "up" on debate theory, but know your opponents aren't, you would be well-advised to minimize the amount of jargon you use, for the use of jargon which your opponents may only halfway understand will probably lead to a muddled debate. And a muddled debate is a debate that frequently escapes your control. If you find yourself debating before a judge who is not well-versed in the jargon, you would be wise to minimize the amount of jargon you use. After all, your goal is to persuade this judge. If he or she cannot totally follow what you're saying, you are not likely to persuade him or her. You could arrogantly say to yourself, "The judge ought to know debate better," and proceed as usual with jargon aplenty. If you did, you would be violating one of the fundamental principles of rhetoric: ADJUST TO YOUR AUDIENCE. The violation would be foolish. Second, those who use jargon *must* realize that, although it is a suitable language for communication among specialists, it is not a suitable language for other situations. The trap of using jargon is that you become able to speak only in that jargon. A jargon-trapped computer scientist would be unable to explain the fundamentals of a programming language or even the fundamentals of computer use in a language other than jargon. A jargon-trapped debater would be unable to discuss public policy without using debate jargon. This trap is one to avoid because several of the benefits of debating as an activity are related to the understanding of and ability to discuss key public policy issues. The trap can totally wipe out these benefits. Therefore, I would advise you to keep the use of jargon reined in, under tight control.

Shorthand in debate takes two forms: first, the use of sentence fragments; second, the use of debate abbreviations. Consider the following brief excerpt from a policy debate:

Go to PMA 3. No motive to circumvent shown. No impact. Go to DA 1. Rather than turn allies off, we keep them by pursuing a consistent foreign policy based on human rights. Turnaround! Go at DA 2. No impact given by 2 NC.

In a very short space, this speaker—a first affirmative rebuttalist—offers us numerous examples of both kinds of shorthand. The second and third "sentences" are not grammatical; they are fragments. The first has an incomplete predicate ("shown" rather than "has been shown"); the second has no predicate at all ("has been shown" omitted). The debate abbreviations PMA, DA, and 2NC are used (as well as a good bit of debate jargon).

Like jargon, shorthand does help the debater move quickly. Like jargon, shorthand is no good if the audience—either the opposing team or the judge—doesn't understand it. Furthermore, like the use of jargon, the use of shorthand can trap you. It may trap you into bad public speaking habits. Good public speakers strive to speak completely, but succinctly; good public speakers strive to minimize abbreviations because they may not be meaningful to all. Whether debating has the teaching of public speaking skills as one of its many goals is a question a few in the field are presently discussing. If you believe debating *should* teach such skills—even if that goal is a secondary one, you probably should try to minimize your use of shorthand.

Whether you choose to minimize the shorthand abbreviations in your speeches or not, you will undoubtedly hear them. Figure 12.1 is a guide to the common abbreviations. Using it, you will be able to decipher the passage above.

Small Points

There are a few other qualities of good delivery that are worth mentioning. If you are aware of these qualities and try to make them a part of your presentation, you should see yourself receiving higher and higher ratings from judges.

1AC—The first affirmative constructive speech or speaker
1NC—The first negative constructive speech or speaker
2AC—The second affirmative constructive speech or speaker
2NC—The second negative constructive speech or speaker
1NR—The first negative rebuttal or rebuttalist
1AR—The first affirmative rebuttal or rebuttalist
2NR—The second negative rebuttal or rebuttalist
2AR—The second affirmative rebuttal or rebuttalist
PMN—A solvency argument used against a needs case: the negative argues that the *p*lan does not *m*eet the *n*eed.
PMA—A solvency argument used against a comparative advantages case: the negative argues, in rather poor English, that the *p*lan does not *m*eet the advantage/s.
DA—A disadvantage
VO—A value objection, i.e., an argument against taking action/s predicated on the value the affirmative team (in a value debate) is defending.

Figure 12.1   The common shorthand abbreviations of debating.

Wit

Debates rarely seem boring to participants: they are very involved in the action; their adrenalin is flowing. The judge in the back of the room may well perceive many debates quite differently. Tired from driving his or her team over 200 miles to the tournament or tired from the coaches' party the night before, the judge may be having a difficult time remaining as alert as he or she *or you* would like. A methodical but dry performance will not keep this judge alert to all of the arguments that are bandied back and forth. If you mix in some wit, you may well keep the judge's attention strongly engaged.

Wit will also give you a chance to come across as a human being, not a debating machine. Coming across as a human being will give you a chance to develop the kind of *ethos* you want and to add *ethos* to the *logos* (logical argumentation) and *pathos* (emotional appeals) you are presenting.

Some warnings about wit. First, restrain yourself from turning a serious discussion of public policy or important values into a comedy routine—or anything close to it. Second, do not make your opponents the butt of your wit. Doing so will lead to bitter debates and will probably destroy the *ethos* you are trying to project and thereby weaken *all* of your argumentation. Third, if you are one of those who simply cannot "pull wit off," don't try. Find some other way—for example, changing your volume and pitch periodically—to keep the judge attentive and responsive.

Eye Contact

Many debaters speak with their eyes glued to their flow sheets or to the floor, *never* looking at the judge. Not only is this noncommunicative behavior, it's stupid behavior. Why? Because you are passing up a valuable opportunity to sustain the judge's attention by periodically looking him or her right in the eyes. Because you are passing up a valuable opportunity to project your *ethos* through the sincere, determined, honest, impassioned looks in your eyes. Because you are passing up a valuable opportunity to find out how you're doing. Not all judges will give you *very* strong signals during a debate, but, with most judges, you can see numerous things that can help you as you speak. For example, if the judge looks puzzled, you should try to explain your argument step by step; if the judge is nodding his or her head impatiently, you should move on, for he probably understands your point and wishes you would stop reexplaining it; if the judge usually "flows" and he isn't flowing an argument you're making, you should offer further explanation until the judge notes it.

Be careful, however, not to overdo "reading the judge." Debaters who do this tend to infer from supposed signals how the debate is going. For example, some judges will begin filling out their ballots before the debate is over. Sometimes, this judging behavior does indeed mean that the judge has reached his decision. However, some judges may simply be writing down a few remarks to the individual performers before those remarks slip their mind. Also, some judges, trying their best to keep a tournament on schedule, will begin writing general remarks on the ballot during breaks between rebuttals and maybe a bit during the rebuttals — remarks that do not presuppose a decision one way or the other. I have known debaters who have seen judges writing and assuming they had already won, relax—and then lose; I have known debaters who have seen judges writing and assuming they had already lost, give up—when they could have won. Other things a judge does can be easily misinterpreted with similar costs. So, look at the judge and pick up on the signals he or she gives; however, don't overdo the looking and especially the inferring.

Avoiding "Noise"

Communications theorists use the term "noise" in a very particular way. "Noise" is anything that interferes with the message, anything that distracts the audience's attention from the message. Debaters need to be aware of the "noise" they may be creating. Below is a partial list of the "noise" you may unwittingly be generating:

- Tapping your pen or pencil on your flow sheet as you speak.
- Too many "ok"s or "you know"s spiced through your speech—to the point where the judge stops listening to the speech and starts counting the "ok"s.
- Walking—defense attorney-like—around the front of the room as you speak—to the point where the judge starts paying undue attention to your movements.
- Excessive gesturing—to the point where the judge starts watching your gestures rather than listening to your speeches.

- Yelling—which will cause your judge to stop listening as he or she mutters, "Why doesn't he calm down."
- Invading the judge's space—i.e., getting so close to the judge that he or she begins to feel uncomfortable.
- Spitting—this behavior usually accompanies "motor mouthing" and can distract the judge from your message especially if you're spitting in the judge's direction.
- Dressing in too revealing a fashion. Skirts that are slit too high, blouses that are unbuttoned too low, pants that are too tight, etc., may be fine for a party, but judges are human. Male judges might be distracted by the sexy attire of female debaters; female judges might be distracted by the sexy attire of male debaters. When distracted, they might miss *the* key argument and, with a smile, give you a loss.
- Your partner's *too* busily working as you speak. If he or she is rummaging too excitedly through your files, that action can detract from what you are saying.

Think of yourself as a message-sending device separated by some space from a message-receiving device. "Noise" is *whatever* intervenes between you and the receiving device. You should try to minimize this "noise" so that communication is as complete as possible.

We have now moved from getting started in debating to fine-tuning your delivery. As we moved from the beginning to the finishing touches, we went through the debating process as you are likely to encounter it: looking at a proposition, researching, devising an affirmative case, writing that case up, refuting in general and refuting affirmative cases, using rebuttal and cross-examination time most effectively, using alogical appeals wisely and appropriately, polishing your performance. All that is left is practice, practice, and more practice.

As we moved from the beginning to the finishing touches, the concept of strategy has come up more and more frequently. Debating is certainly more than just following procedures, although a great deal of your attention early on will necessarily be on procedural matters; debating is also more than analytical thinking, although debating without such thinking is a lame exercise with very little justification. Debating involves strategy. You will learn strategy as you debate. Throughout the latter chapters of this book, I have every now and again offered strategic advice. The four case studies in the next chapter will address some more strategic concerns as well as reviewing fundamentals which are easy to forget.

After reading and studying Chapter 12, you know:

- that you can make rapid delivery effective delivery by conceiving of the speech as a whole and by using "first-time-final" strategies;

- how to reduce your speaking rate a bit by allowing a clear organization to save you time, by not saying everything, by grouping arguments, by zeroing in, and by cutting back on verbosity;
- that debating jargon and shorthand are effective *only if* your audience understands *and* that overreliance on such jargon and shorthand may well detract from the educational value of debating;
- that wit can contribute positively to your *ethos*, that maintaining eye contact with the judge can provide you with valuable information, and that "noise" should be minimized if your speeches are to have the maximum effect.

CHAPTER 13
Four Case Studies

In this chapter, you will:

- read four case studies;
- review some of the fundamentals of debating presented throughout this textbook;
- consider some strategic successes and some strategic errors.

This chapter presents you with four very different case studies. Each should accomplish two goals: first, to review and pull together what this text has presented concerning the various aspects of debating; second, to raise some questions of strategy either addressed by this text briefly or not addressed at all. Studying and discussing each case should further your understanding of debating.

For each case, you are given a summary of the affirmative case, an account of the negative strategy, a review of the debate (complete with a simplified flow sheet), and either a brief commentary or questions.

Case One: Should the Government Maintain Files on Suspected Homosexuals

The Affirmative Case

The resolution calls for the affirmative team to advocate a policy significantly curtailing government information-gathering activities. The affirmative could select one of a large number of government agencies or operations that gather information: the Internal Revenue Service, the FBI, the CIA, grand juries, congressional committees, state vehicle administrations, etc. This affirmative team chose state and local police; they further narrowed the debate by discussing only one kind of information-gathering, recording the arrests of homosexuals for homosexual acts committed in public. The affirmative argued that since these records are distributed throughout law enforcement and leak out from law enforcement agencies to credit bureaus and others, they are the basis of considerable discrimination against homosexuals. The affirmative argued that there was no way the information-sharing or leaking could be effectively controlled; therefore, the only viable solution was to stop the information-gathering by passing a federal law declaring homosexual acts as legal as heterosexual ones and making this federal law supercede any conflicting state statutes.

The affirmative case then was essentially a needs case. Contention (1) presented the problem; contention (2) the alleged harm to homosexuals of discrimination; and contention (3) the inability of the status quo to solve the problem. Then came the plan; then came, as a fourth contention, an explanation of how the plan, by declaring homosexuality as legal as heterosexuality, solved the problem and prevented the harms from occurring.

The Negative Strategy

The negative team decided to have some "fun" with the unusual affirmative case. As an observation, the first negative constructive speaker argued that homosexuality is immoral and quoted from the Bible to prove his point. He then offered a case-side disadvantage: the affirmative plan, he claimed, encouraged immoral behavior and, as a result, weakened the social fabric of America. The impacts would be more crime, more drug use, and more suicide.

Then the first negative responded to the contentions themselves. To contention (1), he offered two responses: (a) the affirmative has shown a problem with information security, *not* with information gathering or criminal proceedings against homosexuals; therefore, the affirmative has justified only a tightening of security, not the affirmative plan; (b) the affirmative has not shown that a significant number of people are affected. To contention (2), he also offered two responses: (a) the cause of discrimination against homosexuals is a public attitude which would operate against suspected gays, information leak or no information leak; (b) the affirmative has not quantified the costs of discrimination so that the judge can see if it is or is not a truly significant concern. To contention (3), the first negative offers a status quo mechanism: lawsuits against agencies which fail to maintain the information security already, as the affirmative admitted in cross-examination, required by law. To contention (4), the first negative offered an argument that eventually proved to be decisive. The harm, he said, stems from the arrest of homosexuals for committing sexual acts in public places (e.g., restrooms, parks). The plan, however, simply puts homosexual acts on the same legal basis as heterosexual acts; the plan does not make sexual acts performed in public places legal since heterosexual acts performed in public places are not legal. Such acts are either forbidden explicitly by state laws or forbidden by public indecency statutes. Since the plan does *not* prevent the arrest of individuals performing homosexual acts in public places, it does not stop the information-gathering, sharing, or leaking; therefore, the plan is absolutely not solvent. After voicing the potentially devastating argument, the first negative offered an "underview": that, since the affirmative plan does not stop the police from establishing records on individuals arrested while engaging in homosexual acts in public, the affirmative team does not significantly curtail government information-gathering and, therefore, is not topical.

The second negative speaker began her speech by extending the first negative observation on the harms of condoning homosexuality by noting that, because it violated fundamental Darwinian principles (she quoted Darwin) of survival, homosexuality was biologically and anthropologically unnatural. Then, the second negative spent a considerable amount of time further developing the first negative's challenge to the affirmative case's solvency. Then, the second negative offered three disadvantages of the affirmative plan. She argued that the plan would (1) deny vital information to police; (2) deny vital information to some employers; (3) cause sexual development problems for young people who would see aberrant behavior seemingly condoned by society. The first and second disadvantages were stressed: the police need to know about lifestyle in order to pinpoint and apprehend those who may be guilty of serious crimes; employers, such as public schools or camps, have justification for denying employment to homosexuals and therefore must have the information.

The negative chose to take the affirmative case head-on. The affirmative defended rights, claiming that the majority's moral judgments should not be imposed on those who dissent from those judgments. The negative argued that rights can and must be limited and that the majority's moral judgment, in this case, should be imposed on dissenters for moral and practical reasons. The negative also pushed the affirmative team to fulfill its *prima facie* obligations: topicality, significance, inherency, solvency. If it were not for the inconsistency between the affirmative's chosen problem area (arrests for acts performed in public) and the proposed plan (giving homosexuals equal legal status with heterosexuals), which calls the plan's solvency into serious doubt, the debate would be interesting and probably close.

The Ensuing Debate

The affirmative team had done its homework fairly well: they had responses and evidence to counter most negative arguments. As the case side of the flow sheet (Figure 13.1) reveals, the second affirmative adequately responded to the first negative's argument against the first three contentions. The first negative rebuttalist tried to resurrect them and succeeded to the extent that the judge was convinced at the end of the negative block that there was, perhaps, *not* a significant case. The second affirmative responses to the (b) arguments under contentions (1) and (2), he argued, were the ones that were not really adequate. These (b) arguments were "presses": i.e., the negative team was pressing the affirmative team to

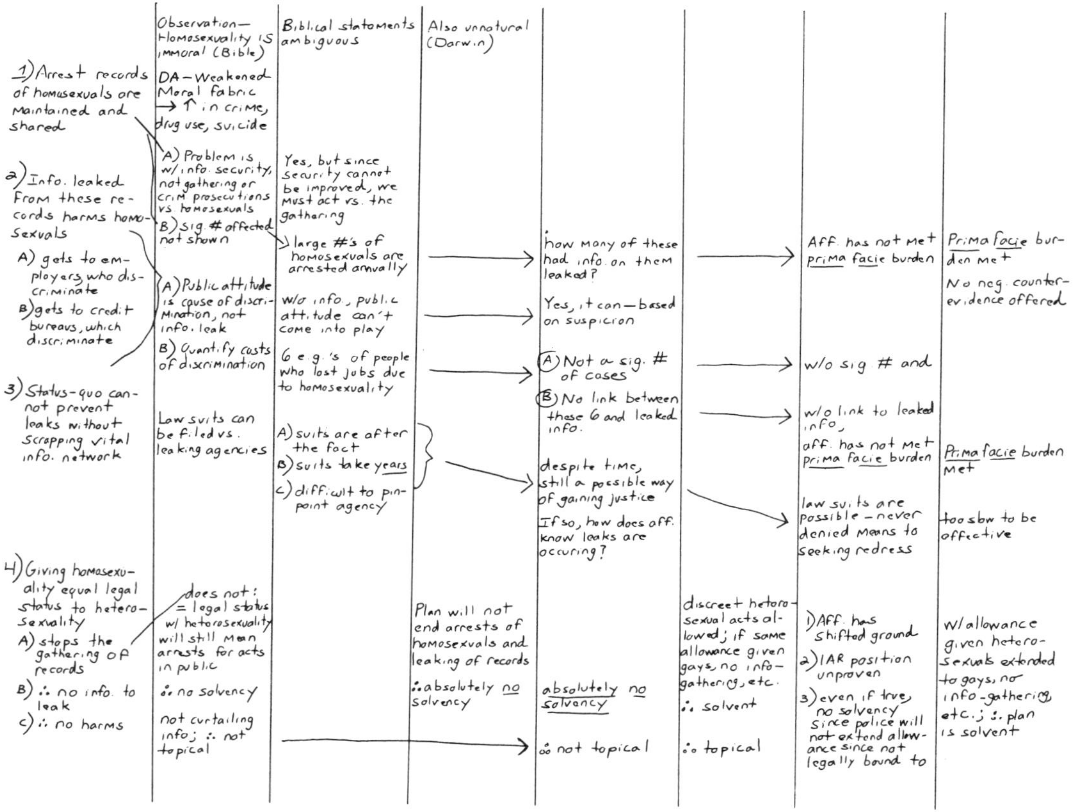

Figure 13.1 Case-side flow sheet for case study one.

meet its obligations and demonstrate that a significantly widespread problem exists and that this problem significantly harmed those who are affected. The second affirmative showed that a sizeable number of homosexuals are being arrested and gave examples of several homosexuals who lost their jobs because of their sexual orientation. As the first negative rebuttalist quite correctly pointed out, first, the affirmative speaker failed to show how many of these arrested gays had information on them leaked to creditors or employers and, second, the affirmative speaker failed to show numbers of victimized homosexuals sufficient to justify the claim of a significant harm and, third, the affirmative speaker failed to link the few examples presented to disclosed arrest records. Going into the summary rebuttals, then, the affirmative is in trouble on case side.

The second affirmative did not fully understand the first negative's response to the claim of solvency (contention (4)) and the topicality challenge that the first negative drew out of it. When the negative solvency argument was reinforced in the second negative's speech, it and the associated topicality challenge became clear to the affirmative team. The first affirmative rebuttalist tried to tackle both, arguing that heterosexuals are, in practice, allowed to engage in sexual acts in public as long as they are discreet, whereas homosexuals are nailed by law enforcement officers, discretion or not. Therefore, by granting equal legal status to homosexuals and heterosexuals, the affirmative plan solves the problems of harassment, arrest, information disclosure, and discrimination facing the gay community. The affirmative case then is solvent and, since it is curtailing information gathering by significantly lowering the number of arrest records, it is topical. Going into the summary rebuttals, the judge has before him—on this crucial pair of arguments—a strong negative stance and a somewhat fuzzy affirmative response.

The first affirmative rebuttalist evidently found the response fuzzy too, for he kept re-explaining it. (Perhaps he was responding to the judge's confused looks.) As a result of this re-explaining, he had less time to respond to the three disadvantages than he would have liked. He was well prepared for the second and third and responded fully, turning both around into advantages. (see Figure 13.2). To the first, he simply said that the second negative had offered no impact, a comment with some merit in the round. Going into the summary rebuttals, the affirmative is in fairly good shape on plan side, despite the brevity of the first affirmative rebuttalist's replies.

The summary rebuttals turned a negative win into a negative romp. The second negative rebuttalist tried to resurrect the disadvantages, but only spent a minute on this chore. The next two minutes were spent demonstrating the lack of significance of the affirmative case. This rebuttalist followed her partner's lead and showed the judge how all the evidence the affirmative team had offered *did not* add up to a *prima facie* case because the evidence left certain crucial claims unsubstantiated. Then, the final two minutes were spent re-presenting the first negative-second negative position on solvency and showing how the first affirmative rebuttalist's response (1) represented a shift in the affirmative team's position,

I = legal status with heterosexuality			
II Federal enforcement though Civil Rights Division of Dept. of Justice against violators			
III Aff speeches for legislative intent			
	DA 1 Deny vital info. to police A) Plan curtails info. gathering B) Info on lifestyle necessary in crime-fighting C) Plan → less effective crime-fighting	No quant. f-ed. impact offered	Yes, there was evidence in a NC says "significantly less effective"	impact never quantified
	DA 2 Deny vital info. to employers A) Plan means info is no longer available B) Info on sexual preference important for some jobs C) "Dangerous" people holding jobs	Info on sexual preference not vital This info. distracts from vital info ∴ if info denied, vital info will be available w/o distraction Turnaround	Info. is vital in schools w/o this info, homosexuals in potentially harmful positions	off removes distracting info. ∴ lets vital info. have its affect
	DA 3 Cause sexual development problems A) Plan will lead to a seeming condoning of homosexual lifestyle B) Young people will see this C) Their seeing it will lead to sexual development problems	On the contrary, seeing it will allow homosexuals to choose that lifestyle without suffering psychologically due to guilt Turnaround	Condoning of homosexuality will → sexual role problems also → psychologically disturbed not getting help	Condoning → tolerant attitude towards gays. → genuine, unrestrained choice of sexual lifestyle

Figure 13.2 Plan-side flow sheet for case study one.

(2) was unproven, and (3) even if true, would only slightly alter the affirmative's solvency problems since the change in law proposed by the affirmative would not necessarily lead to tolerance toward discreet public homosexual acts, especially given the prevailing attitude toward gays among law enforcement officers.

The second affirmative rebuttalist did little but repeat earlier affirmative positions. On the significance of the problem, he argued that it had been adequately proven earlier and noted that the negative team had offered no counterevidence. On the solvency of the affirmative plan, he simply repeated the first affirmative rebuttalist's position and ignored what the second negative rebuttalist had just said in response to it.

Commentary

Much could be said about this debate. I hope you will discuss it at length and draw from it numerous lessons which ought to help you in debating. I want to focus on two lessons—two large lessons, one for the affirmative and one for the negative.

The affirmative team probably chose the wrong model for its case. If you choose the wrong model, the bad choice can prove critical. Here it does.

The affirmative chose the needs case. This model, as noted in Chapter 4, thrusts problems and harms forward. The logic of the needs case also compels an affirmative team using it to argue absolute solvency. As the debate summarized above proved, the affirmative got into trouble in the two areas the "needs case" model tends to push to the forefront: significance of the problem and harms and solvency. Certainly, a good affirmative team using this particular case must know that it will have a difficult time with these two stock issues. Therefore, a good affirmative team would never choose a case structure that draws attention to these areas. The affirmative team can then scarcely be described as a good one, for the team made a critical mistake before the particular debate even began: the team made a mistake in putting its affirmative case together. The affirmative team ought to have chosen to emphasize how its plan *better* protects the rights of homosexuals or how its plan *better* promotes the goal of equal justice for all. To emphasize these chosen points, the affirmative team ought to have chosen either a comparative advantages or a goals case.

The negative team did not panic. This particular case was, in its season, a "squirrel." Negative teams did not expect to hear cases concerning police records on homosexual activities; negative teams were not briefed on such cases. Many a negative team—novice or veteran—would offer the "squirrel case is unfair" argument and little else; many negative teams—novice or veteran—would panic, cease thinking, and offer very little in the way of direct, clashing responses.

"Squirrel cases," however, require thinking, and, in the *vast* majority of cases, thinking reveals one or more *crucial* flaws. This particular squirrel case did not throw the negative team into a panic; both team members thought and, as a result, they managed to pinpoint and exploit flaws in the areas of significance

282   Debating

and solvency. They also thought of other arguments to voice—some good, some mediocre. These other arguments kept the affirmative team busy, too busy to find a way out of its problems demonstrating significance and solvency.

Beginning and even moderately experienced debaters ought to learn these lessons. When you are planning to defend the affirmative side of the proposition, structure your case for the resolution strategically. Do not choose a particular structural model just because you know it well or it *seems* to you *at first glance* that your material will fit that model well. Think of your rhetorical goals and select the structural model which best helps you meet these goals. When on the negative and confronting a "squirrel," *think*. Use the heuristics presented in Chapters 7 and 8; analyze the arguments you are hearing in the ways outlined in Chapter 6. Most important, look for the one or two crucial flaws. Keep in mind that "squirrels" win because they surprise, not because they are excellent cases.

Case Two: Should the U.S. Navy be Revamped?

The resolution calls for the affirmative team to significantly increase United States military commitments. The resolution has been interpreted all season long as allowing the affirmative team to (1) advocate an increase in the number of commitments, (2) advocate a strengthening (in terms of promising more or doing more) of existing commitments, or (3) advocate a strengthening of the United States' ability to meet its present commitments. Cases of the first type might call for a mutual defense treaty with Communist China or expanded military aid to Third World democracies. Cases of the second type might call for the deployment of the neutron bomb in NATO nations or the basing of U.S. troops in Costa Rica. Cases of the third type might call for higher salaries for military personnel (in order to attract more) or the development of the MX missile in racetrack configurations in the western United States.

This particular affirmative team chose the third type of affirmative case and chose to focus not on our ground forces or our nuclear deterrent, but on our navy.

The Affirmative Case

The affirmative team presented a needs case. Contention 1 tried to establish how important sea power is to the nation's ability to meet its military commitments. Subpoint (a) argues that the U.S. economy depends on U.S. sea power and further argues that an economically weak United States is a United States who cannot keep her commitments; subpoint (b) argues that the defense of Europe depends on U.S. sea power; subpoint (c) argues that America's ability to act quickly in trouble spots depends on sea power.

After demonstrating the importance of sea power, the case moves to contention 2, which establishes that a problem exists: that American sea power is on the wane due to misappropriation of funds. The United States spends wastefully on land power, spending scarce resources to defend against unlikely war scenarios and maintaining far too many support services for the present number of combat troops. Furthermore, the United States spends wastefully on sea power by building highly vulnerable large aircraft carriers. The problem of misappropriation is worse in the light of contention 3: Soviet sea power is increasing. The Soviet Union, the contention's substructure argues, has a sea denial, not a sea control, mission (as the United States does). The Soviet Union already has far in excess of the number of vessels necessary to execute this sea denial mission.

To meet this Soviet threat on the high seas, the United States needs to shift from land power to sea power. According to contention 4, this necessary shift is not presently possible because it would be blocked by the Pentagon power structure, which is based on the equality—in money and all else—among the four joint chiefs and the separate departments they represent. Even if the shift in spending from land power to sea power could be brought about, the United States' problems would not end, for the President and the Navy Department are strongly committed to spending naval dollars on highly vulnerable supercarriers.

The affirmative plan outlines the changes that are necessary in naval spending; it also mandates specific cuts in land power spending. "Irrelevant" land units will be eliminated, and the ratio of support units to combat units will be reduced. The savings will fund the naval spending in excess of present spending. The plan also spikes out a potential solvency problem or disadvantage by lifting legal restraints on the National Guard's use in foreign arenas and training the National Guard and the Army Reserve for mechanized (i.e., involving tanks) warfare.

The affirmative case's fifth contention is simply a claim of solvency. By providing more money to the Navy and by mandating strategic changes in naval operations, the affirmative argues it provides the necessary sea power to overcome the Soviet Navy and to strongly back United States foreign military commitments.

The Negative Strategy

As far as the negative team was concerned, there were four *big* flaws in this case: first, the case falsely argues Soviet superiority in sea power; second, the strength of the affirmative argument for sea power should be sufficient to overcome the attitudinal inherency argued in contention (4); third, the affirmative cannot guarantee that its additional money and its new strategy will solve the alleged seapower problem; fourth, the shift away from land power will weaken the U.S. Army and this weakening will be significantly disadvantageous. The first negative speaker chooses to attack the first two flaws; the second negative speaker chooses to attack the second two. Both negative speakers launch a few other lines of argumentation, as the two sides of the flow sheet (Figure 13.3 and Figure 13.4) show; however, these are the four arguments the negative team felt were crucial.

1) Energy Independence is an American goal	→ granted by INC					
2) Relying on Fossil Fuels Will not allow U.S. to meet goal	Affirmative predictions unduly pessimistic	More evidence on fossil fuels' inability to meet goal	Affirmative is basing policy on guesses	More evidence	Affirmative is basing policy on guesses	Still more evidence
3) Solar Energy, with government support now, will allow US to meet goal	Affirmative is basing policy on guesses	More evidence on Solar's ability to meet goal	Affirmative guesses too optimistic and contain too many unknowns	More evidence	Affirmative guesses too optimistic and contain too many unknowns	Still more evidence
	If alternative to fossil fuel is necessary, we have it in nuclear fuel-generated power	INC presented counter-plan. A) it's topical B) it won't meet goal unless large sums of $ are invested C) it is disadvantageous i) safety ii) ecological damage iii) health hazards of wastes	Not a counter-plan but an inherency argument	Negative did present counter-plan; what negative advocated was as much a shift from status quo as affirmative plan is	It wasn't a counter-plan!!	It was a counter-plan and it fails because A) is topical and B) is disadvantageous
				A) is topical		Underviews 1) Since negative offered counter-plan, neg cannot defend status-quo 2) both policies in round justify an affirmative ballot

Figure 13.3 Case-side flow sheet for case study two.

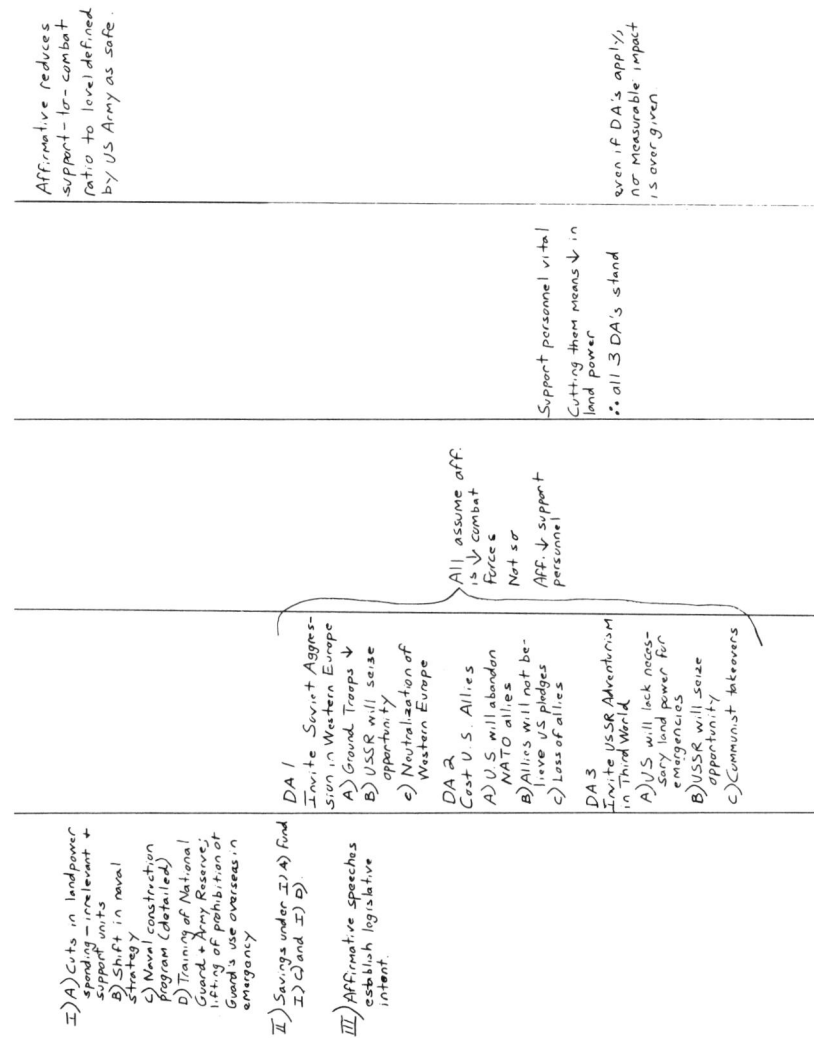

Figure 13.4 Plan-side flow sheet for case study two.

The Ensuing Debate

Winning was not going to prove as easy as the negative team thought, for these "flaws" were areas the affirmative team was fully prepared to debate. Let's trace the four areas of argumentation through the debate.

The first negative argues, with evidence, the Soviet sea power is not as strong in reality as it looks on paper. Many of the submarines listed in the Soviet fleet are of World War II vintage and in drydock in need of *major* repairs; some of the data used in U.S. Department of Defense reports on Soviet power count any armed vessel, whether its primary function is combat or fishing, as part of the Soviet Navy. If the Soviet naval power is accurately assessed, it is significantly below that of the United States, not at par or above, as the affirmative claims.

The second affirmative speaker counters by charging that the first negative speaker has misunderstood the affirmative position. Yes, the first affirmative speaker did read evidence saying that Soviet sea power is equal to or greater than U.S. sea power; however, the real issue is whether the Soviet Union is sufficiently strong to accomplish its sea denial mission. Whether superior, equal, or inferior to the U.S. Navy, the Soviet Navy is sufficiently strong because, according to naval strategy experts, a relatively small navy can effectively deny a nation with a much larger navy the sea lanes.

The first negative rebuttalist, caught a bit by surprise by the second affirmative's response, repeats his original argumentation and tries to refute the second affirmative's position by arguing that, "Of course, size matters." The first affirmative rebuttalist briefly reviews her partner's argument and notes the inadequacy of the first negative rebuttalist's response. The second negative rebuttalist reads two very general quotations from naval officials; the officials say that the U.S. Navy is second to none and can deal with all eventualities. According to this summary rebuttalist for the negative team, these assessments obviously mean that the Soviet Navy is too small for it to be any kind of a threat. The second affirmative rebuttalist simply repeats his original argument, noting the negative team's "continued misunderstanding of the affirmative position in this round."

The first negative uses a fairly standard ploy against a case which seems to be based on attitudinal inherency. He argues that, if the problem is as serious as the affirmative claims, then the attitudes can be overcome. In this particular case, the first negative suggests that the joint chiefs' being devoted to the defense of the United States will cause them to make the necessary adjustments with speed if they are convinced of the need for sea power and the United States' weaknesses in that area. The second affirmative again counters by claiming that the first negative speaker misunderstands the affirmative case's inherency. The second affirmative argues that the affirmative is claiming a "double inherency." The first is structural, not attitudinal: the decision-making structure of the Pentagon, not the views of particular joint chiefs, blocks any movement away from a nearly equal division of defense appropriations. The second comes into play *if* the first fails: if redistribution of funds does occur, then the necessary change in naval strategy will not occur because of the President's and the Navy Department's blind commitment to supercarriers. According to the second affirmative, the first negative misunderstood the first argument when he treated it as attitudinal rather than structural, and the first negative totally ignored the second.

The first negative rebuttalist claimed that "decision-making structure" was a smoke screen and that *both* inherencies were purely attitudinal and that his original argument still stood. The first affirmative rebuttalist ignored the first negative rebuttalist's response and quickly summarized her partner's argumentation. The summary rebuttalist for the negative team, concentrating on "plan side," simply said, "They have no inherency; it's only attitudinal." The summary rebuttalist for the affirmative team insisted again that it was a decision-making structure the affirmative was talking about and read quotations from writers on the Pentagon which *seemed* to suggest that the affirmative's discussion of inviolable decision-making structures had some merit. This same rebuttalist again insisted that the negative team had never directly dealt with the second level of inherency claimed since the opening speech.

The first negative constructive speech pretty much let the affirmative's fifth contention (the solvency claim) slide by. The negative did not initiate its solvency challenge until the second negative constructive speech. There, the negative debater argued that the affirmative team had not met its *prima facie* burden in its initial constructive speech, for the affirmative team had not demonstrated that the extra money and the revised naval strategy would indeed solve the sea power problems facing the United States. The second negative stressed that the affirmative team would have to show absolute solvency.

The first affirmative rebuttalist had the first crack at this solvency challenge and, therefore, felt she had to devote some time to it. She spent two full minutes responding, and her response consisted of strong evidence stating that the money provided by the plan *would* finance shipbuilding and training which *would* solve the sea power problem if that building and training were accompanied by the precise shift in strategy the affirmative team was advocating. The evidence was absolutely on target. What became clear to the negative team (and the judge) at this point is that the affirmative team had not originated the plan but rather adopted as its own a plan of action long advocated by former Senator Taft of Ohio and Senator Hart of Colorado. The borrowing of a plan gave the affirmative its very specific solvency evidence. That evidence, however, tended to come from the same sources as the ones used throughout the first affirmative constructive speech—Taft, Hart, and a few other experts on naval policy. The second negative rebuttalist zeroed in on this evidence: she claimed the affirmative team needed independent validation of its claim, not validation by the same sources that had argued that there was a problem. To prove solvency by quoting the same sources used to establish the existence of the problem, harm, and inherency was a kind of circular reasoning. The second affirmative rebuttalist sloughed off this argument and strongly insisted that the affirmative team had met its *prima facie* solvency burden with strong, on-target evidence.

The second negative constructive speaker offered three disadvantages, all stemming from the cut the affirmative plan mandates in spending on land power. According to the second negative speaker, the affirmative plan will (1) invite Soviet aggression in Western Europe, (2) cost the United States allies, and (3) invite Soviet adventurism, either directly or via proxies, in the Third World. The second negative speaker had a fair amount of evidence to offer: she used evidence she and her partner usually used on the affirmative when justifying a significant increase in salaries for military personnel in order to significantly increase their numbers.

The first affirmative rebuttalist tried to group all three disadvantages together and to claim that none applied to the affirmative plan because of the precise nature of the cuts the affirmative plan mandated. This rebuttalist said, "As my partner noted when cross-examining the second negative, we are reducing the number of troops by reducing the support-to-combat ratio. The troops who will go are support personnel, not fighting men."

The second negative rebuttalist attacked this response head-on. She argued that support personnel are vital and that cutting them significantly would therefore reduce the United States' ability to defend its interests. The three disadvantages, she claimed, still stood.

The second affirmative rebuttalist offered, as an overview, that the affirmative plan reduces the support-to-combat ratio to levels defined by the military itself as acceptable. He did not show how this overview negated the claimed disadvantages; rather he just assumed the application was obvious. This rebuttalist then proceeded to argue that, "Even if the DA's do apply, no measurable impact was given. We don't know how much more likely the Soviet aggression in Western Europe and adventurism in the Third World will be; we don't know how much 'friendship' we'll lose."

Let's go back and consider where each of these four issues stands at the debate's end. On the first issue, the affirmative stance is the one that should win: as the affirmative notes, the negative team did not initially understand the affirmative position; furthermore, once the negative team understood the affirmative position, the negative team met it with rather lame responses. Two occurrences during the round, however, make the affirmative "win" on this issue less than clear-cut. First, the affirmative team may have seemed to the judge to have shifted position between the initial speech and the second constructive speech. Although the affirmative case argued that the U.S.S.R. has enough seapower to accomplish its sea denial mission, some evidence read to support that argument made larger claims, claims which the affirmative team may have been perceived by the judge to have retreated from. Second, the affirmative team rested its case too early: neither rebuttal was used effectively to "sew up" this argument.

On the second issue, the affirmative stance is again probably the one that should win. Initially the negative team did not understand the affirmative's stand on inherency; once the negative team understood the stand, they flat-out rejected it. They rejected it, claiming it was a "smoke screen." The verdict hinges on the extent to which the judge understands and "buys" what the affirmative team is saying about "decision-making structure." The affirmative team has some difficulty explaining the concept, and the judge, after the negative team's last rebuttal, is inclined to go along with the negative team's doubts, not because the affirmative position seems without merit, but because the position was unclear and scarcely evidenced. Then, the second affirmative rebuttal provides lots of evidence. The judge is in a bind. The evidence is now in the round, but it was offered so late that the negative team had no opportunity to respond. The judge might well give this issue to the negative.

On the third issue, the affirmative stance is again probably the one that should win. Even though the first affirmative constructive speech did not make a strong case for solvency, it made the case. And, when pressed for more, the affirmative delivered. The "circular reasoning" argument voiced by the second negative rebuttalist is not really an exposure of affirmative illogic; rather, it is a questioning of the affirmative's reliance on few sources and a call for independent testimony as to the proposal's solvency. As such, it has some merit, but probably not enough to overcome the specificity and conviction of the evidence read by the first affirmative rebuttalist. However, if the second negative rebuttalist's argument is thought by the judge to be an actual exposure of affirmative illogic, then the affirmative team may lose solvency, especially since the second affirmative rebuttalist did not respond adequately to the accusation of illogic.

On the fourth argument, the affirmative stance is again the one that should win. The ingenuity of the plan is that it saves money now spent on land power by cutting support units (not combat units) down to a level certified by the U.S. Army as safe. If the logic behind the plan's cuts is clear, then the affirmative debater should be able to group all the disadvantages together and argue that they do not apply. Unfortunately, that logic only became *slowly* clear in this round, and it may not have ever been as clear as necessary because the affirmative team tended to assume that if it were clear to them, it was of course clear to the judge. Some of the facts necessary to give the judge the degree of understanding the affirmative debaters had were not presented. As a result, the judge's mind is fuzzy as to whether the disadvantages are or are not applicable. The judge just might vote negative.

Commentary

Again, a discussion of this debate could go in any number of directions. And I hope you, your fellow debaters, and your coach or instructor pursue some of these directions. I want to focus on two broad matters.

The first matter concerns plan attacks. Many second negative constructive speakers voice the same plan attacks round after round. Often, they neglect to link these attacks very specifically to the plan under consideration. The plan attacks offered in this debate were ones a second negative debater could use against any affirmative case that "robbed Peter to pay Paul," i.e., took money away from land forces to beef up our ability in some other area. These disadvantages would seem to be appropriate if a case took money from land power to build outer-space weaponry or took money from land power to improve our nuclear capabilities. The second negative, in this debate, did not examine the affirmative plan very closely, for, as his initial premise, he simply argued that "the affirmative cuts land power." A careful examination would have shown him that this link between the specific plan and the disadvantages he wanted to present might not hold. Because he failed to engage in this examination, he left himself vulnerable to an easy affirmative response: that the disadvantages do not apply because, "the affirmative *does not* cut land power one bit." The lesson to be learned by second negative debaters can be put in one word: *think*. Carefully examine the affirmative's plan; do not quickly assume that the plan you are confronting is an x-type and proceed on that assumption and offer the plan attacks you always offer against x-type plans.

The second matter concerns muddled debates. As the summary of each of the four crucial issues should have indicated to you, both teams did a number of things which resulted in considerable muddling. Repeating previously made arguments without acknowledging and/or responding to arguments opponents have offered leads to muddling. Failing to explain arguments fully leads to muddling. Misunderstanding and/or misinterpreting an opponent's position leads to muddling. All of these things happened in this debate and in many actual debates.

Who wins muddled debates? In some judges' minds, the affirmative team has the responsibility to keep its case clear and in the forefront. If a debate gets muddled, the affirmative team is at fault. Therefore, the negative wins: the negative team—perhaps with some help from the affirmative team—has succeeded in bringing the judge to the point where he cannot accept the resolution. In other judges' minds, the first affirmative speech serves as a landmark in the muddle. They will retreat to it and, bringing as much of the actual debate as possible into consideration, decide whether the case is *still* viable at the debate's end. The affirmative team usually has an edge with this kind of judge because the initial speech is usually clear in contrast to much that follows. In other judges' minds, the stock issues serve as a landmark in the muddled round. The judges march the affirmative case past the stock issues and see how the case stands in light of what has been said during the debate. This judging procedure tends to favor the negative, since it allows the negative team the opportunity to win if it has managed to punch one hole which the affirmative team has failed to adequately repair.

Many judges have no set procedures to follow when faced with a muddled debate. They neither vote negative because the affirmative has failed to sustain a *clear* case for the resolution nor retreat to the first affirmative speech or the stock issues and evaluate. They judge impressionistically, or they enter the debate themselves and try to make sense of matters. A judge who judges a muddled round impressionistically is unpredictable. A judge who enters the debate to clarify matters may well end up basing a decision on argumentation he or she has to some extent made. This judge may complete a solvency defense or topicality challenge in clarifying it. The judge's attempts to make sense out of muddle may help the negative team to a victory; they may help the affirmative. There is no telling; this kind of judge is unpredictable.

Who, then, wins muddled debates? There is no answer. These debates, because they are muddled, tend to get out of control. Both the affirmative team and the negative team should be interested in good decisions; both teams have an interest in controlling their destiny in a particular round. When debaters muddle matters, they lose control. And when they lose control, strange things can happen. Decisions become based as much on chance as on the argumentation offered in the round.

Case Three: Should the Government Give Subsidies to the Fledgling Solar Energy Industry?

The resolution requires the affirmative team to advocate a policy which will help assure "energy independence" in the twenty-first century. The affirmative team offers a fairly predictable case and plan.

The Affirmative Case

The affirmative team chooses to use the goals case model in constructing its justification for the resolution. The affirmative begins by announcing (contention 1) that energy independence is an American goal and quotes a series of American presidents. The affirmative team, in its second contention, shows how the present reliance on fossil fuels, even with research subsidies galore, will not allow the United States to meet the goal. Then, the affirmative team shows how solar energy can meet the goal if the solar energy industry is given considerable government support. The plan, a complex one with several different types of subsidies and grants, follows. The first affirmative constructive speaker then concludes by urging the judge to vote for the policy that best meets the important goal of energy independence.

The Negative Strategy

The negative team decided to focus on one aspect of the affirmative case, its conjectural quality. Not only did the affirmative team depend on future projections to indict the present policy which focuses on fossil fuels, but the affirmative team depended on future projections and presently nonexistent technologies to demonstrate the solar energy's ability to meet the goal. The negative decided to argue that (1) the affirmative projections concerning fossil fuels are unduly pessimistic, (2) the affirmative projections concerning the solar energy industry are mere guesses, and (3) if an alternative to fossil fuels is necessary, it is already available in nuclear fuels. The first argument was offered by the first negative speaker as a response to the case's second contention; the second negative argument was offered in response to the case's third contention; the third negative argument was offered during the concluding two minutes of the first negative constructive speech. This argument probably should have been offered as a second major response to the second contention, the first negative speaker arguing that the affirmative team neglected to evaluate a part of the status quo, i.e., nuclear power. Presented where it was and in the manner it was, the argument almost seemed like a counterplan.

Besides repeating and extending the first negative debater's argument that the plan's ability to meet the goal (a kind of solvency) was based on guesses, not facts, the second negative speaker offered a number of disadvantages to adopting the affirmative team's plan. The first affirmative speaker was asked in cross-examination where the money to finance the plan would come from. The first affirmative pointed to three sources: what is presently being spent on other power sources; a tax on solar energy distributed commercially; general federal revenue. Based on this response, the second negative debater built several disadvantages: (1) the bankruptcy of American oil companies; (2) anti-American feelings in the oil-rich regions; (3) greater risk of energy crisis since the plan relies on a single source; (4) an economic slowdown due to the new tax; (5) inflation due to increased federal spending and growing federal deficits; (6) cuts to vital domestic programs and/or foreign programs if the federal government will not support additional spending and permit a growing federal deficit. Each disadvantage was well-developed; for each, some kind of impact was provided by the second negative speaker.

The Ensuing Debate

Let's consider "case side" first. The second affirmative speaker caused some confusion by misinterpreting what was an inherency argument (nuclear power, part of the status quo, can meet the goal) as a counterplan. Beginning with the alleged counterplan, the second affirmative speaker argued that (a) it was topical, (b) it would not meet the goal of energy independence unless outrageous sums of money were invested, and (c) it entailed the significant disadvantages of questionable safety, ecological damage to the water sources used to cool the nuclear reactors, and the long-term health hazard posed by waste materials.

After spending a considerable amount of time refuting a counterplan that was never offered, the second affirmative defended the case. He noted that the goal (contention 1) was granted; then he proceeded to indict fossil fuel energy generation and support solar energy generation with further evidence.

The second negative constructive speaker began her speech with a clarifying observation: she told the judge and the affirmative team members that no counterplan had been presented. She then noted that the affirmative team had mistaken the argument that a status quo mechanism (i.e., nuclear power) could meet the goal for a counterplan which would have to represent a change from the status quo to be the revision of our present energy policy called for by the resolution.

The first negative rebuttalist repeated his partner's comments on the supposed counterplan really being an inherency argument; furthermore, he noted that, as an inherency argument, it had not been refuted. The first affirmative rebuttalist would not admit her partner's mistake. She argued that a counterplan had indeed been introduced. She argued that what the negative team had advocated was a shift in spending from fossil fuel-produced energy to nuclear and, even though nuclear power was part of the status quo, the shift in funding emphasis made the negative team's suggestion a change from the status quo, thus a counterplan, and a topical counterplan to boot. She struck an analogy between the supposed counterplan and the affirmative plan: in both cases, the advocated form of power generation, either nuclear or solar, exists in the status quo; in both cases, the departure from the status quo is the provision of significantly more money for the alternative to fossil fuel generation. Therefore, she argued, if the affirmative plan represents a policy change (something never denied by the negative team), then the negative team has indeed offered a counterplan. She further suggested that the negative team was trying to hide its mistake by now claiming the counterplan was just an inherency argument, the mistake being presenting a blatantly topical counterplan.

The summary rebuttalist for the negative now found herself in trouble. She thought the negative team's intention had been clarified; she also thought the affirmative debaters were the ones with egg on their faces. She tried to get out of trouble by being confessional: "Look, our original intention was . . . " However, the explanation did not wash, and the summary rebuttalist for the affirmative could correctly claim that the counterplan had failed because it had been proven topical and significantly disadvantageous.

The negative rebuttalists, at the same time they were trying to explain that they had not counterplanned, were trying to keep their other case-side arguments alive. They continued to argue that the affirmative's predictions for fossil fuel-generated energy were too bleak and, more important, that the affirmative's predictions for solar-generated were *much too* optimistic and based on several "if"s. The first affirmative rebuttalist simply offered more evidence to support the affirmative assessments. The second affirmative rebuttalist, feeling he had the negative nailed on the counterplan, offered still more evidence to back the affirmative evaluations of fossil fuel-generated and solar-generated energy and then offered two debate-concluding "underviews." First, he argued that the negative had chosen to defend a counterplan, not the status quo; therefore, its arguments in defense of the status quo (i.e., fossil fuel use) and in opposition to the affirmative's bleak evaluation of the status quo should not even be listened to. Second, he argued that the negative had implicitly if not explicitly accepted as a voting standard the best meeting of the goal of energy independence. Of the three policies under consideration, only two can be fairly considered, nuclear and solar, since the negative cannot defend the status quo and a shift to nuclear power simultaneously and be consistent. The policy supported by the affirmative team, solar power, has been proven superior to nuclear, the rebuttalist argued; but, he continued, even if you do not accept the superiority of solar to nuclear, you still must vote affirmative since both the affirmative plan and the counterplan are topical. This complex case-side debate is presented in Figure 13.5.

On case side, the negative team goofed, and the affirmative team exploited the situation. On plan side, the story was different. The first affirmative rebuttalist had six disadvantages to confront. In response to the first, she argued that petroleum would still be necessary for energy, as well as other uses, and that the bankruptcy of oil companies was unlikely. In response to the second, she said the reduction in importation would not be as drastic as the negative claimed and that, as a result, any diplomatic harms would be minimal. She also suggested that, given the 1973 embargo and past price gouging by the oil-rich nations, we should not be reluctant to turn the tables and reduce imports to a trickle. In response to the third disadvantage, she said the sun was a reliable single source and that, therefore, sole reliance on it would not pose any problems. In response to the fourth disadvantage, she argued that the tax would not be large enough to promote a slowdown. Finally, she grouped the fifth and the sixth disadvantages and argued that the needed money could be gained almost totally by cutting subsidies, etc., to companies engaged in research on fossil fuels and by taxing the commercial sale of solar energy.

The second negative rebuttalist accused the affirmative team of being "as hard to pin down as a glob of mercury." When defending the third contention, the affirmative suggests that solar energy will *take over* if given generous subsidies, but when defending against disadvantages, the affirmative team says petroleum will still be needed and not very much money will be needed to encourage the fledgling solar power industry. The negative rebuttalist says he will hold the affirmative to their own "case-side" arguments and assume that solar power will virtually replace fossil fuel- and nuclear fuel-generated power and that solar power will require sizeable initial subsidies. Based on this assumption, disadvantages (1), (2), (4), (5), and (6) still stand.

This rebuttalist also pointed out a contradiction between the first affirmative rebuttalist's responses to the last three disadvantages. In response to the fourth, the affirmative says the tax will be no big deal; in response to the fifth and sixth disadvantages, the affirmative implies that the tax will be substantial enough to supply a large percentage of the necessary incentive money. The affirmative, the negative insists, can't have it both ways: either disadvantage (4) must stand or disadvantages (5) and (6) must stand.

In defense of disadvantage (3), the second negative explained his original position once again. He knows, he says, that the sun is reliable. It was not the sun *per se* he was questioning, but the man-made technology designed to convert the sun's energy into useful power. With no viable nuclear- or fossil fuel-generated power alternatives to solar in future years, the United States runs a real risk. If the solar technology does not develop as predicted, when predicted, the affirmative plan may land the nation in serious trouble.

The second affirmative rebuttalist, who gave a very good summary of "case side," slighted "plan side." As a result, the affirmative team did not adequately

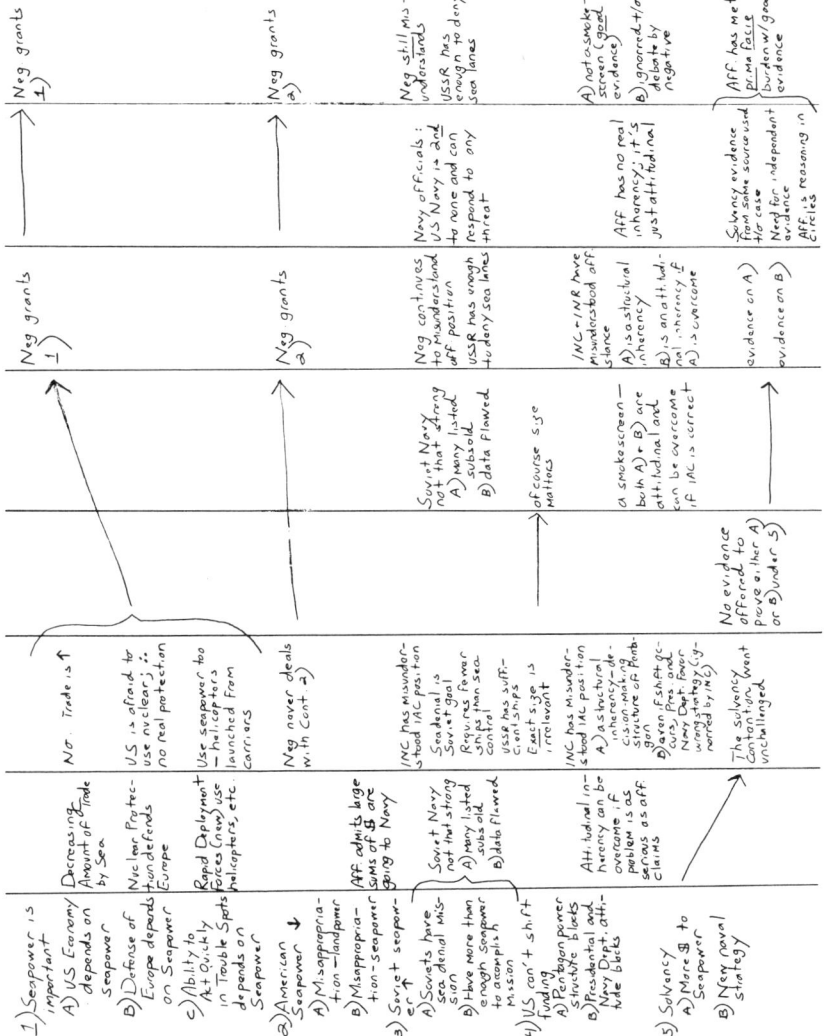

Figure 13.5 Case-side flow sheet for case study three.

wriggle free from the contradictions. The summary rebuttalist for the affirmative team simply said, "We're advocating a middle stance; therefore, the DA's don't apply and there's no contradiction." There may well have been merit to his position; however, the nature of the "middle stance" was not explained, as well as how a recognition of the true affirmative stance affected the disadvantages. On disadvantage (3), the second affirmative rebuttalist said a bit more. He argued that the technology was sure and read evidence to that effect. The plan-side arguments are flowed in Figure 13.6.

So, looking at the entire debate, the judge is in a dilemma of sorts. The affirmative has won case side; the negative has convinced the judge that there is a strong likelihood that a measure of disadvantages (1), (2), (4), (5), and (6) will accrue and has won plan side. The stock issues judge requires that the affirmative carry all of a list of requirements of a valid case. Freedom from significant disadvantages is usually one of the issues on the list. To the extent the judge feels the disadvantages are potentially significant, he or she will probably vote negative. The policymaking judge will be in a real quandary: the plan seems potentially disadvantageous; the counterplan the negative team got stuck with has been beaten with unanswered disadvantages offered by the second affirmative constructive speaker. The best policy in the debate may well be the status quo, but no one is defending it: the affirmative has indicted it; the negative has forfeited its right to defend it when it got stuck defending a counterplan. The policymaker may vote affirmative because the topicality of the counterplan means that there are really two affirmative teams in the debate, or the policymaker may vote negative because no one has succeeded in justifying the resolution, in which case the negative team "lucks out" a victory.

Questions

Again, much in this debate warrants discussion. Rather than comment on it, I invite you to consider the following questions:

1. Did the affirmative team make the best choice when they chose the goals case model?
2. Should the affirmative team have anticipated the nuclear power possibility and addressed it, as well as fossil fuel-generated power, in the opening speech?
3. How could the first negative speaker have avoided getting trapped in a counterplan as he did?
4. Did the second affirmative speaker take the best course when he responded as if the negative team had offered a counterplan?
5. How might the second negative speaker or first negative rebuttalist succeeded in making it clear that the negative team had not presented a counterplan?
6. How wise was the time allocation made by the first affirmative rebuttalist?
7. How should the first affirmative rebuttalist have handled the six disadvantages?

I) Solar Energy Office in Dept of Commerce		Affirmative is hard to pin down
II) Administers II Types of Grants for Different Aspects of Solar Energy Research + Development		defense of contention ③ and defense vs. DA's ① and ② contradict
III) Funding through A) $ currently going to fossil fuel research B) Tax on commercially-sold solar energy C) General federal revenue	DA 1 — Bankruptcy of American Oil Companies	on case side, aff. implies subsidies will be large; contradicts defense vs. DA's ④, ⑤, and ⑥
	Petroleum would still be needed; ∴ no bankruptcies	defense of plan vs. DA ④ contradicts defense of plan vs. DA's ⑤ and ⑥
	DA 2 — Anti-American feelings in the oil-rich regions	Affirmative takes a middle stance on these questions ∴ no contradictions DA's do not apply
	No drastic reduction in imports ∴ minimal diplomatic damage	
IV) Adequate staff, etc.	DA 3 — Greater risk of Energy Crisis	Since oil-rich nations have treated US poorly in past, why should DA 2 matter?
V) Affirmative speeches establish legislative intent		Sun is single reliable source
	DA 4 — Economic slowdown (due to new tax)	The solar technology is questionable; that's why there is a risk.
		Tax rate would not be large enough to cause slowdown
	DA 5 — Inflation (due to ↑ in federal spending and ↑'d deficit)	evidence on how sure solar technology is
	DA 6 — Cuts to vital federal programs	Almost all the $ would come from cuts in subsidies, etc. to fossil fuel and new tax

Figure 13.6 Plan-side flow sheet for case study three.

8. If you were in the position of offering the summary rebuttal for the negative, how would you have proceeded differently?
9. If you were in the position of offering the summary rebuttal for the affirmative, how would you have proceeded differently?

Case Four: Should Political Activism by Religious Organizations Be Restricted?

The resolution in this case is a proposition of value: the affirmative team must affirm the prepolicy value judgment that political activism by religious organizations is disadvantageous. More specifically, the affirmative team must be prepared to argue that a religious group should not be allowed to involve itself in politics, whether it be to advocate prayer in school, an end to federally funded abortions, or a nuclear freeze.

The Affirmative Case

The affirmative team in this debate traced the separation of church and state back to late seventeenth-century epistemology. Recovering from a period of intense skepticism, philosophers at that time came up with a philosophy of knowledge (epistemology) which allowed man to have sufficient certainty to live in this world. These philosophers divided knowledge into different realms: theology, mathematics, politics, etc., and argued that mankind can achieve a different degree of certainty in each. In mathematics, for example, a very high degree of certainty is possible. In theology, on the other hand, a very low degree is possible. Politics falls somewhere in between, closer to mathematics.

When, as a thinker, you worked in one of these fields, your limitations were pretty much set for you, and all who worked with you in the field understood the possibilities and the limitations. If you worked in mathematics, the possibilities of arriving at definite truth were high, the limitations few; if you worked in theology, the possibilities of arriving at definitive truth were low, the limitations numerous and accepted. If disciplinary lines were crossed, epistemological ones were crossed too, and that might be troublesome. A mathematician meddling in politics might believe his political theories had a degree of validity nearly equal to his mathematical theorems. A theologian meddling in politics might believe that a higher degree of certainty was possible.

The affirmative team also took a look at Renaissance and seventeenth-century northern European history. In that history, the team members found numerous examples of where the emotions appropriate to religion were inappropriately carried over into politics. The results were persecution and civil wars.

The lessons of epistemology and history led the affirmative team to argue in its initial speech that the separation of church and state is philosophically and historically justified, for the separation promotes intellectual rigor and domestic peace, and intellectual rigor and domestic peace are valuable. The actual definitive contention would read, "Intellectual rigor and domestic peace are valuable"; the actual designative contention would read, "The separation of church and state promotes intellectual rigor and domestic peace." Subpoint (a) would argue that this evaluation has proved true historically; subpoint (b) would argue that this evaluation is still valid. Further research gave the affirmative team contemporary examples of how intellectual rigor requires separation of church and state—for example, the question of the universe's origin and the definition of death. Further research gave the affirmative team members contemporary examples of how domestic peace requires that the emotions of religion not become mixed with government—for example, sex education, abortion, capital punishment. The affirmative team built these controversial contemporary examples into the substructure of its designative contention. The designative contention would lead to a third contention, a contention affirming the resolution "that political activism by religious groups is disadvantageous." In discussing this third contention, the affirmative team would argue that restraints are necessary because religious groups are presently entering more and more frequently into the political process.

The Negative Strategy

The first negative debater in this particular contest chose to take the affirmative case head-on, by arguing that the separation of church and state is dangerous, not valuable, and by arguing that the increasing activism by religious groups will prove beneficial. She ignored the affirmative's first contention, and she essentially admitted the observation in the third contention while approving and applauding (not criticizing) the increased activism which the affirmative had cited as a justification for legal restrictions.

The second negative debater in this contest chose to examine the kind of policy which affirming the resolution's value judgment would lead to. That kind of policy would have a number of dire results. These she presents in three off-case arguments: (1) a legal restriction will lead to the condoning of immorality; (2) a legal restriction will lead to further restrictions of First Amendment freedoms; (3) a legal restriction will lead to an inferior decision-making process. These she developed well with a fair amount of evidence. Figure 13.7 presents the case-side flow sheet of this debate; Figure 13.8 presents the off-case side.

The Ensuing Debate

Let's consider case side first. The second affirmative constructive speaker emphasizes the two points on which the first negative agreed either by her silence or by her comments: that intellectual rigor and domestic peace are valuable; that political activism by religious groups is increasing. Then, he proceeded to argue that political action by religious groups is undesirable because it could well stand in the way of both intellectual rigor and domestic peace. In other words, he pretty much repeated and expanded on the argumentation in the first affirmative

1) Intellectual rigor and domestic peace are valuable	INC agrees (by her silence)	Intellectual rigor and domestic peace are the values in this debate		
2) The separation of church and state promotes intellectual rigor and domestic peace	The separation is dangerous, not valuable	Separation is in line w/values above	Separation not in line w/values above	New argument in rebuttal
A) historically true	Political action could stand in the way of both intellectual rigor and domestic peace ∴ not valuable		A) Rigor depends on input	
B) still true	Moral considerations are regularly raised in the political process, but in such a way that intellectual rigor and domestic peace are not jeopardized e.g.'s	These moral considerations enter into political discussions because of religious activism e.g.'s	B) Domestic peace depends on all people being heard	New argument in rebuttal
3) Political activism by religious groups is disadvantageous		Moral questions are already being raised More e.g.'s	These questions are being raised thanks to political activism by religious groups	Moral questions come up anyway
A) such activism is growing	INC agrees that activism is increasing			
B) ∴ restraints are necessary	This increase will prove valuable	Restraint on religious groups is in line w/ values above		

Figure 13.7 Case-side flow sheet for case study four.

1) a legal restriction will lead to the condoning of immorality A) plan restricts B) Moral issues will not come up C) Since they are not raised, immorality may well be condoned	Moral issues are raised regularly in policy discussions ∴ a legal restriction → an end to discussion of Moral issues or a condoning of immorality initial premise of argument is wrong	CROSS-APPLY case-side arguments and evidence in response to contention ②	CROSS-APPLY case-side arguments and evidence in defense of contention ②
2) a legal restriction will lead to further restrictions of First Amendment freedoms A) plan restricts B) one restriction leads to others C) results diminution of important American freedoms	Motive for some group to extend this restriction? Mechanism? propensity? evidence inapplicable evidence prejudiced — ACLU is source	Police in '50's & '60's gradually chipped away at suspects rights — e.g. of how a little restriction can lead elsewhere shows motive, mechanism, propensity	20-yr old e.g. is scarcely applicable today does not provide specific motive, propensity, + mechanism
3) a legal restriction will lead to an inferior decision-making process A) plan restricts info. entering process B) less info, poorer decisions C) bad policy will be made, dire results	restriction, on the contrary, will lead to better decision-making because emotions introduced into discussions by religious groups will not interfere	good decision-making is dependent on information restriction → reduced info. flow ∴ inferior decisions	Yes restriction ↛ reduced info. flow because info. enters the process already religious groups also bring emotions into the process restriction gets these emotions out ∴ leads to better decisions

Figure 13.8 Off case-side flow sheet for case study four.

constructive speech. He also briefly responded to the related negative claims that the separation of church and state is dangerous and that activism will prove valuable by arguing that the moral considerations religious groups would raise are raised ordinarily in the political process but in such a way that intellectual rigor and peace are not jeopardized. For example, when federal legislation providing aid to residents of sites where chemical companies many years ago buried toxic wastes is considered, the moral obligation of the government and the chemical companies is certain to come up; when federal legislation providing medical coverage for abortions is considered, the morality of abortion is certain to come up. Political activism by religious groups isn't necessary.

The first negative rebuttalist disagreed. According to her, the moral issues are being regularly raised today only because of activism. If it were not for the political activism of the Roman Catholic Church, the morality of abortion would become lost in the economic question "Can we afford aid?" and the political-economic question "Should government or private enterprise be doing this?" If it were not for the political activism of several Protestant sects, the issue of school prayer and the related question of God's place in the American classroom would have vanished long ago.

The clash between the affirmative and negative positions is clear. The first affirmative rebuttalist does little to advance the argument the teams are clashing over: he just repeats the second affirmative's argument that moral questions are already raised and adds to his partner's examples capital punishment, death with dignity, nuclear weapons development, chemical and biological warfare, orphan diseases, and automobile recalls. In all of these issues, there is a moral dimension and that dimension *is* explored. This rebuttalist does, however, remind the judge that intellectual rigor and domestic peace *are* the undisputed standards of value in the debate, that the separation of church and state has been shown to be valuable based on this standard, and that restrictions on political activism are necessary to maintain this valuable separation.

The summary rebuttalist for the negative team again insists that political activism *is* proving valuable. As far as intellectual rigor is concerned, she suggests that the rigor depends on input and that restrictions on input inhibit rigor rather than ensure it; as far as domestic peace is concerned, she suggests that domestic peace depends on all issues, especially emotionally charged ones, being heard and that restrictions on sharing views endanger domestic peace rather than ensure it. A frustrated people, frustrated because the government is not hearing their heartfelt views, is more likely to riot than a people whose views have been heard and rejected in a democratic process.

The second negative rebuttalist has advanced the debate considerably: we now have an exciting exchange of views on three fronts. Does activism promote or deny intellectual rigor? Does activism promote or deny domestic peace? Does activism bring the moral dimensions of public issues to the attention of elected officials? The summary rebuttalist for the affirmative team chooses to debate only on the third. The first and second arguments, he correctly claims, are based on negative positions taken for the first time in rebuttals. According to the rules of debating, no new lines of argumentation can be initiated in rebuttals: you can extend on arguments already made and respond to arguments already made, but you cannot start an argument from scratch. On the third argument, he repeats the position the affirmative team has been pushing all through the debate: that moral questions enter into the legislative process with or without activism by religious groups. Since this is true, he concludes, and since activism does endanger intellectual rigor and domestic peace, some kind of legal restriction is justified.

The debate on the off-case side is necessarily shorter, since it did not commence until the last constructive speech. The first affirmative rebuttalist responded to all three off-case arguments at some length. In response to the first off-case argument or value objection, this rebuttalist argued, as his partner had, that moral issues are regularly raised in the legislative process and, therefore, an end to activism would not mean an end to the discussion of moral issues and would certainly not mean a condoning of immorality. According to this rebuttalist, the off-case argument falls because its logic is flawed early on by a false premise. In response to the second off-case argument, the first affirmative rebuttalist again questioned the argument's logic. According to this rebuttalist, the negative will have to show a motive and a mechanism and a propensity to use a restriction on political activism by religious groups as a springboard for other restrictions on freedom of speech. The first affirmative rebuttalist also noted that the second negative's evidence which says, essentially, that one curtailment of the constitutional rights granted citizens will necessarily lead to other restrictions was (a) inapplicable because the separation of church and state *is* a constitutional principle, not a departure from the Constitution, and (b) perhaps prejudiced since the source of the cited evidence is the American Civil Liberties Union. In response to the third off-case argument, the first affirmative rebuttalist argued that the contrary was true: rather than a restriction leading to inferior decision making, a restriction would lead to better decision making because emotions would be less likely to intefere. The summary rebuttalist for the negative team tried to reinforce her original first off-case argument by cross-applying arguments made on case side. In defense of the second off-case argument, this final negative rebuttalist cited how police in the 1950s and 1960s gradually chipped away at suspects' rights and privacy rights. This example shows the motive, mechanism, and propensity for turning small restrictions of rights into larger and larger restrictions. The first affirmative rebuttalist's comment on the negative evidence went unanswered. Finally, in defense of the third off-case argument, the second negative rebuttalist argued that good decision making is dependent on full information, that restricting activism curtails information flow, and that curtailed information flow necessarily means inferior decisions. This rebuttalist claims that her opponent did not fully understand the off-case argument.

The summary rebuttalist for the affirmative team recognized, as did the second negative rebuttalist, that the argument over the first off-case argument paralleled argumentation on case side; therefore, he, like the second negative rebuttalist, cross-applied case-side argumentation. On the second off-case argument, this final rebuttalist argued that the example of police department excesses twenty years ago did not provide the motive, mechanism, or propensity for someone to extend the restrictions on the activities of religious groups to more general restrictions on First Amendment rights at present. On the third off-case argument, this final rebuttalist admitted that information was important in the decision-making process, but argued that the information that religious groups provide is already part of the process and enters the process without the intense emotional qualities which that same information acquires in the presentation of religious groups. These emotional qualities, although admirable in many contexts, are a distraction in the decision-making process and can actually lead to bad decisions.

This debate featured a considerable amount of clash. A number of arguments enter the summary rebuttals with two clearly articulated, well-defended positions. Rather than judge this debate for you, I will leave the decision in your hands. The last of the discussion questions which follow will ask you to offer a verdict and—more importantly—explain why you cast your ballot the way you did.

Questions

1. The affirmative team chose intellectual rigor and domestic peace as its values. Do you think they made a wise choice?
2. The first negative constructive speech did not respond to the affirmative's first contention. Why was this failure to respond a mistake? How might the negative team have responded? If the negative team had responded in this manner, how would the debate have been different?
3. There was a very clear clash between the two teams on the question of the value of religious activism in the decision-making process, a clash on case side and off-case side. How might both sides have improved their positions?
4. Critique the first affirmative rebuttalist's handling of the three off-case arguments.
5. The negative team finally got around to addressing the criteria of intellectual rigor and domestic peace, but, as the affirmative team pointed out, the negative did it too late. How does the affirmative's use of a procedural rule to beat an argument sit with you?
6. Were values as fully discussed in this debate as possible? How might the discussion of values been taken further?
7. Whom would you have given the decision to? Why?

After reading and discussing Chapter 13, you know:

- that choosing the wrong structural model for your affirmative case can lead to trouble;
- that "squirrel" cases can be beaten if you remain calm and look for their flaws;

- that, if you are the second negative debater in a policy debate, you should examine the plan you are challenging very carefully before assuming that generic plan attacks are applicable;
- how muddled debates escape the control of *both* teams;
- that a negative team must make its strategy clear to their opponents and judge;
- that *both* affirmative rebuttalists must devote a significant amount of time to the plan attacks or off-case arguments;
- that the negative team in a value debate should almost always question the affirmative's definitive contention.

Glossary of Debate Terms

Absolute Solvency An affirmative plan's ability to totally solve a problem and thereby to totally eliminate the harms that the problem created. See p. 184.*

Add-Ons Advantages to adopting an affirmative plan presented later than the first affirmative debater's constructive speech, usually as an addition to an advantage or advantages presented in that constructive speech. See p. 68.

Affirmative Blocks Outlined responses—usually with evidence—to an anticipated negative argument *or* outlined extensions—usually with evidence—of an argument offered in the first affirmative debater's constructive speech. See p. 193.

Alternative Justifications Case An affirmative strategy in which the first affirmative debater's constructive speech offers two or more separate cases for adopting the resolution, any one of which provides sufficient justification. See p. 77.

Argument-specific Briefs Outlined responses—usually with evidence—to an anticipated argument. See p. 193.

Attitudinal Inherency The affirmative team's claim that a problem cannot be solved, an advantage cannot be accrued, or a goal cannot be met due to the attitudes of those who must take some or all of the necessary action. See p. 71.

Benefits A synonym for advantages, used in a *net benefits case*. See p. 75.

Blocks Outlined responses—usually with evidence—to an anticipated argument *or* outlined extensions—usually with evidence—of a previously established position. See p. 193.

Briefs Outlined responses. See *argument-specific briefs, blocks, generic briefs*, and *case briefs*.

---

* The references at the end of each entry are to the fullest discussion of the concept in the text.

Case Briefs A list of arguments that might be offered against a specific kind of affirmative case. See p. 192.

Case Side The side of a flow sheet on which the argumentation concerning the affirmative's rationale for change or for accepting the resolution's value judgment is tracked; also used to refer to the half of the debate focused on the affirmative's rationale for change or for accepting the resolution's value judgment. See p. 222.

Circumvention A common kind of *solvency* argument in which the negative team argues that some agency has the *motive*, the *mechanism*, and the *propensity* to thwart the plan's success. See p. 183.

Comparative Advantages Case A structural model for a case advocating a policy change which stresses the advantages of a new policy over the *status quo*, the advantages being either performance advantages or problem-solving advantages. See p. 65.

Competitiveness A requisite characteristic of a counterplan meaning one of the following: (1) solving the problem the affirmative team has presented; (2) being unable to coexist with the affirmative plan or being superfluous if the affirmative plan is adopted; (3) solving a problem more significant than the problem the affirmative team has presented; (4) being more advantageous than if both the affirmative plan and the counterplan were adopted. (These interpretations range from the traditional to the radical.) See p. 158.

Constructive Speeches The first and longest four speeches in a debate during which the opposing teams construct their arguments for and against the resolution. See p. 202.

Costs A synonym for *disadvantages*, used in a debate focused on a *net benefits case*. See p. 75.

Counterdesignative Contention The argument, in debating a *value resolution*, that some general course of action other than both what the affirmative is rejecting and what the affirmative is pointing to is more valuable than either. See p. 170.

Counterplan A nontopical, new policy system presented by the negative team as superior to the affirmative plan. See p. 157.

Counterwarrants Justifications for adopting the resolution offered and then refuted by the negative team when that team feels the affirmative's justification does not—usually because of its narrowness—permit the judge to decide if the resolution has merit. See p. 196.

Cross-application Answering an argument by applying an argument or evidence you or your partner have used elsewhere in the debate. See p. 219.

Cross-Examination Debate Association (CEDA) A national intercollegiate debating league founded in the early 1970s in opposition to practices common in intercollegiate debate and in favor of encouraging good communication skills and varied debating experiences. See p. 80.

Definitive Contention The affirmative argument, in a debate on a *value resolution*, that advocates a particular measure of value. See p. 81.

Designative Contentions The affirmative arguments, in a debate on a *value resolution*, that evaluate general courses of action based on the measure of value advocated in the *definitive contention*. See p. 81.

Disadvantages Arguments, typically offered in the second negative speaker's constructive speech, that the policy or general policy orientation advocated by the affirmative team will lead to undesirable results. (*Counterplans* can also accrue disadvantages.) See p. 184.

Enforcement A typical *plank* in an affirmative plan that specifies how the execution of its *mandates* will be ensured in the face of direct and indirect violations. See p. 78.

Extratopical Advantages Advantages of an affirmative plan that accrue to that plan because of action specified in it that exceeds what the resolution calls for. See p. 151.

Fiat Power The affirmative team's right in policy debate to assume that all laws would be adopted and any necessary constitutional amendments would be ratified, thereby focusing the debate on whether the policy *should* be adopted. See p. 14.

Flow Sheets Sheets of paper—usually 8½" × 14"—on which the arguments during the eight speeches of a debate are systematically recorded in such a way that argument and counterargument and counter-counterargument flow horizontally across the page. See p. 222.

Generic Briefs Outlined arguments—often complete with evidence—that could be used in many different debates. See p. 193.

Goals Case A structural model for a case advocating a policy change which establishes a goal that it can meet and the status quo cannot. See p. 68.

Impact A requisite characteristic of advantages and *disadvantages* and, therefore, frequently the final subpoint in presenting them. See p. 185.

Independent Advantages Advantages of an affirmative plan that accrue separately and directly from that plan rather than from another advantage or cluster of advantages. See p. 67.

Inherency A requisite characteristic of a *prima facie* case in *policy debate* and in *value debate*, meaning that the *status quo* or the indicted general policy orientation cannot solve the problem, accrue the advantage, meet the goals, or attain the defined value. See p. 64.

Judicial Paradigm A model for the entire debate based on a courtroom proceeding in which a party is accused, defended, and judged according to a prescribed standard. See p. 145.

Justification A line of argumentation pursued by the negative team which demands that the affirmative team make a case for or justify a particular specification of the resolution—for example, for federal rather than state action, for a total prohibition. See p. 175.

Legislative Intent As a legal term, the intent of legislators, as established by their proceedings, used to clarify aspects of a law. As a *policy debate* term, the intent of the affirmative team, established by their speeches, which could be used—if the affirmative so specifies in its plan—to clarify aspects of their policy. See p. 78.

Legislative Paradigm A model for the entire debate based on a legislative assembly's proceedings in which opposed policy systems are considered and the optimal one is selected. See p. 145.

Mandates The *plank* of an affirmative plan that contains the specific actions the team is advocating. See p. 78.

Meatball D.A.'s Disadvantages which would strike an impartial observer as unrealistic and/or absurd because (1) a long causal chain is part of the disadvantage's logical development, (2) debating rules and/or procedures provide links in that development, or (3) the claimed *impact* is an exaggerated one. See p. 188.

Mechanism A requisite of a *solvency* argument which posits that an agency will circumvent the plan's *mandates*; the means by which the agency will circumvent. See p. 184.

Minor Repair An easily made administrative adjustment to the *status quo* that does *not* entail affirming the resolution. See p. 155.

Motive A requisite of a *solvency* argument which posits that an agency will circumvent the plan's *mandates*; the reason why the agency will circumvent. See p. 183.

National Debate Tournament (NDT) The annual tournament which culminates in debating on a selected national policy topic; the style or mode of debating that exists among schools aiming at a berth at this tournament.

Needs Case A structural model for a case advocating a policy change that establishes that a problem exists, that significant harms derive from this problem, that the status quo cannot solve the problem and prevent the harms, and that a specific plan will. See p. 65.

Negative Block The large chunk of speaking time the negative team has at the core of a debate; the second negative constructive speech plus the first negative rebuttal. See p. 203.

Net Benefits Case A structural model for a case advocating a policy change that argues that the *benefits* of a new policy less its *costs* exceed the *benefits* of another policy less its *costs*. See p. 75.

Observations Originally, arguments of a general nature offered at the beginning of the first negative speech—two common ones being *topicality* and *justification*; more broadly, arguments of a general nature offered at the beginning of any speech. See p. 171.

Off-case Side In *value debate*, the side of a *flow sheet* on which the argumentation for and against the kind of policy the affirmative is advocating is tracked; also used to refer to the half of the debate focused on this argumentation. See p. 204.

Parliamentary Style A semi-serious mode of debating featuring much wit on the part of the participants and cheering, booing, and heckling on the part of the audience. See p. 197.

Plan The specific, detailed policy the affirmative team is advocating in a *policy debate*. See p. 78.

Plan Meets Advantages (PMA) A kind of argument offered in *policy debate* by the second negative speaker against the plan which claims that the plan does not succeed in accruing the claimed advantage(s). See p. 182.

Plan Meets Need (PMN) A kind of argument offered in *policy debate* by the second negative speaker which claims that a plan does not succeed in solving the problem the affirmative team has pointed to. See p. 182.

Plan Side In policy debate, the side of a *flow sheet* on which the argumentation for and against the specific policy the affirmative is advocating is tracked; also used to refer to the half of the debate focused on this argumentation. See p. 203.

Planks The component parts of an affirmative team's plan. See p. 78.

Policy Debate Another name for NDT-style debating in which the flaws and benefits of certain public policies are discussed.

Policymaking Judge A judge who views himself or herself as a legislator choosing between the policies advocated by the two teams in a debate. See p. 228.

Policy Resolution A proposition offered for debate which, if adopted, calls for a policy change along specified lines. See p. 9.

Pre-new Policy (PNP) Resolution A type of proposition offered for debate in *CEDA* or *VALUE DEBATE* which, if adopted, affirms a value judgment which precedes and implies a general kind of new policy. See p. 80.

Pre-present Policy Choice (3PC) Resolution A type of proposition offered for debate in *CEDA* or *value debate* which, if adopted, would affirm a value judgment which precedes and implies a choice between two general present policy orientations. See p. 80.

Pre-present Policy Rejection (3PR) Resolution A type of proposition offered for debate in *CEDA* or *value debate* which, if adopted, would affirm a value judgment which precedes a rejection of a general present policy orientation but implies no definite substitute. See p. 80.

Press A negative strategy which entails calling for specific argumentation and evidence from the affirmative team. See p. 148.

Presumption In *policy debate*, the predisposition favoring—in the *judicial paradigm*—the negative team as defender of the *status quo* and—in the *legislative paradigm*—the negative team as rejecter of change. If the negative team offers a *counterplan*, the predisposition favoring the negative no longer applies. See p. 63.

Propensity A requisite of a *solvency* argument which posits that an agency will circumvent the plan's mandates; the demonstrated likelihood that the agency will circumvent. See p. 184.

Rebuttals The latter four speeches in a debate during which debaters defend and refute arguments offered earlier in the debate. See p. 202.

Significance A requisite characteristic of a *prima facie* case in *policy debate* and in *value debate* meaning that the *status quo* or the indicted general policy orientation either exhibits a major problem which requires solution or can be substantially altered with major benefits. See p. 63.

Solvency A requisite characteristic of a *prima facie* case in *policy debate* and most *value debates* meaning that the advocated policy or general policy orientation will solve the specified problem, will achieve the specified benefits, or will meet the specified goal or value. See p. 64.

Spikes Extratopical provisions in an affirmative team's plan designed to overcome *workability* or *solvency* problems the plan would otherwise have or to overcome *disadvantages* the plan would otherwise accrue. See p. 79.

Status Quo Traditionally, present laws and policies; more recently, the dynamics presently guiding the direction of public policy. See p. 63.

Stock Issues Those matters an affirmative team must convincingly address to present a *prima facie* case, including *topicality*, *significance*, *inherency* or *uniqueness*, *plan*, *workability*, *solvency*, and freedom from *disadvantages*. See p. 63.

Stock Issues Judge A judge who evaluates an affirmative team's case for adopting the resolution based on whether or not it meets all of the *stock issues*. See p. 227.

Straight Negative A perhaps outmoded stance in which the negative team refuses to commit itself to a policy or a value judgment and simply *presses* and refutes what the affirmative team says. See p. 146.

Structural Inherency The affirmative claim that a problem cannot be solved, an advantage cannot be accrued, or a goal cannot be met due to some definite legislative or judicial barrier. See p. 71.

Studies Counterplan A generally applicable *counterplan* calling for further study (and usually specifying the nature of the study) before either rejecting or accepting the resolution. See p. 161.

Systems Analysis A broadly applicable method for viewing and studying phenomena which posit that change is constant, and therefore decisions direct, not initiate, change. Applied to debating, the method requires the reconceptualization of the *status quo* as a dynamic, change-directing system much like, and therefore no more privileged than, the policy system advocated by the affirmative team. See p. 75.

Topicality A requisite characteristic of a *prima facie* case meaning that agreeing with the position the affirmative team takes necessarily entails the adoption of the resolution or, at least, the adoption of the resolution in the particular instance selected by the affirmative team as its example of that resolution. See p. 63.

Turnaround A separate, usually independent justification for voting for the affirmative team, brought about when the affirmative shows that rather than being disadvantageous in a certain area, as the negative team has claimed, the affirmative is really advantageous in that area. See p. 68.

Uniqueness A requisite of an advantage or a *disadvantage*: if an advantage is unique, then the affirmative plan but not the status quo can accrue it; if a *disadvantage* is unique, then the affirmative plan but not the *status quo* can accrue it. See p. 70.

Value Debate   Another name for *CEDA*-style debating in which prepolicy value judgments are discussed, not the *specific* policies those judgments might lead to.

Value Objections (VOs)   Arguments offered by the second negative debater in *CEDA* or *value debate* to the effect that the values promoted by the affirmative team will, if acted upon, result in problems. See p. 190.

Value Resolution   A proposition offered for debate which, if adopted, affirms a prepolicy value judgment. See p. 10.

Workability   A requisite characteristic of a *prima facie* case in policy debate, meaning that the proposed plan must be presented in such a detailed manner so that its day-to-day operations seem feasible. See p. 64.

Glossary of Rhetorical Terms

Anadiplosis A rhetorical scheme in which the last word of a phrase is used as the first word of the succeeding phrase and the last word of the succeeding phrase is used as the first word of the next succeeding phrase, etc. See p. 255.

Anaphora A rhetorical scheme in which a series of phrases or clauses begins with the same word or words. See p. 255.

Antithesis A rhetorical scheme in which parallel phrases or clauses are set in opposition by such words as "yet," "but," "not," "however," and "nevertheless." See p. 255.

Argumentum ad hominem A logical fallacy in which the character of the person making an argument or quoted is attacked rather than his or her credentials or the argument *per se*. See p. 119.

Argumentum ad populum A logical fallacy in which the alleged general belief in a proposition is used as an argument for accepting the proposition. See p. 119.

Asyndeton A rhetorical scheme in which conventionally used conjunctions between joined items are omitted. See p. 256.

Backing A component of an argument, if it is analyzed using Toulmin's methodology; the support that can be offered for the *warrant's* validity. See p. 99.

Brainstorming A *heuristic* activity in which information is rapidly presented by one or several participants without any immediate evaluation or organization of it. See p. 14.

Categorical Syllogism A form of argument in which a defining characteristic of a category is established, the term under consideration is placed in that category, and then the term is concluded to possess the defining characteristic. See p. 135.

Causes   One of the classical *topoi*, or places to look, for argumentation. See p. 126.

Claim   A component of an argument, if it is analyzed using Toulmin's methodology; the conclusion which the entire argument affirms. See p. 99.

Climax   A rhetorical scheme in which a series of parallel-structured phrases or clauses build to a climax. See p. 253.

Condition   A component of a *hypothetical syllogism*; the "if" part of the "if-then" premise. See p. 137.

Consequences   One of the classical *topoi*, or places to look, for argumentation. See p. 126.

Consequent   A component of a *hypothetical syllogism*; the "then" part of the "if-then" premise. See p. 137.

Convergent   A possible relationship among arguments in which two or more arguments which could separately affirm another argument join together to affirm that argument more strongly. See p. 141.

Definition   One of the classical *topoi*, or places to look, for argumentation. Two different types of *definition* are common: the first places the term under consideration into a class or *genus* and then differentiates the term from other members of the class; the second establishes the end or goal of the term. See p. 124.

Differences   One of the classical *topoi*, or places to look, for argumentation. See p. 124.

Disjunctive Syllogism   A form of argument in which the truth of one of two situations is affirmed, the falsity of one is established, and then the truth of the other is affirmed. See p. 137.

Divergent   A possible relationship among arguments in which a single argument or combination of arguments simultaneously affirms a number of independent arguments. See p. 140.

Elements of Choice   Those parts of a discourse that the writer or orator determines—e.g., content, overall organization. See p. 89.

Elements of Convention   Those parts of a discourse that are, to a degree, beyond the writer or orator's control—e.g., grammar and punctuation. See p. 89.

Enthymeme   An unstructured argument with some of the requisite elements in a syllogism stated, and some merely implied. See p. 133.

Epistrophe   A rhetorical scheme in which a series of phrases or clauses end with the same word or words. See p. 254.

Ethos   The character or personality projected when writing or speaking; according to most rhetoricians, it is a powerful, subtle persuasive resource. See p. 250.

Flow Charting   A visual method, adapted from management sciences, for planning or tracing the organization of a discourse. See p. 93.

Grounds   A component of an argument, if it is analyzed using Toulmin's methodology; the evidence for the claim made. See p. 99.

Heuristic   A systematic procedure used to discover information or argumentation. See p. 6.
Hypothetical Syllogism   A form of argument in which the truth of a *consequent* is affirmed if a *condition* is true, the truth of the *condition* is affirmed, and then the truth of the *consequent* is affirmed. See p. 137.
Illicit Process   A logical problem exhibited by a categorical syllogism when the conclusion assumes more general or universal premises than were offered. See p. 136.
Issue-treeing   A visual method for planning or tracing the organization of a discourse. See p. 91.
Jargon   The highly specialized language of a particular field. The term is usually used pejoratively, since writers and speakers frequently use the specialized language before an audience not familiar with the field. See p. 269.
Left-branching Sentence   A sentence in which modifying phrases and clauses are heavily embedded at its beginning. See p. 104.
Linked   A possible relationship among arguments in which two or more arguments *together but not separately* affirm some other argument. See p. 140.
Logos   Argumentation using logical reasoning and/or evidence; one of the three kinds of argumentation, according to Aristotle and classical rhetoricians, the others being *ethos* and *pathos*. See p. 246.
Mid-branching Sentence   A sentence in which modifying phrases or clauses are heavily embedded between the subject and the predicate. See p. 104.
Middle Term   The category mentioned in both premises of a categorical syllogism but not in the conclusion. See p. 135.
Modality   A component of an argument, if it is analyzed using Toulmin's methodology; the degree of certainty claimed. See p. 99.
Necessary Cause   A situation that will necessarily lead to a particular effect whenever the situation is present. See p. 121.
Nestorian Order   An order for arranging a list of arguments, examples, etc., with the most significant last, the second most significant first, and the others in between. (The order is based on the psychology of reader response.) See p. 69.
Noise   In communications theory, anything—aural or otherwise—that interferes with a message reaching and affecting its audience. See p. 272.
Parallelism   A fundamental rhetorical scheme in which related ideas are expressed in the same syntactic form. See p. 106.
Pathos   Argumentation using appeals to the emotions; one of the three kinds of argumentation, according to Aristotle and other classical rhetoricians, the others being *ethos* and *logos*. See p. 246.
Polysyndeton   A rhetorical scheme in which conjunctions are used in places in a series where only commas are required by the conventions of grammar. See p. 255.
Preposition Strings   Modifying clusters in a sentence consisting of a sequence of several prepositional phrases. See p. 103.

Rebuttal   A component of an argument, if it is analyzed using the Toulmin methodology; the admitted conditions under which the *claim* is invalid. See p. 99.

Rhetorical Schemes   Special ways of arranging phrases and clauses to achieve particular stylistic and persuasive effects. See p. 106.

Right-branching Sentence   A sentence in which modifying phrases and clauses are heavily embedded at its end. See p. 104.

Serial   A possible relationship between arguments in which one argument affirms some other single argument. See p. 140.

Similarities   One of the classical *topoi*, or places to look, for argumentation. See p. 124.

Sufficient Cause   A situation that could, but not necessarily will, lead to a particular effect. See p. 121.

Syllogism   A formally structured argument consisting of two premises and a conclusion drawn from them. See *categorical syllogism, disjunctive syllogism,* and *hypothetical syllogism*. See p. 133.

Undistributed Middle Term   A logical problem exhibited in a *categorical syllogism* when the term under discussion is not established in one of the two premises as being a member of the category under discussion. See p. 135.

Warrant   A component of an argument, if it is analyzed using Toulmin's methodology; the general rule of reasoning which justifies the movement from the *grounds* provided to the claim argued. See p. 99.

Appendix: Policy Debate versus Value Debate

Throughout this text, I treat policy or NDT-style debating and value or CEDA-style debating side by side. I treat these two modes or styles of debating that way for a reason: I believe that the common ground between policy and value debate is substantial and that the differences are few and largely superficial. My treatment of these two modes of debating may have, perhaps, blurred them together a bit in your mind. This brief appendix should help you understand the differences between policy debate and value debate.

1. **The Resolution**

A policy resolution calls for the adoption of a *specific* kind of new public policy. A value resolution, on the other hand, makes a prepolicy value judgment. Implicit in all three types of value resolutions (see pp. 80-81) is the rejection of a *general* policy orientation; implicit in PNP and 3PC resolutions is the embrace of a *general* policy orientation. The temporal distance between the value judgment and the rejected and embraced policy orientations tends to give value debate a more philosophical character; the insistence that public policies be talked about in general terms adds to this philosophical character.

2. **Affirmative Case Structure**

Since an affirmative case in value debate *does not* propose a specific policy, the affirmative team does not speak in terms of solving harmful problems, doing a comparatively better job, or meeting a goal. The affirmative case in value debate lacks the specifics that are necessary to validate such definite claims. Instead, the affirmative team defines what is valuable and evaluates general policy orientations according to what has been defined as valuable. The structure of an affirmative case in policy and value debate mirrors the deliberative process of the affirmative team. Thus, in value debate, the case structure tends to be, first, a contention that defines (definitive contention) and one or more contentions that designate (designative contentions). (See pp. 166-170.)

3. Stock Issues

A *prima facie* case in policy debate must be topical, be significant, exhibit inherency, contain a workable plan, prove solvent, and be free from serious disadvantages. Since value resolutions are prepolicy, a *prima facie* case in value debate need not (in fact, should not) contain a plan, workable or otherwise. Since the prepolicy value judgments in PNP and 3PC resolutions do imply a general policy orientation, cases in response to these two kinds of propositions must demonstrate a general kind of solvency. Since the prepolicy value judgments in 3PR resolutions do not imply a general policy orientation, cases in response to this kind of proposition need not demonstrate solvency of any kind.

Disadvantages can be offered against affirmative cases that defend either a PNP or a 3PC resolution (see pp. 189–191); value objections can be offered against affirmative cases that defend all three kinds of value resolutions (see pp. 189–191). Cases must be free from serious disadvantages or value objections to be *prima facie*.

Cases in defense of all three kinds of value resolutions must be topical, be significant, and exhibit a general kind of inherency (see pp. 83–85) to be *prima facie*.

4. Negative Strategies

As in policy debate, the first negative debater may choose to go "straight negative," defend the status quo (PNP and 3PR) or alternative policy orientation (3PC), or defend the status quo (PNP and 3PR) or alternative policy orientation (3PC) with minor repairs. The selected strategy will alter how the first negative debater proceeds in (1) challenging the definitive contention; (2) challenging the indictment of the status quo (PNP and 3PR) or alternative policy orientation (3PC) implicit in a designative contention; and (3) challenging the positive evaluation of a policy orientation implicit in a designative contention in a case in defense of either a PNP or a 3PC resolution. The first negative debater can also offer a counterdesignative contention (see pp. 170–171), having either conceded the definitive contention or challenged it.

The second negative debater can either (1) extend his or her partner's argumentation (all value resolutions); (2) offer disadvantages of the general policy orientation implicit in the affirmative case (PNP and 3PC resolutions); or (3) offer broader value objections to acting on the value/s implicit in the affirmative case (all value resolutions).

5. Cross-examination

Given the name of the organization that introduced value resolutions to intercollegiate debating, The Cross-Examination Debate Association (CEDA), one would expect cross-examination to be an important aspect of value debate. And it is. Since CEDA's founding in the early 1970s, most policy debate tournaments (including the prestigious National Debate Tournament) have added cross-examination to the prescribed format, and cross-examination has gradually acquired importance in policy or NDT-style debating. The purposes and the conduct of cross-examination are now essentially the same in value and policy debating.

6. Delivery

Delivery in value debating tends to be slower; the use of jargon and shorthand is less prominent in value debate than in policy debate. And wit is encouraged more in value debate. In other words, behavior conducive to successful communication, in a debating context *and* in other contexts, is far more prevalent in value debate than in policy debate. The emphasis in policy debate is on presenting as much argumentation as possible to a judge who is adept at taking notes rapidly and accurately; the emphasis in value debate is more on geniune human persuasion. This difference, let me add, is not inherent in either mode.

Index

Add-on advantages, 68
Alternative justifications case, 77–78, 161–162, 204–206
American Enterprise Institute, 23, 38–39
Aristotle, 5, 6, 124–125, 201–202, 246–247

Bibliography Index, 26–27
Biographical information, 54
Briefs, 191–194
Burke, Kenneth, 6, 253–254, 256

Causality, 52, 120–122, 182–183, 215, 235–236
Comparative advantages case, 65–67, 70–71, 74–75, 150–152
  adapted for value debate, 84–86
Computers, 27–28, 58–59
Congressional Research Service, 47–48
Convergent structure, 141–143
Corbett, Edward P. J., 127
Counter designative contention, 166, 170–171, 211–212, 318
Counterplan, 157–161, 207–210, 223, 226
Counterwarrants, 196–197
Court decisions, 42–43, 56

Defending the status-quo, 146–148, 150–151, 155
Defining terms, 10–14, 19, 174
Definitive contention, 81, 166–167, 318

Designative contention, 81, 166–170, 308, 317
Dictionaries, 11–12
Disadvantages, 184–191
Divergent structure, 140–143, 152

Editorial Research Reports, 23
Empirical evidence, 51–53, 116–119, 131, 235
Enthymemes, 133–139
Essay and General Literature Index, 32–33
Ethos, 5–6, 246–247, 250–251, 271–272
Evidence:
  cards, 50, 51, 55–57
  challenging, 115–116
  challenging in cross-examination, 235
  filing, 57–58, 60–61
  incorporating into first affirmative constructive speech, 101–102
  professional use of, 108–109
Excess branching, 104–105
Extratopicality, 150–151

Fiat power, 14, 183
First affirmative rebuttal, 213–221, 241–243
First-time-final strategies, 263–265
Flow charting, 93–94
Flow sheets, 222–226, 278, 280, 284–285, 295, 297, 300–301

320

Flower, Linda S., 7, 91
Formal appeal, 253–257

Goals case, 68–69, 74–75
  adapted for value debate, 81–84
Government documents, 43–47

Handbook evidence, 22
Heuristics, 6
  case structures, 72–73
  challenging the affirmative plan,
    180–186
  challenging a comparative advantages
    case, 150–152
  challenging a goals case, 153–155
  challenging a needs case, 148–150
  challenging plan attacks, 213–218
  divide-and-conquer, 16, 19–20
  flow charting, 93–94
  general heuristic for refutation,
    112–124
  issue-treeing, 91–94
  plans perspective, 15–16, 19
  problems perspective, 14–15, 19
  super heuristic for exploring
    resolutions, 17–19, 20
  topoi, 6, 124–127
  values perspective, 16–17, 20

Independent advantages, 67–68, 151–152
Inherency, 64, 70–72, 148–150
  in value debate, 83, 85
Institutes, 22–23
Interlibrary loan, 28–29, 46
Issue-treeing, 7, 91–94
Issues judge in value debate, 229

Jargon, 269–270, 319
Journal articles, 32, 34–36, 56
Judicial paradigm, 145–146, 202–204
Justification, 175

Law review articles, 41–42, 56
Legislative paradigm, 146, 203–204
Letter of inquiry, 40
*The Library of Congress Subject
  Headings Index*, 23–25
Linked structure, 140–143, 152
Logical fallacies, 119–120, 252

Magazine articles, 30–32, 56
Minor repairs, 155–156
  in value debate, 168–169, 318

Needs case, 65, 73–75, 148–150
Negative block, 203
Nestorian order, 69, 154, 260–262
Net benefits case, 75–77, 162–164,
  206–208
Noise, 272–273

Observations, 171–175
Opinion evidence, 53–54, 116, 118–119,
  130–131, 235
Outlines, 7, 89, 94

Parallelism, 106–107
Pathos, 252–253
Plan, 64, 78–80, 180–186, 189
Policymaking judge, 228–229
Policy resolutions, 9, 10, 317
Pre-new policy resolutions, 80
Pre-present policy choice resolutions,
  80–81
Pre-present policy rejection resolutions,
  81
Preparation time, 203
Presumption, 63, 75–76, 146, 163, 202,
  206–207, 227–228
Primafaciality, 63–64, 318

Question-answer tree, 244–245

Reader's Guide to Periodical Literature,
  30–32, 34
Research notebook, 50–51
Rhetorical schemes, 106–107, 253–256
  anadiplosis, 255
  anaphora, 106, 255
  antithesis, 255
  asyndeton, 256
  climax, 106–107, 253
  epistrophe, 254–255
  parallelism, 106–107
  polysyndeton, 255–256

Serial structure, 140–143, 152
Significance, 63–64, 148–150, 150–151
  in value debate, 83–85
Signposting, 96–97
Skills judge, 229
Solvency, 64, 182–184, 186–187, 189
  in value debate, 83–85
Special interest groups, 39
Squirrels, 178–179, 195–197
Statistics, 37–38, 51–52, 117–118,
  121–122

Stock issues, 63–64
  in value debate, 83–85
Stock issues judge, 227–228
Straight negative, 146–148, 150–151, 155, 318
Summary rebuttals, 221–222
Syllogisms, 133–139
Symposia, 24–25

Think tanks, 38–39
Topicality, 63, 164, 174–175
  in value debate, 83–84

Toulmin, Stephen, 6–7, 98–101, 127–133
Transitional words, 105–106
Turnarounds, 68, 179–180, 216–217, 242–243

Uniqueness, 70–71, 151, 164

Value objections, 190–191, 318
Value resolutions, 10, 80–81, 211, 318

Workability, 64, 180–182, 186, 189

OHIO UNIVERSITY LIBRARY

1993